# BEYOND EROTICISM

## A Historian's Reading of Humor in Feng Menglong's *Child's Folly*

**Pi-Ching Hsu**

**University Press of America,® Inc.**
**Lanham · Boulder · New York · Toronto · Oxford**

4501 Forbes Boulevard
Suite 200
Lanham, Maryland 20706
UPA Acquisitions Department (301) 459-3366

PO Box 317
Oxford
OX2 9RU, UK


Printed in the United States of America
British Library Cataloging in Publication Information Available

Library of Congress Control Number: 2005934177
ISBN 0-7618-3353-6 (paperback : alk. ppr.)

™The paper used in this publication meets the minimum requirements of American National Standard for Information Sciences—Permanence of Paper for Printed Library Materials, ANSI Z39.48—1984

*To Mom and Dad*

# Contents

# Preface

After a decade of teaching, I have come to appreciate humor in a new light. Humor in the classroom helps to entice the interest of the students—although they do not always laugh when they are supposed to. Humor outside the classroom helps to sustain the sanity of the professors—especially when huge piles of student papers are in sight. When I was in college, Aristotle convinced me that comedy was inferior to tragedy; my expressed interest in popular literature met with stern disapproval from my Shakespeare professor. And of course I never heard of Feng Menglong. Then I discovered this disenfranchised intellectual in Professor Victoria Cass's graduate seminar. He who did not win the approval of the mainstream must be mediocre, but Feng Menglong was not mediocre. Admittedly, his philosophy of love could be more refined, and his editorial rigor could be more consistent. But he was still a first-rate transmitter of Chinese culture, and a patriot. Unloved by Ming China, he still loved her and was willing to fight for her. Only a romantic and humorous soul could have taken in his stride the jarring gap between what he gave and what he took.

Throughout imperial China, learned culture and popular culture had been engaged in dynamic interactions. The late Ming saw the pace of such "dialogue" picked up significantly, as a great number of literati writers "went to the people" for sources and inspirations. Some, including Feng Menglong, systematically collected folksongs and folktales, and even contributed their own original works. Many of these collections were lost after the fall of the Ming. In the early twentieth century, May Fourth folklorists reconstructed late Ming popular literature as the once-suppressed, pristine voice of the common people. Recent Western scholarship has shifted the focus to the literati "appropriation" of the culture of the masses. My approach is slightly different. I hope I have done justice to Feng Menglong and to Chinese humor by arguing that when the corrupt imperial court and the hedonistic gentry lost touch with reality and the country was falling apart, the art on the margin, participated by conscientious literati, helped hold Chinese civilization together. Weaving the horizontal and reciprocal element of the essential folk into the vertical structure of social and cultural hierarchy, popular writers such as Feng Menglong expanded the basis of the common culture. Their contributions went beyond an exercise of literary hybridization and had historical ramifications.

I first encountered *Treasury of Laughs*—the third collection of Feng Menglong's *Child's Folly*—when I conducted my dissertation research at Harvard-Yenching Library. My friend Peter, an earnest Harvard doctoral student at the time, sat across the table. When he noticed that I was making great efforts to suppress my giggles, his curiosity was aroused.

"What is it you are reading?"

"I am reading a jest-book."

"I thought you came here to do your dissertation research."

"This *is* my dissertation research."

"Are you serious? How did you get Ann to approve of such a project? And you even got a dissertation fellowship to do it!"

That is why I would like to take this opportunity to thank my advisor Professor Ann Waltner and the University of Minnesota for supporting my rather unconventional dissertation for a History Ph.D., "Celebrating the Emotional Self: Feng Meng-lung and Late Ming Ethics and Aesthetics." The dissertation allowed me to combine my training in literature and history. It laid the groundwork for this volume. I am grateful for the advice of the committee members, Professors Ann Waltner, Edward Farmer, Romeyn Taylor, Byron Marshall, and Chun-Jo Liu. Professor Edward Farmer encouraged me to focus on humor when turning my dissertation into a book.

The transformation turns out to be more work than I have imagined—this is almost a completely different book. Amid the off-and-on writing I am now a decade more "mature" than when I first put my hand to the project. This long stretch of time enables me to not only gain new knowledge and fresh insight but also correct old mistakes, sometimes by chancing upon relevant references while doing unrelated research. It is indeed a humbling experience. Numerous people have aided me in this great undertaking. I am tremendously indebted to Ann Waltner, Kimberly Besio, Sally Scully, and David O. McNeil, who meticulously read the entire manuscript at various stages of my writing, and graced the volume with pages upon pages of insightful comments and suggestions. Several anonymous reviewers helped me refine my argument. Oki Yasushi has generously shared his expertise on Feng Menglong with me over the years. Curator Tai-loi Ma offered valuable advice during my dissertation research at University of Chicago. Peter Ditmanson and Jia-cheng Hsu sent me materials when I requested their labor at local libraries. Gratitude is also due to Susan Mann, Richard Hoffman, Jerald Combs, and Edward Farmer, for their sagacious consultation. My home institution San Francisco State University has patiently supported my research and writing through generous grants of teaching relief and technological support. I would also like to acknowledge financial support from the Robert Pasker and Laurie Pittman Matching Fund for History, which allows me to set up a small word-processing station for the production of the manuscript.

I would like to thank staff of the following libraries for their assistance: East Asian Library and Wilson Library at the University of Minnesota; Harvard-Yenching Library at Harvard University; East Asian Library at the University of Chicago; National Central Library and Taipei City Library in Taipei, Taiwan; Tsukuba University Library in Tsukuba, Japan; J. Paul Leonard Library at San Francisco State University; East Asian Library at University of California, Berkeley.

Last but not least, I thank my husband Chun-hwa Chu, who doubles as my chauffeur, research assistant, and cook when I do intensive research and writing, which, needless to say, has added tremendously to the fun of the work. He also saves me from going bananas by helping me prepare the camera-ready copy of the final product.

Pi-ching Hsu<br>San Francisco, California<br>July 2005

# Notes on Conventions

1. For the sake of consistency, the romanizations of Chinese names and terms given in the Wade-Giles system in quoted texts have been converted to *pinyin*. Well-known terms such as Taoism remain unchanged.

2. *Jinshi* (literally, "presented scholar") was the highest degree of civil service examinations in late imperial China. Occasionally, the date of a person's *jinshi* degree is given in lieu of, or in addition to, his dates.

3. A volume of the traditional Chinese book is divided by *juan* (literally, "scroll"), which is roughly equivalent to "chapter." Each page leaf is folded in half, the first half on the left-hand side and the second half on the right-hand side. Note that traditional Chinese-language books are bound in reverse of English-language books. In citations, 5: 4a denotes the first half of page 4 in *juan* 5.

# Prologue

**"Playing Double-Sixes"**
I'm weaving a white brocade under the window,
Whilst my sweetheart engages my husband in a Double-Sixes game.
Suddenly I hear my husband blurt out,
"Block the gate. I'm catching a pair."
Such a fright he's giving me—
A cold sweat soaks my body, and my hands stop shuttling.
—Feng Menglong, *Shan ge*[1]

This erotic lyric in Feng Menglong's (1574-1646) *Hill Songs* (*Shan ge*) catches a tense moment in a woman's adulterous life. The contrast between the husband's thrill and the wife's terror, the irony of the deluded man's victorious move in the gamble and his lost ground on the sexual front, and the incongruity of an unchaste housewife weaving laboriously while her two bedmates are indulged in a non-physical and unproductive game—the humor in the caricature cannot be missed.

The game Double-Sixes has played a role in an earlier story of the eternal triangle, recorded in the dynastic history of the Tang (618-907). Emperor Zhongzong (r. 683-684) was deposed by his strong-willed mother, Wu Zetian (625-705), who subsequently became China's only female emperor (r. 690-705). While under house arrest, the deposed emperor developed a dependence on his wife, Empress Wei. After Zhongzong regained his throne (r. 705-710), apparently in imitation of her mother-in-law, Empress Wei had her clansmen installed in the government, bossed her husband around, and slept with Empress Wu's nephew Wu Sansi. Completely overpowered by his wife, Zhongzong turned a blind eye to the affair, and even fondly directed Empress Wei's moves when she played Double-Sixes with her lover.[2]

The striking parallel between the Tang tale and the Ming (1368-1644) folksong suggests a possible pollination. However, a significant replacement of the philanderer's contestant in the gamble, along with some face-lifting of the characters, has to occur to make room for the humor in the song. The cuckold is trusting, the adulteress is conscientious, patriarchy still holds, and the commoner husband and wife are not burdened by political obligations of the ruling class, so need not be moral paragons. While narrators of the Tang story categorically condemn the royal couple for his nepotism, her lust, and the decadence they embody, the writer of the Ming song seems more forgiving. One may even sense an implicit empathy toward the woman's courageous pursuit of a forbidden love, as well as the psycho-logical burden she has to bear, at a time when the only sanctified sex is within parentally arranged marriage.

What I have tried to demonstrate above, and will continue to demonstrate in the study, is the possibility of looking beyond the erotic facade of *Child's Folly* (*Tongchi*) and seeing the underlying humor and historical ramifications. This approach is possible because the compiler Feng Menglong was not only a master of erotic stories but also a humorous matchmaker, uniting history and literature, folklore and elite culture. *Child's Folly* is a trilogy consisting of *Hanging Twigs* (*Guazhier*), a collection of some 400 popular songs, *Hill Songs* (*Shan ge*), a collection of 383 folksongs, and *Treasury of Laughs* (*Xiaofu*), a collection of 700-odd jokes. Feng collected oral and written sources of scholarly as well as non-scholarly origins, edited them heavily, and wrote commentaries to reflect on the time, or to express his rather liberal literary or philosophical views. Reading *Child's Folly* could supposedly cure the readers' obstinacy and bring out the child in them.

The greatest appeal of Feng Menglong's works in the late (last century of) Ming commercial press was, at first glance, eroticism. A canny producer of popular literature, he knew how to maneuver titillating sex scenes to satisfy the audience's voyeurism. But he also had a political aspiration, and needed to elevate his literature above and beyond eroticism. He made an attempt to distinguish love from lust, and to maintain that carnal love was healthy and guiltless if it was accompanied by single-minded devotion, whereas loveless sex or uncontrollable lust was harmful and beyond redemption. Although he was not entirely successful in defending that slippery line, his effort warranted him some respectability in what Timothy Brook terms the "gentry society" of the late Ming.[3]

The "gentry society" was a society dominated by a degree-holding elite that had accumulated "symbolic credit" through its cultural capital, social privilege, local undertakings, and representation of a "public" voice independent of the imperial state's magisterial authority. Since the Tiananmen Square Massacre of June Fourth, 1989, Western scholars have debated whether China has ever had a "civil society"—a "public sphere" that mediated between the tyranny of the state and the interest of the people, and whether the "gentry society" was a "civil society." Because Confucian political theory did not conceptualize an antagonism between the state and the people, as in early modern European theories, the discourse on "civil society" might not be a very fruitful approach to the study of China. The reason "gentry society" is of interest here is that localizing public interest in the private sphere, members of the gentry society challenged the state-defined Confucian order by claiming to uphold a higher, more personal yet more authentic, Confucian order. Parallel to the development of the gentry society, a popular literature emerged to mediate between the values of the center and the marginal, between spontaneous human emotions (*qing*) and morally required social, familial obligations (*li*). This historical condition legitimized erotica that claimed to approach human sexuality in a more open and wholesome manner, thus breaking the taboo against sex as a topic of intellectual pursuits. However, as Martin Huang's recent study indicates, many a late Ming writer of erotica led a hedonic sex life that was not nearly as "wholesome" as claimed.[4]

An entry-level degree holder, active in the literati circles and eventually acquiring government assignments late in his life, Feng Menglong earned a membership, albeit a marginal one, in the "gentry society." He participated in the production of what was advertised as "healthy" erotica by satirizing the puritan Neo-Confucian ethic on the one hand, and the loose love ethics promoted by irresponsible pornographic writers on the other hand. A self-proclaimed founder of the "teaching of *qing*," Feng identified *qing*, or "human emotional responses to particular circumstances,"[5] as the fountainhead of all spontaneous and natural feelings, including carnal love and other, more "Confucian" emotions, such as loyalty, filiality, fraternity, and friendship. *Child's Folly* represented the formative stage of the "teaching of *qing*." It celebrated child-like naiveté, which allowed the singers and jesters to see through the incongruity of adult social behavior, and to express their intuitive response in a direct manner. The compilation combined humor and eroticism. Feng took advantage of the ambiguous and transgressive nature of humor to inject both the sensually provocative and a social conscience into the erotic songs and jokes of *Child's Folly*. He extended similar techniques to the other entries of *Child's Folly*—about corrupt officials, pedantic scholars, incompetent physicians, swindler priests, cunning craftsmen, idiots, braggadocios, misers, eccentrics, and so on. The humorous satire reveals the tension and anxiety within the political, educational, judicial, social, and cultural systems of late Ming China. It also reveals some of Feng's own ambiguous attitudes toward gender and class. He might be more enlightened than average contemporaries, but his sense of egalitarianism had its limits.

From the time of Sima Qian (ca. 145-86 BC), Chinese historians have been obsessed with tragic heroes who, despite their integrity, intelligence, and capability, were misunderstood, unappreciated, or wronged. Feng Menglong's humorous tales offer a delightful break from the pathos of this tragedy. Perhaps more than incidentally, Feng also thought of himself as an unappreciated victim of the tyranny of Chinese history. That tyranny should produce humor is not surprising. Humor exposes incongruities and releases tension. Whether humor serves as a vehicle of criticism or as a safety valve, it symbolizes the resilience of a civilization. Feng Menglong's humor both reveals the tension that exists in various spheres of Ming culture and society and gives a view of how the Ming people cope with this tension.

Feng Menglong was a prolific author, editor, and publisher. His career development was similar to many professional writers in the late Ming. Originally aiming to pursue a political career in the civil service, Feng was propelled by his frustration with the grueling examination hall (or "examination hell" if you will)[6] to redirect his creative energy to literary production. Despite his expressed resentment, the outcome of his "Plan B" was spectacular. Feng Menglong's literary world bridged what Robert Redfield calls the Great Tradition and the Little Tradition,[7] creating a middle ground between rationality and fantasy, idealism and pragmatism, elegance and simplicity. His works reflected a mixture of Confucian morality and popular sentiment, filtered through the consciousness of an intellectual who lived in the intersection of the world of literati and the world of the masses.

In the modern times, Feng's most widely studied work is the *Sanyan* (Three Words) collection of vernacular short stories, mostly cautionary tales with romantic plots. *Child's Folly* has also attracted significant scholarly attention, but this trilogy as a whole has yet to be systematically studied. Like Feng's several dozen fictional, dramatic, and lyrical works, *Child's Folly* carries his trademark of eroticism and contains sexually explicit materials. But Feng indicated in his prefatory essays and commentaries that he had the sanity of his fellow Ming people and the integrity of Chinese culture in mind when he compiled *Child's Folly*. While it could be argued that his stated intent was merely a moralistic sugarcoating of the work's subversive content, there was indeed a hidden message.

A search beyond obscenity reveals that many songs and jokes in *Child's Folly* are highly entertaining; besides, they are profoundly reflective of not only the spiritual and material lives of common people in late Ming China but also the social conscience of a disenfranchised elite. Focusing on humor allows an analysis of the social and philosophical aspects of moderately erotic and non-erotic materials in *Child's Folly* while moving away from the most obscene entries that are too offensive to be entertaining.

This volume makes several pioneering attempts. It is the first systematic study of three *non-fictional* collections significant to the study of late imperial Chinese popular culture compiled and edited by the noted *fiction* writer Feng Menglong. It is the first *historical* analysis of Chinese humor that looks closely at the juncture of literature and history. While sexual humor has attracted much scholarly attention, this book highlights mildly erotic and non-erotic materials, selected with a female historian's sensitivities. Focusing on humor as the predominant characteristic of the "tactically forgotten" collections of *Child's Folly*, the book offers a delightful study of the foibles, eccentricities, and anxieties of a broad cross-section of late Ming society.

The book asks how frustration over the competitive civil service examinations, cynicism about human nature and social customs, and exploration of the themes of sexual love played into *Child's Folly*. Particularly, it examines the social criticism hidden behind the laughter, targeting the people of Jiangnan (lower Yangzi valley). Jiangnan in the late Ming was characterized by economic prosperity, social fluidity, widespread literacy, and flourishing of arts and literature, accompanied by corruption, extravagance, mercantilism, philistinism, and heightened social strain. It was a land of "the confusions of pleasure,"[8] and a wonderful source of inspiration for humorous and satirical works.

Chapter One gives an overview of humor in Chinese cultural tradition, and illustrates the validity of studying humor historically. Structural and thematic coherence within the three generically different collections of *Child's Folly* will be analyzed, along with the text's historical ramifications in the context of late Ming China.

Chapter Two explores the historical world where Feng Menglong lived and the literary world which he created. Studying the historical complexity of late Ming Jiangnan alongside the colorful life experience of Feng Menglong helps to explain Feng's transformation from a bohemian to a patriot. Subsequently, the co-existence of humor and seriousness in Feng Menglong's publications will be shown to separate him from most writers of hedonistic literature on the one hand and writers of didactic literature on the other.

Chapters Three and Four are devoted to the translation and analysis of over forty songs and ninety jokes in Feng Menglong's *Hanging Twigs*, *Hill Songs*, and *Treasury of Laughs*. The entries are selected because they are funny even to modern readers. They are also selected because they reflect certain subjective or objective historical truth, or to borrow the phrases of Maram Epstein, they reflect either "historical imaginary" or "historical practices."[9] Contextualized against primary and secondary literature on late Ming culture and society in the Chinese, Japanese, and Western languages, and against Feng's other works, the songs and jokes show their relevance to history and to Feng's intellectual development, especially with regard to his "teaching of *qing*."

The songs are divided into eight categories: authenticity of *qing*, callous men, infatuated women, lover's cross, the woes of marriage, homosexuality, culture of the pleasure quarters, and the way of the world. Playful as they are, the songs are loaded with the sentiments, fantasies, and thoughts of Ming people. Some songs celebrate the "child's folly" in youngsters' passionate pursuit of premarital and extramarital love. Other songs satirize oddities of human behavior in a society full of corruption and pretension—a society where the "child's folly" had been lost. Loss of the "child's folly" is the main theme of the jokes translated and analyzed here. The jokes are divided into ten categories: the ruling class, scholars, fake Neo-Confucian moralists, medicine, clergy, social manners, master-servant relationships, folly of various kinds, children's naiveté, and husband-wife relationships. It will be brought to light that the *Treasury of Laughs* is indeed a treasury, and not just of laughs.

The last part of the study zooms in on the ambiguities of humor and eroticism of *Child's Folly*. As was implied in the title, *Child's Folly* celebrated innocence of the child that was the singer, the jester, the compiler, and Chinese civilization. Permeating the collection was a yearning for the earlier days in the life of the individual as well as of the civilization, prior to moral and value codification—the "prelapsarian" state, if you will. While this thematic framework gave Feng Menglong the liberty to compile sexually and socially tabooed materials, his assertion that "child's folly" had been marginalized and degenerated in his own time made his claim that he was recording the voice of the innocent suspect. Besides, a distinctive voice in the volumes was that of male gentry, who were pushing the limits of Confucian ethic but were neither amoral nor indiscriminate. In other words, they were not "prelapsarian" children.

Popular literature was a common property in the late Ming. Humorous tales were often told and retold, mixing the tellers' materials and the audiences' feedback, before they were settled in printed form. Even then they often existed in multiple collections, with slight variations, and most likely without proper documentation of sources. Some popular texts would generate variant editions, including pirated ones. *Child's Folly* was compiled under similar circumstances. It could be regarded as a collective work by numerous authors, audiences, and editors, put together by a heavy-handed compiler, who tinged the collection with strong personal colors.

The remarkable popularity of *Child's Folly* in the late Ming commercial press signals to the modern historian that the collection's form and content must have struck an accord in the hearts and minds of a large section of contemporary population. The reading public in the late Ming seemed to have an insatiable appetite for folk songs, popular songs, and jokes, and they did not seem to mind if the language was less than chaste. The amorous heterosexual and homosexual lovers, as well as the people of various professions who show up in *Hanging Twigs* and *Hill Songs*, must have reminded the Ming readers of some real people in their society. So must the laughingstocks jumping off the pages of *Treasury of Laughs* be telling stories about their times. Some stories converged with and others diverged from officially sanctified ideology. All stories had complicated meanings hidden behind the laughter. If we are fooled by the loud laughter, we may not hear the subtle message—about frictions real and imagined. So we have to listen carefully.

Analyzing humor is a thankless task. Serious students of humor have been accused of killing their subject of study. Agreeing with Evelyn Waugh's famous analogy that analyzing humor is like dissecting a frog—much is learned but in the end the frog is dead, Peter Duus nevertheless affirms the intellectual value of the humorless "academic scrutiny" of humor. "Most analyses of humor cannot be read for amusement," says Duus. But he quickly adds, "why should they be?"[10] It is a great relief to hear from the expert that analysts of humor need not reproduce the humor in their source material, for humor is not a weapon I am equipped with. (Readers should take this as a warning sign.) I do hope, however, that in the end my frog is still alive. After all, we are living in the age of x-ray, ultrasound, and laser blade. We need not kill the frog to get the anatomy. So let us keep our fingers crossed for the frog.

## Notes:

1. Feng Menglong, *Shan ge* (Beijing: Zhonghua shuju, 1962), 1: 9b. The same version is reprinted in *Ming Qing min ge shi diao ji*, vol. 1 (Shanghai: Shanghai guji chuban she, 1987). All page numbers of *Shan ge* quoted in this study are based on this version.

2. *Jiu Tang shu*, comp. Liu Xu, *Sibu beiyao*, 51: 7a. *Xin Tang shu*, comps. Ouyang Xiu and Song Qi, *Sibu beiyao*, 76: 11b. The former specifies the game to be Double-Sixes; the latter only refers to a gamble. Feng Menglong quotes the latter in his *Qingshi leilue*, *Ming Qing shanben xiaoshuo congkan chubian* (Taipei: Tianyi chuban she, 1985), 17: 24b.

3. The term "gentry society" is coined by Timothy Brook in his *Praying for Power: Buddhism and the Formation of Gentry Society in the Late Ming* (Cambridge, MA: Harvard University Press, 1993).

4. Martin Huang, *Desire and Fictional Narrative in Late Imperial China* (Cambridge, MA: Harvard University Asia Center, 2001).

5. This rendering of *qing* is borrowed from Kidder Smith et al., *Sung Dynasty Uses of the I Ching* (Princeton: Princeton University Press, 1990).

6. Miyazaki Ichisada, *China's Examination Hell: The Civil Service Examinations of Imperial China*, trans. Conrad Schirokauer (New York: Weatherhill, 1976).

7. Redfield defines the Great Tradition and the Little Tradition as follows: "The great tradition is cultivated in schools or temples; the little tradition works itself out and keeps itself going in the lives of the unlettered in their village communities. The tradition of the philosopher, theologian, and literary man is a tradition consciously cultivated and handed down; that of the little people is for the most part taken for granted and not submitted to much scrutiny or considered refinement and improvement." Robert Redfield, *Peasant Society and Culture* (Chicago: University of Chicago Press, 1956), 41.

8. Timothy Brook, *The Confusions of Pleasure: Commerce and Culture in Ming China* (Berkeley: University of California Press, 1998).

9. Maram Epstein, *Competing Discourses: Orthodoxy, Authenticity, and Engendered Meanings in Late Imperial Chinese Fiction* (Cambridge, MA: Harvard University Press, 2001), 2.

10. Peter Duus, "Presidential Address: Weapons of the Weak, Weapons of the Strong—The Development of the Japanese Political Cartoon," *The Journal of Asian Studies* 60, no. 4 (2001): 965.

# 1

# Historicizing the Humor of *Child's Folly*

## 童癡之幽默史觀

There is only one Tower of Misty Rain in the city of Jiaxing, where the visitors can have a good view of the scenery around. On one occasion a resident of Jiaxing drinks with a resident of Suzhou. The Suzhou guy conducts a drinking game. At every round, each person shall name a tourist attraction from his own locale. The person who fails to come up with a site will be punished: by drinking a cup of wine. At the first round, the Suzhou guy says, "Tiger Hill." The Jiaxing guy says, "Tower of Misty Rain." Then the Suzhou guy names at one stretch Stone Lake, Heavenly Scales, Cave Court, Seventy-two Mounts, and so on. The Jiaxing guy runs out of answers right after the Tower of Misty Rain. So he is punished numerous times. When he goes home dead drunk, his wife demands an explanation. He says, "I had a drinking game with a Suzhou friend, where we competed to name tourist attractions from our locales. I lost the game and got drunk." His wife says, "Why didn't you say the Tower of Misty Rain?"

A visitor plans to purchase some Suzhou goods. Somebody tells him, "Suzhou people customarily bargain to get 50% off the original prices. So whatever the asking price, go ahead and offer a half." The visitor believes in the truth of the advice. When he comes to a silk shop, he offers one tael of silver for goods priced at two taels and three quarters of a tael for goods priced at one and a half taels. The shop owner resents it very much and snaps, "If that's your attitude, then you don't need to buy. We might as well give you two bolts of silk on the house." The customer politely folds his hands together, "There. There. I'll take only one bolt."

Huizhou people are known to be stingy. A Huizhou man who sojourns in Suzhou stores self-made salty beans in a narrow-necked bottle, and

> allows himself limited access to only a few beans with chopsticks for each meal. Upon learning that his son is prostituting extravagantly, however, he loses his self-control. Pouring the content of the entire bottle into his mouth, he declares, "There's no point for me to be frugal now."
>
> —Feng Menglong, *Treasury of Laughs* [1]

Never mind the long debate on whether the term "humor" is of English or French origin.[2] In modern English, humor means "the mental faculty of discovering, expressing, or appreciating ludicrous or absurdly incongruous elements in ideas, situations, happenings, or acts."[3] Humor provokes a smile or a laugh. In the first joke, the embarrassing loss of the Jiaxing resident in the drinking game is funny, but his wife's response is even funnier. Alas! There is indeed one and only one tourist attraction in Jiaxing. In the second joke, although the comic butt is the visitor, who takes the words from the horse's mouth a bit too literally—and he goes all the way, yet the most vivid impression the audience might walk away with is perhaps that a smart shopper should never pay full prices in Suzhou. The third joke is, again, Suzhou people making fun of outsiders, whose extreme frugality results in his self-abandoning.

The above three are rare examples of specifically Suzhou jokes in the *Treasury of Laughs*, which in general targets a broad audience. Suzhou, a highly urban city of over one million inhabitants, was the compiler Feng Menglong's hometown. The first joke is built on Suzhou's famous beauty and the renowned Suzhou passion for local tourism, to which Jiaxing cannot compare. The picturesque city of Suzhou on the Grand Canal is dubbed the Venice of the Orient. Dozens of tourist attractions are marked for their seasonal beauties and cultural allures. To the residents of Suzhou, visits to these sites are almost as spiritual as pilgrimages. The second joke hinges on Suzhou merchants' reputation for dishonest pricing and Suzhou buyers' love of bargain. The third joke, on the other hand, is based on a prejudice against Huizhou people, especially the Huizhou merchants sojourning in Su-zhou. Popular image of the Huizhou merchant "was that of the grasping pawnbroker who sued anyone he disagreed with and spent vast amounts of money on commercial sex."[4] In the joke, the father represents the first half of the stereotype; if he loves litigation he must be stingy. The son represents the second half of the stereotype, and Suzhou provides unlimited pleasures for such prodigals. In Suzhou, the despicable Huizhou merchant gets his rightful punishment, so to speak. The three jokes have a geographical and socio-economic-cultural connotation, but they have little political or philosophical implication. Apparently the Suzhou audience would have been entertained a bit more than the outsiders.

When humorous material is contrived out of the blue or built on well-established stereotypes to entertain the audience, as in the above three jokes, there may be little or no correspondence between humor and the current affairs. But humor can also have a hidden agenda that is more serious. When humor is employed as a vehicle for expressions of a subtle nature, which would have otherwise been difficult or dangerous to put in the open, humor is more than entertaining. Many entries of *Child's Folly* are of this "dangerous" nature.

### *Child's Folly*

The universe of *Child's Folly* (*Tongchi*) was a wonderland. It was a world where youthful impulse carried the day, where rules were to be broken, authorities were to be challenged, and fun was to be made of the smart and sophisticated. The child was not to be disciplined and asked to stay within the line. The folly was not to be beaten down and made to correct itself. It was great to be a child (*tong*) in the heart, and it was fine to be infatuated or obsessed (*chi*). In the world of *Child's Folly*, merry-making was not sinful, whereas keeping a straight face was; acting on instinct was not stupid, whereas calculating and scheming were. The compiler was a young, imprudent, and amorous scholar who was frustrated by the world but continued to hold his head high. Suffering repeated failures in his pursuit of a civil service examination degree beyond the entry level, hence unqualified for an official appointment, he vented his anguish in the company of wine, women, and gamblers. Living in both the world of the lettered gentlemen and the world of the common folk, he came to see both worlds differently. He found true value in some seemingly vulgar speech, and, despite his constant assault on elite culture, did not dismiss its value altogether. Taking "*tongchi*" (child's folly) as a common link between the best of both worlds, he put together songs and jokes that, ideally, spoke of a pure and beautiful mind that was free of philistinism and pedantry.

The term "*tongchi*," or "child's folly," was resonant with "*tongxin*" (childlike mind) in the philosophy of Li Zhi (1527-1602), whom Wm. Theodore de Bary calls the "Arch-Individualist"[5] and of whom Feng Menglong was an admirer. Although Li Zhi did not go so far as to proclaim each individual an island apart, he tried to free himself from familial and social obligations by shaving his head and withdrawing to a monastery, thus blocking his incompatible wife, soliciting relatives, and hostile colleagues from his personal life. Such radical behavior called for an intellectual justification. A justification could be found in the "Treatise on the Child-like Mind" in Li Zhi's controversial work, appropriately entitled *A Book to Be Burned*. The treatise argued that the process of elite education associated with the pursuit of practical knowledge, moral principle, and social reputation made people forget who they really were. Because their minds were blocked up by the accumulative information coming from without, they lost their intuitive, innate knowledge; therefore, whatever they said, did, and wrote was insincere and inauthentic. To go back to the original self, one had to recover the "unmistakably pure and true" mind one had as a child.[6] Knowledge, principle, and reputation were important ingredients for the Confucian "perfection of adulthood"; acquisition of these indicated people's readiness to take up the responsibilities that society expected of them. To Li Zhi, however, they corrupted people's minds and lured them away from selfhood.

Two millennia prior to Li Zhi, Lao Zi and Mencius had discoursed on "the mind of a new-born baby." But Lao Zi's version (primal energy) had a touch of mysticism, and Mencius' version (innate goodness) had a moral connotation. Unlike the great Taoist and Confucian thinkers, Li Zhi did not philosophize. His motivation was to liberate people's bodies and minds, pure and simple. Feng Menglong was greatly influenced by Li Zhi. In *Child's Folly*, Feng contended that spontaneous expression of true feelings was lost in elitist literature, which was full of artificiality with regard to both the producer's heart-and-mind and the product's form-and-content. He proposed that one find true feelings in the unpolished voice of the simple folk, who still possessed the "child's folly." It is noteworthy that Feng's "folk" were not limited to the unlettered peasants and workers. Included in *Child's Folly* were works of elite authors who, in Feng's judgment, were as spontaneous as the non-gentry authors. They were rich in emotions (*qing*), and they refused to conform to rigid norms (*li*) of behavior and utterance. In the spirit of what Wm. Theodore de Bary terms "individualism and humanitarianism,"[7] these intellectuals wanted to break free from the shackles of convention and liberate themselves intellectually. They found in folk literature a subjectified, privatized world where objective, external rules collapsed. They not only read folk literature but also contributed to it.

It is well known that *Hanging Twigs* and *Hill Songs* were the first (*yi nong*) and second (*er nong*) collections of *Child's Folly*. From a collection of over seven hundred jokes entitled *Jueying sanxiao*

(*Three Laughs That Break the Chin Strap of Your Hat*), we learn that the *Treasury of Laughs* was the third collection (*san nong*) of *Child's Folly*, and that it had already been published by 1616. In the preface to *Three Laughs*, Hulu Sheng complained that the jokes in *Xiaolin ping* (*Commentary on the Glove of Laughter*) were of mixed qualities and the comments absurd, while most jokes in *Xiaozan* (*In Praise of Laughter*) were not funny and the comments pedant. The one jest-book he found acceptably funny and zestful was the *Treasury of Laughs* in the trilogy *Child's Folly*, although of course it was not as good as the *Three Laughs*, which might have been compiled by Hulu Sheng himself under a pseudonym.[8] For the purpose of this study, what is most noteworthy is the reference to the *Treasury of Laughs* as the third collection of *Child's Folly*. In *Xiaofu*, 13: 3b, Feng Menglong cites Hulu Sheng's comment on a joke about a son-in-law who succeeded in the examination with the help of his powerful father-in-law. I locate the joke and the comment in the renowned *Sishu xiao* (*Jokes on the Four Books*), which contains several sources of the *Treasury of Laughs* entries. Given Hulu Sheng's credential in the late Ming jest-book industry, his statement that *Treasury of Laughs* was part of the *Child's Folly* trilogy should be reliable.

*Child's Folly* was compiled in Feng Menglong's youth, when he frequented courtesans' quarters, gambling houses, and wine shops, and collected his materials on the side. His ingenuity at combining work and pleasure inspired a folk story. A Mr. Wang opened a wine shop in the dead end of a quiet lane in Suzhou (he could not afford a better location because of his small budget). Although the wine was good, the business was bad. As he was pondering what seemed to be his only option—closure, his cousin Feng Menglong paid a visit. After listening to Wang's problem, Feng wrote a few words on the shingle of the wine shop, "Anybody who can inscribe on the wall a proverb about something that can be said but not done will be treated with free wine." The news spread fast, and people swarmed to the wine shop, writing and reading proverbs such as "Picking a bone in the egg." Mr. Wang's business improved, and Feng got to collect a bunch of proverbs as raw materials for his popular literature.[9] The story sounds like fun, but in reality Feng's sensational work (and pleasure) associated with the production of *Child's Folly* enraged his gentlemanly father and brother, and won him an infamous reputation.

*Child's Folly* indeed contained some off-color materials that would have embarrassed Feng's "decent" family, but it also had a serious intent. It illustrated the rebellious young Feng Menglong's notion that "child's folly" could be an excellent prescription for the ailments of his times, which he ascribed to unnatural suppression of spontaneous emotions and desires. The three collections shared some common thematic features. Recurring subject matters of *Child's Folly* included:

1. Articles for comfortable, elegant living, ranging from daily necessities, food, and stationary, to toys and decorations, to the moon and the stars.
2. People of all walks of life—courtesans, students, teachers, officials, weavers, servants, craftsmen, merchants, vendors, physicians, peasants, fishermen, monks and nuns, beggars, and so on.
3. Social customs, folk beliefs, and human nature.
4. Romantic love.
5. Sex—heterosexual, homosexual, and bisexual.

Love and sex were perhaps the most prominent topics, and they were not treated with any of the subtlety expected of literati novels, such as the eighteenth-century masterpiece *Dream of the Red Chamber*, where lads and lasses agonized over constant misunderstanding and quarrelling, being awkward in expressing their amorous feelings. In *Child's Folly*, men and woman were not a bit too shy to flirt, get naked, and throw themselves into ecstasies.

The crudeness of eroticism in *Child's Folly* should not surprise us. It seemed natural for the lower body to get more exposure in the lower form of literature. The sensational descriptions of love-making in *Hanging Twigs* and *Hill Songs* and the prominent sexual jokes in *Treasury of Laughs* accorded with the crude consumer culture of late Ming commercial press, a crudity which Feng endeavored to counter in his later, more mellow works, especially fiction and plays. But in *Child's Folly* Feng made no apology for crude eroticism. Carnal love and spiritual love were two sides of a coin. He saw no reason to separate them—why put the latter on a pedestal and put a taboo on the former? With the fusion of physicality and spirituality the focus of *Child's Folly* moved above and beyond the lower body.

Many love songs in *Hanging Twigs* and *Hill Songs* illustrated positive examples of "child's folly" in common people's, especially young women's, spontaneous, almost primitive passions for sexual love out of wedlock. A departure from Neo-Confucian norms of constraint and modesty, such headlong passions were appropriated by Feng Menglong as examples of true love (*qing*). A young woman who took a lover behind her mother's back was as gutsy as a filial daughter who rescued her father from the jaws of a tiger—both acted courageously out of deep feelings. On the other hand, most jokes in *Treasury of Laughs* illustrated negative examples of people who lost "child's folly" in pursuit of fame and wealth, criteria for earthly success. Out of blind conformity to normative conventions, narrow-minded value judgments on the basis of marketplace morality, the desire to appear better than one actually was, or insensitive absorption in self-interest, a person became hypocritical, philistine, pretentious, greedy, or stingy. Feng sympathized with the child-like behavior and disliked the grown-up. By reversing the worldly practice of praising the socially sophisticated and successful and looking down upon the socially naive and base, the three collections of *Child's Folly* broke the established rules of the mundane world.

Besides their contents, the three collections of *Child's Folly* also shared some formal similarities. The language was witty, humorous, sarcastic, and unrestrained; phrases in Suzhou dialect—Feng Menglong's native language—and plays on words, especially puns, were employed frequently. Puns were a marked characteristic of Suzhou folk literature. It was a particularly powerful linguistic device to escape the established meanings of words. Besides humorous effects, the employment of puns in the language of *Child's Folly* enhanced the language's challenge to standard forms.[10] By extension, the word-play, which toys with the ambiguity of language, was a challenge to the establishment and the authorities. Walter Redfern says of puns, "Experimental psychologists have shown quantifiably what most people know instinctively and by experience: that it is authoritarian personalities who most dislike and reject ambiguity. Hence the double meaning practiced in all forms of underground literature."[11]

The non-standard, elusive, and at times provocative and subversive nature of the language added a touch of popular, folkloric (as opposed to elite, canonical) literature to the collection. Such language appealed to the taste of a general audience. But the literary allusions which appeared occasionally, and the commentaries attached to some entries, written in non-transparent classical Chinese, were rather sophisticated; they seemed to be oriented toward a more exclusive, elite audience. Perhaps Feng was self-conscious about his position in the literary pantheon. He might be a popular writer, but he was also an aspiring participant in the civil service exams. The latter was at least as important as the former, and he wanted to demonstrate his scholarship wherever he could.

Despite the thematic continuity, the generic difference between the first two (*yi nong* and *er nong*) and the third (*san nong*) collections of *Child's Folly* cannot be ignored. The word *nong* (literally, "to play with") indicates a connection with musical performance, so the song collections fit the description better than the jest-book. It was possible that the original design of *Child's Folly* included only

*Hanging Twigs* and *Hill Songs*, and adding *Treasury of Laughs* to form the trilogy was an afterthought. Folksongs, popular songs, and jokes were not incompatible. They all belonged to a sensitive oral tradition that the imperial courts regarded as significant political capital worthy of systematic gathering, as will be discussed later. They were also common forms of entertainment in the pleasure quarters. Besides, their difference in genre was somewhat diminished in the late Ming, when fiction, drama, poetry, prose, songs, and jokes shared so much in common in both form and content that strict generic distinctions were breaking down. Richard John Lynn contends that renowned Ming writers Xu Wei (1521-1593) and Tang Xianzu (1550-1616) "thought of all literary art as one and did not, as far as their basic assumptions were concerned, greatly distinguish among verse (*shi*), lyrics (*ci*), drama (*qu*), and prose (*wen*)."[12]

Andrew Plaks observes the frequent infusion of vivid "painterly" details in *xiaopin* ("vignettes," "essays of minor appreciation," or "literature on the minor key"), a new form of writing that emphasized individualistic perception on casual topics such as travels, pets, personal collections, and hobbies.[13] Given the generally short length and transgressive nature of the songs and jokes in the three collections of *Child's Folly*, Feng Menglong could well categorize all of them under the loose label of *xiaopin*. They were fun and light and harmless, but they went straight from the hearts of the authors to the hearts of the audiences, and could probably carry much more weight than "serious" utterances.

It befitted Feng Menglong to compile such a playful yet serious work. Feng was, in the words of his eulogist, an unrestrained learner of the Way who "turned laughs and curses into writings that were as blazing as the rosy clouds."[14] Although in the eyes of several "authoritative" critics in late imperial China, Feng was just a "jester among versifiers," and his works were "extremely frivolous," "funny talk having nothing to do with the 'major elegance,'"[15] Feng has now been acknowledged as a giant in late Ming literature. He played a significant role in the printing and publishing of the deluxe editions of the popular novels *Shuihu zhuan* (*Water Margin*, or *All Men Are Brothers*) and *Jin Ping Mei* (*Golden Lotus*, or *The Plum in the Golden Vase*). According to the novelist and playwright Li Yu (1611-1680), Feng was the first person to group *Romance of the Three Kingdoms* (*Sanguo zhi yanyi*), *Water Margin*, *Journey to the West* (*Xiyou ji*), and *The Plum in the Golden Vase* together under the now standard collective appellation *Sida qishu* (*Four Masterworks of Ming Novels*).[16]

Feng was also an excellent creator of literature. He was a prolific writer whose brush moved freely between classical and vernacular language, between popular and elite genres, between serious and entertaining subject matter, and between solemn and playful voices. The variety of his writings and compilations is astonishing: vernacular short stories, folk songs, novels, thematic anthologies in classical language, *chuanqi* (Southern drama), poetry and *sanqu* (art songs), contemporary history, examination handbooks, jokes and riddles, gambling guides, and a gazetteer. The best-known compilation of this prolific writer may be the *Sanyan* (*Three Words*), a fine collection of 120 vernacular short stories from Ming and earlier sources in three volumes: *Gujin xiaoshuo* (*Stories Old and New*, c. 1620)—also known as *Yushi mingyan* (*Illustrious Words to Instruct the World*), *Jingshi tongyan* (*Comprehensive Words to Admonish the World*, 1624), and *Xingshi hengyan* (*Constant Words to Sober the World*, 1627). *Sanyan* attracts modern scholars' attention because while being highly entertaining, the stories allow us to have a glimpse of the spiritual and material lives of common people in Ming China.

While a great number of *Sanyan* short stories have been translated into English (some of them in multiple versions),[17] the majority of the some 780 songs and 700-odd jokes in *Child's Folly* have not been rendered into English (there is a German translation of *Hill Songs* by Cornelia Töpelmann and a Japanese translation of *Hill Songs* by Oki Yasushi).[18] But to a historian, *Child's Folly* is no less valuable than *Sanyan* as a remarkable window on the behavior and mentality of Ming people. Reading the three collections of *Child's Folly* against one another and against other historical texts reveals a considerable degree of consistency, which validates it as a reliable source. By translating and analyzing more than one hundred and thirty entries of *Hanging Twigs*, *Hill Songs*, and *Treasury of Laughs*, focusing on humor and its historical meaning, this study hopes to highlight the juncture of history and literature.

## The Deep Structure of Humor

Philosophers, psychologists, sociologists, anthropologists, ethnologists, and literary critics have long been intrigued by the deep structure of humor, and their research findings vary. A significant point of divergence in scholarly opinions about humor centers round whether humor helps to maintain or subvert the established social and cultural patterns. Some, following the lead of Mikhail Bakhtin, see humor as a safety valve, which, through the release of tensions, helps to reduce the tensions and thereby sustain the existing cultural values and social structure. Others, such as Mary Douglas, regard humor as sort of an "anti-rite,"[19] which, by giving symbolic expression to the inconsistencies and irrationalities of the dominant patterns, disrupts the order and harmony imposed by standard rites.

There seems to be a grain of truth in both views. When personal flaws and social problems are brought out repeatedly in a hilarious manner, the matter may be trivialized; the audience may be bored, numbed, or made to feel that the flaws and problems are somehow universal and inevitable, and hence, acceptable. As people simply laugh it away, the flaws and problems need not be corrected. A possible example of humor helping to maintain the dominant structure is the ever-popular political sitcom. Michael Mulkay contends, "In so far as laughter and amusement are substitutes for serious political action, it seems likely that action designed to produce political change will be stunted rather than stimulated by the political sitcom."[20]

On the other hand, a suitable dose of humor may effectively expose the incongruities between appearance and essence, ideal and reality, norms and alternatives, and bring the defects of the dominant patterns into sharp focus. After the laughter subsides, critical consciousness may be awakened. Humor plays on the ambiguity of words and worlds. In an age when "the objective view of life has broken down and the need is felt to justify the subjective criteria of judgment," observes N. J. Jacobs, a philosophical use of humorous paradoxes may "bring to the surface some unexpected neglected aspect which would rouse us from our mental torpor."[21] In his study of the Japanese political cartoon at the turn of the twentieth century, Peter Duus finds that humor can work both ways. The political cartoon could serve as "a weapon both of the weak and the strong, as easily deployed in defense of the state as in an attack upon it."[22]

Other areas of disagreements on the ontology of humor concern questions such as whether humor is the exclusive property of the masses, and whether laughter liberates people from fear and anxiety. Bakhtin gives an affirmative answer to both. He differentiates popular culture from learned culture and assigns laughter only to the former. In his study of epic and novel, Bakhtin contends,

> It is precisely laughter that destroys the epic, and in general destroys any hierarchical (distancing and valorized) distance. As a distanced image a subject cannot be comical; to be made comical, it must be brought close. . . . Laughter has the remarkable power of making an object come up close, of drawing it into a zone of crude contact where

> one can finger it familiarly on all sides, turn it upside down, inside out, peer at it from above and below, break open its external shell, look into its center, doubt it, take it apart, dismember it, lay it bare and expose it, examine it freely and experiment with it. Laughter demolishes fear and piety before an object, before a world, making of it an object of familiar contact and thus clearing the ground for an absolutely free investigation of it.[23]

Bakhtin's rather one-sided view does not bear scrutiny. Cultural historians have found ample evidence of humor among monks, philosophers, and statesmen, and they question if laughter and fear are mutually exclusive. Aaron Gurevich, for example, points out that one of the main aspects of popular culture in Europe of the Middle Ages was fear of going to hell after death. He says, "[P]recisely because the majority of the people could not rid themselves of this fear of eternal damnation, their fear was, to some extent, psychologically balanced by their attitude towards laughter and happiness. Joy and fear were intrinsically and intimately interconnected."[24]

Despite all the contention, most scholars seem to agree that humorous material is capable of inducing a smile or a laugh because it touches on some recognizable contradictions, conflicts, or incongruities existent in the objective and/or subjective universe common to the humorist and the audience. If the humorous reference were alien or unfamiliar to the participants, it would not work. Since humorous discourse is often an outgrowth of the strains and tensions within historically specific social structure, cultural heritage, political system, personal relations, and collective mentality, it has historical meanings and can be studied as such.

## Historical Study of Humor

Jacques Le Goff justifies a historical approach to humor and laughter in the following passage:

> I hope to validate an initial, very general, observation, but one that we should not neglect because we think it banal: laughter is a cultural phenomenon. Depending on the society and period, attitudes to laughter, the ways in which it is practised, its objects and its forms are not constant but changing. Laughter is a social phenomenon. It requires at least two or three persons, real or imagined: one who causes laughter, one who laughs and one who is being laughed at, quite often also the person or persons one is laughing with. It is a social practice with its

> own codes, rituals, actors and theatre. . . . As a cultural and social phenomenon, laughter must have a history.[25]

Le Goff suggests that the study of humor include "on the one hand a history of values and mentalities and on the other a history of literary and artistic representations: a history of laughing and of making us laugh."[26] The former approach is contextual and the latter, textual. Taking these approaches one would find that the ruling discourse on humor changes over time, so do the producers of humor and the judgments on what is and is not funny.[27] Humor is neither transcultural nor ahistorical.

As a historical material, humorous discourse has an advantage, as well as disadvantage, over "serious" discourse. As Arthur Koestler observes, "The pattern underlying all varieties of humour is 'bisociative'—perceiving a situation or event in two habitually incompatible contexts."[28] Humor provokes laughter when it succeeds in fooling its victim. The audience is steadily led to anticipate something, which the punch line at the very end abruptly contradicts. The delayed revelation seems hilarious and preposterous, but is inherently probable. Otherwise it would be farcical and not truly funny. Unlike the coherent and consistent structure of serious discourse, which assumes unitary meanings, humor calls for a duality or even multiplicity of opposing meanings. This inner logic of "bisociation" makes humorous discourse a better medium than the serious discourse to depict the fluid complexities of the real world, which is full of ambiguities, contradictions, and surprises. Michael Mulkay contends that humor is "either consistently inconsistent or inconsistently consistent," a literature whose "interpretative openness" "seems more accurately to reflect or reproduce or allow for the multiple realities of the social world." In this respect, humor is "superior to ordinary, serious discourse, which is premised on an implicit denial of the fact that we live in a world of multiple meanings and multiple realities."[29] Paradoxically, even though we appreciate the merit of humorous material, when we use it for historical analysis we have to employ the opposite mode—the serious discourse. Due to the inevitable gap between the two modes—and the serious mode is inferior—we can only try to approach our evasive material, and are in danger of failing to get a full grip on it.

## Humor in Chinese Culture

Although scholarly attention to humorous discourse does not compare favorably with that paid to "serious" discourse, still, humor is recognized as a proper subject of scholarly inquiries, and research on humor in Western cultures has been voluminous. The same statement, however, cannot be made about humor in Chinese scholarship. Chinese historians have paid little attention to humorous material. This negligence may be explained by the bountiful supply of material in the "serious" mode, the persistent marginalization of humorous discourse in mainstream culture, and the linguistic as well as cultural barriers. It does not indicate a real shortage of humor in Chinese culture.

The equivalent of "humor" in modern Chinese is *youmo*, an existing Taoist term which the twentieth-century Chinese writer Lin Yutang borrows to transliterate (rather than translate) "humor"—he cannot find an exact Chinese equivalent to the English word. Originally denoting a serene and quietist state, the classical phrase *youmo* bears little resemblance to its modern counterpart. Lin Yutang justifies his choice of word by pointing out that the highest form of humorous utterance must be subtle (*you*) in its connotation, which is to be appreciated quietly (*mo*) by the receptive listener.[30] Chinese, according to Lin, were capable of this kind of humor. Lin's rendering reminds us of the humor of Zen masters, whose deliverance is often obscure and cryptic—for the enlightened minds only.[31]

Observing the exotic look of the term *youmo*, the May Fourth writer Lu Xun (1881-1936) laments, "'Humor' (*youmo*) is evidently not an indigenous product of China, nor are the Chinese a people good at humor."[32] Lu Xun and Lin Yutang were prominent opponents, but Lu's dismissive comment on Chinese humor was not simply a personal attack on Lin. The fact that the intellectual humor of magazines founded by Lin Yutang on the models of *Punch* and the *New Yorker* failed to draw enough readers in China to survive[33] seemed to justify Lu Xun's pessimism. However, the unfavorable condition for humor at that historical moment largely resulted from the harassment of censorship by various (humorless) political authorities, including the Nationalists, the Communists, and the Japanese Imperialists. The Chinese lack of humor is hardly a timeless truth. *Youmo* as humor is indeed new to China, but indigenous terms such as *guji* and *huixie* have signified funniness and playfulness since ancient times.[34] They can be regarded as approximation of "humor."

Although humorous materials were often classified as *xiaoshuo* (petty talk) and treated rather derogatorily by bibliographers, humor was a vehicle employed frequently by "serious" writers. Philosophers in China's Axial Age[35] used humorous anecdotes and parables "to explicate their doctrines, deflate their opponents, or to touch upon some ineffable and mystic truth."[36] Without knowledge of the term "bisociation" they nevertheless practiced the principle of loosening up the link between signifier and signified to enlighten their audience. The following is a good example:

> Zhuang Zi was one day fishing, when the Prince of Chu sent two high officials to interview him, saying that his Highness would be glad of Zhuang Zi's assistance in the administration of his government. The latter quietly fished on, and without looking around replied, "I have heard that in the state of Chu there is a sacred tortoise, which has been dead three thousand years, and which the prince keeps packed up in a box on the altar in his ancestral shrine. Now do you think that tortoise would rather be dead and have its remains thus honored, or be alive and wagging its tail in the mud?"
>
> The two officials answered that no doubt it would rather be alive and wagging its tail in the mud; whereupon Zhuang Zi cried out, "Begone! I too elect to remain wagging my tail in the mud."[37]

Zhuang Zi was not the only great thinker who tried to get himself "off the hook" politically by employing humor. The Grand Historian Sima Qian gingerly hid his criticism of the unstable emotions, arbitrary decision-making, and nepotism of his boss Emperor Han Wudi (r. 141-87 BC) in the inconspicuous "Guji liezhuan" (Biography of the Jesters) in his monumental *Shiji* (*Records of the Grand Historian*). But the political connotations of the jesters could not have escaped the notice of the ruling class. According to the twentieth-century Chinese scholar Rao Zongyi, bureaucrats called *baiguan* were established since high antiquity to collect critical remarks and humorous talks on the street for the purpose of gathering public opinions.[38] This institution was similar to the Music Bureau established by Emperor Han Wudi around 120 BC to collect popular songs and ballads in order to observe people's likes and dislikes and gather intelligence on possible "poetic omens" that portended dynastic decline.[39] Similar to the Western oracular tradition, the ditties or prophetic songs sung by ordinary children in the "streets and lanes" could be politicized as "satire directed against the ruling class by the ruled." Among the common targets of the satire were "greedy officials, avaricious members of the royal family, and conscription officers in the countryside."[40] The governmental collection of songs and jokes served the function of public opinions poll.

In the early fifth century, Prince Liu Yiqing (403-444) sponsored the compilation of *Shishuo xinyu* (*New Account of Tales of the*

*World*). The compilation "begins with a somewhat sober depiction of civic and personal virtues, continues through a series of special topics like recluses, outstanding women, technicians, artists, and eccentrics, and ends with a colorful catalogue of human folly and vice."[41] Regarding the *Shishuo xinyu* as more than an entertaining anthology of tales, but a historical writing mirroring standard history such as the *Shiji*, numerous imitators continued the legacy of *Shishuo* well into the modern era.[42]

Humor can be found in Chinese literature of various genres. In *Asian Laughter: An Anthology of Oriental Satire and Humor*, Leonard Feinberg puts together more than two hundred pages of Chinese humorous materials in English translation in the following categories: jokes, anecdotes, poetry, drama, short stories, novels, essays, and proverbs. The anthology is, of course, far from exhaustive.

The above review of humor in Chinese history indicates that rather than non-existent, humor is a notable element of Chinese culture. Lin Yutang proposes a "dangerous, sweeping generalization," which he believes "may nevertheless be true." "All good, pervading, solid lasting humor," contends Lin, "is based on a philosophy, a way of looking at things. We say the Chinese are humorous because they are philosophic." He further identifies Confucianism, or what he terms "a philosophy of common sense," as the philosophical foundation of Chinese humor.[43]

Lin Yutang's theory is a bit difficult to follow. How can common sense be the basis of humor? Common sense is, by definition, "ordinary," "unreflective," and free from "intellectual subtlety."[44] Doesn't humor require a *special* intellectual perception? As for Confucianism being a "philosophy of common sense," isn't it against all practical common senses to, for example, prioritize moral integrity over personal gains, and lay down one's life for a cause from which one oneself can obviously not benefit? But Lin Yutang apparently defines "common sense" a bit differently. He says,

> All popular folk humor, I believe, is more or less alike, depending on a common assent as to what is to be laughed at—the miser, the cheat, the quack doctor, the mother-in-law, and, above all, the henpecked husband—and on a sudden ease of tension which provides the comic relief. Thoughtful humor, however, is based on the perception of human errors, incongruities, cant, and hypocrisy, which admittedly are shared by all of us. The comic spirit is that human understanding which, being higher than academic intelligence, rises above the confusion and self-deception of our common notions, and points its finger at life's sham, futility, and follies. The true comic genius is really a

> higher, because subtler, form of intelligence because it sees what the others do not see, and under the cloak of fun exercises the criticism of man's ideas. Man is a laughing animal, an honor doubtfully shared by anthropoid apes, and that is why to err is bestial, but to laugh at our errors is human. Only that culture which, by its own intellectual richness, rises above itself through its more penetrating minds to exercise criticism of its ideas, vogues, and fetishes could qualify for the name of a human culture.[45]

So there seem to be two different kinds of humor, which require two different kinds of common sense. It takes only ordinary common sense to construct or to recognize stereotypical laughingstocks such as the miser, and so on. But it takes a more philosophical, and in the Chinese case, the Confucian, common sense to participate in "thoughtful humor." The more extraordinary kind of common sense required by the thoughtful humor is good, sound, rational judgment that is pure, simple, and childlike, and is therefore not corrupted by biases, misperceptions, and philistinism. This higher form of common sense enables one to take a macrocosmic view of the world, to see through the illusions of life, and to escape the trap of "the confusion and self-deception of our common notions" by laughing heartily at "life's sham, futility, and follies," including the follies of one's own thought, character, and behavior. A good humorist is not to be fooled by these follies. From this perspective, Confucianism may be termed "a philosophy of common sense," and common sense so defined can be regarded as the philosophical foundation of Chinese humor.

George Kao also sees a philosophical dimension of Chinese humor. He maintains, "Chinese humor, to a greater degree than that of any other people, sees the ludicrous in the pathos of life. It is the result of a philosophical reaction to adversity coupled with innate optimism about the future."[46] The pages of four millennia of Chinese history, beginning with the Shang dynasty, have doubtless been filled with human tragedies due to the perennial occurrences of political tyranny, dynastic revolutions, foreign invasions, economic crises, famines, plagues, among other man-made and natural disasters. Without a sense of humor it would have been virtually impossible for the Chinese to survive all the adversity that life presented them. Pessimism is not absent from Chinese culture; it has a strong presence from time to time. But China could not afford to dwell on pessimism. The civilization has to rely on an optimistic and humorous attitude toward life to get through the tyranny of its history. Here Confucianism again stands out. Relative to the other two major thought systems in China—Taoism and Buddhism—Confucianism has a stronger affirmation of the meaning of life in the here and now and a more optimistic outlook on humanity. The Confucian values of a distinct this-worldly nature may be part of what Lin Yutang means by "common sense." And it may well be Confucian humor that has contributed to the tenacity of the Chinese people and the longevity of the Chinese civilization.

Lin Yutang praises Confucius profusely for his sense of humor. To Lin Yutang, Confucius' humor was a natural development of his humanity. Confucius was flesh and blood, he was rich in emotions, and he was not afraid to show his "human" traits—the *Analects* recorded Confucius laughing, crying, singing, castigating, and cursing. He mocked his disciples, he mocked himself, and he mocked his contemporaries for their affectation, hedonism, incompetence, and vices. But even though his talents were unappreciated by any of the potential employers of the time, he did not cry out in total despair. Rather, he kept his spirits high. This resilience was the origin of Confucius' humor.[47]

There is a good reason why Lin Yutang singles out Confucius in his discussion of Chinese humor—Confucius has been canonized as the Utmost Sage, the Model Teacher of All Time, and as such he seems to have always kept a straight face. If even the Sage has a human and humorous side, how much more so do ordinary Chinese? Indeed Confucianism does not monopolize humor in Chinese culture. Taoists and Chan (Zen) Buddhists are also noted for their humor because of their love of paradoxes. Chinese philosophers, writers, and artists are often very playful with their material, even when they have a serious intent. Henry Wells observes that Chinese humor may "at times be childlike but never childish."[48] Comedy is childlike; it celebrates life. Farce is childish; it ridicules life. Good humor is comic, but not farcical. Humor in Chinese culture "ranges from the macabre to the highly refined, from burly outspokenness with freedom from inhibition to subtle and delicate understatement, from extravagance to intimation. It may be tart but never quite acidulous. . . . It presumes a moment of happiness and a sense of well-being. . . . It takes positive pleasure in contemplating life's unreasonableness."[49] Chinese humor is healthful; it maintains sanity.

But Chinese humor eludes the Western world. Henry Wells points out a characteristic of humor which is embedded in the Chinese language:

> Their language itself abounds in intimations implicit in their written characters and in the halftones of its extraordinary inflections. Hence

> the incongruity at the root of all humor lies peculiarly at the root and germ of Chinese humor. This is less outspoken or obvious than ours, less dependent on verbal wit and even less conspicuously resting on the surface than humor of the Hindus or the Japanese. The refractions are peculiarly delicate, the emanations singularly subtle. For this very reason the field cannot be too often studied and explored.[50]

And perhaps for this very reason Chinese humor has *not* been studied often. No matter how witty the puns and allusions are, they do not translate into humor in another language: the cultural link between the jester and the audience is missing.

This missing link explains why it is so difficult for English readers to laugh while reading texts such as *Jokes on the Four Books* (*Sishu xiao*), attributed to our "Arch-Individualist" Li Zhi,[51] and *Laughs to Keep One Awake (Seisuisho)*, compiled between 1615 and 1623 by Anrakuan Sakuden (1554-1642).[52] After having been translated into English, with painstaking annotations, the humor of the two texts is inevitably lost.

The *Jokes on the Four Book* is a sixteenth-century Chinese joke book, a crafty parody of the *Four Books* (*Analects*, *Mencius*, *Great Learning*, and *Doctrine of the Mean*), Confucian Classics which constitute the standard curriculum of civil service exams in late imperial China. It is probably one of the sources for Feng Menglong's *Treasury of Laughs*. Truncating the text of the (deadly serious) Classics for hilarious comic effects, *Jokes on the Four Books* is oriented toward an audience well versed in the highly ambiguous and paradoxical classical Chinese. The *Laughs to Keep One Awake* is a Japanese joke book roughly contemporary to the *Treasury of Laughs*. Although similar in format to *Treasury of Laughs*, *Laughs to Keep One Awake* relies too heavily on linguistic incongruity to touch off laughter in an audience that is not literate in Japanese puns and literary allusions.

Readers of this study need not worry. *Child's Folly* was oriented toward a much less exclusive audience, and the content went well beyond literary themes. Despite the frequent flaunting of the authors' ingenuity in wordplay, the works contained plenty of humorous materials that involved neither complicated puns nor obscure allusions. Blessedly for the historians, the materials were both humorous and rich in historical connotations.

*Child's Folly* provoked laughter through plays on words, surprising contrasts, and exhibitions of incongruities in the social behavior of Ming people. Some of the heroes and heroines in *Child's Folly* were funny because they naively failed to understand social conventions, and some others, because they understood the conventions *too* well. The latter lost their innocent "child's folly"—Feng Menglong's version of Li Zhi's "childlike mind"—when they strove to gain more profit and respect than they were entitled to. As Henry Wells contends, "When a work of wit and trenchancy shows moral indignation on one hand or tender sympathy on the other it veers away from pure humor, becoming in the first instance satirical, in the second romantic."[53] Some of the entries of *Child's Folly* could be termed romantic: they poked fun at intellectually or physically challenged persons while allowing sympathy. But many other jokes inhibited empathy toward the spiritually inferior comic butts. These could be regarded as satire which was intended to expose human folly and social ailments, so as to persuade the audience to take a moral stand transcending marketplace morality and earthly conventions.

As a professional writer, Feng Menglong wrote first and foremost for entertainment. Any works that bore his name sold well, attesting to their strong appeal to the taste of the general public at that time. It is this popularity that makes his writing a good source to study the general sentiments of his time. Moreover, Feng's writings also projected his intellectual conscience as a mediator between the core and the periphery of Chinese culture and society. Feng's heavy editing significantly toned down the vulgarity and obscenity of his source material, but he deliberately left traces of vulgarity and obscenity to retain the works' folk colors and to make a point about culture and society.

Feng was critical of those who tended to polarize culture and society as "high" and "low." The result of such polarity, he warned, was that high culture would become ever more gaudy and low culture ever more bawdy, leaving the fabric of culture and society hollow. He therefore urged concern and respect for the people and culture of the periphery, lest they slip into total obscurity, and he suggested that hackneyed scholars invigorate themselves by learning from simple commoners. As we shall later see, the value of such an editorial approach is contestable: as Feng tried to bridge the higher and lower strata of culture and society, in the eyes of some of his modern critics, he altered the "authentic" folk literature rather than preserve it. Feng's strongest defense, on the other hand, may be Alan Dundes' definition of folk literature around a broadly defined "common tradition" shared by all the participants, crossing class lines.[54]

Because Feng Menglong was a well-rounded compiler, *Child's Folly* presents a remarkably wide spectrum of funny snapshots of Ming China. The snapshots captured images of a society that was full of tensions and ambiguities, but still possessed the capacity to make fun of itself. An intellectual exploration of the complicated stories behind the stories promises to be exciting and rewarding. I hope readers of this volume will find that this is a promise that holds true.

## Notes:

1. Feng Menglong, *Xiaofu*, *Ming Qing shanben xiaoshuo congkan chu bian* (Taipei: Tianyi chuban she, 1985), 13: 8b-9a; 11: 9a; 8: 6a-b.

2. Jan Bremmer and Herman Roodenburg, "Introduction: Humour and History," in *A Cultural History of Humour: From Antiquity to the Present Day*, ed. idem. (Cambridge: Polity Press, 1997), 1-2.

3. *Webster's Third New International Dictionary of the English Language, Unabridged* (Springfield, MA: Merriam-Webster, 1986), 1102.

4. Brook, *Confusions of Pleasure*, 127.

5. Wm. Theodore de Bary, "Individualism and Humanitarianism in Late Ming Thought," in *Self and Society in Ming Thought*, ed. idem (New York: Columbia University Press, 1970), 188-225.

6. Li Zhi, "Tongxin shuo," in *Fen shu* (Taipei: Heluo tushu chuban she, 1974), 97-99.

7. Wm. Theodore de Bary, "Individualism and Humanitarianism in Late Ming Thought," 145-247.

8. Hulu Sheng, "Ji *Sanxiao* lue,"*Jueying sanxiao*, compiled by Kaikou Shiren and commented by Wendao Xiashi, Ming edition preserved in the College of Liberal Arts in Tokyo University. The exact reference to *Treasury of Laughs* is "*Xiaofu* among the three collections (*san nong*) of *Tongchi*" (*lue*: 2a). Since *Hanging Twigs* is the first collection of *Child's Folly* and *Hill Songs* is the second collection, *Treasury of Laughs* must be the third collection. See Oki Yasushi, "Fu Muryu 'Sanka' no kenkyu," *Toyo Bunka Kenkyujo kiyo* 105 (1988): 208. For bibliographic information on the *Jueying sanxiao*, see Hidetaka Otsuka, "*Zetsuei Sansho* ni tsuite," *Todai Chutetsubun Gakkai ho* 8 (June 1983): 159-62. My gratitude to Oki Yasuishi for sending me copies of the above materials.

9. Liu Yonglong and Su Conglin, *Jiuling xiaohua* (Taipei: Yushu tushu chuban youxian gongsi, 1994), 173-75.

10. I owe this insight to conversation with Kimberly Besio, Patricia Sieber, and Ding Naifei, April 1995.

11. Walter Redfern, *Puns* (Oxford: Basil Blackwell, 1984), 10.

12. Richard John Lynn, "Alternate Routes to Self-Realization in Ming Theories of Poetry," in *Theories of the Arts in China*, eds. Susan Bush and Christian Murck (Princeton: Princeton University Press, 1983), 333.

13. Andrew Plaks, *The Four Masterworks of the Ming Novel: Ssu-ta ch'i-shu* (Princeton: Princeton University Press, 1987), 35. For a detailed discussion of *xiaopin* essays, see Cao Shujuan, *Wan Ming xingling xiaopin yanjiu* (Taipei: Wenjing chuban she, 1988). For an anthology of *xiaopin* in English, see Yang Ye, *Vignettes from the Late Ming: A Hsiao-p'in Anthology* (Seattle: University of Washington Press, 1999).

14. Wang Ting, "Wan Feng Youlong," in Chen Hu, *Liyou ji* (Qiaofan Lou congshu), *shang*: 16b.

15. Zhu Yizun, *Ming shi zong* (n.d.), 71: 23a-b. *Siku quanshu zongmu tiyao, juan* 132, "Zi bu Zajia lei," in *Guoxue jiben congshu si bai zhong*, edited by Wang Yunwu (Taipei: Commercial Press, 1968), 2739.

16. Li Yu, "Sanguozhi yanyi xu," in "Li Liweng piyue Sanguozhi," *Li Yu quanji* (Zhejiang: Zhejiang guji chuban she, 1992), vol. 10, 1. For Feng Menglong's involvement in the commercialization of these novels see Oki Yasushi, *Minmatsu no hagure tsishikizin: Fu Muryu to sosu bunka* (Tokyo: Kodanshya, 1995), 140-45.

17. The most accessible collections are Cyril Birch, *Stories from a Ming Collection: The Art of the Chinese Story-Teller* (New York: Grove Weidenfeld, 1958); John Lyman Bishop, *The Colloquial Short Story in China: A Study of the San-yen Collections*, Harvard Yenching Institute Series 14 (Cambridge: Harvard University Press, 1956); William Dolby, *The Perfect Lady by Mistake and Other Stories by Feng Meng-lung (1574-1646)* (London: Elek, 1976); Y. W. Ma and Joseph S. M. Lau, eds, *Traditional Chinese Stories: Themes and Variations* (New York: Columbia University Press, 1978); Yang Hsien-yi and Gladys Yang, *The Courtesan's Jewel Box: Chinese Stories of the Xth-XVIIth Centuries* (Beijing: Foreign Languages Press, 1957); Yang Hsien-yi and Gladys Yang, *Lazy Dragon: Chinese Stories from the Ming Dynasty* (Beijng: Foreign Languages Press, 1994); Shuhui Yang and Yunqin Yang, trans., *Stories Old and New* (Seattle: University of Washington Press, 2000); and Shuhui Yang and Yunqin Yang, trans., *Stories to Caution the World* (Seattle: University of Washington Press, forthcoming).

18. Oki Yasushi translates twelve entries of the *Hill Songs* and two entries of the *Hanging Twigs* in Oki Yasushi, "Women in Feng Menglong's 'Mountain Songs,'" in *Writing Women in Late Imperial China*, eds. Ellen Widmer and Kang-i Sun Chang (Stanford: Stanford University Press, 1997), 131-43. Victor H. Mair translates two entries of the *Treasury of Laughs* and three entries of its sequel *Expanded Treasury of Laughs* in *The Columbia Anthology of Traditional Chinese Literature*, ed. idem (New York: Columbia University Press, 1994), 662-64. Jon Kowallis translates thirty-seven jokes from the *Treasury of Laughs* and twenty-one jokes from the *Expanded Treausry of Laughs* in *Wit and Humor from Old Cathay* (Beijing: Panda Books, 1986), 95-128. There is a German translation of the *Hill Songs*, Cornelia Töpelmann, *Shan-ko von Feng Meng-lung: Eine volksliedersammlung aus der Ming-zeit* (Wiesbaden: Franz Steiner, 1973), and a Japanese translation, Oki Yasushi, *Fu Muryu sanka no kenkyu: Chugoku Mindai no tsuzoku kayo* (Tokyo: Keiso shobo, 2003).

19. Mary Douglas, *Implicit Meanings* (London: Routledge & Kegan Paul, 1975), 102.

20. Michael Mulkay, *On Humor: Its Nature and Its Place in Modern Society* (Oxford: Basil Blackwell, 1988), 195.

21. N. J. Jacobs, *Naming-Day in Eden* (London: Gollancz, 1958), 150.

22. Duus, 989.

23. Mikhail Bakhtin, "Epic and Novel: Toward a Methodology for the Study of the Novel," in *The Dialogic Imagination: Four Essays by M. M. Bakhtin*, ed. Michael Holquist, trans. Caryl Emerson and Michael Holquist (Austin: University of Texas Press, 1981), 23.

24. Aaron Gurevich, "Bakhtin and His Theory of Carnival," in *A Cultural History of Humour*, ed. Bremmer and Roodenburg, 57.

25. Jacques Le Goff, "Laughter in the Middle Ages," in *A Cultural History of Humour*, ed. Bremmer and Roodenburg, 40.

26. Ibid., 42.

27. Bremmer and Roodenburg, "Introduction," in *A Cultural History of Humor*, 6-7.

28. Arthur Koestler, *The Act of Creation* (London: Arkana, 1989), 95.

29. Mulkay, 219.

30. Lin Yutang, "Youmo zahua," in *Qingsuan yueliang: Yutang youmo wenxuan, xia*, edited by Lin Taiyi (Taipei: Lianjing chuban shiye youxian gongsi, 1994), 254.

31. Because the question and answer between the Zen master and the student is to arouse the student's doubt, so as to induce him to seek and get the answer on his own, the pivotal saying of the Zen master could be "thoroughly unexpected and unthinkable by ordinary convention, even cryptic or humorous, with an endless potential of application to various situations." See Nan Huai-Chin, trans. Thomas Cleary, *The Story of Chinese Zen* (Boston: Charles E. Tuttle, 1995), 121.

32. Lu Xun, "Cong fengci dao youmo," in *Lu Xun xuanji* (Hong Kong: Wencai chuban she, 1968), 195.

33. Leonard Feinberg, ed., *Asian Laughter: An Anthology of Oriental Satire and Humor* (New York: John Weatherhill, 1971), 4-5.

34. See Gaylord Kai Loh Leung's entry on *ku-chi* (*guji*) in *The Indiana Companion to Traditional Chinese Literature*, ed. William H. Nienhauser, Jr. (Bloomington: Indiana University Press, 1986), 482-84.

35. Karl Jaspers coins the term "Axial Age" to refer to the intellectual breakthroughs developed out of the tension between the transcendental and mundane orders in the first millennium before the Christian era. The evolutions took place in Ancient Israel, Ancient Greece, Early Christianity, Zoroastrian Iran, early Imperial China, and the Hindu and Buddhist civilizations. For a comprehensive discussion of the Axial Age civilization in China see S. N. Eisenstadt, ed., *The Origins and Diversity of Axial Age Civilizations* (New York: State University of New York Press, 1986), 291-373.

36. Jon Kowallis, *Wit and Humor from Old Cathay*, 5.

37. "Independence," *Zhuang Zi*, translated by Herbert A. Giles, Lin Yutang, and others, in *Asian Laughter*, ed. Feinberg, 43-44.

38. Rao Zongyi, "Lun xiaoshuo yu baiguan: Qin jian zhong 'baiguan' ji Ru Chun cheng Weishi wei 'ouyu wei bai' shuo," in idem, *Wen Che* (Taipei: Xuesheng shuju, 1991), vol. 1, 253-60.

39. James J. Y. Liu, *Chinese Theories of Literature* (Chicago: The University of Chicago Press, 1975), 65.

40. Anne Birrell, *Popular Songs and Ballads of Han China* (London: Unwin Hyman, 1988), 102.

41. Richard B. Mather, entry on *Shih-shuo hsin-yü* (*Shishuo xinyu*) in *Indiana Companion*, 704. Also see his *Shih-shuo hsin-yü: A New Account of Tales of the World* (Minneapolis: University of Minnesota Press, 1976).

42. Nanxiu Qian, *Spirit and Self in Medieval China: The Shih-shuo hsin-yü and Its Legacy* (Honolulu: University of Hawai'i Press, 2001).

43. George Kao, ed., *Chinese Wit and Humor* (New York: Coward-McCann, 1946), xxx.

44. *Webster's Dictionary*, 459.

45. George Kao, xxxiii.

46. Ibid., xxi.

47. Lin Yutang, "Si Kong Zi," in *Qingsuan yueliang*, 97-102.

48. Henry W. Wells, *Traditional Chinese Humor: A Study in Art and Literature* (Bloomington: Indiana University Press, 1971), 4.

49. Ibid., 5.

50. Ibid., 228.

51. Ching-sheng Huang, "Jokes on the Four Books: Cultural Criticism in Early Modern China," Ph.D. diss., University of Arizona, 1998.

52. Miles Kenneth McElrath, Jr., "The Seisuisho of Anrakuan Sakuden," Ph. D. diss., University of Michigan, 1971. I am grateful to Robert Borgen for bringing this reference to my attention.

53. Wells, 217.

54. See, for example, Alan Dundes, *Folklore Matters* (Knoxville: The University of Tennessee Press, 1989).

# 2

# Feng Menglong and His World

# 馮夢龍的世界

Feng Menglong was not only a man who lived in Jiangnan in the late Ming, but also a man *of* Jiangnan in the late Ming: his heartbeat resonated with that of his time and his surroundings. He was also a heavy-handed editor who projected his ego very strongly in his compilations: he felt free to alter the words, structure, and even the story line of his material as he saw fit, and to talk to his audience directly. The person, the world he lived in, and the world he created formed an interlocking trio. A temporal and spatial overview of the historical context of *Child's Folly*, along with a biographical study of Feng Menglong's life, writing, and thought, will help us analyze the text of *Child's Folly* more comprehensively. Conversely, a comprehensive textual analysis of *Child's Folly* will add to our understanding of Feng Menglong and his world.

## Late Ming Jiangnan: The Promised Land of Laughs and Tears[1]

The late Ming saw the peak of several literary genres. Besides jokes, erotica, and tales of the shrew, the period also produced a great number of autobiographies[2] as well as oneiromancy and stories about dreams[3]. For the historian as detective, the popularity of these literary genres gives clues to a high level of anxiety: anxiety about the unknown in a rapidly changing world; anxiety about keeping up in a competitive world; anxiety about self-identity in an intrusive world; anxieties about the tension between expectations and performances, dream and reality, and duties and desires in a liberating yet demanding world; and anxieties caused by frictions between the sexes and among segments of society in an alienating world. The anxiety seemed to be particularly high in the Jiangnan area.

In his physiographic study of late imperial China, G. William Skinner constructs eight "macroregions" of China: Northwest China, North China, Upper Yangzi, Middle Yangzi, Lower Yangzi, Yun-Gui, Lingnan, and Southeast Coast.[4] Among these, the Lower Yangzi, or Jiangnan, has attracted the greatest scholarly attention, and for good reason.

Late sixteenth-, early seventeenth-century China was an integral part of the emerging world economy. Massive amounts of silver flowed into China from Japan and Spanish-America in exchange for China's luxury goods—silk, brocade, cotton textiles, ceramics, copper cash, gold, precious stones, mercury, and tea, to name but a few.[5] Within China, domestic trade also flourished. Regional and specialized products such as the ceramics of Jingdezhen, the brushes of Hangzhou, the paper of Anhui, and the bamboo, wood, lacquer, and tallow of western Zhejiang enjoyed a reputation on an empire-wide scale.[6] Commercial prosperity accelerated cultural accomplishments. Jiangnan, the fertile region south of the Yangzi River between modern Shanghai and Nanjing, was the economic and cultural center of China of the day. It was a highly commercialized region in which the arts and humanities flourished, on a par with those of the northern Italy of the Renaissance.

But the picture of Jiangnan in late Ming China was not all rosy. Timothy Brook writes, "For upper gentry, large landowners, and rich merchants, the late Ming was a time of cultural brilliance, innovative ideas, and endless pleasure—also a time of confusion and anxiety. At the other end of the social scale, the anxious poor survived at the edges of this prosperity as short-term tenants, wage laborers, domestic servants, woodcutters, and seasonal migrants."[7] Tremendous tensions and contradictions could be found in the culture of Jiangnan. Social fluidity gave rise to anxiety over blurred class lines. The booming economy raised concerns over moral decadence. Widespread literacy and popularization of education sharpened a sense of discrimination against the undereducated. The flourishing of various schools of arts, syncretic religions, and philosophical thoughts heated up the debates over orthodoxy and heterodoxy. Ironically, fluidity did not translate into tolerance.

Three groups of people dominated the cultural scenery of Jiangnan: well-to-do merchants interested in raising their social status through possession of *objets d'art* and association with literati; literati frustrated by the stifling examination system and dangerous official careers in an imperial court characterized by mediocre rulers, factional strife, and personalization of politics;[8] and courtesans acquainted with literati through their literary and artistic talents, in addition to a feminine charm absent from most women of more "orthodox" upbringing. The presence of courtesans often served to smooth out the awkward transactions between the merchants and the literati. A conversation between the renowned Suzhou scholar Wang Shizhen (1526-1590) and his colleague Zhan Jingfeng demonstrated their views of the undignified interdependence of scholars and merchants: Wang Shizhen observed that Huizhou merchants went after Suzhou literati like flies attracted by mutton. Zhan Jingfeng retorted that Suzhou literati also went after Huizhou merchants like flies attracted by mutton.[9] Such cynicism notwithstanding, culture and commerce intertwined in the thriving markets in published books, tutorial services, performing arts, works of calligraphy and painting, antique bronzes, contemporary ceramics of renowned kilns, among other "superfluous things" (to borrow Craig Clunas's phrase) which were not for daily use but for pleasure and for display of taste and wealth.

Suzhou, in modern Jiangsu province, was particularly prosperous among the cities of Jiangnan. In terms of cultural and economic achievements, even the capital city of Beijing was no match for Suzhou. Evidence of Suzhou's leadership in fashion can be found in the popularity of the term "hint of Su (*Su yi*)." The Ming scholar Xue Gang traced the origin of the term to a Hangzhou magistrate, who in 1596 was so offended by the flamboyant footgear of a man under his jurisdiction that he ordered him flogged and "cangued." The cangue was a heavy wooden stock with a hole in the middle, which a convict of minor offense in imperial China was required to wear around the neck for a period of time, as a way of punishment.[10] Without an existing name for the crime, which was to be posted on the cangue for public view, the magistrate invented the term "hint of Su" to refer to the offense of following the decadent fashion of Suzhou.[11]

Song Maocheng, on the other hand, believed the "hint of Su" to originate from a mistaken interpretation of an official's comment on the imperial son-in-law's essay. The commentator praised the essay for its "exuberant hint of Su," meaning the eloquent writing style of Su Shi (1037-1101), one of the most popular Song dynasty writers in the Ming, along with his almost equally famous father and brother, collectively called the "Three Sus." Courtiers, and even the emperor, misunderstood the comment as a reference to the unconventional and refreshing style characteristic of Suzhou artifacts, outfit, and customs. Therefore the "hint of Su" acquired a positive meaning and became a fad. An exemplification of the fad of *Su yi* was to seat host and guest East-West rather than South-North, to break up the convention of assigning a hierarchical relation through seating arrangement.[12]

Whichever the origin of the term, *Su yi* came to serve as an index of one's fashion sense. Certainly not everybody approved of it. Zhang Dai (1599-1684?), a native of the neighboring province of Zhejiang, was indignant over his fellow countrymen's blind imitation of Suzhou fashion. "When the Suzhou people fancy tall hats and wide sleeves, the Zhejiang people follow suit. Before everybody in Zhejiang manages to catch on, however, the hats in Suzhou have turned short and the sleeves have turned narrow. Therefore Suzhou people often make fun of Zhejiang people for our failure to catch up. Indeed [if all we do is imitate] we won't ever catch up!"[13]

Zhang Han (1511-1593),[14] a Zhejiang scholar-official from an artisan background, expressed a different uneasiness with Suzhou's fashions:

> Concerning the customs of the populace, in general people south of the Yangzi are more extravagant than those north of it, and no extravagance south of the Yangzi surpasses that of Suzhou. From of old, the customs of Suzhou have been habituated to excess and splendor and a delight in the rare and strange, to which the sentiments of the people there are invariably drawn. The garments made in Suzhou are splendid, as if to be otherwise would be uncultured. The vessels made in Suzhou are beautified, as if to be otherwise would be valueless. The whole world appreciates the garments of Suzhou, and Suzhou gives garments still more craftsmanship. The whole world values Suzhou vessels, and Suzhou gives vessels still more craftsmanship. In this way the extravagance of Suzhou customs becomes even more extravagant, so how can the desire of the world for the objects of Suzhou be stifled and turned to moderation? It is easy to turn people from moderation to excess, but it is hard to turn them from excess back to moderation.[15]

We see in the above statement an anxiety over the "spiritual pollution" entailed by over-commercialization. Such anxiety had a classical origin. Frugality was a traditional virtue which, vigorously observed by the whole empire, was supposed to keep people's minds contented and social order secured. Extravagance aroused materialistic desires and corrupted people's minds; it should not be encouraged.

To the Ming court at Beijing, on top of this classical concern over extravagance, there might have been a more contemporary apprehension of Jiangnan, whose "subversive" potential had been under official vigilance ever since the dawn of the dynasty. After the Ming founder Zhu Yuanzhang (Taizu, the Hongwu emperor, r. 1368-1398) established his imperial seat in Nanjing,[16] at least 59,000 "wealthy households" of eastern Jiangnan were moved to Nanjing and their lands converted into "official fields," which the government then rented to tenants.

In addition to nurturing the poor peasantry and populating the new capital, there seemed to be a third motive behind this move of Taizu's: to punish wealthy gentry of Jiangnan for having supported Zhang Shicheng (1321-1367), one of Taizu's rivals in competition for the throne.[17] Suzhou, having been the power base of Zhang Shicheng, was particularly severely punished. Taizu levied a tremendous tax upon Suzhou, which devastated its economy for a century.[18] It was not until the 1430s that the economic sanction was officially relieved,[19] and not until the latter half of the century that Suzhou gradually recovered its economic prosperity. But up until the sixteenth century, according to Matteo Ricci, the district was still "heavily patrolled and guarded, as the fear of rebellion from this quarter [was] greater than from anywhere else in the kingdom."[20]

No late Ming emperors demonstrated a distrust of Jiangnan as explicitly as Emperors Yongzhen (r. 1723-1735) and Qianlong (r. 1736-1795) of the succeeding Qing dynasty (1644-1911).[21] But the Ming court could not have been unaware that after Beijing replaced Nanjing as the nation's primary capital in 1421, the government of Nanjing had gradually become the haven of officials in disfavor and a center of political dissent was formed in the area. With their tremendous economic power and prevailing intellectual influence, the rich merchants, independent-minded literati, and political dissidents in Jiangnan could well pose a potential threat to the central government in Beijing.

The anxiety over commercial prosperity and extravagant lifestyle of Jiangnan was in strong evidence in the discourse among officials and intellectuals in the late Ming.[22] Their concerns were not imaginary: corrupted social customs and heightened social strain were real problems. In the late Ming the pursuit of extravagance went so far that it was no longer possible to enforce the sumptuary laws established by Emperor Taizu: palace musicians emulated the attire of civil officials, maidservants in wealthy families imitated the costumes of ranking ladies, even poor scholars found it difficult to resist the temptation to wear colorful clothing. Some people were simply ignorant of the sumptuary laws, and others took pride in violating the legally and ritually sanctified class distinction.[23] But this was not the most serious social problem.

The most serious social problem came from a side effect of mercantilism—unequal distribution of wealth. Not only was there a disparity in wealth between the rich and the poor, but the rich, being able to purchase power, were able to evade corvée duty and taxation and transfer the tax burden to the poor, making the poor even poorer. Clashes between the rich and the poor sometimes resulted in terrifying riots.[24] Now, after a lapse of about four centuries, William Atwell is in agreement with the apprehensive Ming officials when he observes, from a global perspective, that the bullion flowing into China after the middle of the sixteenth century "facilitated high levels of public expenditure, rapid urban growth, and intense economic competition, all of which proved to be socially and politically disruptive."[25]

But the diversified culture of the late Ming did not allow skeptical views of commercial activities to monopolize the discourse. An alternative view was proposed by Lu Ji (1515-1552), who came from a wealthy office- and land-holding family based in Shanghai. Reviving a pro-commercialization theory contained in the "Treatise on Extravagance" (*Chimi pian*) in the miscellany *Guan Zi*, which had been dormant in China for almost two millennia since its last appearance around 190 BC,[26] Lu argued eloquently that frugality was associated with poverty and extravagance, with richness. Jiangnan was an excellent example of the latter condition:

> Today the wealth of the nation is concentrated in the Jiangnan area. Nowhere else will we find people more extravagant than those of Suzhou and Hangzhou, where numerous people till no land but taste the most delicious food, weave no thread but wear the most beautified clothes. This is because the custom there is extravagant and a large number of people there are pursuing secondary occupations. Just take the lakes and mountains of Suzhou and Hangzhou as examples. In accord with seasonal events, the rich people of Suzhou and Hangzhou tour these scenic spots in decorated pleasure boats and in sedan chairs. Tasting plenty of delicacies and mellow wines, they also enjoy singing and dancing performed by their entourage. This is surely extravagant. But few people recognize that a great number of sedan-chair carriers, boatmen, singsong boys, and dancing girls rely on the lake- and mountain-tours for a living. Hence, "the loss of one party is the profit of the other." If extravagance means dumping one's wealth in the ditch and squandering it to no avail, then it is advisable to prohibit extravagance. In reality, however, what is generally referred to as extravagance is no more than the luxurious spending of wealthy merchants and powerful families in the maintenance of huge houses, carriages, and horses, and in the enjoyment of food, drink, and clothing. When they are extrava-

> gant in food, the tiller and the cook share the profit; when they are extravagant in clothing, the weaver and the dealer share the profit.[27]

According to Lu Ji, the lavish life-style of Jiangnan stimulated production and created jobs; it was of wide benefit and thus deserved a warm welcome from the government and society alike.

The debate over the merits and demerits of commercialization was just one of the many expressions of scholarly reflection on the restless social and intellectual landscape of late Ming China. Two forces were simultaneously at work. On the one hand there was a tendency toward breaking the traditional boundaries between elevated and base social status, between high and low literature and arts, and between orthodox and heterodox behavior and ideology. On the other hand, there was an equally evident counter-force to harden the lines of discrimination. These two trends were not mutually exclusive or completely at odds: they interacted with each other and generated new theories, new practices, and new interpretations.

High social mobility and cultural fluidity made many late Ming literati apprehensive. To keep vigilance against what they regarded as philistinism, many resorted to binary categorization: whatever they stood for they elevated as "orthodoxy"; whatever they stood against they condemned as "heterodoxy." Such an attitude was reflected in the proliferation of scholarly works aiming at establishing an authoritative classification of poetry, painting, connoisseurship, and so on. Those who did not believe in the established "orthodoxy," on the other hand, stressed originality and creativity. Instead of following the old-fashioned and unimaginative "orthodoxy," argued the latter group, one should be true to one's authentic self and follow one's own individual nature.

The intellectual history of late imperial China was highly complex. But we shall simplify it here for a macroscopic view. In the field of philosophy, the "conservatives" were mostly followers of the relatively objective and elitist Cheng-Zhu (Cheng Yi (1033-1107) and Zhu Xi (1130-1200)) school, or "learning of principle" (*lixue*), while the "liberals" were mostly sympathizers of the relatively subjective and popularist Wang Yangming (1472-1529) school, or "learning of the mind" (*xinxue*). Although the Ming court sanctified a dogmatic version of Cheng-Zhuism as state orthodoxy, neither the Cheng-Zhu school nor the Wang Yangming school enjoyed overwhelming dominance in the field of philosophy.

Similar observations can be made on other intellectual undercurrents of the time, such as the archaic movement and its counterpart, which may be loosely termed the "romantic" movement. The archaic movement was spearheaded by the Former Seven Masters and the Latter Seven Masters, who promoted emulation of the prose of the Qin (221-206 BC) and Han (206 BC-AD 220) and the verse of the High Tang (713-765).[28] Such a neoclassical mode of writing attracted a huge following. But it also had its enemies. Critics of the archaic movement argued that this mode of writing was anachronistic and it stifled individual creativity. Rather than model themselves on previous format, the "romantics" developed new styles that were informal in structure and spontaneous in mood. They drew inspirations from folktales, folksongs, and jokes. To borrow the metaphor of Michael Holquist, while the neoclassicists "appropriated" the prose of Qin-Han and the poetry of High Tang masters by "ventriloquating" them, the romantics did likewise with popular literature.[29] However, while the neoclassicists deliberately mimicked classical models, the romantics did not self-consciously mimic literature of the masses. As Kathryn Lowry surmises, part of the romantic writers' motivation to look at popular literature was the pursuit of "authenticity," or "the concern to pin down an understanding of actual, ordinary and unelevated forms of expression." [30] Such pursuit was polemic to imitation.

The Ming romantics did not romanticize incessant cravings for the unattainable, as some Western Romantics, such as Johann Wolfgang von Goethe (1749-1832), did. But many Ming romantics did glorify passion and individual aspirations. They also demonstrated nostalgia for the good old days of primitiveness, before Confucian Classics were canonized and, in effect, rigidified ethic and aesthetic judgment. The "romantic" mode of writing permeated into poetry, drama, art songs, fiction, and *xiaopin* essays, generating a formidable countercurrent to the archaic movement. Although originality, creativity, and cardinal Confucian values were important for both the neoclassicists and the romantics, the two schools appeared to despise each other, and neither had decisive dominance in the literary field.

That the line of discrimination, between what belonged to "this culture of ours"[31] and what did not, was thin, fluid, and hard to settle demonstrated the multifarious nature of late Ming culture. That the literati insisted on drawing the line on their own terms also illustrated the tension among different schools. Such tension was in general healthy, and it rendered the intellectual field ever more lively. Jiangnan, where artists, writers, and thinkers congregated, was a center for such highly charged intellectual activities.[32]

There were quite a few good reasons why Jiangnan could attract a huge number of artists and men of letters: the beautiful scenery of the mountains and lakes and the charming congregation of singing girls and dancing ladies, both great sources for artistic inspiration; the comfortable life of big cities; the generous sponsorship of wealthy merchants; the easy access to good writing and painting utensils; the numerous publishing houses and art studios; the flourishing markets in cultural products; and the density of urban population. But there was also a dark side of the story: Jiangnan was able to absorb many talents partly because Beijing was not. There were some male literati, such as painters Shen Zhou (1427-1509) and Qiu Ying (d. 1552?), who voluntarily chose an artistic career over an official career because of their natural bents.[33] Female artists and poets, on the other hand, did not have that option. But in an age when the civil service examination was the standard "ladder of success" for educated males, a great majority of male intellectuals did not voluntarily choose culture over office. They were either rejected by the examination system, as the population and number of competitors grew,[34] or they were repelled by the undesirable political condition in the Ming court after they finally elbowed through the "thorny gates."[35]

The political sector of the late Ming proved perfectly capable of creating factionalism and controversies, but hopelessly incapable of solving them. Take the troublesome Wanli reign (1573-1620) as an example. After the emperor stopped holding audiences in 1589, he refused, for thirty years, to respond to petitions and left his officials to sort out one controversy after another, including such vital issues as the appointment of the heir apparent and the role of eunuchs in collecting special mining and market taxes.[36] The "increasing sclerosis in the heart of the bureaucracy"[37] since the Wanli reign cooled the political aspiration of some intellectuals while arousing strong resistance in others. Many demoralized literati reoriented their talents and energies toward the arts and humanities, occasionally venting their frustrations in their works, but in general turned their backs on politics. Some intellectuals were so disillusioned they lost their faith in principles and resorted to hedonism and moral relativism. The worst kind of educated men, not so much frustrated by politics as by their failure in the examinations, went so low as to become notorious troublemakers, stirring up disputes, instigating lawsuits, and leading protests, much to the indignation of their socially concerned peers.[38] Widespread literacy and popularization of education now became a curse, because far too many such pseudo-scholars were produced.

Disillusioned but still interested intellectuals, on the other hand, organized study groups to discuss the Five Classics[39] and criticize current affairs of the nation—activism in which Feng Menglong took a part. Among the most prominent study groups was the Ying She. Founded in 1624 in Suzhou by Zhang Pu (1602-1641), Zhang Cai (1596-1648), and Yang Tingshu (1595-1647), the Ying She later joined forces with other study groups all over the country and formed, in 1629, the famous restoration society Fu She.[40] From time to time study group members were drawn into political disputes.

A prominent example of this involvement was the 1626 Suzhou incident, which occurred during the reign of the muddleheaded Tianqi Emperor (r. 1621-1627), a virtual puppet of the notorious eunuch Wei Zhongxian (1568-1627). On his way to consolidate his power Wei needed to purge his political opponents, especially members of the Donglin fundamentalist reform movement.[41] In 1622, an official of the Donglin party Zhou Shunchang (1584-1626), in a time-honored form of protest, returned to his hometown Suzhou on extended leave of absence. In the same year, Feng Menglong was allegedly implicated in the publication of a fictional work critical of Wei and forced into seclusion, although this is very likely a case of mistaken identity on the part of modern researchers.[42]

Zhou Shunchang kept up his criticism of Wei Zhongxian and in 1626 Wei ordered Zhou's arrest. Suzhou literati, many of them Ying She members, made great efforts to rescue Zhou. After the attempts failed, Suzhou literati rallied a mass demonstration in which both students and commoners participated. During the demonstration government agents were killed. As a retaliation five commoners were executed, many others were exiled to the frontier, and the students were degraded or dismissed. If not for the natural calamities following the Suzhou incident—thought to be a correlative sign of heavenly wrath—the retaliation could have been more severe. The murder of Zhou Shunchang in a Beijing prison and the abortive demonstration effort deeply demoralized the outraged intellectuals.[43] Although the death of the Tianqi Emperor and the accession of the Chongzhen Emperor (r. 1628-1644) created a more favorable political climate for the reformist intellectuals, it was all too late to alter the downward slide of the Ming fortune.

Early Qing emperors and *kaozheng* ("evidential research") scholars often attributed the downfall of the Ming dynasty to Wang Yangming's heterodoxy. Benjamin Elman has argued forcefully that, contrary to its rather disparaging image in traditional Chinese historiography, the philological *kaozheng* scholarship was not an intellectuals' escapist response to the Manchu literary inquisitions. Rather, the *kaozheng* movement was the intellectuals' vehement self-examination and self-criticism, aimed at correcting the faults of late

Ming hedonism and moral relativism, as well as the apolitical and imprecise scholarship. The Qing emperors, in an effort to justify their take-over of China and to suppress individualistic sentiment in Jiangnan, happily sponsored such intellectual self-blame.[44]

Intellectual self-examination and self-criticism did not start with the Manchu take-over, however. It started in the late Ming, when intellectuals attempted to supplement the learning of principle, or learning of "moral substantiality and metaphysical truth," with the learning of practicality, or the "pursuit of objective, empirical investigation" such as statecraft.[45] In a way, *kaozheng* scholarship was an outgrowth of late Ming learning of practicality. The eminent *kaozheng* scholar Huang Zongxi (1610-1695), for example, was a member of the Fu She and his father Huang Zunsu (1584-1626) a Donglin martyr. Neither the Donglin nor the Fu She intellectuals were able to save the Ming dynasty. But it is a bit far-fetched to blame Li Zhi and other non-traditional intellectuals for the downfall of the Ming dynasty.

It is difficult to assess the responsibility for the fall of the Ming. The most immediate cause was, of course, Li Zicheng's (1605?-1645) mass rebellion in the desolate north.[46] The self-aggrandizement of the gentry in the forms of tax evasion, land annexation, and illegal acquisition of personal dependents, even forced slavery, had added hardships to a peasantry already impoverished by poor harvests. The 1641 official report that "in large areas of the north thirty percent of the inhabitants had starved to death, thirty percent had succumbed to plague, and the remainder had become bandits"[47] might be an exaggeration, but the situation was doubtless bleak. Under such circumstances Li Zicheng's propaganda for equalization of wealth and elimination of corruption certainly sounded appealing. It is debatable whether Li Zicheng's rebellion counts as a "peasant uprising." Li himself was not a peasant; he was an unhappily laid off postal worker. The rebellion did not erupt in the south, where the gentry's suppression of the peasantry was most severe. And Li's promises of social and economic redress did not hold.[48] But whatever the nature of the rebellion, the Ming government was ill equipped to deal with it.

In response to numerous domestic and ethnic rebellions as well as the military threats from the Manchus, the Ming government had, between 1618 and 1636, raised taxes seven times.[49] The tax increases drew silver away from important sectors of the Ming economy such as Jiangnan, but did not enrich the governmental revenues significantly, due to official embezzlement.[50] This fact, complicated by the sharp decline in bullion imports from international trade and the series of devastating natural disasters in the late 1630s and early 1640s in connection with the Eurasian "Little Ice Age,"[51] put the Ming economy in a poor position to cope with the military expenses for the Li Zicheng rebellion.[52] But before that final collapse, the Ming court had accumulated enough "bad karma" to deserve the undoing: it had almost completely alienated its own people.

The Ming was an age of autocracy.[53] When the founding emperor Zhu Yuanzhang continued the Mongol practice of flogging officials in public, and in 1380 abolished the office of prime minister, the relation between the Confucian scholars and the imperial court was changed.[54] Gone was the "benevolent despotism" of the Song (960-1279).[55] And gone was the unquestioned honor and prestige of the Chinese scholarly class. After the Eastern Depot (*Dongchang*), staffed by palace eunuchs, was established in 1420 at the order of Emperor Yongle (r. 1403-1425) to survey the regular secret police (the Embroidered Uniform Guard, *Jinyi wei*), the gentry's basic sense of security was also threatened. In their capacities as the spies, purveyors, and secretaries of the autocrat,[56] eunuchs were capable of placing the scholar-officials at their mercy. Meanwhile, eunuchs were also subject to the scholars' jealousy, prejudice, and misunderstanding. Antagonism between the scholar-officials and the eunuchs intensified as the latter expanded in number and power. Autocracy in the early Ming was still tolerable because the autocrats were at least capable of minimizing political malpractices and social injustice. In the late Ming, juvenile, absentee,[57] and incompetent autocrats, along with the aggrandized factionalism, corruption, misappropriation, and abuse of power among officials, underlings, and eunuchs, as well as escalating social injustice, proved just too much for both the officialdom and the populace to bear. The resentment was so wide and severe that it was impossible for the Ming court to keep claiming that the Mandate of Heaven was with it.

While failing to resolve its internal tension, the government also failed to release the tension outside the court: tension between the rich and the poor, the powerful and the powerless, and the urban and rural areas. Tension needed to be released in one way or another, if not by the action of the government, then by the action of the masses themselves. The latter often took violent forms: sectarian religious uprisings, tenant rebellions and bondservant rebellions.

James Tong's study of Ming collective violence shows a distinct spatial-temporal pattern of rebellions and banditry, concentrating on the two coastal provinces of Guangdong and Fujian during the reigns of Zhengde (1506-21), Jiajing (1522-66), Tianqi (1621-27), and

Chongzhen (1628-44). There is a rational explanation for this pattern. When bad times increased the hardship in a subsistence economy and weak regimes decreased administrative rigor in famine relief and law enforcement, the suffering masses in peripheral areas were more likely to choose to become outlaws. Rebellions of the White Lotus and Maitreya societies often corresponded to agrarian crises and governmental dysfunction. In response to crises stemming from heavy taxation, poor harvests in times of natural disasters, devastation of pirates and bandits, and exploitation of land-holding gentry, the millenarian White Lotus-Maitreya societies offered distressed peasants what the government could not: a spark of hope for the advent of a new world order.[58]

Revolts against imperial clansmen and the tenant and bondservant revolts in Jiangnan and the southeastern coastal area are best understood in terms of conflicts between different social strata, but their occurrence also signified Ming China's failure to mitigate social tensions. Likewise, food riots, anti-tax rebellions, and armed conflict between natives and outsiders or between employers and employees signified governmental incapacity to cope with social change.[59] Governmental armies offered common people no consolation in the wake of revolts. Lacking provisions and discipline, they often turned looters themselves.[60]

Too many contradictions existed in Ming China. On the surface, economy was booming, society was fluid, and culture flourished. But amid all these, the roots of disharmony—heightened social strain and worsening human relationships—were growing. The reactionary and faction-ridden government not only failed to alleviate the tension and anxiety but also in effect accelerated them. The crisis in the age of prosperity did not escape the keen observation of Feng Menglong.

## The Obscure Informant

Feng Menglong would be an unlikely historical informant in "positivistic" historiography—historical writings that rely mainly on "serious" discourse in elite sources about verifiable and "significant" events, institutions, and personages. Feng was a "marginal" figure who lived in Changzhou, and was registered in Wuxian, Suzhou prefecture,[61] in the declining years of the Ming dynasty. He never passed the civil service examination at the provincial level, which would have qualified him for an official appointment, and had to make a living by seeking patronage from the great merchants of Jiangnan. He did not opt for the career of a "city hermit" or "mountain man," who sold works of art at high prices in the name of an "amateur." The "amateur" artists allegedly created paintings, calligraphies, and writings only for in-groups, and received gifts rather than payments. In this way they retained their literati pride and their integrity. Perhaps contemptuous of such hypocrisy, Feng instead chose to become a "professional" writer of popular literature—a "marginal" occupation in the Ming because of the genre, the audience, and the cash reward.

Late Ming China had a flourishing market in popular literature, including fiction, joke books, riddles, almanacs, family encyclopedias, children's primers, know-how manuals, law texts, route guides, religious tracts, and so on. They were often heavily illustrated and written in vernacular or simple classical language to meet the reading needs of the wider, semi-literate audience.[62] Some were well written and well printed. Others were notoriously degrading, especially the pornography. As Timothy Brook points out, "Confucian teachers were right to fear that noncanonical reading would bring students under the wrong influences, for popular literature did corrode the edges of the canon."[63]

Partially victimized by the negative image of popular writers and partially due to his untraditional mode of behavior and iconoclasm, Feng Menglong could not find himself an eminent position among men of letters. The official history of the Ming dynasty (*Ming shi*) did not mention Feng Menglong's name. We find late Ming and early Qing references to him only sparingly: a few poems about him by his friends; some scanty mention in local gazetteers of his "tributary student" (*gongsheng*) status, his examination handbooks, and his short political career[64]; and some rather harsh literary critiques. His friends described him as a talented scholar, sincere friend, frustrated student, devoted teacher, conscientious author, admirable bureaucrat, and unconventional character.[65] "Authoritative" critics such as Zhu Yizun (1629-1709) commented that Feng "was good at verses that brought a smile to your face, and occasionally hummed a tune of facetiae. Although he could not be called a poet, he could be regarded as a jester in the writing circles."[66] The *Siku quanshu* (*Complete Library of the Four Treasuries*)[67] cataloguers treated him similarly. They described his anthology of classical stratagem, *Zhi nang* (*Sack of Wisdom*), as "extremely frivolous," and his anthology of classical tales of humor, gossips, and witticism, *Gujin tan gai* (*Survey of Talk Old and New*), as "funny talks having nothing to do with the 'major elegance' (*daya*)."[68] These early Qing critics put him squarely outside of the mainstream.

The Manchu court banned many of Feng's works overtly because they were erotic and subversive, but, covertly, also because he was a Ming loyalist who compiled historical accounts about the fall of the Ming house and participated in the Southern Ming (1644-1662)[69] effort to restore the Ming dynasty. The ban seemed to be effective: original copies of many of Feng's works are no longer extant in China. During the New Culture and New Literature Movement of 1915-1927 (better known as the May Fourth movement, named after the politically-oriented student movement of 1919), when scholars attempted to reconstruct Feng Menglong's works in their efforts to find the "voice of the people," they had to rely heavily on the Japanese collections.

Nagasawa Kikuya speculates the intensive Japanese interest in Feng Menglong's works might have to do with the fact that Feng's works provided the Japanese with firsthand information on the fall of the indigenous Ming and the rise of the Manchu Qing.[70] Nagasawa wrote in 1928-29, when Japan was developing aggression into Manchuria, so he might have read the politics of his time into the Ming-Qing transition. W. L. Idema is perhaps also impressed by Feng's loyalty to the Ming when he points out, in his study of Feng's prefaces to the *Sanyan*, that Feng might have intended to make a political statement when tracing the origin of the genre of vernacular short story back to the Southern Song. "The Southern Song, living unconcerned in peace while it should have reconquered the North [from the Jurchens], must have been an image to [Feng] of his own Ming dynasty, slowly retreating from Manchuria."[71]

Haiyan Lee aptly points out that when China was in a semi-colonial state, the May Fourth "rescue mission" of popular literature, such as Feng Menglong's works, had a nationalist agenda:

> Through folklore studies, May Fourth intellectuals fashioned their self-identity vis-à-vis a reified notion of the Chinese "people." But, "people," particularly the peasantry, was a profoundly ambiguous entity, both seductive and dangerous, both the object of longing and regulation. One of the questions that deeply troubled the intellectuals was whether or not the average peasant was capable of love or sympathy. The folklorists offered the most affirmative answer, mitigating Lu Xun's bleak view [of the unfeeling, cowardly, and chauvinistic Chinese peasantry] and reinventing rural society as a site of emotional authenticity, pastoral nostalgia, and communitarian harmony. Drawing inspiration from European and Japanese folklore studies, the folklorists projected folk culture as a vital alternative tradition suppressed by Confucian orthodoxy and threatened by modernity. They embarked on

a rescue operation aiming to save the endangered folk culture from its enemies old and new and to appropriate it for modern emancipatory goals.[72]

In the 1950s, Feng's colloquial fiction, hinting, as it did, at the sufferings of commoners at the hands of exploitative gentry and government underlings, was extolled by Chinese scholars in the People's Republic as "the expression of a nascent bourgeois ideology, opposed to the conservative ideology of the gentry" in feudal China. In the 1960s, however, the same "bourgeois" literature of Feng's was criticized as sharing the "exploiting" and "suppressive" ideology of the feudal gentry, perhaps because of its inherent Confucian didacticism.[73]

So scholars in different spatial and temporal frames have ignored, marginalized, or politicized Feng Menglong in accordance with their own agenda. The historical Feng Menglong has thus been obscured.

The hidden agenda notwithstanding, thanks to the May Fourth Movement, Feng Menglong was rediscovered and his works were gradually patched together from extant copies found in China and Japan.[74] Scholars both in China and in the West have painstakingly traced the sources of Feng's fictional works.[75] And thanks to the pioneering work of Japanese scholar Shinoya On[76] and Chinese scholar Rong Zhaozu,[77] and the more recent research by Lu Shulun[78] and Patrick Hanan,[79] among others, a rough outline of Feng Menglong's life can now be reconstructed.

## Feng Menglong's Life and Intellectual Development

Feng Menglong was an untraditional character springing from a traditional household. Born into an educated family,[80] Menglong, his painter elder brother Menggui,[81] and his poet younger brother Mengxiong,[82] were recognized as the "Three Fengs."[83] While nothing irregular was reported of his two brothers, the rebellious second son's merry-making resort to the courtesans' quarters and gambling houses, and subsequent publication of "indecent" songs and jokes (*Child's Folly*) and gambling guides, smeared his reputation. Two of Feng Menglong's gambling guides are extant: *Paijing* (*Classic of Cards*), in thirteen sections, and *Madiaojiao li* (*Rules of the Madiao Games*), in ten sections.[84] In the Qing dynasty, *Paijing* was still held to be a classic among gamblers.[85] According to a *biji* (note-form literature) anecdote, after the publication of Feng's *Guazhier* and *Yezi xin dou pu* (probably an alternate name of *Madiaojiao li*[86]), "frivolous youngsters were completely carried away, some of them even went bankrupt because of it." Public criticism was so severe that, probably around 1613,[87] Feng had to seek protection of General Xiong Tingbi (1569-1625), the former education intendant in Nanjing, who lived in temporary retirement at that point.[88] Xiong was famed to be very strict with the students,[89] which makes his favorable treatment of Feng's case in the anecdote more remarkable. The implication was that only a truly discriminating eye could recognize a true talent who did not fit in the society.

Judging from his frequent resort to the city's pleasure quarters, the young Feng Menglong seemed to have indulged only in sport. Nonetheless, he produced in the 1620s his celebrated *Sanyan* collection of cautionary tales, something that would not embarrass his family. He wrote some of the stories himself, rewrote, adapted, polished, and reprinted some others from both classical and vernacular sources, and in some cases combined several short tales of separate origins into one longer story.[90] A comparison of some of the *Sanyan* stories with the originals suggests that Feng Menglong was an editorial genius—without his re-creation these mediocre stories would have long been forgotten. The *Sanyan* is a treasure house of the record of daily life in Ming China, in both mental and material dimensions. It provides a precious supplement to the official documents.

As a literary work the *Sanyan* is truly the crown jewel of vernacular short stories in premodern China. The language is lively and elegant, the plotting is well done, and the descriptions of the characters are delicate down to the psychological details. Feng Menglong created some of the most admirable heroines in the history of Chinese literature. Prompted by love (*qing*), they showed courage, wisdom, and a perseverance that far exceeded the performances of their male counterparts. Feng Menglong also created some of the most admirable heroes in Chinese literature. Out of true friendship, these men readily sacrificed their lives, as well as their wealth, for their best friends.

Meanwhile, Feng Menglong was also engaged in more "serious" literary activities. Specializing in the Classic *Chun Qiu* (*The Spring and Autumn Annals*, dating from the Eastern Zhou period, one of the Confucian Five Classics) since his youth,[91] Feng joined a special *Chun Qiu* study group in Huang'an and Macheng, Hubei province, between 1612 and 1617, and again in 1620.[92] He subsequently wrote at least three examination handbooks on the *Chun Qiu*: *Linjing zhiyue* (*Guide to the Spring and Autumn Annals*, 1620),[93] *Chun Qiu dingzhi canxin* (*New Light on the Central Ideas of the Spring and Autumn Annals*, c. 1623),[94] and *Chun Qiu hengku* (*A Spring and Autumn Annals Thesaurus*, 1625).[95] There might have existed a fourth handbook on the

*Chun Qiu* entitled *Bieben Chun Qiu daquan* (*The Alternative Edition of the Great Compendium of the Spring and Autumn Annals*).[96] In 1630 he published his *Sishu zhiyue* (*Guide to the Four Books*).[97] Written by an exam candidate who never achieved a degree further than the most basic level of *shengyuan*, Feng's handbooks nevertheless enjoyed great popularity, judging from his continuous publication on this subject. In fact, the gazetteer of his native place, *Suzhou fuzhi*, mentioned Feng's *Zhiyue* and *Hengku* particularly as the two crucial books most important for examination candidates specializing in the *Chun Qiu*.[98] The *Hengku* became a standard work during much of the Qing dynasty.[99]

Feng Menglong's expertise on the *Spring and Autumn Annals* also propelled him to rewrite Yu Shaoyu's popular historical novel *Dong Zhou lieguo zhi* (*A Fictionalized History of the States in the Eastern Zhou*). Feng claimed to be correcting factual mistakes of the old version in a "scientific" spirit to achieve greater historicity. It would, however, be a mistake to see the author of the *Xin Lieguo zhi* (*New History of the States*) as a predecessor of the scientifically minded Qing *kaozheng* scholars. While Feng was correcting objective historical mistakes, he was also injecting subjective moral assertion, and he probably drew from folk tradition as much as from more orthodox historical sources in his reconstruction. As Robert Hegel suspects, when novelists in late imperial China modified existing works "in the name of greater historicity," they might well be asserting their own moral judgment by romanticizing history as it should be to criticize the present.[100] Barred from active service of the state, the writers of historical romances "expressed their personal frustrations and anxieties by attacking the very structure of power in Chinese society at the time, e.g., the Confucian moral order nominally, *but in their minds not actually*, practised."[101] Feng's historical romance can be viewed in the same vein.

Feng's sojourn in Huang'an and Macheng was significant to his intellectual development. Macheng was where Li Zhi became a "Confucian monk" in 1588 and published his controversial *Fen shu* (*A Book to Be Burned*) in 1590. Huang'an was where Li Zhi lived before he moved to Macheng. Although Li Zhi had died in 1602, his influence must still be strong when Feng visited the region in the 1610s and 1620s. Among Feng's close friends in Huang'an and Macheng were the descendants of the prestigious Geng family, with whom Li Zhi had lived. Many of Feng's works bore the marks of Li Zhi's influence. It is likely that Feng had admired Li in his youth, and the Macheng experience reinforced this admiration. During this period, Feng organized a literary society called Yun She (Metrical Society).[102] A poem by Qian Qianyi (1582-1664) suggests that Feng was the leader of a seven-member literary society—after the Seven Wise Men of the Bamboo Grove in the Six Dynasties (220-589). The group included Qian, Wen Zhenmeng (1574-1636), and Wen's nephew Yao Ximeng (1579-1636); all three held the *jinshi* degree, which hinted at the quality and status of this group.[103] We are not sure if this group was the Yun She or if it was yet another group that Feng organized.

Feng Menglong was well connected with the scholars of his day. At least eighty of his acquaintances can be documented. Most of them were from Jiangnan and Hubei and many were Fu She members.[104] Scholars have speculated that Feng himself might also have been a Fu She member, although his name does not appear on extant Fu She lists.[105] In 1630, at the age fifty-six, Feng Menglong was finally given a chance to fulfil his political ambition. He was selected by his locality as a "tributary scholar" (*gongsheng*), thus becoming eligible for political appointment.[106] He served one term as assistant instructor in the district of Dantu, Jinjiang Prefecture, perhaps from 1631 to 1634.[107] He then became magistrate of Shouning County, in Funing Prefecture, Fujian Province from 1634 to 1638. The *Funing fuzhi* (*Prefectural Gazetteer of Funing*) describes him as an exemplary magistrate: "His government was simple, and recourse to the law was rarely called for. He honored, above all, literary and cultural endeavors. He treated his people with benevolence, and the scholars with etiquette."[108] Feng's contemporary Xu Bo, a Fuzhou scholar renowned for his library Hongyu Lou (Red Rain Tower),[109] wrote in his preface to Feng Menglong's *You Min yincao* (Draft Poetry During Sojourn in Fujian): "When Mr. Feng is off duty, he is either writing a book or composing a poem. Of all fifty-seven magistrates in Fujian, there is none as leisurely as Mr. Feng, but there is none as able as Mr. Feng either. This is because although Mr. Feng indulges himself in poetry, the pains he takes to regulate the administration and settle the lawsuits far exceed all the other magistrates."[110]

During his tenure as magistrate Feng compiled *A Provisional History of Shouning* (*Shouning daizhi*) in two *juan*, prefaced spring of 1637.[111] The more conventional title should have been *Shouning xianzhi* (Gazette of Shouning County). Feng used the word *dai* (to wait) instead of *xian* (county), because, as he stated in the preface, the current version was only provisional; he was waiting humbly for a perfect version in the future. Apparently, even as a bureaucrat, Feng would not simply follow the convention.

The convention of gazetteer-compilation was to treat the subject matter impersonally. Feng observed the "scientific" part of the convention by correcting the mistakes in the previous compilation, giving a more precise description of Shouning's history, geography, administration, economics, customs and culture. But he disregarded the convention against subjectivity by including a number of personal accounts of his life as Shouning magistrate. Without including a section on "Art and Literature" in the gazetteer, he nevertheless managed to put eight poems he composed in various sections. It seems curious that Feng chose to record his personal accounts in a public document rather than write a separate book (although he was not unique—Magistrate Zhang Tao, for example, also compiled a rather personalized gazetteer of She County in 1609[112]).

If Feng had hoped that by recording his compassion and accomplishments in the gazetteer he would enhance his chance of being remembered by posterity, he was mistaken. All copies of the *Shouning daizhi*, except one, were to disappear from the face of the earth. Moreover, perhaps due to Feng's improper format, the later Shouning magistrate Zhao Tingji did not make use of Feng's version when he revised the gazetteer in 1686, more conventionally entitled *Shouning xianzhi*. Zhao's edition was the only Shouning gazetteer that was passed down to posterity in China, and there was no mention of the accomplishments that Feng had proudly recorded in the *Shouning daizhi*. Zhao might judge Feng's accounts to be exaggerated. Or Feng might be black-listed in the Qing. Fortunately, through the only extant copy in Japan, modern editions have now been made available in China and Taiwan, and more is known about Feng Menglong through his autobiographic accounts in the *Shouning daizhi*.

According to the *Shouning daizhi*, seeing the poor educational facilities in the mountainous area of Shouning, Feng Menglong lectured on the *Sishu zhiyue* himself. Despite his frustration with the locality's destitution and savagery (banditry, female infanticide, superstitious treatment of diseases, and so on), with unreasonable higher authority, with unsatisfactory regulations, and with his hopeless clerks, Feng managed to make some changes for the better, even at his own expense. Feng's unique administrative style can be illustrated in his efforts to lessen the people's bureaucratic burdens, to curb the practice of female infanticide, and to get rid of lawless elements. Observing that common people could not afford the bureaucratic surcharges related to the compilation of the Yellow Register of Population and the welcoming and sending-off of officials, he petitioned to renovate the system so as to give the people a break from these harassing "conventions."[113]

Fujian was notorious for female infanticide; "even the wealthiest families killed baby girls after the second one."[114] Rather than reprimand his people for breaking the law, which they did, Feng pleaded with their conscience. In his official proclamation he first asked a rhetorical question: "Those of you who are fathers, think to yourselves: if people did not keep baby girls, how could you ever have a wife? Those of you who are mothers, think to yourselves: if people did not keep baby girls, how could you ever have a life?" He then reached down to a more practical line of persuasion: "Furthermore, boys are not necessarily filial, and girls are not necessarily unfilial. If you are well-to-do, raising the girl would not cost you a fortune. If you are poor, you may keep the girl for the time being and give her up for adoption when she is eight or nine. She will be worth several ounces of silver. Raising her will not be an unrewarding labor." And finally he announced the reward for those who reported the crime or agreed to adopt the girl and the punishment for those who committed the crime or concealed their neighbor's crime.[115] When the custom was so widespread, he knew law and ethics alone would not work and he needed to be more low-keyed in communicating with his people.

But what really made Magistrate Feng interesting was that he was trying to imitate the "wise magistrates" in his *Sanyan* stories when he listened to legal cases. The *Shouning daizhi* recorded triumphantly that Feng on one occasion detected a case of false accusation and on another occasion captured a cunning villain. He did this by playing the legendary Judge Bao or Judge Dee[116] in real life: he made detective tours in disguise and adopted wise strategies and tactics.[117] Fiction and reality merged in this writer-turned-magistrate.

The Ming court cannot be said to have been appreciative of Feng's talent and ability. Feng had continuously failed the exams prior to his appointments, and his posts were very minor ones. But this did not prevent Feng from devoting his loyalty to the Ming. He was engaged in the reformist political activity of the Fu She and the restoration efforts of the Southern Ming during the final years of China's last indigenous imperial dynasty. Now an overt patriot, he recorded the eventful final moments of the dynasty in his *Zhongxing shilu* (Veritable Records of the National Restoration, 1644). He soon incorporated this into a larger compilation *Jiashen jishi* (Records of the Year Jia-shen, 1644). In 1645 he reissued the *Zhongxing shilu* under the new title *Zhongxing weilue* (Grand Designs of the National Restoration), with minor modifications.[118]

In his preface to the *Zhongxing weilue*, Feng Menglong recorded his excitement upon hearing the rumor that the Ming generals Wu Sangui (612-1678) and Hong Chengchou (1593-1665) were about to jointly resist the Qing and restore the Ming. Hindsight proves Feng's excitement wrong-headed—both Wu and Hong defected to the Qing. Lu Shulun criticizes Feng for making a "childish" mistake in historical judgment and turning, in his old age, into a "counter-revolutionary" in the great movement of Li Zicheng's "peasant uprising."[119] Whether Feng was a counter-revolutionary or a patriot is, of course, a contested point between Marxist and non-Marxist historians.

Feng Menglong's death was shrouded in mystery. Some believe he was martyred in an anti-Qing battle in Fujian in the southeast coast of China in 1645. Some believe he escaped to Japan after the fall of the Ming and lived for a few more years. Citing writings of Feng's friends about his death, Lu Shulun dismisses both theories and believes Feng died at home in 1646 of natural causes—a heartbroken loyalist who knew the restoration enterprise was doomed.[120]

## Feng Menglong and Hou Huiqing

A producer of erotic literature, Feng Menglong had a colorful love life himself. He frankly admitted he was a "lady-killer" among courtesans, who often showered him with souvenirs.[121] But he was discreet about his most serious romantic affair with the courtesan Hou Huiqing. The earliest mention of Hou appears in the *Hill Songs*. Feng introduced Hou as a "famous courtesan," as he did other courtesans, and praised her for her exquisite discrimination—she compared herself to a clearheaded examiner who knew how to rank her clients—in the tone of an admirer without specific indication of intimacy.[122] It was not until Hou left Feng to marry someone else that Feng poured out his feelings toward her publicly.

According to his friend Dong Sizhang (1586-1628), after the loss of Hou Huiqing, Feng Menglong no longer visited the courtesans' quarters. He composed thirty poems under the title "Yuanli shi" (Poetry on sorrow over separation). Members of his literary society responded with their own poems of lament. We can imagine how a "decent" Confucian moralist would have judged such display of male sentimentality: it was comical, even preposterous. But in the late Ming, this conduct was acceptable among the "romantics." These poems were collectively printed in the *Yutao ji* (*Record of Anguish*), which unfortunately is no longer extant.[123] Luckily, in his revised edition of *Hanging Twigs*[124] Feng recorded the last of his thirty "Yuanli" poems:

The craze for poetry, the obsession with wine, no more!
In my sickness I often shut my doors in daytime.
The utmost torture in one's entire life
Is to try to summon the soul at the *yuanyang* grave.[125]

*Yuanyang*, the Mandarin duck, mates for life, and is hence a symbol of conjugal felicity. "The *Yuanyang* Grave" is the title of several plays whose stories vary. In one story, a scholar is too timid to ask for his parents' permission to marry his beloved courtesan. The despondent courtesan perishes and the remorseful scholar takes his own life. Their bodies are buried together, and the local people call the site the Yuanyang Grave. In another story, a scholar is so infatuated with a courtesan he pines away. In still another story, a courtesan dies broken-hearted after her scholar-lover abandons her for a gentlewoman.[126] The invocation of the "*yuanyang* grave" in the above poem has led to some scholarly speculation that Hou suffered a tragically early death, but that was not the case—she actually deserted Feng, an "unromantic" fact that can be deduced from other sources.

The *sanqu* ("free songs" or art songs) collection *Taixia xinzou* (*Celestial Songs Played Anew*) contains six verses under the title "Yuanli ci" (Lyric on sorrow over separation)[127] and six verses in "Duan'er yibie" (In memory of our separation on the second day of the fifth month),[128] which Feng clearly stated were written for Hou. In the "Yuanli ci" Feng complained that since Hou only took him to be a substitute lover to fill in the gaps in her emotional life, he had risked his reputation for her in vain. He blamed her for failing to cherish their tender relationship and for making him, an amorous youngster, spend the long nights alone. He recalled how he was numbed by her apparent lack of remorse at her departure. He also lamented that the potential wealth promised by a scholar's learning was just a dream in comparison with a merchant's actual wealth, and that Heaven did not understand the principle of correct matchmaking. The last reference suggests that Hou Huiqing might have married a merchant—it is no wonder why so many villains in Feng Menglong's courtesan-scholar romances are merchants. In the "Duan'er yibie" Feng expressed how much he still missed Hou after losing her for a full year. He did not know whether she was happy or not, but he knew for certain he was miserable and he was afraid the next year would be even more unbearable. In addition to these two sets of songs, there are six verses in "Yuanmeng" (Troubled by dreams),[129] five verses in "Youhuai" (Thoughts),[130] and four verses in "Shiji" (Vow on courtesans)[131] which might also be related to Feng's loss of Hou.

The modern Chinese scholar Gao Hongjun has made a rather shocking discovery concerning Feng Menglong and Hou Huiqing's love story. Gao believes the person for whom Hou deserted Feng was none other than Yuan Zhongdao (1570-1623), the younger brother of Yuan Hongdao (1568-1610), renowned founder of the Gong'an school of expressive poetry.[132] There is the possibility, therefore, of learning more about Hou's life and romantic-tragic story.

From "Fang ge zeng ren" (Singing a song as a gift), "Nei ji" (Letter from my wife), and "Da" (Reply) in Yuan Zhongdao's collected work *Kexue Zhai qianji* (*The Former Collection of the Kexue Studio*),[133] the following story can be gathered:

In 1595, a year after failing the provincial examination for the third time, Yuan Zhongdao abandoned himself to the company of singing girls from the seventh to the ninth month. He was then robbed, stricken by illness, and forced to beg in Suzhou's pleasure quarters. A courtesan took care of him, and in the fifth month of 1596 he took her as his concubine. In the ninth month of that year, his wife sent him a letter congratulating him for acquiring a new mate and urging him to return home for the sake of their children. In reply, he wrote that the new woman was of lowly status and, knowing little about the wifely duties of sewing, weaving, and cooking, was no fit companion for him. He urged his wife to start brewing some nice wine in preparation for his return, which, he promised, would be no later than the coming spring—it was time for his next provincial examination attempt.

The mystery woman abandoned by Yuan Zhongdao turns out to be somebody called Huiqing. Yuan Zhongdao made two references to her by name in the *Kexue Zhai qianji*, one in a poem entitled "Bie Huiqing" (Saying good-bye to Huiqing), the other in the twelfth of his fifty-eight "Ganhuai shi" (Poems on aroused emotions).[134] Huiqing was described as a talented singing girl in Suzhou who pitied Yuan Zhongdao when he was in distress. Yuan eventually left her and never returned—he justified his heartlessness by stating that women were all a bad karma that held him down. Gao Hongjun believes this woman to be Hou Huiqing, who deserted Feng Menglong to marry Yuan Zhongdao and was herself in turn abandoned by Yuan. The problem with this theory is that at the time when Feng compiled the *Hill Songs*, which must be after 1596 (for in a note to the song "Country folk" (Xiangxia ren), Feng said "I still remember in 1596 . . ."[135]), Feng did not seem to have been separated from Hou Huiqing, judging from his casual reference to her. So it seems unlikely that Hou deserted Feng in 1596. If Oki Yasushi's dating of the *Hill Songs* at between 1611 and 1616 is correct,[136] then Hou probably did not even know Feng in 1596. Most likely, Feng's lover Huiqing was different from Yuan's lover Huiqing.

The investigation about the relations of Feng Menglong, Hou Huiqing, and Yuan Zhongdao incidentally points to a significant divergence between the love ethics of Feng and Yuan. In the biographies of his elder sister and the mothers of his friends, Yuan Zhongdao displayed great respect for their talents and virtues.[137] But he did not seem to hold the same attitude toward his wife, his concubines, and his other sexual partners, male and female. To him, they were the objects of his desire, a desire he had trouble controlling, hence his "bad karma." Yuan's sense of misgiving is understandable: like many late Ming hedonists, he fell a prey to a sexually transmitted disease (which was commonly referred to as "blood disease"). Despite the acute pain associated with the disease, Yuan could not get away from sexual indulgence. He confessed, "Repentance sometimes makes me wish that I could completely reform myself. However, I gradually forget about this once the symptoms of the disease begin to recede. I soon again start to indulge myself in sexual pleasures as before."[138] This unrepentant hedonist once expressed the wish of constructing a three-story residence, where he could "do meditation on the top level, read Buddhist sutras and Taoist texts on the second, and enjoy the company of prostitutes on the ground floor."[139] He wanted to have it all.

Feng Menglong did not profess to separate love and sex, and shared little of the hedonists' ambivalence about erotic pleasure and spiritual redemption. To him, sex with love was healthy, for which no redemption was needed; sex without love was unhealthy, for which no redemption was possible. Karma was no excuse for prostitution, nor would Feng categorize all women in the pleasure quarters as objects of loveless sex. He treated the courtesans he befriended as real human beings with real feelings, and even regarded some of them as his *zhiyin* (bosom friends, literally, "people who appreciate my music"),[140] and held in contempt courtesans who sold their love through mere commercial transactions. That was probably why the betrayal of Hou Huiqing ripped his heart: his infatuation with a fallen woman of impeccable virtue, something he celebrated so much in his romantic writings, was unrequited in real life.

Patrick Hanan mentions that in the summer of 1617 there appeared a "flower register" entitled *Wuji baimei* (The Hundred Most Beautiful Courtesans of Suzhou). Feng Menglong was depicted as the lover of Liu Hanxiang, the ninth courtesan in the ranking. According to the flower register, after Feng went to Hubei, the girl's affection for him cooled.[141] The historical Feng Menglong did go to Hubei in the 1610s, but no mention of Liu Hanxiang is found in Feng's extant works. The *Wuji baimei* states that Feng Menglong gave the name Liu Pian (courtesy name Hanxiang) to the courtesan,[142] which suggests that Feng might be the virgin courtesan's first sexual partner, who had the right to give her a new name. Feng might or might not have completely stopped visiting courtesans after his heart-wrenching separation with Hou Huiqing, but after all the publicity it seemed unlikely for the flower register to casually associate Feng's name with another courtesan. It may therefore be assumed that Feng's affair with Liu Hanxiang might have preceded that with Hou Huiqing. The *Celestial Songs Played Anew*, which contained the sorrowful songs of the jilted Feng Menglong, was published in 1627. Feng's separation with Hou should not have occurred too much earlier, perhaps within a decade. In all likelihood, Feng Menglong's love affair with Hou Huiqing probably occurred in the 1610s-1620s, around the time of the compilation of *Child's Folly*.

## The *Qing-Li* Dichotomy and Feng Menglong's "Teaching of *Qing*"

The love story of Feng Menglong and Hou Huiqing illustrated Feng's rich emotions (*qing*). In fact, *qing* was such a central concept in Feng's writing that he proclaimed himself founder of the "Teaching of *Qing*." The word *qing* cannot be adequately translated into one English word. In Chinese discourse, *qing* has two basic meanings.[143] It can mean feelings, emotions, sentiments, sensitivity, or passion—the inner activities of the heart-and-mind, the total human responses to various experiences and conditions. It can also mean essence or actual circumstances; in opposition to appearance or falsity, *qing* was the real condition of things as well as of inner human reality.

Many intellectuals in the late Ming associated *qing* with unobstructed spontaneity of human nature, manifested in love or friendship, and original creativity of the human mind, as feelings or sensitivity. As the former, *qing* was to be celebrated as an important literary theme; as the latter, *qing* was to be celebrated as an integral part of literary production. On the basis of *qing*, Xu Wei contrasted the poetry of the pastoral past with that of the utilitarian present. He stated:

> The poetry of the ancient people originated in *qing*; they did not fabricate *qing* in order to compose poetry. Therefore there was poetry but no poets. Only in later times did poets emerge. Nowadays the topics and styles of poetry are numerous, but most poems are composed through fabrication of *qing* which is not there originally. The purpose of writing poetry with fabricated *qing* is to seek fame. Seeking fame in poetry, one inevitably ends up imitating poetic styles and plagiarizing beautified diction. When this happens, the substance of poetry is lost. Therefore I say presently there are poets but no poetry.[144]

Although Xu Wei did not articulate what he meant by the "poetry of the ancient people," he seemed to be referring to verses by anonymous authors, such as the folksongs in the *Book of Odes*. The "poets of the present" probably referred to the neo-classicists, who emulated the High Tang models. Xu Wei's distinction between true "poetry" and fake "poets" is based on several criteria: the presence or absence of true feelings, the absence or presence of practical purpose of composition, and the absence or presence of poetic formalism. This idea is close to the Romantic theory that poetry is a formulation of the intuitive perceptions of "primitive" people, who are free from the self-imposed limitations on freedom, a characteristic of contemporary civilization.

Tang Xianzu identified *qing* as the most crucial element of human nature and the key to human existence. He expounded, in the preface to his romantic play *Peony Pavilion*, "We do not know where *qing* comes from. However, once *qing* has arisen and taken deep roots in one's heart, it can bring death to the living and life to the dead."[145] In the context of *Peony Pavilion*, *qing* referred to love between man and woman. The heroine pined away after having an erotic dream, and was brought back to life when her dream lover appeared in real life.[146] Such "enchantment of love" disrupted not only the life of the fictional heroine but also those of many female readers of the play who modeled their lives after hers.[147]

To render the *Peony Pavilion* a more didactic interpretation, some commentators in late imperial China endeavored to read moral lessons into the heroine's dream of love. Chen Jiru (1558-1639) argued that the carnal love between husband and wife was the beginning of human relations and foundation of moral nature, and the dream was a vehicle for enlightenment. Therefore the erotic dream was not subversive in essence. Rather, Tang Xianzu had the ingenuity to "turn dream into wakefulness and transform love into moral nature."[148] Lu Ciyun, who lived at the turn of the eighteenth century, hinted that the dream of love was a metaphor for human attachment, and had to be transcended.[149] But Wai-yee Li is not convinced. She dismisses such moral readings and points out that Tang Xianzu "seems to be saying that *qing* is of such vastness and force that it rebels against the hierarchy of *xing* [human nature], *qing* [emotions, manifestation of human nature], and *yu* [desires, excessive emotions]."[150] In other words, *qing* is beyond human control and human discourse. It is neither moral nor immoral, and its power is formidable. Love, in both the spiritual and the physical aspects, transcended the boundaries between life and death, between illusion and reality, and it made extraordinary things happen.

Feng Menglong appreciated *Peony Pavilion* for its masterful dramatization of the marvelous work *qing* could do. But he did not approve of the nonchalant and frivolous behavior occasionally displayed by the male protagonist. Using the metrical irregularities of Tang Xianzu's original work as an excuse, Feng rewrote *Peony Pavilion* under the new title *Romantic Dream*, where he "straightened up" the young man, making him a more responsible and sincere romantic hero.[151] Feng's revision is understandable in light of the rivalry between Tang Xianzu's Linchuan School and the Wujiang School headed by Feng's prosodic teacher Shen Jing (1553-1610). The Wujiang School emphasized metrical perfection and plain diction in form, and advocated the traditional virtues of loyalty, filial piety, chastity, and righteousness in content. Heroes created by Wujiang playwrights were not supposed to behave like libertines, even for a fleeting moment, whereas Tang Xianzu's romantic heroes were somewhat beyond good and evil.

The postulation of *qing* as "the primary and essential condition of life"[152] in the writings of Tang Xianzu was part of a late Ming intellectual trend to redefine *qing* and cast it in a more positive light than the puritan Neo-Confucians would have. Moralists such as Zhu Xi in the Song and Lü Kun (1536-1618) in the Ming regarded sexual love—*qing* narrowly defined—as a subversive and disruptive force capable of confounding social order and hierarchical relations. Both Zhu and Lü acknowledged the positive value of the *qing* that was moderate and without sexual connotations. But both also saw a danger in intimate *qing* between man and woman which could lead to the relaxation of domestic rules of propriety and undermine the segregation of the two sexes.[153] However, romantic writers, not unaware that *qing* was both liberating and threatening, "practiced a sleight of hand." In their fictional works, "the protagonists' most deeply felt desires, which initially challenge hegemonic moral codes, are eventually made to express the highest Confucian values of filiality, loyalty, and chastity; true *qing* resolves any tensions between authentic self-expression and orthopraxy."[154] Feng Menglong sums up this Machiavellian treatment in his preface to *Comprehensive Words to Admonish the World*, "the rhapsody concludes on a stately note." This celebration of *qing* was not an isolated phenomenon in the intellectual circles. It was both a producer and a product of the late Ming commercial market for romantic literature on love and friendship, which in turn was closely related to the rapid social and cultural changes of the time.

In the social landscape of late Ming China, intellectual discourses placed conjugal relations and friendship above the other three of the "five human relations": lord-subject, father-son, and brotherhood. As the state became obsessed with the regulation of sexual behavior,[155] the society became obsessed with foot-binding and market in concubines, courtesans, and prostitutes. Meanwhile, women assumed growing leadership in religious activities and the printing press. A heightened sense of appropriate gender relations seemed a natural development. As the "ladder of success" into officialdom, commerce, and industry became more dependent on social networks beyond the family, and intellectuals sought to assert selfhood through association with like-minded fellows,[156] the importance of friendship stood out. In this social and cultural topography, *qing* was significantly redefined along more personal and secular lines. Rather than an abstract entity, *qing* in late Ming romantic literature now denoted love of the self, friends, family, and by extension, society at large.

With the acclamation of *qing* as a positive force of life came the attack on *li* as a negative imposition on life. A concept cherished by Song Neo-Confucians such as Cheng Yi and Zhu Xi, *li* was reason, principle, and "the human social expression of the inherent patterns of the cosmos."[157] Because of the all-encompassing *li* the cosmos operated in a rational and orderly fashion; humans, being part of the cosmos, should also observe *li* lest chaos should prevail.

But many intellectuals in the late Ming seemed to lose faith in *li*. The diminished authority of *li* might have something to do with the diminished prestige of independent Neo-Confucian lineages since the early fifteenth century. With the execution of the renowned Neo-Confucian Fang Xiaoru (1360-1424) and his network at the hand of Emperor Yongle, the tradition of intellectual lineages, which claimed to transmit *li* from master to disciple through several generations, was destroyed. What followed was a court-imposed exam curriculum of Neo-Confucianism, instituted by people who had little or no connections with the prestigious tradition of transmission of *li*.[158] As the "doctrinally narrow conception" of *li*, constructed by the autocratic state in the name of "Cheng-Zhu orthodoxy,"[159] became rigid and alienating, and the focus of publishing shifted from Classics to romances,[160] *li* lost its intellectual appeal to the general populace. Because *li* had been so caught up with authoritarianism, it had to be abandoned in the vocabulary of literature of a more "romantic" bent, where autonomy of the human will and action was celebrated. In the writings of the romantics, *li* was stripped of its philosophical essence and degenerated into strict nominal rules inflicted on the individuals. It now signified prescribed moral principle and obligations that allowed for no expediency.

Confucius said, "Broaden me with literary culture (*wen*); restrain me with ritual propriety (*li*)" (*Analects*, VI.27). While a true Confucian gentleman can be expected to achieve a perfect harmony between literary exhilaration and ritual constraint, the balance can be easily tipped in a less perfect person. The tension between *wen* and *li* is so strong that the survival of the Chinese civilization could be threatened when *wen* and *li* are not in harmony. "Too much *li* leads to empty formalism and spawns a dry proliferation of rites.... An excess of *wen* can produce too much feeling and emotion, dissolving correct boundaries and confusing proper discrimination with an ever-broadening circle of aesthetic and literary possibilities."[161] The tension between *qing* and *li* in late Ming discourse can be regarded as a logical result of the potential conflict between literary culture and ritual propriety within Confucianism, aggravated by changing meanings of words and changing historical conditions.

The celebration of *qing* can also be understood in the context of a Ming conception that women, being physically secluded and barred from the civil service exams, which tested students' literary achievement as well as "political correctness," embodied purer and more autonomous sentiments and intellect. Women were therefore morally and artistically superior to men. In her study of late imperial Chinese fiction, Maram Epstein identifies the discourse of *qing* as an iconography. Reversing the hierarchy of *yin* and *yang*, the discourse on *qing* "promoted the feminine and the natural as markers of moral and spiritual authenticity," and pitted it against a ritualism which was "mechanical, even false."[162] While the state orthodoxy, the learning of the public moral virtue of *li*, was *yang*, authenticity actually lay in the *yin*, the discourse on the private feelings, *qing*.

Feng Menglong was an active participant in the discourse on *qing*. *Child's Folly* represented the formative stage of his theory of *qing*, which culminated in his anthology of classical love stories, *Qingshi leilue* (*A Classified Outline of the History of Love*, abbreviated as *Qingshi* or *History of Love*). *History of Love* interprets phenomena in the human, supra-human, and sub-human territories from the single perspective of *qing*. Feng contrasts *qing* and *li* sharply in the following passage in the *History of Love*:

> With regard to all matters of loyalty, filiality, chastity, or heroism, if one acts solely from moral principle, then one's action will certainly be forced; if, however, one acts on the basis of utmost feelings, then one's action will certainly be sincere. . . . An ordinary intellectual only knows that *li* restrains *qing* but does not know that *qing* maintains *li*.[163]

Moral actions are admirable only when they spring from true feelings coming from the inside, rather than being a result of externally imposed pressure.

Romantic writers in the late Ming by and large defined *qing* as carnal love. Feng broadened that definition of *qing* to include love of a wide spectrum of subjects: sweethearts, spouses, friends, parents, children, siblings, superiors, inferiors, neighbors, homeland, state, and so on. Philosophically, he regarded *qing* as the foundation of admirable personality and noble action: if you are incapable of true love, you would not be a good person, nor would you act heroically for a cause. Literarily, he saw *qing* as the wellspring of authentic literature: if you do not have strong feelings about a subject, you cannot write a good piece of work on it.

Feng described himself as an unrestrained "*qing*-crazy person" in his youth, who cherished true feelings in a person more than anything else. Perhaps frustrated by his repeated defeats in the examination hall, our compiler of *Child's Folly* was propelled to seek the company of courtesans, drunkards, and gamblers, people who had come down in the world just like him; some of them he found more sincere in their feelings than many educated men.

It seemed natural for the rebellious young man Feng to challenge tradition and orthodoxy. But then Feng's learning in the Classics was recognized by the intellectual circles in Macheng, which must have provided him with some consolation and enabled him to reexamine the value of tradition. The middle-aged Feng became less rebellious.

Finally, the urgency of national crises turned the "bohemian" in youth into a patriot in old age.

Throughout his life Feng Menglong was never apologetic for having been defiant of orthodoxy. He believed the current politics did not work because the uncorrupted scholar-officials stuck rigidly to the rules and failed to take timely and expedient actions and the corrupted officials and underlings ignored the needs and feelings of common people. The current educational system did not work because the hackneyed schoolmasters were wrongfully taken to be the authorities, and the students were trained to be uncritical. Pedantry and conformity to the rules could not save the country. The times called for people who not only had the courage to stand up against the so-called "orthodoxy," but could also do it effectively.

Feng was also never apologetic for being amorous. He asked: If one could not devote love to one's sweetheart and friendship to one's companion, how could you expect this person to devote loyalty to the country? In Feng's discourse, *qing* acquired the status of Wang Yangming's "*liangzhi*" (innate knowledge/act of goodness). As "spontaneous emotional responses to particular circumstances," *qing* gave rise to devotion, devotion gave rise to heroic action, and heroic action gave meaning to life. If a person was without *qing*, he/she ceased to be a human being. In this regard Feng anticipated Bakhtin, to whom life is "the dialogue between events addressed to me in the particular place I occupy in existence, and my expression of a *response* to such events from that unique place. When I cease to respond, when there are—as we say so accurately in English—*no signs of life*, I am dead."[164]

Nor was Feng ever apologetic for being devoted to popular literature, the literary form that most of his contemporary literati despised. He contended in his prefaces to the *Sanyan* that popular literature was at least as good as elite literature in its dual function of self-expression and transformation of people's minds. But popular literature was the more natural and more effective of the two forms. It took its raw material from the masses and was therefore closer to the real-life experiences of the masses. It was written in a plainer language, so its impact on the people's minds was more direct.

Feng's challenge to orthodoxy, his celebration of *qing*, and his advocacy of popular literature were closely related. If writers employed intricate reasoning and delicate diction, as was generally required by elite literature, their feelings would be obstructed and would not flow out of their mind-and-heart spontaneously. Such literature, as the preface of Feng's *Stories Old and New* pointed out, might appeal to the "literary mind," but not to the "common ear," for most people did not have enough literary training to understand such literature. His concern about the common people and his stress on the spontaneous expression of feelings made it logical for him to devote himself to popular literature. His protest against the authorities' repression of feelings in the name of "orthodoxy" also prompted him to "take the true love between man and woman as an antidote for the fake medicine of nominal rules," as he stated in his preface to the *Hill Songs*. Moreover, in a time when pretension, falsity, hypocrisy, stinginess, indifference and heartless calculation seemed to characterize human relations, his teaching of *qing* could be a "cure" to the "ills of the age": if everybody acted according to his/her feelings and conscience, society would be sound. An optimistic outlook on life indeed!

## Notes:

1. This phrase is inspired by Emmanuel Le Roy Ladurie, *Montaillou: The Promised Land of Erro*r, trans. Barbara Bray (New York: Vintage Books, 1979).
2. Wu Pei-yi, *The Confucian's Progress: Autobiographical Writings in Traditional China* (Princeton: Princeton University Press, 1990).
3. Lienche Tu Fang, "Ming Dreams," *Tsing Hua Journal of Chinese Studies* 10, no. 1 (1973): 55-73.
4. G. William Skinner, *The City in Late Imperial China* (Stanford: Stanford University Press, 1977).
5. William S. Atwell, "International Bullion Flows and the Chinese Economy Circa 1530-1650," *Past and Present* 95 (May 1982): 68-90.
6. Craig Clunas, *Superfluous Things: Material Culture and Social Status in Early Modern China* (Urbana: University of Illinois Press, 1991), 56-58.
7. Brook, *The Confusions of Pleasure*, 153-54.
8. What is meant by personalization of politics is that the authorities made judgment on a political proposal not on the basis of its own merits, but on the basis of the political alignment of the drafter.
9. Zhou Hui, *Er xu Jinling suoshi*, in *Biji xiaoshuo daguan*. Cited in Chen Wanyi, *Wan Ming xiaopin yu Ming ji wenren shenghuo* (Taipei: Daan chuban she, 1988), 71.
10. For an illustration of the cangue see Philip A. Kuhn, *Soulstealers: The Chinese Sorcery Scare of 1768* (Cambridge, MA: Harvard University Press, 1990), 8.
11. Xue Gang, *Tianjue Tang bi yu, juan* 1. Cited in Chen Wanyi, 65.
12. Qian Xiyan, "Su yi," *Xixia, juan* 3. Cited in Chen Wanyi, 66.
13. Zhang Dai, "You yu Yiru ba di," *Langhuan wenji*, *juan* 3. Cited in Chen Wanyi, 67.
14. See Lienche Tu Fang's biography of Zhang Han (Chang Han) in *Dictionary of Ming Biography* (1368-1644) (*DMB*), eds. L. Carrington Goodrich and Chaoying Fang (New York: Columbia University Press, 1976), 72-74.

15. Zhang Han, "Bai gong ji," from *Songchuang mengyu*, preface dated 1593, in *Wulin wangzhe yizhu*, *Congshu jicheng san bian*, 4: 15b. Translation modified from Clunas, *Superfluous Things*, 145.

16. The third Ming emperor, Yongle, moved the primary capital from Nanjing to Beijing but kept Nanjing as the secondary capital. See Edward L. Farmer, *Early Ming Government: The Evolution of Dual Capitals* (Cambridge: Harvard University Press, 1976).

17. *Ming shi*, ed. Zhang Tingyu, in *Xin jiaoben Ming shi bing fubian liu zhong*, ed. Yang Jialuo (Taipei: Dingwen shuju 1975), *juan* 77. *Ming shilu*, *Taizu shilu*, 24: 7a. Frederic Wakeman, Jr., "The Price of Autonomy: Intellectuals in Ming and Ch'ing Politics," *Daedalus* 101, no. 2 (1972): 37-38.

18. The *kaozheng* (evidential research) scholar Gu Yanwu (1613-1682), however, argues that Taizu levied heavy taxation only on the confiscated land and not on the private land of innocent people. He regards it unfair to accuse Taizu of punishing the Suzhou people for the sake of Zhang Shicheng: Suzhou paid higher taxation because it happened to have a higher percentage of confiscated land. See Gu Yanwu, *Tianxia junguo libing shu*, 1901 *Tushu jicheng chubian*, 15: 21b-22a.

19. Taizu's successor Emperor Jianwen (r. 1399-1402) lifted the economic sanction, but the next emperor Yongle soon restored the old tax. In 1430 Emperor Xuande reduced the tax on the "official land" by twenty to thirty percent. In 1436 Emperor Zhengtong leveled the taxation on the "official land" and the "private land." See *Wuxian zhi* (1933; rpt. Taipei: Chengwen chuban she, 1970), 44: 2b-3b. But according to Gu Yanwu, until his days the heavier taxation was still not completely relieved because of the negligence of officials in charge. See Gu, *Tianxia junguo libing shu*, 18: 4b.

20. Matteo Ricci, *China in the Sixteenth Century: The Journals of Matthew Ricci: 1583-1610*, trans. Louis J. Gallagher (New York: Random House, 1953), 317-18.

21. For a case study of Emperor Yongzhen's distrust of Jiangnan, see Jonathan D. Spence, *Treason by the Book* (New York: Penguin, 2001). For the case of Emperor Qianlong see Philip A. Kuhn, *Soulstealers*.

22. Clunas, "Anxieties about things: Consumption and class in Ming China," *Superfluous Things*, 141-65.

23. Lament over the violation of sumptuary laws can be found in Zhang Han's *Songchuang mengyu*, Fan Lian's *Yunjian jumu chao*, Shen Defu's *Wanli yehuo bian*, Gui Zhuang's *Gui Zhuang ji*, among others. See Liu Zhiqin, "Wan Ming shifeng manyi," *Shehui xue yanjiu* (March 1992): 107-111.

24. For a 1582 Hangzhou riot against tax injustice see Chen Xuewen, "Ming dai yici shimin yishi de xin juexing: Wanli shi nian Hangzhou bingbian he minbian yanjiu," *Zhejiang shehui kexue* (February 1992): 61-64.

25. William S. Atwell, "Some Observations on the 'Seventeenth-Century Crisis' in China and Japan," *The Journal of Asian Studies* 45, no. 2 (1986): 227.

26. The "Chimi pian" was written during the Qin-Han transition, when merchants first emerged as a significant social force in China. See Guo Moruo, "'Chimi pian de yanjiu," *Nuli zhi shidai*, 2nd edition (Beijing, 1973), 148-201. Also see Lien-sheng Yang, "Economic Justification for Spending—An Uncommon Idea in Traditional China," *Harvard Journal of Asiatic Studies* 20, nos. 1-2 (1957): 36-52.

27. Lu Ji, *Jianjia Tang zazhu zhaichao*, in *Jilu huibian*, 204: 3a-b. Cf. Lien-sheng Yang's translation in "Economic Justification for Spending," 51 and Pei-kai

Cheng's translation in "Reality and Imagination: Li Chih and T'ang Hsien-tsu in Search of Authenticity," Ph. D. diss., Yale University, 1980, 44-45.

28. The Former Seven Masters were Wang Jiusi (1468-1551), Li Mengyang (1472-1529), Wang Tingxiang (1474-1544), Kang Hai (1475-1540), Bian Gong (1476-1532), Xu Zhenqing (1479-1511), and He Jingming (1483-1521). The Latter Seven Masters were Xie Zhen (1495-1575), Li Panlong (1514-1570), Xu Zhongxing (1517-1578), Zong Chen (1525-1560), Wang Shizhen (1526-1590), Liang Youyu (1522-1566), and Wu Guolun (1524-1593).

29. Michael Holquist, "The Politics of Representation," in *Allegory and Representation*, ed. Stephen J. Greenblatt (Baltimore: The Johns Hopkins University Press, 1981), 163-83.

30. Kathryn Lowry, "Excess and Restraint: Feng Menglong's Prefaces on Currently Popular Songs," *Papers on Chinese History* 2 (Spring 1993), 97.

31. I borrow this phrase from Peter K. Bol, *"This Culture of Ours": Intellectual Transitions in T'ang and Sung China* (Stanford: Stanford University Press, 1992).

32. For a cultural history of Ming writers and artists, see Uchiyama Chinari, *Mindai bunjinron*. Tokyo: Mokujisha, 1986.

33. Shen and Qiu were registered as professional painters and never as students of the district school. See Richard Edwards, entry on Shen Chou [Shen Zhou] in *DMB*, 1174.

34. While there was no limit to the number of the lowest degree holders (*shengyuan*), the quotas were fixed at the provincial (*juren*) and metropolitan (*jinshi*) levels. Only those who passed at least the provincial examination or obtained a *gongsheng* degree either by purchase or by recommendation were eligible for official appointments. Considering the population growth and the popularization of education, which expanded the pool of examination candidates, the quotas were proportionally shrinking. From this perspective, Jiangnan actually suffered more of the examination hell than other districts of China. See Ho Ping-ti, *The Ladder of Success in Imperial China: Aspects of Social Mobility, 1368-1911* (New York: Columbia University Press, 1962), 173-85, 232-34.

35. I borrow the phrase "thorny gates" from John W. Chaffee, *The Thorny Gates of Learning in Sung China: A Social History of Examinations* (Cambridge: Cambridge University Press, 1985).

36. See the biography of the Wanli emperor Zhu Yijun by Charles O. Hucker in *DMB*, 324-37 and Ray Huang, *1587: A Year of No Significance* (New Haven: Yale University Press, 1981).

37. Clunas, *Superfluous Things*, 5.

38. The uncorrupted administrator Hai Rui (1513-1587) was most critical of the trouble-making *shengyuan* or *xiucai* (budding scholars), the numerous lowest-degree holders the unsound Ming examination system produced. See the discussion in Joanna F. Handlin, *Action in Late Ming Thought: The Reorientation of Lü K'un and Other Scholar-Officials* (Berkeley: University of California Press, 1983), 58-59. Hai Rui's attack on the unworthy shengyuan was later echoed by Gu Yanwu. See Gu Yanwu, "Shengyuan lun," in *Tinglin wenji*, 1: 17a-22a, *Gu Tinglin xiansheng yishu shi zhong* (Taipei: Jinxue shuju, 1969).

39. The Five Classics are *Shijing* (*Book of Odes*), *Shujing* (*Book of Document*), *Yijing* (*Book of Changes*), *Liji* (*Book of Rites*), and *Chun Qiu* (*Spring and Autumn Annals*). They were part of the examination curriculum.

40. See William S. Atwell, "From Education to Politics: The Fu She," in *The Unfolding of Neo-Confucianism*, ed. Wm. Theodore de Bary (New York: Columbia University Press, 1975), 333-67.

41. The Donglin Academy was founded in 1604 by Gu Xiancheng (1550-1612) and other like-minded upright scholar-officials. Their goal was to root out the evil influences at court cast by Wei Zhongxian's corrupt "eunuch party," as well as moral laxity of their colleagues. Unlike the Ying She and the Fu She, many Donglin members were from official backgrounds. For more information on the Donglin movement see Charles O. Hucker, "The Tung-lin Movement of the Late Ming Period," in *Chinese Thought and Institutions*, ed. John K. Fairbank (Chicago: University of Chicago Press, 1957), 132-62; John W. Dardess, *Blood and History in China: The Donglin Faction and Its Repression* (Honolulu: University of Hawaii Press, 2002). The struggles between Wei Zhongxian and the Donglin party inspired the production of a large number of fiction and drama; see, for example, Oki Yasushi, "Minmatsu Konan ni okeru shuppan-bunka no kenkyu" (Research on the printing press in late Ming Jiangnan), *Hiroshima Daigaku Bungakubu kiyo*, vol. 50 *Tokushugo* no. 1 (1991): 122-32.

42. For discussions of the alleged incident see Lu Shulun, "Feng Menglong de 'yi yan de zui' han 'shu ji gou dang,'" *Liaoning Daxue xuebao, zhexue shehui kexue ban*, 1981.6: 83-84; Ju Jun, ed., *Feng Menglong shiwen* (Fuzhou: Haixia wenyi chuban she, 1985), 68. Tai-loi Ma believes the author implicated in this political struggle was actually Feng Menglong's friend Wen Zhenmeng, on whose behalf Feng wrote two formulary essays that mentioned the incident in the first person, hence the misunderstanding. See Tai-loi Ma, "Feng Menglong yu Wen Zhenmeng," *Zhonghua wenshi luncong*, 1984.1: 137-39.

43. For the Suzhou incident see Kaidu chuanxin (The True Story of the Promulgation), which is translated with an introduction in Charles O. Hucker, "Su-chou and the Agents of Wei Chung-hsien, 1626," in idem, *Two Studies on Ming History*, Michigan Papers in Chinese Studies no. 12 (Ann Arbor: Center for Chinese Studies, University of Michigan, 1971), 41-83.

44. Benjamin Elman, *From Philosophy to Philology: Intellectual and Social Aspects of Change in Late Imperial China* (Cambridge: Harvard University Press, 1984).

45. Wm. Theodore de Bary, "Introduction," in *Principle and Practicality: Essays in Neo-Confucianism and Practical Learning*, eds. idem and Irene Bloom (New York: Columbia University Press, 1979), 25.

46. For a study of the late Ming rebellions see James Bunyan Parsons, *Peasant Rebellions of the Late Ming Dynasty* (Tucson: The University of Arizona Press, 1970).

47. Mary M. Anderson, *Hidden Power: The Palace Eunuchs of Imperial China* (Buffalo: Prometheus Books, 1990), 258.

48. For a discussion of the nature of Li Zicheng's rebellion see Kwang-Ching Liu, "World View and Peasant Rebellion: Reflections on Post-Mao Historiography," *The Journal of Asian Studies* 40, no. 2 (1981): 295-326.

49. Ray Huang, "Fiscal Administration during the Ming Dynasty," in *Chinese Government in Ming Times: Seven Studies*, ed. Charles O. Hucker (New York: Columbia University Press, 1969), 117-19.

50. Frederic Wakeman, Jr., "The Shun Interregnum of 1644," in *From Ming to Ch'ing: Conquest, Region, and Continuity in Seventeenth-Century China*, eds. Jona-

than D. Spence and John E. Wills, Jr. (New Haven: Yale University Press, 1979), 44-47, 77-78.

51. During the seventeenth century, colder temperature and significant shifts in global wind patterns had a devastating impact on agricultural production in Europe, China, and Japan. See Atwell, "Seventeenth-Century Crisis," 225-27, and Frederic E. Wakeman, Jr., "China and the Seventeenth-Century Crisis," *Late Imperial China* 7, no. 1 (1986): 5-6.

52. Atwell, "International Bullion Flows," 88-89.

53. For the formation of Ming autocracy in the founding era see John W. Dardess, *Confucianism and Autocracy: Professional Elites in the Founding of the Ming Dynasty* (Berkeley: University of California Press, 1983).

54. Charles O. Hucker, *The Ming Dynasty: Its Origins and Evolving Institutions*, Michigan Papers in Chinese Studies no. 34 (Ann Arbor: Center for Chinese Studies, the University of Michigan, 1978).

55. Despite all this, the concept of "oriental despotism" still does not apply to Ming China, where the emperor was still subject to certain institutional and ideological restraints to his whim. See Romeyn Taylor, "Rulership in Late Imperial Chinese Orthodoxy," and Edward L. Farmer, "The Dragon's Tether: Theoretical Limits on Imperial Power in Ming China," papers presented in the Conference on "Absolutism and Despotism in Early Modern Eurasia" at University of Minnesota, October 26-28, 1989.

56. For a brief summary of the eunuchs' roles see Frederic Wakeman, Jr., "The Price of Autonomy," 40.

57. Jiajing and Wanli emperors each held only a single audience with their ministry heads. See Frederic Wakeman, Jr., "China and the Seventeenth-Century Crisis," 12.

58. Hok-lam Chan, "The White Lotus-Maitreya Doctrine and Popular Uprisings in Ming and Ch'ing China," *Sinologica* 10 (1969): 211-33.

59. James W. Tong, *Disorder Under Heaven: Collective Violence in the Ming Dynasty* (Stanford: Stanford University Press, 1991).

60. Feng Menglong's preface to *Jiashen jishi*, in *Xuanlan Tang congshu*, *xu*: 5b-14a records the soldiers' looting at the fall of the Ming and his criticism of Ming court's faulty military policy.

61. This information is given by Feng Menglong himself in the *Shouning daizhi*. About the problems surrounding the identification of Feng Menglong's native place see Ye Ru's discussion in "Guanyu Sanyan de zuanji zhe," in *Ming Qing xiaoshuo yanjiu lunwen ji* (Beijing: Renming wenxue chuban she, 1959), 31-33.

62. For definition and discussion of the vernacular and classical languages, see Patrick Hanan, "Language and Narrative Model," in *The Chinese Vernacular Story* (Cambridge, MA: Harvard University Press, 1981), 1-27.

63. Brook, *The Confusions of Pleasure*, 168.

64. The references appear, respectively, in *Suzhou fuzhi* (1743 edition), 39: 12b; *Suzhou fuzhi*, 54: 12b, quoting *Jiangnan tongzhi* (1737), 165: 43b; and *Funing fuzhi* by Li Ba et al., *juan* 17.

65. See Tai-loi Ma, "Feng Menglong youpeng jiaoyou shi kaoshi," in *Zhongguo tushu wenshi lunji* (Taipei: Zhengzhong shuju, 1991), 329-36.

66. Zhu Yizun quotes one poem by Feng Menglong in his *Ming shi zong*, slightly inaccurately (Feng's original poem appears in Mao Jin, "He youren shi

juan," in *Yinhu yigao*, *Yusahn congke*, 6b-7a), and attaches this comment. See Zhu, *Ming shi zong* (n.d.), 71: 23a-b.

67. For a study of the compilation of *Siku quanshu*, see R. Kent Guy, *The Emperor's Four Treasuries: Scholars and the State in the Late Ch'ien-lung Era* (Cambridge, MA: Council on East Asian Studies, Harvard University, 1987).

68. *Siku quanshu zongmu tiyao, juan* 132, "Zi bu, zajia lei," 2739.

69. For the Southern Ming see Lynn A. Struve, *The Southern Ming 1644-1662* (New Haven: Yale University Press, 1984).

70. Nagasawa Kikuya, "'Sangen' 'Nihaku' ni tsuite," *Shibun* 10, no. 9 (1928): 12-36 & 11, no. 5 (1929): 21-29.

71. W. L. Idema, *Chinese Vernacular Fiction: The Formative Period* (Leiden: E. J. Brill, 1974), 37-38.

72. Haiyan Lee, "Tears That Crumbled the Great Wall: The Archaeology of Feeling in the May Fourth Folklore Movement," *The Journal of Asian Studies* 64, no. 1 (2005): 59.

73. Idema, XLIV.

74. An original printed text of Shan ge was discovered in Huizhou, Anhui in 1934. Based on this text, in 1935 Chuanjing Tang in Shanghai published a typeset *Shan ge*, edited by Gu Jiegang. Zhongyang shudian in Shanghai subsequently published *Huang Shan mi*, including "Shan ge," "Huang ying er," "Mi yu," "Guazhier," and "Jiazhutao." The first modern edition of *Gujin xiaoshuo* was published by the Commercial Press in 1947, based on the Tianxu Zhai edition. The earliest modern edition of *Jingshi tongyan* was published in installments during 1935 and 1936 in the *Shijie wenku* edited by Zheng Zhendo, based on the Jianshan Tang edition (preface dated 1624). The earliest modern edition of *Xingshi hengyan* was published in 1936 as an addition to the *Shijie wenku* series, based on the Ye Jingchi edition (preface dated 1627). See Hanan, *Chinese Short Story: Studies in Dating, Authorship, and Composition* (Cambridge, MA: Harvard University Press, 1973), 228. Shanghai Zhonghua shuju published *Guazhier* in 1961 with a preface by Guan Dedong and *Shan ge* in 1962, also prefaced by Guan Dedong.

75. For example, Sun Kaidi, "Sanyan Erpai yuanliu kao," *Guoli Beiping tushuguan guankan* 5, no. 2 (1931): 11-62; Tan Zhengbi, *Sanyan Liangpai ziliao*, 2 vols. (Shanghai: Shanghai guji chuban she, 1980); André Lévy, *Inventaire Analytique et Critique du Conte Chinois en Langue Vulgalire, Mémoires de l'Institut des Hautes Etudes Chinoises*, vols. 8-1, 2, 3, 4 (Paris: Presses Universitaires de France, 1978, 1979, 1981, 1991).

76. Shinoya On, "Min no shosetsu 'Sangen' ni tsuite," *Shibun* VIII (1926), no. 5: 309-19, no. 6: 375-96, no. 7: 468-79.

77. Rong Zhaozu, "Ming Feng Menglong de shengping ji qi zhushu," *Lingnan xuebao* 2, no. 2 (1931): 61-91, and "Ming Feng Menglong de shengping ji qi zhushu xu kao," *Lingnan xuebao* 2, no. 3 (1932): 95-124.

78. The bulk of Lu Shulun's research on Feng Menglong, conducted in the 1960s, was published posthumously in the monograph *Feng Menglong yanjiu* (Shanghai: Fudan Daxue chuban she, 1987). The editor attributes Lu's reluctance to have it published earlier to unfavorable political climate: Feng Menglong's status was ambiguous for a while in China. Lu's earlier papers on Feng were published under the pseudonym Ye Ru.

79. Most notably *The Chinese Short Story* and *The Chinese Vernacular Story*.

80. We do not know the name of Feng's father, but we know that he was a close friend of Wang Jingchen (1513-1595). Wang was a Confucian philosopher of Suzhou known for his filial piety and humanity. Feng's father was presumably of similar character. See Feng Mengxiong's colophon to Wang Jingchen, *Si hou bian*, 1924 edition.

81. Xu Qin, *Ming hua lu, juan* 8, *Congshu jicheng chubian*, vol. 317, 88.

82. Chen Jisheng's *Tianqi Chongzhen liangchao yishi* (rpt. Beijing: Zhonghua shuju, 1958) records 10 poems (under 8 titles) of Feng Mengxiong in *juan* 8, 1081-82.

83. Ye Ru, "Guanyu Feng Menglong de shengshi," in *Ming Qing xiaoshuo yanjiu lunwen ji*, 35.

84. Feng's "Madiao pai jing" of 13 sections is preserved in *Xu Shuofu*, ed. Tao Ting, *jiu* 39 (rpt Taipei: Xinxing shuju, 1964), 1759-62.

85. See the vernacular short story, "Jue xinkeng lingui cheng caizhu," in Zhuoyuan Ting zhuren, *Zhaoshi bei, Hanben Zhongguo tushu xiaoshuo congkan* (Taipei: Tianyi chuban she, 1974), 98.

86. Rong Zhaozu, "Ming Feng Menglong de shengping ji qi zhushu xu kao," 103.

87. Rong Zhaozu dates this crisis at "either a few years prior to 1619, or between 1620 and 1621." See Rong, "Ming Feng Menglong de shengping ji qi zhushu xu kao," 103. According to a recent study by Gao Hongjun, Xiong Tingbi was assigned the education intendant in Nanjing in 1611; he got acquainted with Feng Menglong in 1612, and was temporarily dismissed in 1613. Gao's chronology seems reasonable. See Gao, "Guazhier chengshu kao ji Feng Menglong, Hou Huiqing lianli yuanwei," *Tianjin Shida xuebao, sheke ban*, 1992.2: 40.

88. Niu Xiu, "Yingxiong judong," *Gusheng xu bian*, in *Biji xu bian* (Taipei: Guangwen shuju, 1969), vol. 39, 256-58.

89. *Ming shi, juan* 259, 6692. *Xu Biaozhong ji* (Taipei: Chengwen chuban she, 1971), 2: 1b.

90. For Feng Menglong's role in the writing and editing of the Sanyan and the periodization of the source stories see Patrick Hanan, *The Chinese Short Story*.

91. See Feng Menglong's introduction and Feng Mengxiong's preface to *Linjing zhiyue*.

92. It was common for young scholars in the Ming to join a study group in order to have their examination preparatory essays read and criticized by their fellow students and teachers who were expert with "eight-legged" essays. These study groups also collaborated with bookstores to have the collections of students' essays published. See Atwell, "From Education to Politics," 337. Huang'an and Macheng were known for its Chun Qiu expertise. For the dates of Feng's sojourn in Huang'an and Macheng see Lu Shulun's entry on Feng Menglong in *Zhongguo lidai zhumin wenxue jia pingzhuan*, vol. 4 (Jinan: Shandong jiaoyu chuban she, 1985), 458.

93. A copy is preserved in the Academia Sinica, Taipei, Taiwan.

94. There is a copy in the Naikaku Bunko.

95. There is a copy in the Harvard-Yenching Library.

96. The *Bieben Chun Qiu daquan* of 30 *juan* is listed in *juan* 30 of *Siku quanshu zongmu tiyao*, 611.

97. An incomplete edition is preserved in the Beijing Library.

98. *Suzhou fuzhi*, 54:12b, quoting *Jiangnan tongzhi* (1737), 165: 43b.

99. Hanan, *Chinese Vernacular Story*, 82-83.

100. Robert E. Hegel, "Unpredictability and Meaning in Ming-Qing Literati Novels," in *Paradoxes of Traditional Chinese Literature*, ed. Eva Hung (Hong Kong: The Chinese University Press, 1994), 147.

101. Ibid., 155.

102. See Jin Demeng, "Feng Menglong sheji kao," *Zhonghua wenshi luncong*, 1985.1: 281-84; Yao Zheng, "Feng Menglong yu Yun She chengyuan mingdan," *Zhonghua wenshi luncong*, 1987.1: 279-82.

103. Qian's poem was composed for Feng's seventieth birthday, entitled "Feng Erzhang Youlong qishi shou shi," in idem, *Muzhai chuxue ji*, ed. Qian Zeng, *Jindai Zhongguo shiliao congkan* (Taipei: Wenhai chuban she, 1984-87), 713. For the poem's suggestion of the existence of a seven-member group see Tai-loi Ma, "Feng Menglong youpeng jiaoyou shi kaoshi," 335-36.

104. Lu Shulun, *Feng Menglong yanjiu*, 69-78. This list is not exhaustive.

105. The earliest scholarly discussion about Feng's connection with Fu She is perhaps Hu Wanchuan, "Feng Menglong yu Fu She renwu," *Zhongguo gudian xiaoshuo zhuanji*, vol. 1 (Taipei: Lianjing, 1979), 123-36.

106. *Suzhou fuzhi*, 39: 12b. 1630 was a year of great success for Fu She members in examination and political appointments. It is not clear whether Feng acquired the *gongsheng* because of his connection with Fu She.

107. We know this from Feng's own reflection in his *Shouning daizhi* (copy preserved in the Ueno Library), 1: 17. The 1683 *Dantu xianzhi*, 21: 24b, records his tenure as during the Tianqi reign. But the *Dantu xianzhi* dating was wrong. See Hanan, *Chinese Vernacular Story*, 224.

108. *Juan* 17 of *Funing fuzhi* by Li Ba et al. Translation slightly modified from Mowry, 34.

109. See Lienche Tu Fang's entry on Hsü Po [Xu Bo] in *DMB*, 597-98.

110. Xu Bo, "Shouning Feng Fumu shi xu," in *Hongyu Lou ji* (manuscript preserved in Shanghai Library), quoted in Lin Ying and Chen Yukui, "Feng Menglong si nian zhixian shenghuo de shilu: Shouning daizhi pingjie," *Zhonghua wenshi luncong*, 1983.1: 210.

111. The only extant original copy of the *Shouning daizhi* was preserved in Ueno Library in Tokyo. Modern typeset editions have recently been published in both China and Taiwan. There are two comprehensive studies on *Shouning daizhi*: Lin Ying and Chen Yukui, "Feng Menglong si nian zhixian shenghuo de shilu: Shouning daizhi pingjie"; Y. W. Ma (Ma Youyuan), "Feng Menglong yu Shouning daizhi," *Xiaoshuo xiqu yanjiu*, vol. 3 (Taipei: Lianjing, 1990), 141-80. Patrick Hanan has a brief discussion of *Shouning daizhi* in his *Chinese Vernacular Story*, 85-86.

112. The vision projected in Zhang Tao's gazetteer provides a point of departure for Timothy Brook's *Confusions of Pleasure.*

113. Feng, *Shouning daizhi*, "Liyi," B1a-b.

114. *Fujian tongzhi*, 1871 edition, *juan* 35. For a discussion of the custom see T'ien Ju-k'ang, *Male Anxiety and Female Chastity: A Comparative Study of Chinese Ethical Values in Ming-Ch'ing Times*, *Monographies du T'oung Pao*, vol. XIV (Leiden: E. J. Brill, 1988), 30-31.

115. Feng, *Shouning daizhi*, "Fengsu," A 51a-52a.

116. Magistrate Bao Zhen of the Song dynasty and Prime Minister Di Renjie of the Tang dynasty are dramatized as sagacious, even divine, judges in Chinese fiction. The formal is more famous in China; the latter is more famous overseas. Robert

van Gulik adapts the Di Renjie tales into a famous series of English-language detective stories entitled *The Judge Dee Murder Mysteries*, which has been translated into some twenty different languages.

117. Feng, *Shouning daizhi*, "Yusong," A39b-40b; "Quanjie," B56b-57a.

118. The early-Qing list of books to be burned also includes a *Zhongxing congxin lu* by Feng Menglong. See *Qing dai jinhui shumu si zhong, Guoxue jiben congshu si bai zhong*, 49.

119. Lu, *Feng Menglong yanjiu*, 30.

120. Ibid., 6-9.

121. Feng Menglong, *Guazhier*, in *Ming Qing min ge shi diao ji*, vol. 1 (Shanghai: Shanghai guji chuban she, 1987), 5: 54a. Part of the section has been published in my article, "Courtesans and Scholars in the Writings of Feng Menglong: Transcending Status and Gender," *Nan Nü* 2, no. 1 (2000): 40-77; used with the permission of Brill Academic Publishers.

122. Feng Menglong, *Shan ge*, 4: 31a-b.

123. See Dong Sizhang's statement in the *Taixia xinzou* (modern facsimile edition without a preface, n.d.), 7: 13b.

124. Since Feng did not express any sense of resentment in his *Shan ge* entry on Hou Huiqing, it seems Hou still befriended Feng when *Shan ge* was completed. *Guazhier* appeared before *Shan ge*, which makes the inclusion of the "Yuanli" poem in the *Guazhier* very strange. A logical explanation, it seems to me, is that the original texts based on which Zhonghua shuju reconstructed the *Guazhier* must contain some revisions Feng made after his loss of Hou Huiqing. A further indication that our version of *Guazhier* is not the first edition, but a revised one, can be found in Feng's note to the song "Zhang" (Accounts) (*Guazhier*, 3: 25a) in which he stated that this song was a gift from the *pipa* (lute) player A Yuan who, upon learning of Feng's effort to expand his edition of *Guazhier*, presented this song as an addition to the volume.

125. Feng, *Guazhier*, 2: 14a.

126. I am grateful to Yao Hai-hsing for providing me with information on the various "Yuanyang Grave" plays.

127. *Taixia xinzou*, 7: 12a-13b.

128. Ibid., 11: 24a-25b. In 11: 24b we see a note on the margin saying that in the old *Wanzhuan ge* collection there were only two verses in this set.

129. Ibid., 7: 27a-28b.

130. Ibid., 10: 23a-24a.

131. Ibid., 10: 24a-25a.

132. Gao Hongjun, "Guazhier chengshu kao ji Feng Menglong, Hou Huiqing lianli yuanwei," *Tianjin Shida xuebao, sheke ban*, 1992.2: 39-44.

133. Yuan Zhongdao, *Kexue Zhai qian ji* (Taipei: Weiwen tushu chuban she, 1976, modern facsimile edition of the original preserved in the Central Library, Taipei, Taiwan), 2: 16b-18a, 18a-b, 19a-b.

134. Ibid., 2: 40a-b, 5: 5a-b.

135. Feng, *Shan ge*, 5: 36b.

136. Oki Yasushi, "Fu Muryu 'Sanka' no kenkyu," *Toyo Bunka Kenkyujo kiyo* 105 (February 1988): 208-09.

137. Pei-kai Cheng, "Wan Ming Yuan Zhongdao de fufu guan," *Research on Women in Modern Chinese History* 1 (June 1993): 201-16.

138. Yuan Zhongdao, "Xin lu," in *Kexue Zhai ji*, ed. Qian Bocheng (Shanghai: Shanghai Guji chuban she, 1989), *juan* 22, 954-55. Translated by Martin Huang in *Desire and Fictional Narrative in Late Imperial China*, 11.

139. The tenth of Yuan Zhongdao's fifty-eight "Ganhuai" poems, in *Kexue Zhai ji, juan* 5, 192. Translated by Martin Huang in *Desire and Fictional Narrative*, 19.

140. For Feng Menglong's relations with courtesans see Oki Yasushi, "Fu Muryu to Gijo," *Hiroshima Daigaku bungakubu kiyo* 48 (January 1989): 71-91.

141. Hanan, *Chinese Vernacular Story*, 90. His source is Wanyu Zi's *Wu ji baimei*, 1617 edition (Hosa Bunko, Nagoya).

142. Cited by Oki Yasushi in *Minmatsu no hagure tsishikizin: Fu Muryu to Sosu bunka* (Tokyo: Kodanshya, 1995), 106. Oki suspects Wanyu Zi, the author of *Wu ji baimei*, might be Yu Wanlun, who might have written a preface to Feng's *Guazhier*.

143. For a discussion of the discourse on *qing* throughout Chinese literary history see Siu-kit Wong, "*Ch'ing* in Chinese Literary Criticism," Ph.D. diss., Oxford University, 1969.

144. Xu Wei, "Xiaofu shi xu," in *Xu Wenchang san ji* (Taipei: Central Library, 1968), 19: 29b-30a. Trans. Modified from Chih-ping Chou, *Yüan Hung-tao and the Kung-an School* (Cambridge, MA: Cambridge University Press, 1988), 19.

145. Tang Xianzu, "Mudan ting ji tici," in *Tang Xianzu ji*, ed. Xu Shuofang (Beijing: Zhonghua shuju, 1962), 1093.

146. For an English translation of the play see Cyril Birch, trans., *Mu-tan t'ing—The Peony Pavilion* (Bloomington: Indiana University Press, 1980).

147. Dorothy Ko, *Teachers of the Inner Chambers: Women and Culture in Seventeenth-Century China* (Stanford: Stanford university Press, 1994), 68-112.

148. Mao Xiaotong, ed., *Tang Xianzu yanjiu ziliao huibian* (Shanghai: Shanghai guji chuban she, 1986), 2.855.

149. Ibid., 2.681.

150. Wai-yee Li, *Enchantment and Disenchantment: Love and Illusion in Chinese Literature* (Princeton: Princeton University Press, 1993), 61.

151. For a discussion of Feng Menglong's alterations of the romantic hero Liu Mengmei in his Romantic Dream, see Catherine Swatek, "Plum and Portrait: Feng Menglong's Revision of The Peony Pavilion," *Asia Major* 3rd series, 6: 1 (1993): 127-60.

152. C. T. Hsia, "Time and the Human Condition in the Plays of T'ang Hsien-tsu," in *Self and Society in Ming Thought*, ed. Wm. Theodore de Bary, 276.

153. For Lü Kun's distrust of sexual love in gender relations, see Katherine Carlitz, "The Social Uses of Female Virtue in Late Ming Editions of Lienü Zhuan," *Late Imperial China* 12, no. 2 (1991): 117-52, and idem, "Desire, Danger, and the Body: Stories of Women's Virtue in Late Ming China," in *Engendering China: Women, Culture, and the State*, eds. Christina K. Gilmartin, et al. (Cambridge, MA: Harvard University Press, 1994), 117-21.

154. Epstein, *Competing Discourses*, 87.

155. The Ming dynasty was a watershed in the regulation of sexuality. The state "extended chastity honors to martyred victims of attempted rape, expanded the death penalty to cover all rapes between status equals, imposed a stricter standard of evidence for rape conviction, and banned consensual homosexual sodomy for the first

time." Matthew H. Sommer, *Sex, Law, and Society in Late Imperial China* (Stanford: Stanford university Press, 2000), 308.

156. Ronald Dimberg, *The Sage and Society: The Life and Thought of Ho Hsin-yin* (Honolulu: The University Press of Hawaii, 1974), 75-118; Joseph McDermott, "Friendship and Its Friends in the Late Ming," *Family Process and Political Process in Modern Chinese History* (Taipei: Institute of Modern History, Academia Sinica, 1992), 67-96.

157. Personal communication with Peter Bol, October 1991.

158. Peter Ditmanson, "Intellectual Lineages and the Early Ming Court," *Papers on Chinese History* 5 (1996): 1-17.

159. Thomas Wilson, *Genealogy of the Way: The Construction and Uses of the Confucian Tradition in Late Imperial China* (Stanford: Stanford University Press, 1995), 24.

160. Brook, *Confusions of Pleasure*, 62-65, 129-34, 167-71.

161. Stephen W. Durrant, *The Cloudy Mirror: Tension and Conflict in the Writings of Sima Qian* (Albany: State University of New York Press, 1995), xiv.

162. Epstein, 7.

163. Feng Menglong, *Qingshi leilue*, 1: 41b. Translation modified from Hua-yuan Li Mowry, *Chinese Love Stories from Ch'ing-shih* (Hamden: Archon Books, 1983), 38.

164. Michael Holquist, *Dialogism: Bakhtin and His World* (London: Routledge, 1990), 48-49.

# 3

# *Hanging Twigs* and *Hill Songs*:

## The Triumph and Trial of Emotions and Desires

## 掛枝兒及山歌

Feng Menglong revealed his amorous nature in the love songs written after his loss of the courtesan Hou Huiqing, as recorded in the *Hill Songs* and the *Celestial Songs Played Anew*. Feng's friend Dong Sizhang commented that these songs were "forced upon him by extreme emotions; they contained absolutely no set phrase of lovesickness."[1] The editor of the *Celestial Songs Played Anew* also commented that Feng's songs were "devoid of linguistic brilliance, but surpassing other people's works in one area, that is, genuineness (*zhen*)."[2] The songs demonstrated a straightforward and unreserved outpouring of Feng's sorrow and grief. He did not employ literary allusions or beautiful phrases to describe his feelings of loss. Nor did he display the emotional modesty that was expected of a traditional Confucian gentleman. In other words, artificiality was absent from the literary expression of his feelings and from his handling of emotions. This genuineness in emotions and their expressions was also the spirit behind the compilation of *Child's Folly*.

The compiler of *Hanging Twigs* and *Hill Songs* was a romantic "bohemian." He took the forbidden love of young couples as a symbol of the individual's courageous challenge to social decorum and Confucian patriline. The youthful lovers were passionate, redheaded, and rebellious. They could not be constrained. The folkloric and comical nature of the folk and popular songs allowed the editor to side with the unestablished and inexperienced and celebrate their "child's folly." The mood of the songs was in line with Northrop Frye's theory on "the mythos of spring: comedy." "The obstacles to the hero's desire," says Frye, "form the action of the comedy, and the overcoming of them the comic resolution. The obstacles are usually parental, hence comedy often turns on a clash between a son's and a father's will. Thus the comic dramatist as a rule writes for the younger men in his audience, and the older members of almost any society are apt to feel that comedy has something subversive about it."[3] Clashes between the will of the children and the parents were indeed a recurring theme in *Hanging Twigs* and *Hill Songs*. However, the protagonists were not fathers and sons, but mothers and daughters, and the focal point of their clashes was, appropriately, love and marriage. The mothers were determined to protect the daughters' reputation, but the daughters would not sacrifice carnal love for an empty name, hence the conflict of interest and a battle of wit and will, in which the younger women always got the upper hand.

## Preface to *Hill Songs*

Although the universe of *Hanging Twigs* and *Hill Songs* was full of subversive elements, Feng Menglong invoked well-established Chinese cultural tradition to justify his position:

> From the beginning of writings and records, each age has had its songs and rhymes. What the grand historians presented [in their collections of songs] included both the *feng* (airs) and the *ya* (elegance). This was super. However, since Chu laments and Tang regulated verses competed [with songs] for beauty and gusto, the voices of the common people expressive of their nature and feelings were no longer included in the realm of poetic endeavor. Such songs were distinguished as the *shan ge* (hill songs). They refer to songs sung by farmers in the field and youngsters in the village on the spur of the moment, with which officials and literati do not concern themselves. As long as these songs were not included in the realm of poetic endeavor and were not the concern of officials and literati, their influence became increasingly eclipsed, and the minds of the singers also became increasingly shallow. The hill songs popular today are all but tunes on amorous themes. Even though that is the case, [we see that] love songs amidst the mulberry on the banks of the river Pu[4] were censured in the "Guofeng" (Airs of the States) [of the *Book of Odes*] yet Confucius recorded them. He saw that, as these were expressions of genuine feelings, they should not be eliminated. Although the hill songs are extremely vulgar, are they alone not the descendants of the airs of Zheng and Wei?[5] Besides, in our degenerate times, there may be false poetry and prose, but there are no false hill songs. It is because the hill songs do not vie for social preeminence with poetry and prose that they do not trifle with falsity. Since they do not trifle with falsity, isn't it fine for me to collect them in order to record what is genuine? Or, [through my collection] people

of today may ponder that the songs presented by the grand historians in high antiquity were like that, and those remain among common people in recent times are like this. In this sense perhaps this volume can also be a collection via which to discourse on affairs of the times. In terms of taking the true love between man and woman as an antidote for the fake medicine of nominal rules, the merit of this collection equals that of *Hanging Twigs*. For this reason I recorded the *Hanging Twigs* first, and then the *Hill Songs*.

—Feng Menglong, Preface to *Shan ge*[6]

The main argument was that marginalization of love songs resulted in the falling of their quality. By extension, sanctions against carnal pleasure, which had to be justified by procreation in orthodox teachings, drove it underground and made licentious monsters out of people. Both were unhealthful and, in the context of the *Book of Odes*, un-Confucian. "Nominal rules" (*ming jiao*), literally "teaching of names," usually referred to Confucianism, because Confucius emphasized the "rectification of names" or making names and reality conform. Here *ming jiao* referred more narrowly to the superficial application of Neo-Confucianism, in which nominalism took priority over substance. Originally prescribed to cure social ailments of moral decadence, *ming jiao* instead worsened the ailments because of wrongful application, which resulted in oppression of human emotions and desires. To rescue people from this "fake medicine," Feng prescribed the antidote of genuine *qing*, here referring specifically to forbidden love, mostly under feminine initiation.

Oki Yasushi contends that women's sexual aggression, exemplified by the love songs in *Hill Songs*, was a prominent feature of folk literature and was a legacy of matriarchy in high antiquity.[7] Ernestine Friedl suggests that in order for matriarchy to exist in any society, women have to have the following overt power: "(a) the control of the production and, even more importantly, of the domestic and extradomestic distribution of strategic economic resources; (b) rights to participation in political, ritual, and religious activities and to leadership in them; and (c) the degree of autonomy enjoyed in decisions concerning sex relations, marriage, residence, divorce, and the lives of children."[8] Based on textual and archaeological evidence, some Chinese scholars argue that prior to sedentary agriculture, men in China moved about, hunting and fishing, while women controlled the homestead, collecting and planting. Myths about fatherless dynastic founders in high antiquity suggest that women might have multiple sexual partners, so motherhood was more easily established than fatherhood. Children lived with their mothers and took the mothers' surnames.

The Chinese word for "surname" is of the woman radical—yet another support of the possibility of matriarchy. Clan exogamy was based on the matriline, so cousins on the mother's side could not marry each other, while cousins on the father's side might. Up until the Spring and Autumn period (722-481 BC), women still presided over sacrificial ceremonies and arranged children's marriages. The eldest daughter did not marry; she remained at home to carry out family rites and was called "child of the shaman" (*wu er*).[9]

Western scholars also find evidence of women's religious and political power in ancient China. According to Edward Schafer, Nü Gua, the cultural hero who patched up heaven when a corner of it collapsed, was a dancing shamaness whose main job was to make rain.[10] Michael Loewe finds report of the "child of the shaman" in Shandong as late as the Han dynasty.[11] Although a consensus is yet to be established, scholarly opinions support at least a possibility of matriarchy in China's high antiquity. No matter whether Feng Menglong made a connection between matriarchy and women's sexual aggression, in a time when patriarchy had been firmly established for two millennia, a celebration of women's sexual initiative constituted a challenge to the established norm of the society.

The content of *Hill Songs* was brazen and sensational; however, the rhetoric of the preface was quite conventional. Feng Menglong sought to place the love songs in the mainstream of China's cultural tradition, claiming that being spontaneous expressions of genuine feelings, they were the legitimate descendants of the airs of Zheng and Wei, which Confucius included in the *Book of Odes*. The appeal to the highest authority signals to his readers the strength of his conviction.

Traditionally, there were two theories concerning the origin of the *Book of Odes*. Sima Qian proposed, in his *Shiji* (*Records of the Grand Historian*), that in ancient times there were more than three thousand poems. Confucius eliminated a good portion of them, recorded only three hundred and five poems that were applicable to Confucian ethics, and set them to music, so as to harmonize the songs with ritual propriety and to perfect the kingly way.[12] Ban Gu (32-92 AD) proposed an alternative theory in the *Han shu* (*Dynastic History of the Han*). Following the "Wang zhi" (Kingly institutions) section in the *Book of Rites*, Ban stated that in ancient times, officials were sent to various regions of China to collect popular songs, in order to give the ruler an idea of local customs and morals. Therefore Confucius recorded a cluster of songs from the Zhou period and selected some old songs from the Shang times, along with some current songs from his hometown Lu, totaling three hundred and five songs. Because the songs existed not only in written form but also in oral form, they survived the First Emperor's book burning.[13]

The major difference between the theories of Sima Qian and Ban Gu is that Sima Qian stresses a conscious action of selection and elimination on Confucius' part when he compiled the *Book of Odes*—he scratched out nine-tenths of ancient songs for didactic reasons. Ban Gu's theory, that Confucius compiled the *Book of Odes* as a window on local customs and morals, was preferred by Feng Menglong. Feng did not explicitly challenge Sima Qian's theory that the *Book of Odes* was a selective collection. But his argument that Confucius recorded the love songs of Zheng and Wei because he "saw that as these were expressions of genuine feelings, they should not be eliminated" diverged from Sima Qian's statement that the selection was based on didactic considerations.

In dominant Han Confucian hermeneutics, love songs in the *Book of Odes* were interpreted as political allegories intended to satirize current affairs. Such an interpretation may remind Western readers of the controversies surrounding the Song of Solomon.[14] Since Ouyang Xiu (1007-1072) of the Song dynasty pointed out that some love songs in the *Odes* might simply be love songs, the allegorical interpretation had been seriously challenged. Feng Menglong's preface to the *Hill Songs* was a natural product of the development of *Odes* studies since the Song challenge of the Han allegorical interpretation.

The Song scholar whose interpretation of the *Book of Odes* exerted the strongest influence on Ming *Odes* studies was Zhu Xi. Zhu Xi on several occasions expressed a distrust of the didactic "Major Preface" and "Minor Prefaces" to the *Odes*, especially the latter.[15] He entertained certain skepticism about Confucius' deletion of songs in the *Odes*; he suspected it to be legendary. He found Confucius a loose editor, for some of the songs were nicely done while some others were not.[16] Unlike Sima Qian, who believed the three-hundred-odd songs in the *Odes* to be motivated by the sages' sense of indignation,[17] Zhu Xi believed the *ya* (elegance) and *song* (odes) poems were authored by elites in the imperial court for courtly and ceremonial reasons, and the *feng* (airs) poems were written by common people.[18]

What motivated the poets to sing, Zhu believed, was mostly "expression of the *qing* which was stimulated by objects, and deliverance of the poet's feelings and nature."[19] He disagreed with his spiritual teacher Cheng Yi's attribution of the airs of Zhounan and Shaonan to the education-minded Duke of Zhou. Rather, he was in agreement with Ban Gu's belief that the licentious songs in these airs were love songs between man and woman and that Confucius recorded them as a showcase to demonstrate the excessive evil desires and bad social customs which had resulted from the rulers' failure to educate the people.[20]

Zhu Xi employed the theory of *zheng* (correctness/orthodoxy) and *bian* (change/deviation) in his criticism of the *Book of Odes*. "Correct" poetry provided "models for virtue" and "warnings against vice" and expressed feelings that were restrained and magnanimous. Such poetry taught ethical values through positive examples. "Changed" poetry was the product of a society that deviated from correct norms. Such poetry was full of unrestrained and even demonic sentiments, but through negative examples, it could serve the positive function of redressing wrongs and thereby rectifying society.[21] One can argue that Zhu Xi was replacing one didactic interpretation of the *Book of Odes* with another. He could justify Confucius' recording of the love songs with his *zheng-bian* theory, but he did not appreciate the "unrestrained and demonic" sentiments as they were. He thought the airs of Wei were barely tolerable, since in those songs it was men who flirted with women, but the airs of Zheng were truly intolerable, because in most of the songs it was women who flirted with men![22] Zhu Xi's chauvinistic view notwithstanding, he still contributed to the Chinese understanding of the *Odes* by decisively stripping them of allegorical camouflage and recovering the original appearance of the love songs. He firmly established the non-elite authorship of the love songs and shifted the interpretation of poetry from the didactic *yan zhi* (verbalization of intent) tradition to the expressive *yuan qing* (inspiration by emotions) tradition.

Because Zhu Xi's interpretation of the *Odes* was regarded as orthodoxy in the Yuan and the Ming, it helped develop a theory that the songs in the *Odes* were expressions of genuine feelings sung by women, girls, humble men, and youngsters in the "lane and alley." It was exactly because the minds of these people were unsophisticated and their learning was limited that their feelings could be this genuine and their poetry could be this natural. It then followed that popular and folk songs of every age were worth collecting because of their genuineness. Many writers before Feng, such as the dramatist Li Kaixian (1502-1568), were enthusiastic about adapting and imitating popular songs and putting them into print.[23] Through such activities they not only recorded the "voice of the people," but also added to that voice. Yu Wanlun (1578-1618, *jinshi* 1613), the writer of a preface to Feng Menglong's *Dazaogan* (perhaps an earlier edition of *Guazhier*)[24] claimed to have collected about two hundred popular songs himself. Anonymous collections of little-edited popular songs were also in vogue.

Feng Menglong's preface to the *Hill Songs* can be regarded as a synthesis of the studies of the *Book of Odes* since Zhu Xi and the practices of song collection in the late Ming.[25] By looking at the folk and popular songs as vocalization of genuine feelings he stressed the expressive, author-oriented, function of the songs. By pointing out the social value of the songs as an index of popular sentiments he emphasized the songs' affective, audience-oriented, function.

Feng wished to preserve the songs in a primitive form, but he also felt compelled to polish, edit, and comment on them, as well as to include works by himself and his literati friends. This causes many modern scholars' concern about the authenticity of the songs in the *Hill Songs* and *Hanging Twigs*, wondering if these songs were truly of popular, as opposed to elite, authorship and readership. But this problematic seemed to have concerned Feng Menglong very little, since he did not want to present popular and folk songs as exclusively the commoners' property. It was, in Feng's opinion, due to the elites' mistake of separating the popular from the elite forms of culture and abandoning the former that popular culture became exclusively the commoners' property.

## The Question of Authenticity

Feng Menglong took pains to break the established dichotomy of elite and popular literature, arguing that the dichotomy did not exist in high antiquity, when culture was a complete whole. After the dichotomy was established, however, both elite and popular cultures suffered degradation. In an age when the popular *feng* (airs) and the elite *ya* (elegance) were equally valued, the two cultures were allowed to enrich each other, and the great poetic anthology *Book of Odes* appeared. After officials and scholars canonized certain elite forms of poetry, such as rhapsody and regulated verses, the perfection in the writing of such poetry became a stepping-stone for social and political advancement, to which the elites now paid exclusive attention. The folk, popular forms of poetry, irrelevant to one's social and political success, were ignored and marginalized. Consequently, interactions between elite and popular cultures were halted. The result was twofold. First, the elite literature lost its liveliness and vitality and the popular literature lost its spiritual guidance. The former then became increasingly artificial and the latter increasingly shallow. Second, the ruling elite gradually lost track of the likes and dislikes of the masses. Feng proclaimed an intention to bring the two traditions back in contact, so that they could again nourish and inform each other. In a way, he claimed to be doing what a responsible government should be doing, building bridges rather than tearing the nation apart.

According to Feng, the central value of folk and popular songs was the quality of *zhen* (genuineness, authenticity). In keeping with late Ming "individualism" and "romanticism," this *zhen* referred to the immediacy and sincerity of an individual's unmediated emotional expression; it also denoted an expressive form which was autonomous and which stood in opposition to canonized forms.[26] Folk and popular literature was the best place to look for *zhen*, since considerations of literary skill and social prominence, which could do harm to stylistic and intentional genuineness, were irrelevant in the realm of popular and folk literature. However, Feng did not regard *zhen* as a faculty exclusive to non-scholarly people; literati with a spark of naiveté could also appreciate as well as produce works that were genuine. For example, in the *Hanging Twigs* Feng recorded a series of songs by literati authors in response to an anonymous song entitled "Sending My Lover Off," translated below:

**"The original song"**
Sending my lover off,
All the way to No-Tin Road.
I protest to you, the potter my love,
How come the same kiln produces two different goods?
The brick is so thick,
And the tile so thin.
The thick one is the other person,
And the thin one is me.

**"The courtesan Feng Xisheng's *fan'an*"**
Don't be mad at the potter.
Truly the brick is thick,
And the tile is thin,
But they are both clay, all the same.
I'd say the tile's actually dearer than the brick.
The brick's used to pave the floor down below;
The tile's used to build the roof up above.
His feet stamp upon the other person,
And his head upholds you on top of everything.

**"Feng Menglong's *fan'an*"**
If it is indeed as you said,
How can I not be mad at the potter?

The brick is thick,
And the tile is thin.
If they're both the same clay, then
Making her brick and me tile
Is not without ill intention.
Even though you put me on top of your head, potter,
I've got to shelter you from wind and rain.
And how is the one under your feet at a disadvantage?
There's vacuity between your head and the roof,
But no distance between your feet and the floor!

**"Master Mount White Stone's *fan'an*"**
I plead with you, my fair lady,
Not to be angry with the potter.
Be it that the brick is thick,
And the tile is thin,
Who would not say they are clay, all the same?
Giving her thickness, and you thinness,
Therein lies my good intention.
I wear you on top of my head,
And thanks for shielding me from all the wind and rain.
I stamp steadily upon her,
So as not to allow anybody to throw her at you.
Although you and I appear to have a thin relationship,
Our love will last a long, long time.
However thick my tie with her may look like,
It's no comparison with my love to you.

**"Qiu Tianshu's *fan'an* # 1"**
In my view, lady and potter,
The two of you need not fret.
The brick is thick,
And the tile is thin—
You've both testified to its truthfulness.
Whether the potter's thick or thin with the ladies,
Is none of my business, but
The bricks are each square and fair,
Nicely level and substantial;
The tiles are laid one upon the other,
Overlapping and queer.
Do you mean to say that we should be thick with the queer one,
And be thin with the one that's firm and solid?

**"Qiu Tianshu's *fan'an* # 2"**
Upon hearing this,
I'm even angrier with you, potter!

Bricks and tiles are both clay,
To make one good and the other bad,
I can't forgive you for that!
Why do you make the bricks level and solid,
And make the tiles curve and queer?
Since you've differentiated between the plain and the queer,
You're at liberty to be thick or thin with us.

**"Qiu Tianshu's *fan'an* # 3"**
The potter,
Having listened to her complaints for a long while,
Steps forward and makes a bow.
I can't but laugh at you, my fair lady,
For being so sensitive,
And so suspicious.
Whether the product is thick or thin, sideways or straight,
I didn't intend to make it one way or the other.
But the body of the brick has to be flat and square,
And the body of the tile has to be curve and queer.
If you know one has to be square and the other queer,
You would not resent my making her thick and you thin.
(*Guazhier*, 4: 36a-37a)

Each of these seven songs served as a response to the previous one. The author assumed the voice of the jealous lady, the double-faced potter, or the busy body of a mediator. They employed the metaphor of brick and tile to compare the two women involved in the eternal triangle. The tone was humorous and the imagery was plebian.

Personification of articles such as bricks and tiles was a common device in the *Hanging Twigs* and *Hill Songs*. Nanny Tang (Tang Pozi, hot-water bag) and Madam Zhu (Zhu Furen, bamboo pillow), for example, appeared in the *Hill Songs* (8: 61b-63b) as two women seeking the favor of the same man. In the summer, the man relied on the bamboo pillow (Madam Zhu) to keep cool in the bed; in the winter, he relied on the hot-water bag (Nanny Tang) to keep warm inside of his quilt. This caused the two utensils to become rivals for the man's affection. Such personification had a comic effect.

But occasionally, personification was employed in a tragic story. For example, "Door God" in *Hill Songs* (9: 70a-71a) gave a graphic description of how a faded poster of Door God, a deity to ward off evil and bring in wealth, was scraped away on New Year's Eve to make way for the new poster. As the homeowner sprinkled cold water on the old Door God, poked a broom at him, tore his clothes, and finally ripped up his face, the Door God's once handsome looks and faithful services to the homeowner were all but forgotten. Oki Yasushi suggests that the abusive handling of the Door God was a metaphor for woman battering.[27] If the songs directly depicted family discord or physical abuse, they might be too painful to read. Endowing homely objects with feminine sensibilities brought home to the "woman problem" while keeping it at a safe distance. This literary device also added folk colors to the lyrics.

The series of songs on the potter and his lady friend cited above was called *fan'an* or "overturning a case," because each singer tried to make an argument to counter the argument of the preceding singer. It took wit and humor to create memorable *fan'an* works. Feng made it clear that these *fan'an* songs were written by renowned literati, rather than by anonymous folk singers, but he had no problem incorporating them in the *Hanging Twigs*. After recording the songs, he quoted Dong Sizhang's comment, "The more it overturns, the more ingenious it gets. Therefore we know that literati's minds are like a well of spring that never dries out" (*Guazhier*, 4: 37a-b). These works were imaginative and zestful, and their language was plain and colloquial. They vividly sang of the emotions of two bickering lovers and bystanders who tried, apparently with little success, to mediate. Like the imitative artifacts which some celebrated Ming artists proudly counterfeited to demonstrate their technical ability to recreate the original,[28] the imitative popular songs also carried their literati authors' pride of authenticity. In Feng Menglong's view, it was the "authentic" essence of popular literature, rather than the "folk" origin of the author, that really mattered.

## *Hanging Twigs* and *Hill Songs*

"Hanging twigs (*guazhier*)" was originally a tune of urban songs popular in north China. Its basic structure is 8-8-7-5-5-9, meaning eight syllables in the first line, eight syllables in the second line, seven syllables in the third line, and so on. The mood of the song was usually merry and sensual, and the language was polished. *Guazhier* gradually spread to the south, probably through traveling bureaucrats, merchants, and the entourage of singsong girls associated with them. Eventually this urban tune was introduced to the rural areas and was no longer an exclusive property of city dwellers.[29] At the turn of the sixteenth and seventeenth centuries, *guazhier* fascinated people "south and north, male and female, old and young, high and low," and came into vogue nation-wide.[30]

"Hill songs" (*shan ge*) had been popular in the Suzhou area since the tenth century, and attracted tremendous literati attention in the late Ming.[31] Its basic structure is 7-7-7-7, but there are also variations that can go to great lengths. For example, "The Incense-Burning Lady" recorded in *Hill Songs* (9: 74b-77b) contains more than 1,400 words. The prototype of *shan ge* was erotic songs sung during agricultural work, or during folk festivals where song competitions provided young men and women an opportunity to find a sexual partner. From its mountainous place of origin, the *shan ge* was probably introduced to the city of Suzhou through village women who went to the city to work in the ever-growing textile industry, and through boatmen who constantly traveled between rural and urban areas. Gradually, the folk songs were urbanized and could also be heard in pleasure quarters.[32]

While more conservative writers were alarmed by the popularity of the sensational songs[33] and more avant-garde writers, such as the Gong'an poet Yuan Hongdao, incorporated the songs in their own poetic composition, Feng compiled *Hanging Twigs* and *Hill Songs* to preserve almost eight hundred folk and popular songs. Many post-May Fourth researchers suspect the songs were not real folksongs, but literati imitations (*ni shan ge*). Andrew Plaks, for example, suggests that the songs be "read as literati exercises in the imitation of popular song," and that Feng's claim of authenticity be understood as "just one jaded connoisseur's reconstruction of popular expression, and not any simple gathering of pristine material."[34] Besides the songs Feng noted were by literati authors, other songs could have been collected from printed texts[35] as well as oral sources—from the singing girls, city dwellers, boatmen, and villagers in the Suzhou area,[36] and on the occasion of hill-song festivals.[37] Since Feng was a heavy-handed editor, the material was indeed not "pristine." However, Plaks's description "literati exercises in the imitation of popular song" better fit another of Feng's song collection *Oleander* (*Jiazhutao*) than *Hanging Twigs* and *Hill Songs*.

*Oleander* was a collection of one hundred and twenty imitation folk songs, generally believed to be written by Feng Menglong. The term *Jiazhutao* literally means "a hybrid of peach and bamboo," which refers to the typography of the *Oleander* verse: four four-syllable lines typical of *Book of Odes* songs inserted between four seven-syllable lines typical of Tang regulated verse. It is probable that the four-syllable lines are compared to bamboo leaves for their thinness and the seven-syllable lines are compared to peach blossoms for their richness.[38] This collection is an intricate literati exercise hybridizing elite and popular literature, to borrow Shuhui Yang's terms.[39]

As the preface of *Oleander* points out, "Three lines of [existing] hill song and one line of [existing] *shi* poetry are interspersed with four lines of new *ci* lyric." The last line of each verse has to be the final line of a poem from the *Qianjiashi* (Poetry of A Thousand Writers), and the last word of the verse has to be used in the beginning of the next verse.[40]

The structure of *Hanging Twigs* and *Hill Songs* are much looser than that of *Oleander*. Very likely Feng Menglong compiled *Oleander* separately from *Hanging Twigs* and *Hill Songs* to differentiate self-conscious literati imitation of folk songs from literati edited folk songs by authors with the supposedly natural quality of "child's folly." Feng registered his suspicion that some of the songs in *Hanging Twigs* and *Hill Songs* were poor literati imitations, judging from their unnatural though neat style, while others he included in spite of, even because of, their bad taste, which certified their lowly origins. Some of the songs could be termed "dissolute" (*yin*) and "vulgar" (*bi*), yet, like the literary critic Wang Guowei (1877-1927) three centuries after him, Feng Menglong valued them because they were the intimate expressions of the singers' true feelings. Feng contended that the singers could not help but sing their feelings out, and the listeners could not help but be touched, because they both had true feelings, including erotic feelings.[41]

The eroticism of the hill songs might have an anthropological explanation. Originally sung by agricultural laborers at work in the hilly areas, *shan ge* was a medium to convey amorous feelings, a form of self-entertainment, and a homeopathic charm to pray for good harvests. Feng recorded in the *Survey of Talk Old and New* a folk belief that saying obscene words while planting parsley would have the magic power of enhancing the fertility of the plants. He also warned that failure to say obscene words for fear of violating Confucian ritual propriety would devastate the growth of the plants.[42] His argument could be backed up by the *Book of Odes*.

According to Marcel Granet, an analogy between the roles of the maternal soil and the productive mother existed in the time of the *Book of Odes*, "when houses and villages belonged to the women." Granet reconstructs that world in the following passage:

> They ruled there, bearing the title of mothers. Guardians of the seeds, they kept them in the dark corner where they spread their mats for the night. . . . They conceived, in the house of their birth, at the contact of the seeds which seemed to hold life in themselves. Between the mothers of the family, the garnered seeds and the domestic soil, a commu-

> nity of attributes was established. Near the seeds and the bed a confused multitude of ancestral souls seemed to dwell in the maternal soil, waiting for the time of reincarnation, while at the same time the Earth itself appeared to be a Mother, giving fertility to women, and receiving it from them.[43]

Spring was the season that drummed up the process of conception and fertilization. Festivals were held in the open field, when love songs were sung and young men and women had their romantic nights out. The initiative came from the women, and the words were loaded with sexual implications. The legacy of this primitive and matriarchal culture was carried on in hill songs, which, retained mostly among ethnic minorities in mountainous and hilly areas, were comparatively unaffected by the development of urban, patriarchal culture in the central kingdom. Such marginalized and supposedly less "tainted" culture was what interested Feng Menglong.

*Hanging Twigs* and *Hill Songs* each recorded slightly less than four hundred songs. Feng divided the songs in the *Hanging Twigs* into ten categories: intimacy, merrymaking, lovesickness, parting, grudge, complaint, affection, objects, sarcasm, and miscellany. He divided *Hill Songs*, again, into ten chapters. The first four chapters were quatrains on illicit love. Next came quatrains on miscellaneous themes, quatrains about objects, followed by medium-length songs on illicit love, long songs on illicit love, and long songs on miscellaneous themes. The last chapter was hit songs from Tongcheng, Anhui province, which were introduced to Suzhou by traveling merchants from that famous commercial center in the North.

*Hanging Twigs* and *Hill Songs* glorified a "prelapsarian" state of mind and practices prior to the establishment of legal and ritual norms and the canonization of cultural and literary forms. Ethically, it was a world beyond constraints of morality, and aesthetically, it was a world beyond concerns over style. Feng Menglong modified the songs quite a bit, but the form and content of many songs remained coarse and sensational. The songs by literati authors were more refined, but they also demonstrated a certain degree of defiance of the establishment. Most of the entries were love songs, but quite a few entries were plainly social criticism. Altogether they sang of the dreams, cravings, frustrations, and observations of the people, at times romantic and at times satirical. They also reflected Feng's ethical and aesthetic view on *qing* in his early years.

A translation and analysis of selective songs from the *Hanging Twigs* and *Hill Songs*, which are humorous, witty, or satirical, will illustrate Feng Menglong's vision of the trial and triumph of human emotions and desires. The songs are divided into eight categories for analytical purpose.

### *1. Authenticity of Qing*

**"Sending Off"**
Sending my love off,
I walk him a long way out of the door.
I enjoin him a thousand times,
And urge him ten thousand times:
"Come back early.
You know I don't have a single relative at home.
And on my body is inflicted a sickness;
In my belly I am having a baby.
If I want salty and sour food,
Who on earth will buy it for me?"
(Feng Menglong's Comment) This is most transparent, most rustic, and also most genuine (*zhen*).

(*Guazhier*, 4: 35a)

A woman was having a baby out of wedlock, and the baby's father was leaving. In urging her lover to come back early, she brought up the point that he was the only one who would buy her "salty and sour food," a quencher of morning sickness. The song was a lovely exemplar of *zhen*, genuineness or authenticity. The woman did not need to go to a great distance to find a reason why she needed him at her side: salty and sour food was such an immediate object of desire to her physically. And mentally, the food represented a focal point through which she, the baby, and the man were conjoined. She desired the food because of the baby; the baby was in her body because of the man. The fact that the baby was illegitimate and that she did not have a relative at home intensified her reliance on him.

All songs are not equally genuine. Feng praised the above song as being most genuine (*zhen*) because of its most transparent (*qian*) and rustic (*li*) expression. This comment stood in clear contrast to his comments on some more refined or more intricate works, comments like "this work is not free of literary tone" (*Guazhier*, 7: 66b), "this song cannot be said to be missing the point, but it lacks naturalness" (*Guazhier*, 8: 75b), and "this is extremely neat, but the neater it gets, the farther away it is from being natural—this must be a work by a scholar" (*Guazhier*, 8: 77a). A work that was overly neat and literary must have gone through intensive polish. Therefore it could not be *zhen* or natural any more.

Besides *zhen*, *qi* (surprise, extraordinariness, or marvel) was another important criterion in Feng Menglong's aesthetics. Feng was appreciative of *qi*, but he regarded *zhen* as a more significant criterion than *qi*. This preference can be seen from the following examples:

**"Flirtation"**
My cute nibbles grabs me outside of the window.
His mouth quickly bites at my powdered perfumed cheeks;
His hands hurriedly rip off my fragrant silk girdle.
Big brother,[44] wait for a while!
I am only afraid somebody may pass by.
If after a while nobody comes,
Then you can untie my pants at your will.

**"Flirtation"**
Handsome sweetheart, I love your amorous charms,
Moving my heart, fulfilling my wishes,
That's why I make merry with you.
Who would have known that you are a cutthroat "bandit incarnate"?
Regardless of good time or bad time,
No sooner do you enter the door than you hold me in your arms.
If somebody happens to see us,
Sweetheart, what should I do?

(Feng Menglong's Comment) This is also genuine (*zhen*). The above two songs are without any marvelous (*qi*) imagination. But they are as natural as colloquial language. They are the patterns of nature between heaven and earth. Why do we have to apply rouge to a peony?

(*Guazhier*, 1: 5a-b)

The women complained in a coquettish manner about their lovers' disregard of social censorship under the spur of sexual impulse. While complaining about the men's lack of the sense of shame, the women did not see their sexual desire as guilt. The revelation of the women's inner passion for sexual pleasure exposed the superficiality of the constraints of social decorum. The language of the songs was simple and forthright, yet they described vividly the women's ambivalent feeling toward their illicit sexual lives. As Feng put it, the songs were not marvelously imaginative (*qi*), but were very genuine and natural (*zhen*)—such were "the patterns of nature between heaven and earth," which need no adornment.

The "Sending off" song below was both genuine (*zhen*) and marvelous (*qi*). It had a surprising turn of the story, which added a touch of humor but did not diminish its naturalness:

> **"Sending Off"**
> Sending my love off,
> I walk him all the way to the Red Sun Road.
> My love cries.
> I cry.
> The donkey driver also cries.
> Donkey driver, why are you crying?
> He answers:
> "The one who is leaving is unwilling to leave;
> The one who is crying is concentrating on tears.
> You two are flirting with each other,
> And my donkey is suffering."
> (Feng Menglong's Comment) The donkey driver lives by the donkey, therefore his love for his donkey is the most genuine love. Compare this donkey driver to lovers nowadays: before she will love him, she wants him to love her first; then once she loves him, she is afraid he doesn't know that she loves him. So they each puts on a display of love to satisfy the other, and each forces the appearance of love in order to avoid criticism by other people. No more than twenty or thirty percent of all this is true love. In name, she and he are in love, but in actuality they are not as in love as the driver and his donkey. How fine that line is—"The donkey driver also cries"! The language is funny, but the meaning is biting. Of all the "Sending Off" songs, in my view this one tops the list.
>
> (*Guazhier*, 4: 37b)

Feng seemed a bit too harsh on the lovers in the song. Just because the donkey driver said they were flirting does not necessarily mean that they were simply "forcing the appearance of love." But Feng's commentary can be regarded as a critique of cloying sentimentality. He seemed to be arguing that most people were not absolutely genuine in *qing*. They were more concerned about being loved and loved back than loving unconditionally. In the song, the lovers' prolonged maudlin over a brief separation might be too excessive to be genuine. The crying scene might be a sign that they were feeling insecure, and therefore they needed to show evidence of love to the other party as a test of the other party's love. Or it might be a display of their love to the onlooker. Compared with such artifice, concluded our sarcastic commentator, the most basic love built on practical needs between the donkey driver and the donkey was more genuine.

Whether one's *qing* is genuine or not is judged by both action and motivation. Similar behavior may be motivated by different reasons, and the *qing* involved may or may not be genuine, as shall be seen in the following two songs in the *Guazhier*:

**"Sending a Letter"**
No sooner does the messenger walk out of the door
Than I ask my maid to summon him back.
When you see him, be sure not to tell him that I am upset with him.
Although he is not nice,
I have my own arrangement.
If you unravel his lack of *qing*,
It'll only make his *qing*-absent heart doubly bad.
(Feng Menglong's Comment) "Don't unravel this, so that I can make my own arrangement." This woman is truly an old hand.
(*Guazhier*, 5: 40a)

**"Sending a Letter"**
The messenger walks out of the door a little too soon.
I hurriedly ask my maid to call him back.
I haven't given you my special instruction:
When you see him, don't say that I am losing weight because of him.
Presently he is not feeling well.
If you let him know my condition, it'll add to his worry.
So, if he asks about my health,
Just say I've never had any ailments.
(Feng Menglong's Comment) How can she not be losing weight?
(*Guazhier*, 2: 16a)

Both women asked the messengers not to reveal their conditions to their lovers, but for different reasons. It was out of her wish to keep her lover under control that the first woman refrained from complaining. Therefore Feng commented that she was truly adept at handling man-woman relations. The woman in the second song, on the other hand, genuinely did not want to worry her lover with the information that she was losing weight because of lovesickness. A love so deep was very consuming; therefore Feng jokingly commented that no wonder she was losing weight.

**"Smile"**
Southeast wind begins to blow sidewise,
A fair, fresh flower blooms among leaves.
Young lady, do not smile in such a frolicsome manner.
Not a few instances of illicit love begin with a smile!

**"Glance"**
I am thinking of enticing you into having an affair with me.
No need for matchmaker; no need for bride-price.
The fishing net catches the fish in the meshes;
A thousand *zhang*[45] of silk cloth is woven on the shuttle.
["Meshes" is a pun on "eyes"; "shuttle" is a pun on "sideways glance"]
(*Shan ge*, 1: 1a)

The above two songs are the opening entries of the *Hill Songs*. Feng Menglong commented, "No smiles allowed. No glances allowed. These are the 'Neize' (Rules of the Inner Chamber) of 'Zhounan'" (*Shan ge*, 1: 1b). "Zhounan" is a section in the "Guofeng" (Airs of the States) chapter of the *Book of Odes*. The section is well known for being full of licentious songs. "Neize" is a chapter in the *Book of Rites*. The chapter is about rules of sex-segregation. Feng appeared to be arguing that, although the songs in the *Hill Songs* were amorous, their ultimate goal was to caution men and women against violation of ritual propriety. By demonstrating the danger of excessive *qing* and inappropriate physical contact, the songs taught men and women to restrain their *qing* and abide by the ritual codes. However, it is questionable that Feng was serious about the alleged didactic function of the *Hill Songs*.

## 2. *Callous Men*

**"Patience"**
Iron cannot iron out the frown between my brows.
Scissors cannot scissor off the distress in my heart.
Embroidery needle cannot embroider *yuanyang* buttons.
You and I both have a mind on it,
But in front of people, it's hard to put our hands to it.
If you are my destined love,
Big brother, be patient and wait for the time to be ripe.
(*Guazhier*, 1: 2a)

In his comment Feng Menglong quoted a passage from *Xuetao Ge Waiji* (*Outer collection of the Snow-Wave Tower*) which reminds readers of the womanizing Don Juan, "A wife is not as good as a concubine. A concubine is not as good as a maid. A maid is not as good as a courtesan. A courtesan is not as good as a secret love. A consummated affair with the secret love is not as good as a failed attempt." He then added, "Only someone deep in *qing* can come up with such words."

The list of possible sexual partners in the quotation was in descending order of legitimacy and accessibility. The more legitimate and accessible the partner, the less exciting the conquest. Following this logic, the most desirable women were indeed those who were not only dangerously illegal to pursue but were, after some serious efforts, proven to be hopelessly beyond reach. In Ming China, a wealthy man was allowed legal sexual access to his wife, his concubines, whom he could acquire only if he was over forty and without an heir—but this condition was generally ignored, and his maids, as long as he did not dally with the wanton thought of confounding the hierarchical order of these women's status. A wife had the authority to limit her husband's access to the concubines, who were customarily under her control. A concubine had the authority to limit her master's access to the maids, whose children fathered by the master, unlike her own, were not automatically acknowledged as the family's offspring.

Sex with a maid won less social approval than sex with a concubine, and sex with a concubine won less social approval than sex with the wife. Sex with women outside of the wall of the family compound was a risky business. One's reputation could be ruined if one was not discrete. A man could visit a courtesan's boudoir, if he had the quality to win over her heart—a Ming courtesan was comparable to a geisha in Japan in that she did not need to offer sexual service to a lesser client. But "domesticating" a courtesan was undesirable. No matter how beautiful and talented a courtesan was, her feminine virtue was questionable in the public eye. A few courageous men, such as Chen Zilong and Qian Qianyi, did marry talented courtesans, and their love stories were highly publicized.[46] These, however, were the exceptions, not the rule. As for sex with "decent" women such as somebody's wife, somebody's unmarried daughter, or a widow, it was a criminal act punishable by the law.

In a time when the government displayed unprecedented interest in regulating its subjects' sexual behavior, Feng Menglong's list, which proportionated desirability to illegitimacy, was not only immoral but also illegal. But Feng did not condemn this hedonistic view. Rather, he seemed to regard it as romantic. The love game between man and woman was made all the more interesting by the factors of illegitimacy and risk; continued desirability of a woman was sustained by her prolonged unattainability.

**"Beautiful Wife"**
An extremely beautiful wife in his arms is not worth a dime.
He's seduced an ungainly woman to share his bed.

> Such are things due to the confusing 500-year-old karmic account,
> To discard the gold and embrace the brick.
> (Comment) "If the love of my lord's not based on looks, then how am I supposed to array myself?" How very unfair—this matter of the world!
>
> (*Shan ge*, 5: 41b)

Ordinary reasoning would lead us to assume that when a man abandons his wife for a mistress, the new woman must be better-looking than the old one. But this is not always the case, as is exemplified by the song. The singer laments that a man could actually be so silly as to "discard the gold (his beautiful wife) and embrace the brick (his ungainly mistress)." It is interesting to note that the mistress is compared to a brick, a metaphor which also appears in the series of *fan'an* songs discussed earlier. In those songs, the brick is compared favorably with the tile from the jealous lady's perspective, although other people might disagree. In this song the brick is obviously inferior to the gold, except in the eyes of the unfaithful husband. Such incredible phenomenon, according to the singer, could only be explained by the confounded fate, which has its roots in "the confusing five-hundred-year-old karmic account," a mess perhaps even the gods could not straighten out. The main point of the song is evidently not the cliché that beauty is only skin-deep. More likely, the song points to a mystery in extramarital affairs: even if the wife seems superb in other people's eyes, the husband somehow finds an emptiness in his heart which can only be filled by another woman, however inferior she might look to an objective judge.

Feng Menglong quotes in his commentary a Tang poem entitled "A Sigh in the Spring Palace," attributed to Du Xunhe (*jinshi* 891).[47] In the poem, a comely palace maid complains that beauty causes her grief, as she comes to the realization that beauty is not what really wins over the emperor's heart. To prove her point, she alludes to the famous *femme fatale* Xi Shi.

Xi Shi lived in the last century of the Spring and Autumn period, when rival states of China maneuvered diplomacy alongside warfare. The legend had it that Xi Shi's husband Fan Li, a subject of Gou Jian, the King of Yue, presented her as a gift to the enemy Fu Chai, the King of Wu. She successfully bewitched Fu Chai, causing him to neglect the affairs of the state, and to finally lose his kingdom and his life to Gou Jian. Mission accomplished, Xi Shi reunited with Fan Li. Together they retired from politics and engaged in commerce, accumulating enormous wealth.

In the light of Confucian matrimonial ethics, it would seem astonishing for Fan Li to volunteer his wife's sexual service, and to reclaim her "used" body after the "loan period" was up. But stratagem was of supreme importance in this age, Confucianism was yet to cast influence on Chinese culture, and the southern states of Wu and Yue were in the margin of Chinese civilization. In this historical context, wifely chastity was of little significance. However, Feng Menglong was apparently deeply troubled by the tension between loyalty and chastity in the Xi Shi legend. In his historical romance *New History of the States*, Feng took great pains to dismiss any hint of a romantic relationship between Xi Shi and Fan Li. Xi Shi was just one of the two beautiful commoner girls Fan Li recruited to bewitch Fu Chai. Because Xi Shi so captured Fu Chai's heart, the other girl, Zheng Dan, died of jealousy. After Fu Chai's death, Gou Jian took Xi Shi back to the state of Yue. Gou Jian's wife, perhaps fearing the effect of Xi Shi's charm on her husband, secretly dropped Xi Shi in the river. Meanwhile, sensing that Gou Jian was not a ruler who was willing to share the glory of his victory with his meritorious subjects, Fan Li stealthily took a boat and disappeared into the waters of the Yangzi delta. Because both Xi Shi and Fan Li disappeared into the waters, Feng explained, people erroneously put these two together and rumored that Fan Li and Xi Shi eloped after the Yue victory over Wu.[48]

The length to which Feng went to dismiss the marital relationship between Xi Shi and Fan Li reflected Feng's insistence on wifely chastity. The majority of Chinese intellectuals, however, did not seem to share Feng's obsession with the vexing issue of Xi Shi's split loyalty toward two husbands. The Chinese fascination was mostly directed toward Xi Shi's great success as a *femme fatale*. Some believed her remarkable beauty was what captured Fu Chai's heart. Others believed her looks were actually not out of the ordinary; what really fascinated Fu Chai was something deeper down—some mysterious feminine charm which other women could not even begin to imagine, let alone imitate. This mysterious charm might not work on every man, but when it worked, it worked fabulously.

The poem "A Sigh in the Spring Palace" represented the latter view, that Xi Shi was more charming than beautiful. Facing the competition with a woman with the magical charm, even a great beauty might suffer woeful disappointment in her effort to win or to maintain a man's love, however incredible this might seem in other people's eyes. By citing this poem in his comment, Feng expressed his sympathy with the uncertainty of women's fate and also demonstrated his understanding of men's complicated desires in women.

## *3. Infatuated Women*

**"Affair"**
We are having an affair, and don't you panic.
Should we be caught in the act, I alone will bear the responsibility.
Before the judge I'll fall on my knees and my breasts, and tell the truth.
Setting my teeth firmly, I'll insist that I seduced a lover.
(Feng Menglong's Comment) This woman is full of chivalrous spirit.
(*Shan ge*, 2: 15b)[49]

Women in the *Hanging Twigs* and *Hill Songs* were more determined than men in their pursuit of love. When it comes to romance, the hero pales before the heroine, because the heroine, being confined to the domestic sphere, is not corruptible by considerations of external factors such as fame, wealth, and power. The infatuated women focused their thoughts so intensively on love that they were easily cheated by the wind and mistook the shadows of flowers and trees on a windy night to be their lovers knocking on the door (*Guazhier*, 1: 8a-b). When their lovers did come knocking on the door, they employed all sorts of clever devices to cheat their mothers, who kept a close eye on their amorous daughters but to no avail. Here are some examples from the *Hill Songs*:

With her parents nearby and her unknowing lover approaching, a witty woman borrowed the words of a children's song to give her lover a hint about her parents' presence. Sensing the timid lover was about to be frightened into retreating, she quickly sang another children's song to instruct him to hide among the bushes and wait for the right moment (1: 6b-7a). She did not want to get caught, but she still wanted to have a good time.

Another woman, for fear of arousing her parents' suspicion, advised her lover not to sneak into her bedroom through the back door. Rather, she asked him to pluck a feather off a chicken in her family farm, so that she could take the chicken's cry for help as an excuse to "put on a single-layered skirt" and rush out to drive the wild predator away (1: 7a).[50] The woman was very smart indeed. She killed two birds with one stone, demonstrating her filial devotion to the family's well-being and satisfying her sexual pleasure; both were done "in the open," so to speak. One wonders if the woman chooses this strategy because she fully understands that the most dangerous way may be the safest way, or if she, like the author of *Outer Collection of the Snow-Wave Tower*, is also thrilled by the risk of the act.

In a third song, a smart mother had strewn lime powder all over her daughter's bedroom floor to detect any presence of a man. But the even smarter daughter carried her lover on her back, so as not to leave her lover's footprints on the floor (1: 8a).[51] Readers of mystery and detective novels are well aware of the importance of footprints in the investigation of a crime. If the mother in the song were more sensitive than an amateurish detective, she might have discovered the unnatural distance between her daughter's footprints due to the weight of her burden. But that seems beyond the mother's intelligence, so we need not worry for the daughter. In the romantic universe of *Hanging Twigs* and *Hill Songs*, the wisdom of the older generation was no match for that of the younger generation.

The woman in the following song was lovingly protective of her clumsy lover:

**"Walking My Lover Out"**
I walk my lover out, shoulder by shoulder.
Brightly shines the light from Mother's bedroom.
I open my robe to shield my lover,
Passing through Mother's room, two as one.
I walk him to the kitchen,
He accidentally kicks the fire-tongs.
Mother asks, "Little wretch, what's the noise?"
I answer, "The lamp holder drops to the floor,
And the dog stealthily licks the oil."
I walk him to the edge of the eaves,
He accidentally kicks a stone brick.
Mother asks, "Little wretch, what's the noise?"
I answer, "A snake coils around a clam,
And drops into the ditch."
I walk my lover to the middle of the yard,
The dog at the front gate bites and barks twice or thrice.
I stretch my jade-like hands to pick up the golden-haired dog,
Don't bite my sweetheart, nor alarm my Mom.

(*Shan ge*, 3: 25b)

What an eventful short trip between the young lady's bedroom and the front door of her family compound! Each accident caused by the clumsy young man created a tense moment. Both the dangerous condition and the clever solution contributed to the comic effect of the song. Notably, the sole hero was the witty and amorous young lady. She took the center stage, foiled by the two clowns. Neither the old woman nor the young man could rival the young woman in this romance where the final triumph belonged to the youthful and the feminine.

When women set their hearts on love, they did not mind taking the initiative, despite the feminine virtue of modesty conventionally expected of their gender. Female sexual aggression is exemplified by the heroines in the next two songs.

**"Affair"**
The southeastern wind blows, touching off his worries.
The man says, "It's hard to seduce the charming lass of 16, 17,
Just as it's hard to lay my hands on something under boiling water,
Or to put a loose thread through a hole without a needle."
Hearing him, the woman says, "Don't worry.
My tender age is perfect timing for a love affair.
You can ladle out the boiling water to get to your object.
Twist the thread, thread a needle, and you can put it through."
(*Shan ge*, 2: 15a)[52]

**"Affair"**
The woman combs her hair till it shines like a lacquer bowl,
In the presence of others she stretches her foot to seduce a man.
In the past it was the man who seduced the woman,
But in the brave new world it is the woman who seduces the man.
(*Shan ge*, 2: 15a)[53]

In the first song, the adventurous lass encouraged the hesitant man to have an affair with her while she was young. "Don't be intimidated by the difficulties," she seemed to be suggesting, "They are not as hard to overcome as you thought, especially with my active collaboration." Our heroine clearly demonstrated stronger determination than our hero in their search for romance.

In the second song, the woman physically made the first move. This aggressiveness was allegedly justified by the changed times. The time when men had to take the initiative in a love affair was past. In the new social atmosphere of late Ming China, women could also take the initiative. The statement should not be taken at face value, however. As discussed earlier, women's sexual aggression might be a legacy of matriarchy in high antiquity, but it had long been suppressed by a patriarchal social system and Confucian decorum. The popularity of romantic literature in the late Ming stimulated discourse on a more open gender relation, but there was no evidence of a sexual revolution that "liberated" women. In the light of *Child's Folly*'s connection with the culture of the pleasure quarters, perhaps the song was both defiant and seductive.

The above songs are about illicit love affairs. A possible by-product of an illicit love affair is an unplanned pregnancy. This unpleasant situation was realistic enough to inspire several songs. A pregnant unwed teenager was worried about being punished by her mother (*Guazhier*, 1: 10b). A number of pregnant women expressed strong anxiety over their physical changes, which were bound to betray their secrets (*Shan ge*, 1: 11b-12a). The woman in the following song affectionately examined her illegitimate baby boy:

**"Pregnancy"**
The lady's tummy hurts; she sips the ginger soup.
In the middle of the night she delivers an illegitimate child.
With her slim jade fingers she holds the baby to the lamp.
He half resembles me, half my lover.

(*Shan ge*, 1: 12a)

In the last resort, an unwed mother committed infanticide:

**"Pregnancy"**
The lady instructs the little brother amour,
I can't keep you, for I don't have a husband.
When you learn of the wedding date of my lover and me, if ever,
Please come back to my tummy—it's our bonds.

(*Shan ge*, 1: 12b)

Abortion and infanticide were considered immoral deeds and were harshly censured by religious institutions, but the practices were widespread among impoverished and illicit couples. Women were made to bear most of the blame. Midwives were entrusted with the tasks so routinely that they suffered a bad name in the medical circles. Because the souls of the prematurely terminated fetuses and babies were believed to suffer confinement in a Buddhist Purgatory for Those Who Died Through Injustice (*wangsi cheng*), they allegedly resented their mothers and would cause them all sorts of grief. But unlike late-twentieth-century Japan, Ming China did not provide commercialized religious rituals to appease the menacing fetus.[54] So the sorry mother had to find her own way to cope with her guilt and her fear. In the above song, the woman decided to get rid of her illegitimate child. To comfort herself as well as appease the resentful spirit, she made an agreement with her unwanted child: if she would eventually become her lover's legitimate wife, she wanted the baby to come back and be their legitimate child. But this agreement might be as uncertain as her future with the man.

The women in the *Hanging Twigs* and the second half of *Hill Songs* at times displayed sophisticated sentiments such as bashfulness, coquetry, melancholy, and sentimentality, which probably reflected their urban backgrounds. Women in the first half of *Hill Songs*, on the other hand, were earthy, passionate, bold, dominant, and fearless, a possible reflection of the ethnological background of hill songs' rural origin.

### *4. Lover's Cross*

**"Sneeze"**
Sitting in front of the dresser,
I suddenly sneeze.
Which means, my lover must be thinking of me.
I should send him a letter.
But then I wonder,
Has he thought of me just this once?
Since I parted with you,
Everyday my tears drop like strings of pearls.
At this rate of my longing of you,
I reckon you must have sneezed like rain!

(*Guazhier*, 3: 23b-24a)

It was a common superstition in China that if somebody thought of you intently you would sneeze. A similar superstition also existed in Japan. In the pleasure quarters of Yoshiwara, the superstition among courtesans and prostitutes was: "sneezing once someone is saying good things about you, sneezing twice someone is saying bad things about you, sneezing three times someone is in love with you, and sneezing four times you have a cold."[55] In the above song only the romantic meaning was invoked. When the woman sneezed, she immediately interpreted it to mean that her lover was longing for her from afar. The depiction of the thoughts of this lonely and sentimental woman was full of interesting twists and turns. At first she took delight in her lover's thought of her. Then she got a bit upset—the sole occurrence of sneeze since their parting indicated he had not been thinking of her before, whereas she had not stopped thinking of him. But then her thought turned comical. Her ceaseless longing for him translated into incessant sneezes of this faithless lover—it served him well!

Feng Menglong identified the author of "Sneeze" as his associate Dong Sizhang, and praised him for his original imagination and amorous characteristic. It did not bother Feng that the author was an elite man rather than an illiterate woman, although the latter would have seemed a more ideal creator of such a song.

**"Dreaming"**
The dream that I just had was so funny;
I dreamed that you were flirting with another woman.
I woke up to find you still in my arms,
But I can't sweep the dream away from my mind.
Let me hold you tight while I fall back to sleep.
Yet I'm afraid though you're by my side while I'm awake,
You might be gone again while I'm dreaming.
(Comment) What harm does it do if he's gone in your dream? The thing to fear is that he's gone when you wake up.

(*Guazhier*, 2: 13b)

The commentator was more practical-minded than the singer. It was silly to dread an imaginary rival; what should be feared was a real one, one that the commentator maliciously suggested might actually exist. While the commentator realistically expressed a man's view, the singer did not realistically express a woman's view. Any woman in love may once in a while dream about her lover's sneaky affair with a mystery woman—a subconscious projection of her sense of insecurity. She may find her dream unfounded and laugh at herself at a later point. But the immediate response right after she wakes up is most likely lingering anger with the man who dares to betray her, be it dream or reality. The singer, however, displayed no trace of resentment toward the innocent offender. She only revealed her passionate desire to possess him in both dream and reality. The song was apparently meant to entertain a male audience, who wanted to be loved but had little patience with women's somehow irrational sensitivity.

**"A Slip of Tongue"**
My cute lover, in his sleep,
Lets slip incriminating utterance about a secret love.
Every single word, every single sentence,
I hear it right, with no mistake.
In the middle of the night, I wake you up,
Cursing you for your hunger of sex.
Your body's next to mine, but
Your heart's longing for her.
From now on,

Even if you display a hundred kinds of tenderness,
All hundred kinds are fake.

(*Guazhier*, 5: 52b-53a)

Here the man was found out to be double dealing. What he managed to hide while awake, he exposed in his dream. But he would not be truly punished. The woman claimed she would never trust him again, but she did not threaten to leave him. Rather, her coquettish complaint appeared little more than a device to entice his apology, accompanied by his "hundred kinds of tenderness."

Jealous uproars resulting from erotic dreams are a recurrent theme in love songs and sexual jokes. In Zhao Nanxing's (1550-1628) *Xiaozan* (*In Praise of Laughter*), a man named Zhao Shijie allegedly woke up in the middle of the night and told his wife, "I just had a dream, in which I had sex with another man's wife. I wonder if you women also dream of such stuff?" His wife replied carelessly, "What difference does it make if you are a man or a woman?" Enraged, Zhao gave his wife a good beating. So there was a saying, "Zhao Shijie rises in the middle of the night to beat the difference [out of his wife]."[56] It was all right for men to have erotic dreams, but not all right for women, who were supposed to be "different." The wife was punished for failing to know and observe the difference.

**"Trashing the Pillow"**
At the third watch I suddenly tear my pillow to threads.
Since I slept on you, I have been husbanded for merely half a month.
Was it because the hour was inauspicious when I made you?
I'll pick a good day anew
To make another pillow that will make a market.
If this man will come,
I'll reward you with my slender waist.

**"Beating the Maid"**
Lovesickness, how it hurts!
Oh, I've become so skinny.
At midnight I get up and beat my maid.
Maid, why's it that I'm skinny and you're also skinny?
I am skinny because I miss my love.
You are skinny for what reason on earth?
Is it that the one I love,
With him you also have a relation?
(Comment) "Trashing the Pillow" and "Beating the Maid" depict the women's states of mind when they are extremely lonely and bored. The songs are marvelous (*qi*) as well as genuine (*zhen*).

**"Beating the Maid"**
Love sickness, how it hurts!
Oh, I've become so skinny.
At midnight I get up and beat my maid.
Maid, why's it that I'm skinny and you're plump?
The maid answers the mistress,
How very thoughtless you are!
You have a lover to long for,
And whom should I be longing for?
(Comment) She beats the maid if she's skinny, and she beats the maid if she's plump. The mistress is truly a difficult person. Even the mister must be scared of her!

(*Guazhier*, 3: 31a-32a)

"Trashing the Pillow" and "Beating the Maid" describe the petulant moods of women who miss the company of their lovers. While the women are in a cross mood, whatever crosses their path might be fired at. In the first song, the woman vents her anguish on her pillow, and in the second and third, the maids are victimized by the mistress's lovesickness. At the end of "Trashing the Pillow," the heroine has a renewed hope—perhaps making a new pillow would change her fortune for the better. Her wish that the new pillow—a prop in the intercourse—might "make a market" suggests that she might be a prostitute. At the end of the first "Beating the Maid," the heroine is still angry—she reveals her suspicion that her skinny maid might also have a relation with her lover. The anger is carried over to the second "Beating the Maid" song, where it is the plump maid who is beaten, perhaps because she is in a better shape than her mistress. The last two songs show a woman with a dreadful propensity for violence—she does not need a good reason to beat her maids.

"Trashing the Pillow" and "Beating the Maid" are "marvelous" as well as "genuine" in Feng's opinion. The stories involve twists and turns to the audience's surprise—that is why the songs are "marvelous." The language is plain, the expression is straightforward, and the emotional development is natural—that is why the songs are "genuine." Readers are captured by the dramatic beginnings and compelled to follow the women's flow of thought very closely to find out what is going on.

## *5. The Woes of Marriage*

**"Prosecution of Adultery"**
The words of ancients do not always earn respect.
How difficult! A fair lady is allowed to marry only one man.
If we could get Empress Wu Zetian to amend the *Great Ming Code*,
Who in the world would dare to prosecute adultery?
(*Shan ge*, 1: 11a)

Feng Menglong commented, "This is a new piece by my friend Su Zizhong.[57] Zizhong is an honest and sincere scholar, yet he has such an extraordinary thought! A literary man's mind can go in any direction, can't it?" The fact that the author of the song was an "honest and sincere" scholar sharpened the song's sarcastic nature: even an "honest and sincere" scholar would comment on an unorthodox matter such as adultery in a joking manner. Wu Zetian, China's only woman-emperor, was censured by Chinese historians for her licentious conduct both before and after the ascension. Before, she was the imperial consort of two emperors who were father and son; after, she had a couple of famous male consorts who were elder and younger brothers. She was also believed to have quite a few other lovers. Chastity was apparently not a concern to Wu Zetian. What made traditional Chinese historians even more uncomfortable was that she seemed to become more licentious as she grew older.

In the *History of Love* (*Qingshi*), Feng Menglong listed Wu Zetian in the category of "Degenerates," which contained largely pre-Ming scandalous anecdotes from within the ruling class. After an entry in the "Monsters" chapter about an old woman who was remarried at the age of seventy-two and was able to give birth to two children afterwards, Feng commented that the old and licentious Wu Zetian could also be regarded as a "monster," like the old woman in the tale. But Wu Zetian was worse than a "monster"; she was a "degenerate." As an emperor, who was required to be a paragon of virtues, her filthy behavior could cast a more profound evil influence on the people than any ordinary "monster."[58]

A comparison of Feng's attitude in the *History of Love* with his attitude in the *Hill Songs* indicates that his attitude in the *Hill Songs* was more ambiguous. In the *Hill Songs* he and his friend Su Zizhong were making fun of both Wu Zetian and the law against adultery: if the current emperor were an adulterer himself, he would have understood why people committed adultery and would sympathize with them. Feng could be making fun of the adulteress for making an ingenious argument to rationalize her irregular behavior. But the tone was ambiguous enough so that his sympathy could also be with the non-conformist who refused to take rules for granted.

Ambiguity can also be detected in the next song:

**"Blessing"**
In the second month vegetable flowers are yellow everywhere.
The old man and the old woman go to burn incense.
The silly turtle murmurs and murmurs in his mouth,
He only prays that the gods will bless his wife.
How would he have known that silently,
His wife is praying for the blessing of her own lover?
(Comment) This is truly a silly turtle!

(*Shan ge*, 2: 15b-16a)

This is indeed a comical picture, and the fact that the adulteress was an old woman makes it even funnier—who would have thought that a woman of that age could still be so amorous? On the other hand, if the guilty party were the man, no matter whether he was young or old, it is not funny. Cuckoldry is comical because it involves a reversal of gender hierarchy. Feng did not comment on the woman's adultery directly. He simply lamented the stupidity of the "turtle," the cuckold. It is hard to tell whether he had sympathy with the cuckold in addition to mockery. It is even harder to tell how he felt about the adulteress. But the song seemed to be making fun of both the husband and the wife. The adulteress evidently triumphed over her husband, taking advantage of his love, his trust, and his stupidity, but she could not get away with it in front of the gods.

Other adulteresses in the *Hanging Twigs* and *Hill Songs* could not keep their composure as calmly as this old woman. They were frightened to death that their husbands would find out what was going on, and they were on constant alert for gossips. This did not prevent them from continuing the affair. They were just nervous. Feng himself wrote two songs about adulteresses' abnormal public behavior. In one song the woman was afraid that her neighbors would talk, therefore she flattered them and bribed them; she even enjoined her maid to be extra careful not to offend them. In the other song the woman did the opposite: she tried to frighten her neighbors into silence by swearing (*Shan ge*, 1: 10b-11a). Feng did not take a moralistic tone and condemn adultery as an immoral and shameful crime. His approach was covert and humorous, pondering how adultery, besides matrimony, affected one's social relations.

**"Crying Over Seven Husbands" (to the tune *Qingjiang yin*)**
Cobbler Zhang, Blacksmith Zhao, Carpet-knitter Wang, Tinsmith Kong,
Archer Lu, Mister Coffin-maker, and Ferryman Sun,
Come on, you all, to eat the soup and rice.
My heaven, heaven, heaven, heaven, heaven, heaven, and heaven.
(*Shan ge*, 5: 40b)

A woman was offering sacrifices—soup and rice—to her seven deceased husbands. She first called out to them individually by their occupational appellations, and then designated each of them a collective name, "heaven."

In the Cheng-Zhu orthodox teaching, a husband was heaven to his wife; since heaven could not be replaced, a woman should not be remarried. Cheng Yi seemed to have a somehow more balanced view when he cautioned against widower-remarriage as well as widow-remarriage, on the ground that marriage was a life-long bond, which should not be broken on the death of either the wife or the husband.[59] But Zhu Xi seemed to care less about fairness. Zhu regarded it appropriate for the husband to have concubines even when the wife was still alive, while the wife was to have only one husband, alive or dead, because the husband was the heaven to the wife, and there could only be one heaven.[60]

The woman in the above song had seven husbands and therefore seven "heavens." The song made fun of the woman who survived so many husbands: she must have been extraordinarily tough. But the song also made fun of the Cheng-Zhu analogy between heaven and husband: it could not be taken seriously. Feng Menglong's brief comment that "the words were amusing" does not automatically tell us where he stood in this matter. But it seems clear that he was by no means a guardian of the Cheng-Zhu orthodoxy.

**"In Dread of Wife"**
He was born a henpecked husband,
How laughable, for god's sake!
She's neither the father, nor the mother,
And she's not a robber, either.
But seeing her, he trembles with fear,
Listening to her lecture, with a humble heart.
An alcoholic, he's forced to tell people he cannot drink;
A sensualist, he's forced to tell people he suffers impotence.
If he dares to step out of the line a bit,
Several nights of uproar await him.

(*Guazhier*, 9: 98a)

**"In Dread of Wife"**
I'm not afraid of Heaven,
I'm not afraid of Earth,
I'm not even afraid of Mom and Dad.
I'm only afraid of that ferocious wife of mine.
My wife is truly hard to converse with.
She's the jealous Zeus,[61] flesh and blood;
She's the mischievous Raksasi,[62] in real life.
If one half sentence gets on her nerves,
Numerous slaps swish across my face.

(*Guazhier*, 9: 98a)

Henpecked husbands and shrewish wives are popular stereotypes. Their comic effects come from the sharp reversal of gender hierarchy in a patriarchal society such as imperial China. As shall be seen later, the popularity of the comic shrew reached a peak in the seventeenth century, probably a symptom of male anxiety in the face of rising female prominence in non-domestic spheres such as religion and literature, and increasing male incompetence amidst the hellish examination competitions and bloody political struggles.

In the above two songs, the men were completely overpowered by the supposedly "weaker sex." In the first song, the fact that the wife was not supposed to be frightening, as she was no father, mother, or robber, was established up front. But contrary to the established understanding, the husband trembled under her sway. Although he liked wine and women, he had to make self-negating excuses to turn down his friends' invitations to wine shops and whorehouses. The wife was apparently a smart woman. Only by forcing her husband to make those dramatic claims would future invitations be permanently blocked. Here we see two opposing forces in the husband's nature—henpecking and masculine desires—at war, and the result was a complete loss of masculinity.

Ritual texts advised the Chinese to be in awe of Heaven, Earth, Emperor, Parents, and Teachers. The man in the second song was not in awe of these legitimate authorities. The omission of the emperor and the teacher could be explained by the general populace's little contact, and therefore little concern, with these two. However, he was in awe of his wife (*fang xia*). The term *fang xia* literally means "*under* the house"; ironically, his wife seemed to be *above* everything. She was so ferocious that just carrying out a conversation with her could put the husband in danger. She was compared to the baleful star

Great Year (Zeus) and the anthropophagous demon Raksasi, neither of which humans could afford to cross. Furthermore, she was jealous and mischievous, which added difficulty to daily dealings with her. All of this somehow justified this unruly man's—note his defiance of Heaven, Earth, Mom, and Dad—incongruous dread of his domestic inferior.

> **"Lament Over Solitude"**
> In the sky there are lots of stars but not lots of moons;
> In the world there are also lots of mismatches.
> Look! The lass of two times eight sleeps with her feet drawn,
> And the lad of two times ten does not have a wife.
>
> (*Shan ge*, 3: 23a)

The number of stars does not match with the number of moons. Likewise, some people are bound not to find spouses. In the song, the woman of sixteen and the man of twenty were both single and lonely; how nice if they could just find each other! But given the historical shortage of marriageable women in China due to female infanticide and concubinage, the man could be expected to remain single much longer than the woman.[63]

> **"The Monk"**
> In the sky there are lots of stars but not lots of moons.
> The monk is singing hill songs in front of the door.
> The priest asks, "Master, what would make you happy?"
> The monk answers, "To grow my hair and take a wife."
>
> (*Shan ge*, 5: 36a)

Buddhist monks had to take the tonsure and a vow of celibacy. Taoist priests took neither. When the Taoist priest asked the Buddhist monk what would make him happy, the monk answered he would be happy if he could have some hair and a wife, just like the priest.

In the universe of *Child's Folly*, celibacy—a suppression of sexual instinct—was a marked target of ridicule. Celibacy was believed to drive the practitioner in the opposite direction. In *Hanging Twigs*, a young Buddhist nun found celibacy hellish and fantasized leaving her hair to grow and marrying a cute young man. A young Buddhist monk fantasized mating with the female bodhisattva, and "the two bald heads of ours would grow old together" (*Guazhier*, 10: 101b). The wish of the young monk was doubly incongruous: it was profane to fantasize having sex with a bodhisattva, and a bodhisattva was by no means "bald"—she was always portrayed to have a full head of hair.

As shall be seen later, the *Treasury of Laughs* satirized the Buddhist clergy's rule of celibacy even more hilariously: the monks and nuns were portrayed almost as sex maniacs!

But matrimony might not be the best alternative to celibacy in the mind of the compiler of *Hill Songs*. After recording "The Monk," Feng threw in a cynical comment on the monk's innocent wish to "grow hair and take a wife." He said, "Taking a wife may turn out not to be so happy a thing after all. The monk is still a layman with this regard" (*Shan ge*, 5: 36a). Whether this is the voice of experience is hard to tell. Almost nothing about Feng Menglong's married life is recorded in his own works or in the works of his friends. He had a son named Feng Yu, who shared his interest in art songs.[64] It is unclear if Feng Yu was Feng Menglong's biological son or adopted son, and if Feng Yu's mother was Feng Menglong's wife, concubine, or somebody else. The absence of any reference to Feng Menglong's wife, or concubine, for that matter, as well as the rich references to Hou Huiqing and several other courtesans, seem to be sure indications that Feng was not a happily married man. Of course, this does not necessarily mean that he was a victim of an unhappy marriage.

### 6. *Homosexuality*

**"The Moon Has Risen"**
Waiting for my lover in a rendezvous till the moon's high in the sky,
And a homeless wanderer is taking shelter at my front gate.
If you would like to take my bedroom it's fine with me,
I'd rather be the one sleeping in front of the gate.

(*Shan ge*, 1: 5b)

The woman's lover was apparently late for the date, but she did not resent that. What she resented was that while she was waiting for him in front of her house, a homeless man was also there, and was evidently not leaving. This man would certainly get in the way when her lover showed up. So she was willing to give up her bedroom to the man in order to clear the scene.

This heterosexual love song reminded Feng Menglong of a funny story about a homosexual man, which he proceeded to record:

A poor student took his servant to attend an exam. On the road he saw a house with the door slightly open ajar. Darkness had fallen. He and the servant entered the house and asked to stay for the night. The hostess—who certainly did not expect to see *him*—refused, on account of her single status. But the student and his servant would not leave. Unable to drive the unwelcome guests away, she locked herself up in her bedroom and cursed, until she was exhausted and fell asleep. The student was getting bored, and cold, and hungry, when he heard knocks on the door, which got ever more urgent as the student hesitated. Finally, the student opened the door only slightly to see what was going on. A man handed him a bowl of stewed pork feet from the opening of the door and said, "I'll go get a pitcher of wine. Wait for me." Shortly the wine came—it was nicely heated. The student grabbed the wine and quickly shut the door, but the man outside was quicker—he already put a foot in the door. The student exerted himself and held the door. The man outside murmured some amorous words, and then suddenly grabbed the student's hand to touch his erect penis. The student was turned on; he also grabbed the man's hand to touch his own erect penis. The man was panicked and ran away. He certainly did not expect the person inside to be anybody other than his sweetheart, and he was probably not interested in homosexual sex. The student heartily consumed the food and wine with his servant, had a good night's sleep, and left the woman's house at the crack of dawn without saying goodbye. He even took the bowl and pitcher left by the man to a restaurant to exchange for a nice breakfast.

Though he did not plan it, by taking advantage of an unknown couple's illicit affair, the student got a free room, a free dinner, a free breakfast, a homosexual arousal, and a good laugh. It was indeed a very good deal. Feng Menglong described the student's character as *guji*, "grotesque" or "humorous," and the event as *qi*, "strange," "extraordinary," or "marvelous." The narrator was not in a hurry to pass moral judgment. What interested him the most was the surprising twists and turns of the story, summed up in the word *qi*. Most readers would agree that the climax of this *qi* tale was reached when the student put the stranger's hand on top of his erect penis.

The word *qi* is a magic word in a branch of late Ming aesthetics which preferred the strange to the ordinary, the marginal to the mainstream, and the small to the large. The appreciation of *qi* could be applied to rock collecting, calligraphy, painting, poetry, essays, and fiction.[65] Feng Menglong commented on the song "Herd Boy and Weaving Maid," "If there is one word in a literary work which is competitive in the category of *qi*, the work is worthy of immortality." The beauty of *qi* lay in spontaneity, or the feeling of effortlessness and casualness. "Like the song of a child, the tune just happens to be in accord. If the word is inserted purposefully, it is an evil way to do composition" (*Guazhier*, 7: 69a). Ingeniously picked and positioned, as if it should have been there naturally, one single marvelous word could open up a whole world of fantastic strangeness, like the "eye" in Zen poetry.

Strangeness did not necessarily reside in the sphere of the supernatural, such as ghost stories and tales of miracles. It could also be found in the vicissitude of lives of ordinary people. The life of the poor student in the above story might not be characterized as ordinary, but his playfulness, his homosexuality, and his chance encounter with the couple were all humanly plausible. Ling Mengchu (1580-1644) contended in the preface to his fiction *Pai an jing qi* (*Slapping the Table in Amazement*), "People only know that what exists beyond [the perceptions of] our ears and eyes, such as ox-demons and snake-spirits, are strange. They do not know that within [the perceptions of] our ears and eyes, in our daily life, there are also numerous wonders and curiosities that lie beyond ordinary logic and reason."[66] The student's homosexual arousal under the unusual circumstances is qualified to be a specimen of life's "numerous wonders and curiosities that lie beyond ordinary logic and reason." He seems always to be able to make the best of the situation.

But not everybody was able to make the best of any situation. Feng Menglong told a story about another homosexual man, who had a hard time fitting into a heterosexual marriage. Feng's friend Zhang Fengyi (1527-1613), a famous dramatist, had a young homosexual partner. After getting married the "traditional" way, the young man lost a lot of weight. Zhang Fengyi was humored by his miserable state and composed a song to poke fun at him.

**"Pet Boy"**
The bridegroom is truly crossed by a baleful star.
Look at his face—not much flesh.
Thinking about how hard it is to be a husband,
You might as well come back to be a wife.

(*Shan ge*, 5: 37b)

Male-male sexuality, euphemized as "passion of the cut sleeve," was socially acceptable in the late Ming, so long as it was not adopted as a total alternative to heterosexuality—which would have conflicted with the filial duty of procreation.[67] The Ming literatus Xie Zhaozhe and the Italian Jesuit Matteo Ricci both reported on the prominent presence of male prostitutes, although as Giovanni Vitiello points out, while the former seemed amazed and even amused by the phenomenon, the latter was totally scandalized.[68] With powdered faces and rouged lips, and wearing male clothing on top and female garments underneath, male prostitutes adopted a deliberately incomplete female persona. This enabled the cross-dressed handsome boys to enchant their clients through the creation of a sexually ambiguous fantasy world of "physical and psychological transvestism."[69] No wonder the upright Jesuit was scandalized.

In addition to male prostitution, some wealthy gentry took the possession of young, male sexual slaves as a fashionable practice. This relationship was different from homosexual love as understood today. Rather, it was closer to sodomy, with clear hierarchical asymmetry between the two partners. The penetrator was often the senior in age, wealth, and power, hence the "husband"; the penetrated male was often reduced to a female in the sexual relationship, hence the "wife." In the above song, Zhang Fengyi's former partner apparently was the penetrated prior to his marriage, and now he was the penetrator, and he was losing weight. There might not be a connection between the two, but Zhang mocked him along the lines anyway. The fact that the song became "a hit," as Feng Menglong reported, testified to the considerable degree of social acceptance of male-male sex.

But lawmakers had a very different view. As Matthew Sommer points out, "sexual union between males was understood not in terms of the polarity of sexual orientation, but rather in terms of the polluting gender inversion of the penetrated male."[70] Male-male sex was legally regarded as sexual penetration "out of place," and the Ming government "banned consensual homosexual sodomy for the first time" in Chinese history.[71] However, law was one thing, and practice was another. The existence of the law did not mean that people would stop doing it; what it probably meant was that too many people were doing it.

Because anal sex diverges from the norm, mockery of such style of sexual intercourse is a recurrent theme for humor in *Hanging Twigs*, *Hill Songs*, and *Treasury of Laughs*. In *Treasury of Laughs* alone, there are eighteen jokes on homosexuality. On several occasions the jesters associate passion for anal intercourse with fondness for excreta. As Ching-sheng Huang points out, this reduction of homosexuality to scatology could be regarded as insulting.[72] Other entries on homosexuality, although less disgraceful, contain quite a bit of graphic and obscene language. Although the overall tone of the entries seems hilarious and non-judgmental, the scatological touches and the indication that the compiler is laughing along with the audience hint at Feng Menglong's "straight" sexual orientation.

Since the main purpose of the entries on homosexuality in *Child's Folly* is little more than pure amusement, and they lean heavily on the sexual rather than emotional side of such relations, it is necessary to look elsewhere for a clearer indication of Feng Menglong's opinion on homosexual love. The best place to look is perhaps Chapter 22, "Qing wai" (Outer or Homosexual Love) in the *History of Love*. But it is noteworthy that the compiler of *History of Love* was a more mature man than the compiler of *Child's Folly*. A certain degree of inconsistency between his attitudes in the two collections is to be expected. For one thing, he was more serious and more philosophical in the *History of Love*.

As Lee Hua-yuan Mowry has observed, Feng Menglong arranged the forty entries of the chapter "Qing wai" into fifteen categories, which followed the same general pattern that guided the other chapters on heterosexual love.[73] The implication was that homosexual love and heterosexual love were parallel to each other, although the word *wai* (outer) signified that homosexual love was outside of the norm. The word *wai* might also be a reference to the men's "predilection for fondling with the external" (*hao wai pi*) in association with homosexual sex. Feng did not make a sweeping generalization about male-male sexuality. He disapproved of emperors who had sexual relations with both males and females: that was a sign of excessive lust and moral decadence. He was disgusted by rulers who granted political powers to their male consorts: that was a sign of poor judgment and abuse of imperial authority. He quoted a proverb, "If there are no handsome boys in the residence, this must be a decent household" (*Qingshi*, 22: 24b), to express his disapproval of sodomy in gentry families. But he praised partners of genuine homosexual love who were truly devoted to each other. Their "abnormal" (*wai*) sexual orientation was by no means a cause of discrimination in Feng's highly positive evaluation of their love (*qing*). The best example was "The Story of Scholar Wan" (*Wan Sheng zhuan*) (*Qingshi*, 22: 7a-8a).[74]

Scholar Wan fell in love with a lad named Zheng Mengge—it was love at first sight. Although on their second encounter Zheng had been worn out by the hardship of life due to the severe poverty of his family, Wan loved him even more. He nurtured the boy back to his former beauty, and those young men who before had ridiculed Scholar Wan's ugly boy friend now competed to flirt with the boy. But the couple took no notice of other people. When Zheng reached adulthood, Wan arranged marriage for him, gave him a third of the Wan estate, and invited Zheng's parents to live with them. "Five out of every ten nights" Zheng slept with Wan, and the other nights he slept with his wife. If Zheng's wife was unhappy about the arrangement we hear nothing of it: Feng reported total gratitude from the entire

Zheng family. Feng also reported no complaint from Wan's wife. In fact, she was not mentioned at all, and the readers are left to wonder if Wan was ever married.

At the end of the story, Wan disclosed, to his "inner relative" Mr. Tian and his friend Mr. Yang, his wish to be buried with Zheng in the event of his death. The term "inner relative" is a bit ambiguous. It could mean a relative from the mother's side or from the wife's side. If Mr. Tian was from the wife's side, then Wan had a wife, and she was from a prominent clan, since Mr. Tian was addressed as *gongzi* (son of duke), an indicator of his elevated social status. Scholar Wan was reported to be of moderate means. He was at most a middle-class man. If he did have a wife from a prominent clan, and the wife's family seemed to accommodate his "passion of the cut sleeve" in life as well as in death, it would be truly amazing.

But Feng was not interested in telling more about Scholar Wan's life. His focus was so sharply on the deep sense of commitment and devotion between Wan and Zheng that nothing and nobody else seemed to matter very much. Feng emphasized that Zheng was comely, but was by no means a great beauty. Physical attraction alone could not explain Wan's infatuation with Zheng. And yet Wan fixed his love on Zheng and never swayed. There must have been a spiritual dimension to it. Single-minded dedication unto death, be it heterosexual or homosexual love, such as that between Wan and Zheng, was well received in the circles of *qing*-crazy intellectuals.

Romance had its risk. In *History of Love*, Feng Menglong recorded a possible case of sexually transmitted disease ("blood disease") among homosexual men. Zhang Youwen and Zhang Qianren were homosexual lovers. Youwen died of "blood disease." Qianren vowed never to have another homosexual lover, in memory of Youwen. But he broke the vow, and also died of "blood disease." Qianren's uncle, the homosexual dramatist Zhang Fengyi, dreamed that it was Youwen who came to take Qianren to the underworld.

Feng Menglong registered his uncertain suspicion about a possible link between anal sex and the fatal "blood disease" when he pointed out that as a counter case, Zhang Fengyi was still healthy at over eighty (*Qingshi*, 22: 21b-22b). Feng Menglong did not describe the symptoms of the "blood disease," but Yuan Zhongdao, the bisexual poet and hedonist, described his own symptoms in some detail. "I am suffering from a blood disease as a result of my promiscuous life in my youth," said Yuan. "Whenever the disease begins to strike, I have problems breathing, and my stomach aches as if there were pieces of stone inside me; I cannot sleep; I am frightened out of my wits when I find myself spitting blood, believing that I am about to die."[75] The symptoms seemed to bear some similarity to AIDS, but that could not be ascertained.

Homosexuality could run in the family. Feng Menglong reported two generations of homosexual men in the case of Zhang Fengyi and his nephew Qianren, and again in the case of Yu Wanlun and his father Yu Huali (*Qingshi*, 22: 1a-b). Feng did not wonder whether the family tradition was due to inheritance or imitation. It just seemed natural to him.

Feng made a slightly pedantic statement on homosexuality in the general commentary on Chapter 22 of *History of Love*. Compared with the playful and amoral Feng Menglong in *Child's Folly*, here Feng retained his sense of humor, but also revealed a more serious and moralistic side.

> The Historian of Love says: Food, drink, men, and women—herein lie human beings' biggest desires. A beautiful lass can tangle a tongue; a beautiful lad can ruin an elder. Hence the warning [in the *Zhanguo ce* (Strategics of the Warring States)]: beware of these two kinds of beauty. Xin Bo [an official in the court of King Huan of Zhou (r. 718-696 BC)] was deep in both heterosexual and homosexual love. From the above classical allusions we know that love of men and love of women have long been discussed side by side. And yet men who love only men and men who love only women have sneered at each other, though neither group appears to have the upper hand. I have heard Minister Yu Huali say that sex with a woman is for procreation and sex with a man is for pleasure. He argues that all under heaven, the colors of males are superior to the colors of females: Among the feathered species, from phoenix and peacock to chicken and pheasant, beautiful patterns and colors are both the male's privilege; that is also true with the luster of the coats of dogs and horses. He even proclaims that if males could produce offspring, then there would be no use for females. Alas! There are indeed men who love men to this extent, so how can we talk only of love of the creatures in the inner quarters (*nei*)? *Kong Cong Zi* records that when Zi Shang had an audience with the King of Wei, the King's favorite courtier, of beautiful beard and eyebrows, stood by the side of the King. The King told Zi Shang, "If beard and eyebrows could be loaned, I would not be stingy with loaning them out to you." Well, to go so far as to favor a courtier just because he has beautiful beard and eyebrows—I do not know what the foundation of his *qing* is!
>
> (*Qingshi*, 22: 29b-30a)[76]

Feng Menglong cautioned against discrimination based on sexual orientation: heterosexuality, homosexuality, and bisexuality had all been well documented historically. He apparently disagreed with Minister Yu's extreme statement on male superiority, though he was amused enough to record it at length. He flatly disapproved of homosexuality between ruler and courtier. What was possible between Scholar Wan and the young man Zheng was impossible between the King of Wei and his male favorite, who was reduced to "beautiful beard and eyebrows" in Feng's rhetoric. When political power was at stake, homosexual love lost its authenticity.

## 7. *Culture of the Pleasure Quarters*

**"Clamor"**
In this trade,
Ten measures of true love,
Can only be counted as three.
How could you strike
Right at the center of the drum?
No wonder you're apt to
Cause a clamor for no good reason.
I'm in essence a flower in the wall and willow on the roadside,
How can I avoid dallying with butterflies and playing with bees?
If I behave, as you wish,
Like a virtuous woman, a chaste wife,
I'm afraid you won't be able to recognize my face!

(Comment) There is a "three-syllable dictum" in the "Green Tower" (Red Light District): *hong* (heating), *hong* (coaxing), and *hong* (clamoring). It is said that heating is like fire, coaxing is like a spell, and clamoring is like a tiger. In the ambience of golden goblets and sandalwood castanets, embroidered drapes and perfumed quilts, hungry eyes send waves, and hot bowels are about to boil. This is the so-called "heating." The army of powder gets your soul bewitched. The fairy of flowers gets your nostrils drunk. The passion is as strong as liquor. The vow is as heavy as mountain. Such tricks of coaxing are a hundred kinds. Then the wishes are too luxurious to fulfill. The promises are too weighty to keep. Jealous uproars are hard to take. Empty manger is easy to jump. The pledge of love onto death is brought to an abrupt end with a clamor. That is why the singer chants, "Ten measures of true love can only be counted as three." If you can understand the meaning of it, you will be doing ok.

(*Guazhier*, 5: 51b-52a)

Feng Menglong's advice to visitors of the pleasure quarters that true love was hard to find among courtesans complied with the conventional wisdom. Equipped with dazzling outfits and make-up, enchanting techniques of words, songs, wine, and body movements, not to mention a sensual and inviting bedroom setting, the courtesans employed all sorts of charms to bewitch their patrons. But their promises of love should not be taken seriously. As long as the man played along, with the clear understanding that cheating was part of the courtesan's job description, he would be able to maintain a harmonious relationship with the female entertainer. Once he showed his green eye, the romance would be spoiled, and he would be ridiculed. Perhaps Feng should listen to his own advice!

**"Tearing Up the Handkerchief"**
My handkerchief,
My handkerchief,
Who's torn it up?
Tell me quickly,
Tell my quickly.
Don't hide the truth from me.
If you still would not say,
You'll be in big trouble.
The handkerchief itself is a petty object,
But the intention of the handkerchief giver is exuberant.
If you smear my handkerchief,
You're smearing me!
(Comment) I have observed that women in the Green Tower often take the private gifts they receive for granted. They may abuse the objects, or give them away: they do not seem to cherish them very much. But if they occasionally give people a fan or a kerchief, they act as if there is something precious and secretive about the gift. Ages later they would still check and see if the receivers continue to have the keepsakes in their possession. The silly men thereupon take the keepsakes to be precious and secretive and store them away in their safes. Some go so far as to retain the keepsakes even after the givers are already gone, foolishly cherishing the objects as if the women's perfume still lingered around them. How ridiculous! In my youth I used to be in the company of courtesans, and I received quite a few handkerchiefs containing the poetry of some other guys—apparently gifts to the courtesans, which were passed on to me. When the men wrote the poetry on the handkerchiefs, they expected the handkerchiefs to be kept in the courtesans' chests as souvenirs of their everlasting romance. How would they have known that the women were to give them away without much hesitation? Therefore, the rubbish about the handkerchief

means nothing more than a cliché, so it is quite all right to have it torn up.

(*Guazhier*, 5: 54a)

The singer of the song was a courtesan who just found out that the handkerchief she had given to her lover was torn up. She immediately suspected that it was the act of a jealous foe. She was angry about the existence of the other woman, about that woman's jealous caprice, and about the man's refusal to expose her. But in the eyes of the commentator, the handkerchief did not mean as much as she claimed. All the fuss about the handkerchief was but a game to make the silly man feel guilty. A wise man would not be trapped.

It is noteworthy that Feng's comment deliberately revealed his rich experience with the courtesans and his popularity among them. In Feng's opinion, frequent visitation to the pleasure quarters was nothing to be ashamed of; it was even something to celebrate. That was because the romance of a love-imbued courtesan and a frustrated scholar joining through empathy was highly idealized in the late Ming.[77] The idealized courtesan embodied romantic chivalry and headlong passion. Frailty might be the name of her trade, but she defied that name by demonstrating her determination to sacrifice everything for the unrecognized talent for whom she fell. Such a courtesan might be a rare find, but she was worth the search. So Feng felt he did not need to be apologetic.

**"Anger with the Courtesan"**
The silly turtle,
For no good reason,
Falls for an untidy courtesan.
She's simply able to
Sing a bit of music and
Drink a bit of wine.
What are you praising her for?
When I see her coming my way,
I can't help but get angry.
Her looks are so-so,
Her figure is no good.
Even if you love her voice to death,
The voice is of no good use in bed.

(Comment) I have heard from the elders that forty years ago, the courtesans in the Wu area all walked on foot to their destinations, followed by their attending lute carriers. When they saw civil officials and military officers, they would bow to pay respect. Recently this tradition has been maintained only in the north, and in the south it's all but gone.

> The situation in Suzhou is the worst. Singsong girls cannot sing. Musical entertainers cannot play instruments. If the woman has a comely look, she would be revered like the Queen Mother of the West, and praised like the bodhisattva Guanyin. She gives orders at her will, and people follow her wishes submissively. If the woman happens to chant a couple of syllables in harmony with the music, people are stunned as if she is as good a singer as a wondrous phoenix, and prostrate themselves in front of her. Otherwise, people would acclaim that so-and-so is in a superior class and so-and-so is of good quality. Thereupon in the filthy Green Tower no girls are reckoned to be trashy. The more generously you request their service, the worse their quality becomes. The more courteously you treat them, the poorer their skill becomes. The so-called lute players on the pleasure boats are but blind chantresses and singing beggar women. They are singsong girls and musical entertainers in name, but in actuality they cannot even compare to blind beggar musicians. If the man in the song indeed chances upon a courtesan with a good voice, I'd say go ahead and "love her voice to death." However, the words that come out of the mouth of a jealous shrew is something I do not dare to believe.
>
> (*Guazhier*, 5: 56b-57a)

The woman in the song flew into a temper because her lover had been attracted to a courtesan who, in her opinion, had no merit other than her ability to "sing a bit of songs and drink a bit of wine." But the commentator was skeptical about her judgment. Not that he did not believe the courtesan could be as unseemly as she described, but that he did not believe the courtesan could sing as well as she implied. Here Feng Menglong expressed a low opinion of contemporary courtesan culture and nostalgia about the good old days when courtesans had the proper skill and the proper conduct. But his sentiment need not be taken seriously: he might have had too high a standard. In the eighteenth century, literati were to look back to the seventeenth century with real nostalgia: courtesan culture went into a dramatic decline after the fall of the Ming.[78]

Feng Menglong's high standard of courtesan virtue can be inferred from his narration of the story of Zhang Runsan in the *Guazhier*. The courtesan Zhang Runsan, falling in love with a merchant surnamed Cheng, promised Cheng her hand. The merchant was moved by the courtesan's love and spent all his fortune on her. That was a deadly mistake. The merchant went bankrupt, became a beggar, and thus could not afford to visit the courtesan any more. Knowing the embarrassing situation Mr. Cheng was in, Miss Zhang offered Cheng all her savings and asked him to invest the money wisely, so that they might be able to have a future together. Unfortunately, as was predictable for an inconsistent merchant, Cheng was not a reliable man. He quickly spent all the "easy money" he got in another courtesan's house! The heart-broken Zhang Runsan, learning of the hopeless situation, summoned Cheng and proposed a double suicide. Cheng did not want to die, but realizing that the wine Zhang was drinking had been poisoned, he grabbed the carafe and drank the rest of the contents. When Zhang Runsan's "mother," the procuress, discovered the two bodies, she immediately fed the young woman with the fresh blood of goat (what a resourceful granny!), and Zhang was revived. When they in turn tried to revive the man, he was already beyond remedy. The merchant's father brought the case to the magistrate of Changzhou, who happened to be the Gong'an poet Jiang Yingke (1556-1605). Since Jiang Yingke's tenure as Changzhou magistrate lasted from 1592 to 1598,[79] the date of the story could be safely put in the 1590s. The magistrate, true to his poetic sentiment, sympathized with the courtesan. The case was dropped, and Zhang Runsan was released. When the story spread around, Zhang's reputation as a romantic heroine soared up to the sky. But the whole event ended in anticlimax: she married, of all possible candidates, a silk merchant—how could a silk merchant truly appreciate her? (*Guazhier*, 5: 41a-43a).

Feng Menglong admired Zhang Runsan's earlier dedication but lamented that her story did not have a suitably tragic ending. She could have been remembered as a chivalrous courtesan, had she perished at the drinking party, but she survived, and worse still, she did not keep her chastity for her deceased lover. This turn of events is indeed a pity, at least aesthetically. But Feng's lament went beyond aesthetic concerns. He evidently deemed unethical the courtesan's failure to hold on to *qing*, when he criticized her for being faithless (*fuxin*). Modern readers would find Feng's comment on the courtesan overly harsh, since her merchant lover's faithlessness was the cause of the double suicide to begin with. Concerning sexual relations, traditional Chinese writers tended to demand a higher moral standard for women than for men, and Feng was no exception. But, to balance this prejudice a little bit, Feng also acknowledged that he would be even more disturbed by the outcome of the story if it were the merchant who survived—what an excrescence that would be![80]

The overall picture of courtesans painted in the *Guazhier* was distinctive from that depicted in the courtesan-scholar romance in the *Sanyan* and the *Qingshi*. The courtesans in the *Guazhier* were "flowers in the wall and willow on the roadside." They could not be expected to stand up to the moral standard of chaste wives hidden in the inner quarters of the family compound. Pretentious and capricious, they lacked deep feelings and genuine emotions. They were not the sort of people who possessed the intuitive "child's folly." Aside from problematic virtue, Feng even called into question their basic artistic skill and etiquette. This was in direct contrast with the idealized image of the talented and love-imbued courtesan whose beauty, virtue, and artistry were exclusively devoted to one worthy man alone throughout her entire life. In many *Sanyan* and *Qingshi* stories, devoted courtesans endured all sorts of hardships to be lifelong soul mates of their scholarly lovers. Their unsurpassed virtue redeemed their bodies as sexual commodities.[81] As Feng commented in the *Qingshi*, simply because female entertainers were often compared to "peach and willow trees on the roadside" did not necessarily mean that they could not be expected to "possess the bones that could bear up under the winter chill," like the cypress, symbol of wifely chastity (*Qingshi*, 1: 42a).

Genre is a possible explanation for the two glaringly different images presented by the same writer. The frail courtesan who succumbs to the evil of the trade may seem more realistic than the strong-willed courtesan who transcends her social station, but both images are based partly on stereotypes and partly on personal observation—needless to say, not all courtesans are the same. The frail type predominates the popular songs, and the strong-willed type predominates the fiction, because the former fits better in the comic, satirical mode, and the latter is more appropriate in romance of tragic twists and turns. Interestingly, the merry whore in the popular song is locked in an unhappy relation with her clients, while the suffering courtesan in the romance is either rewarded with a happy marriage or, failing that, a fine reputation.

The courtesans in the *Guazhier* who are not bogged down by ethical obligations or emotional attachment can be regarded as the *bian*, or negative examples, in Zhu Xi's poetic terminology. They deviate from the model of "child's folly." But Feng Menglong's criticism of them sounds more cynical than didactic. He was not a second Zhu Xi.

## *8. The Way of the World*

**"Guest Entertainer"**

You who entertain the guests in death rituals,
Let me ask you why you busy yourself so much.
There is a death in somebody else's house,
Why are you wearing the mourner's cap,

Listening to the sound of the castanets,
And running around so diligently?
Those who come are not your friends,
Nor are those who go your families.
They have nothing to say to you when you're about to leave,
Except to please take off the mourner's white round collar.
(*Guazhier*, 9: 98b)

It was a custom in late-Ming Suzhou for non-literati families to hire civil service degree holders as fake clansmen to entertain friends and families during memorial services. The deceased might or might not be comforted by the presence of a fake gentry clansman, but the living members could not bear to make public knowledge the clan's failure to produce any student, so they resorted to this face-serving device. Mourning was an important ritual around which the relationships within the Chinese family were constructed and reconstructed. By acting as family members in strangers' funerals, these "guest entertainers" allowed themselves to be artificially grafted onto other people's lineages. It was highly inappropriate in the Confucian mode of conduct. Besides, true Confucians were supposed to see themselves as members of the "guilt society," not members of the "shame society."[82] Moral conscience should be more important than social face. The "guest entertainers" violated ritual propriety and participated in the shallow game of the wrong kind of society, all for but a little material gain. They were mocked for being thrice removed from the Confucian model.

**"Mountain Man"**
If you ask me about the mountain man,
The mountain man doesn't live in the mountain.
He's just brazen-faced. Oh, how shameless!
Writing a few stanzas of bad poems,
Wearing the Confucian cap,
Claiming to be a law-abiding citizen,
Presenting his name cards everywhere, he says,
A certain gentleman in the capital
Has recently sent a letter to this humble subject.
A certain gentleman in the village
Is the bosom friend of this humble subject.
Before I leave, by the way,
I have a plea on behalf of my relation,
But it's all for the sake of justice, and
I have no cash reward to present you.

(Comment) The song delineates a complete picture of the mountain men's tricks. It can be passed down to later generations along with the "Song of the Mountain Man" by Mr. Zhang Boqi [Zhang Fengyi]. I have also heard of a joke, which says: A man is assigned to be the magistrate of the County of One Single Resident. One day, the magistrate goes out, carried by his only subject. In the middle of the trip, it begins to drizzle. The magistrate improvises a poem,
*My fate is bitter and my office lowly: what can I say?*
*In the midst of drizzles I am just carried on the back of a man. . . .*
He has not figured out the second half of the poem when his only subject asks to finish it:
*My mouth yells to clear the way and my shoulders carry the sedan chair.*
*My hand drags the flogging stick and my feet travel to and fro.*
The magistrate exclaims, "Well, I am impressed!" The single resident abruptly puts the magistrate down on the ground and salutes him with folded hands, saying, "I do not dare to hide it from you. In fact, the mountain man of this county is also little me." Alas, the poem composed by the mountain man really suits him well. The mountain man is good only for carrying the magistrate. Confucius lamented, "The *gu* (an octagonal goblet) is unlike a *gu*. [Can it still be called *gu*?]"[83] I feel sorry that "mountain" is no mountain, and "man" is no man. So I attach my note here to voice my opinion.

(*Guazhier*, 9: 95b-96b)

Feng Menglong's opinion on the so-called "mountain man" was evidently low. He described the mountain man as sort of a Jack of all trades among the lower strata of literati. *Shanren* or "mountain man" was originally an honorable appellation referring to talented people who, for some lofty reason, refused to serve the government and retired to the mountains to become hermits. The term "mountain man" not only denoted the location of his residence but also signified his lofty personality and his detachment from the mundane affairs of the dusty world. However, by the mid-sixteenth century, the "mountain man" had become a distinctive social category with a very different meaning. Any educated man without a government position (unemployed or retired) or even a scholar-official disinterested in politics could claim to be a "mountain man." The new "mountain man" did not live in the mountains. If he did, that would have made it too inconvenient for his patrons to place orders for his artwork and deliver payments (euphemized as "wetting brushes" to reduce the unpleasant connotation of commercialism), or for his powerful associates to visit him and discuss current affairs.

Although the mountain man did not go to the mountains, a successful mountain man would be able to make the mountains go to him. Artificial mountains in beautifully landscaped gardens created cosmic energies inspirational for artistic creativity and instrumental in the purification of body and soul. Just as there were "true" Neo-Confucian moralists and "fake" Neo-Confucian moralists, there were "true" mountain men and "fake" mountain men in late Ming China. The "true" mountain men were respected for their superb literary and artistic talent, and for their sense of detachment from the political intrigues and mercantile philistinism that plagued late Ming state and society. Although they lived in the cities, sold their talent, and pursued comfortable material lives, they approached the lofty spirit of their ancient predecessors, and would not bow to wealth and power. The "fake" mountain men, on the other hand, could not afford to harbor such lofty spirit. Possessing questionable talent, lacking inherited estate, and stumbling along the road to examination success, the "fake" mountain men would have difficulty acquiring the comfort of life they desired without playing some abject games. They cultivated connections with the rich and famous and paid homage to the powerful. They gossiped about their critics and flattered their admirers. Manipulating their borrowed fame, they sold their artwork at inflated prices and interceded in legal cases for personal profits.[84] Because of their dubious character, the fake mountain man became a marked target of ridicule in late Ming literature.

In the *Hill Songs*, Feng Menglong included a lengthy "Song of the Mountain Man," of more than eight hundred characters. The song was commonly attributed to Zhang Fengyi and was believed to imply specific people of some fame. Perhaps to help refute the troubling rumors, Feng clarified that Zhang Fengyi was not the original author: he simply revised an existing song and made it famous. The song took the form of a conversation between a mountain man and the God of Earth. The mountain man visited the Temple of the God of Earth. Because of the way the mountain man was dressed, the God of Earth at first mistook him to be a colleague. Upon realizing who the visitor really was, the God was annoyed. "What is this busy body doing here? Very suspicious!" thought the God. The God demanded that the mountain man explain himself: why he disturbed the peace and quiet of the locality, and why he paid a visit to his temple. The mountain man replied:

> My dear, dear, venerable God of Earth,
> I'm such a person that

If you call me fake I'm not fake, and
If you call me true I'm not true, either.
Regarding poetic composition I can't mock the wind nor dally with the moon.
Regarding calligraphy I can do neither standard nor script style.
It's all because of poor business
That I enter your sacred gate.
Alas! I want to do trade but I lack principal.
I want to teach but I can't find the school.
I want to be a fortune-teller but I know nothing about the Five Phases.
I want to be a physician but I understand nothing about the Six Pulses.
I was born to have a weak composition:
I have neither the legs nor the shoulders
To carry heavy loads.
And I was born with a foul mouth
That damages others as well as myself.
After counting out all thirty-six strategies in the book,
I can't but attach myself to a mountain man of some renown.
After I don't know how many sittings with him,
And how many snacks of wonton boiled in wine,
He finally agrees to send in my name,
And take me to have an interview with a big potato.
Though I don't dare to wish to spread my name to the Four Seas,
I'd be delighted to heap honor upon myself,
To shock all those friends and relatives,
And to astonish all those neighbors in the village.
To help fulfill the wish I'm paying homage to the gods,
It's not that I'm here for nothing.

Unhappy about what he heard, the God of Earth called the mountain man a disgusting and shameless gyp. He accused him of abusing his personal connections to line his pockets when interceding in legal cases in the name of upholding justice. The mountain man sweated upon learning that his sin was known to the gods and asked for a divination: would he be able to escape retribution? The God of Earth gave him a two-sentence advice: "Where you can let go of your grip, let go. Where you can spare a victim, spare him." With this the song ended on a satirical note (*Shan ge*, 9: 79a-81b).

Far from having a sense of detachment from the mundane affairs of the dusty world, the fake mountain man was an active contributor to the dust of the world. Because the term "mountain man" had been contaminated by these pretenders, some literati deliberately distanced themselves from any association with that name.[85]

**"Deceiving Mother"**
Mother keeps an eye on me like a tigress,
I keep Mother ill-informed of my goings-on.
It's like missing the thief in front of the police station,
The archers patrol day and night, but all in vain.
(Comment) Recently archers are in the habit of collaborating with thieves. I'm afraid they are imitating this young lady.
(*Shan ge*, 1: 7b)

The mother in the song wished to keep her daughter's suitor away, apparently to prevent a premarital scandal. The problem was that her wish clashed heads-on with her daughter's interest. The young lady acted as her lover's liaison, so the mother had difficulty getting rid of the amorous man. The daughter compared the situation to that of police work: when the patrolmen were in league with the thieves, the villains would never get caught. Feng Menglong's comment indicated that this was not just a metaphor, but a fact. Matteo Ricci confirmed this in his journal. "Thousands of night watchmen in the cities roam the streets sounding a gong at regular intervals. Yet, despite this, and the fact that the streets are closed with iron bars and locks, it frequently happens that houses are thoroughly ransacked by night marauders. This probably happens because the watchmen themselves are robbers or are in league with the robbers, and the result of frequent thieving is that others are engaged to watch the watchmen."[86] Ricci's report sounds almost like a joke: what if the men hired to watch the watchmen also needed to be watched? The Ming state's ineffective improvisation was lamentable.

**"Excess"**
In the sky, when there are too many stars the moon's not bright.
In the pond, when there is too many fishes the water's not clear.
In the court, when there's too many officials the law's chaotic.
When the lady has too many lovers her heart is in disarray.
(*Shan ge*, 4: 31a)

The message: more is not necessarily better. Excess starlight outshines the moon. Excess fishes muddle the pond water. Excess officials in the imperial court confound the laws and regulations due to conflicting personal interests and counterproductive factional struggles. Likewise, when the young lady has excess lovers she is confused in her heart.

The quiet insertion of the political comment in this otherwise quite innocent folksong is interesting. It seems that the excess stars, fishes, and lovers all conspired to flank the excess officials and smuggled them onto the stage without attracting too much unwanted attention. Feng Menglong further directed the attention away from the political criticism when he cited in the appendix a conversation with the "famous courtesan" Hou Huiqing. Feng asked Hou if her heart was in disarray, since she knew so many men. Hou answered she had an examination desk in her heart, whereby she ranked all her clients and perhaps even picked her future spouse: her heart was absolutely not confused. As a repeated failure in the examination hall who always attributed his misfortune to muddleheaded examiners, Feng expressed admiration for Hou's cool judgment, which he respected over those of the state officials. Little did he know that he would end up failing the examination with Hou Huiqing as well.

**"The Bow-Shaped Crescent"**
The bow-shaped crescent moon shines upon the nine provinces:[87]
Some families are happy, others sorrowful.
In some families, husband and wife share the conjugal bed,
In others, family members scatter to other provinces.
(Appendix) A *xiucai* (entry-level civil degree holder) is ranked "C" in the triennial evaluation examination. His servant composes a song to make fun of him:
The bow-shaped crescent shines upon the nine provinces:
Some families are happy, others sorrowful.
In some families, the son is awarded red satin,
In others, the son is beaten till blood comes out.
Only my young lord gets the perfect grade:
He's free of happiness and also free of sorrow.

(*Shan ge*, 5: 36b)

The "Bow-Shaped Crescent" was a popular tune. People could freely fill in the words using a fixed formula. According to Feng Menglong's vernacular short story, "Fan Qiuer's Dual Half-Moon Mirrors Round off Again" (*Jingshi tongyan*, Ch. 12), the song quoted in the text of *Shan ge* was produced during the transition between Northern and Southern Song, in the twelfth century. When the Jurchens took over North China and brought an end to the Northern Song, the Song imperial court moved to the South and established the Southern Song. Amidst the chaos of the war, many Chinese residents in the North tried to escape to the South. Quite a few of them became separated with their families. The song recorded the varied fortunes of the Chinese families during the Diaspora. It was a very sad song. But the song Feng cited in the appendix was of a very different nature. It poked fun at a mediocre student whose score was neither good enough for an award nor bad enough for a beating. As we shall later see, entry-level degree holders in the Ming were required to take triennial evaluation exams. They were given grades on a scale of A-F. A and B students would receive material rewards; C students would receive neither rewards nor punishments; D students would receive a beating; E student would receive a demotion; and F students would lose their student status (and along with it, their gentry privileges). With a score in the middle range, the student in the song was indeed "free of happiness and also free of sorrow." One only wonders if the servant would be so bold as to sing the song in front of his "young lord."

**"Country Bumpkin"**
The country bumpkin has no idea about the convict in cangue.
Suddenly catching sight of one, his tongue sticks out.
He doesn't know if the man's head is so hard it penetrates the stock,
Or if inside the stock grows such a man.
(Comment) Don't say that country bumpkins are all stupid. They can be extremely smart. I still remember in the year of *bingshen* (1596) a countryman sailed a small boat home while singing songs. In the darkness of the night his boat happened to bump against the boat of a prefectural judge. The judge said to him, "If you can sing a song impromptu on the theme of this event, I shall release you." The countryman let out his voice and sang,
*"The sky's dusky, the sun's set, all around it's pitch-black.*
*The head of the small boat bumps into the head of the big boat.*
*Alas! This little man's a wheat-eating mouth from the countryside,*
*Who's ignorant of the way of the world.*
*Oh, what a headless trouble I've gotten myself into!*
*I beg you, the Lord of the Azure Sky,*
*Don't hack my head off my body, please."*
The judge was greatly pleased. He sent the countryman away with the reward of a pitcher of wine.

(*Shan ge*, 5: 36b-37a)

The cangue, as we have seen in the previous chapter, was a wooden stock, which a convict of minor offense was required to wear around the neck for public display. The country bumpkin in the song was ignorant of laws and punishments, hence his amazement at the sight of it.

Feng recounted the humorous tale about the countryman and the prefectural judge in conjunction with laws and punishments. The countryman might not have known the law very well, but the judge certainly did. When the countryman's boat bumped into the judge's boat in the darkness of the night, it was a small accident which did not warrant a punishment: nobody was hurt and no boat was damaged. But the difference between the status of the two parties meant that if the elevated official wanted the abject commoner punished, he could well make out of it a case of disrespectful conduct against the authorities. The judge decided to make the countryman decide his own fate. Here the judge somehow demonstrated a sense of humor: since the country bumpkin got himself into trouble while singing a hill song, to get himself out of the trouble he had to sing another hill song. This turned out to be easy for the countryman, who was evidently a good hill song singer. The wordplay on "head" that he improvised on the spot was both smart and appropriate. It was the *head* of the small boat that bumped into the *head* of the big boat. The implication was that the humble offender in the small boat was at the mercy of the respectable offended in the big boat. The trouble was *head*less. It was headless because it happened out of the blue. It was also headless because the worst scenario would be for the offender to lose his head. But of course this was an exaggeration—his offense by no means deserved decapitation. When the folk called the official Lord of the Azure Sky—the human incarnation of the unfailingly just and righteous divine judge—and pleaded with him not to hack his *head*, the judge was made to acknowledge that this was no big deal. He not only released his prisoner but also rewarded him with wine for his performance.

The law was designed to uphold justice and maintain social order, but its enforcement could be arbitrary. In Feng's tale the wit of the countryman saved his skin. But what if he failed to come up with a satisfactory performance? A covert social criticism lies herewith.

## Romantic Heroism

*Hanging Twigs* and *Hill Songs* present by and large an unrestrained depiction of intimate feelings and carnal desire, and the tone of Feng Menglong's commentary tends to be playful, at times hedonistic. But the two song collections are not typical of erotic literature popular in the late Ming book market. Many late Ming authors of pornographic erotica make a pretense that their absorbing depiction of sexual pleasure is an eye-catching device to captivate readers until they are struck by the sudden revelation of retribution that the philanderers are doomed to suffer. They claim that eroticism is the means, and sexual containment is the end.[88] Such rhetoric is little more than sugarcoating. Feng Menglong seems a bit more mindful of his social responsibilities. As is discussed above, some entries in

*Hanging Twigs* and *Hill Songs* contain social satire on the ills of the age, others reflect on the problems of human nature. Even the erotic songs reveal the complexity and problematic nature of human emotions and desires, exposing the deficiency of puritan Neo-Confucian ethics, which center on emotional moderation with little regard to individual variations.

Neo-Confucian philosophers, such as Zhu Xi, advocated channeling emotions and desires through ritual propriety so that they would abide by the Golden Mean and harmonize with Heavenly Principle. Because the "Golden Mean" requires moral cultivation, second nature takes priority over spontaneity. Because the "Heavenly Principle" endorses sex-role segregation and gender hierarchy, romantic impulse is tabooed and women's well-being is compromised. Although Zhu Xi's ethics is not exactly oppressive, it "falls short of actually encouraging an emotionally rich life," in the words of Donald Munro.[89] Feng Menglong is not unaware of the wayward propensity and destructive potential of *qing*, human emotional responses, but he chooses to emphasize its creative power and constructive function. In *Hanging Twigs* he illustrates the positive force of *qing* in the following statement:

> It is said, "The guts for sex are as big as heaven." It is not so. I would say, "The guts for *qing* are as big as heaven." Everything under heaven relies on guts, and guts rely on *qing*. Yang Xiang was a feeble teen-age girl; yet she had the strength to beat the tiger [who had her father in its mouth and cause the pained animal to drop its victim alive].[90] That was because her *qing* got the better of her, as she was eager to rescue her father from suffering. The gatekeeper of the ancient state of Qi was a base subject whose heel was mutilated as a punishment for a crime he had committed. Yet he had the courage to assault the horses [of King Jing's carriage, to protest the king's unkingly manner of leaving for court as late as noon, with hair uncombed, and in company with women].[91] That was because his *qing* got the better of him, as he was eager to correct his king's misbehavior. From this point of view, why can't we say that the guts for loyalty and filiality are also as big as heaven? I give all such guts a collective name, "the guts for *qing*." When testing my theory on the people of the world I find that mediocre people always pass the buck, not because they lack in guts, but because they are short of *qing*. Alas! My theory is proven to be right.
>
> (*Guazhier*, 1: 4b-5a)

Feng makes little distinction between "lower" emotions, the basic human drive and arousal, and "higher" emotions, the sublimation of the former. Nor does he differentiate between the physical and spiritual dimensions of emotions. According to his theory of "the guts for *qing*," *qing* allows people to take bold action on the spur of the moment, exerting strength which they normally do not have. They are able to perform with prowess not because they have guts, but because they have deep feelings toward the recipient of the deed. Herein lies the connection between romanticism and heroism.

In the *Sanyan* collection of vernacular fiction, Feng Menglong modifies his "romantic heroism" slightly to the right. He tells juicy tales of forbidden love but also warns of the danger of licentiousness and stresses the personal and familial responsibility of love. If the *Hanging Twigs* and *Hill Songs* treat the social tension inherent in carnal love by siding with the young lovers in opposition to the seniors and the authorities, the *Sanyan* circumscribes carnal love a bit and treats the tension with more subtlety. C. T. Hsia calls this "regulated hedonism."[92] "Having examined, with a thoroughness not to be found in the traditional Chinese moralists and philosophers, all the beautiful and ugly aspects of passion," says Hsia, "the storyteller comes out with a plea for health and sanity: he is for the individual insofar as he respects the instinctive integrity of passion and deplores the condition of sexual deprivation, but he is for society insofar as he points out the dangers of compulsive lust and excessive dissipation."[93] Love does not need to start with a lawful marriage, but it has to end in one, and in the process the heroes and heroines have to demonstrate their undying devotion, overcome trying obstacles, and win social recognition, otherwise death, murder, or disgrace awaits them.

Closely associated with undying passion is the spirit of chivalry, both being romantic and heroic. Chen Jiru spelled out the connotations of chivalry in the following passage:

> In life, spirit and will, discernment and courage, operate hand in hand and spur each other on. A son who is chivalrous will be filial, an official who is chivalrous will be loyal, a woman who is chivalrous will be chaste, and a friend who is chivalrous will be dependable. Only the chivalrous will rescue another from penniless obscurity, provide support in time of crisis, and defuse disputes between others. Only the chivalrous will avenge grievances and reward kindness. Only the chivalrous will right wrongs and restore justice, only the chivalrous will overcome disaster.[94]

Sure enough, besides tales of love, the *Sanyan* also tells stories of chivalry and friendship. In "Yang Jiaoai Forsakes His Life for the Sake of His Friend" (*Yushi mingyan*, Ch. 7) and "Fan Juqing's Friendship in Life and Death" (*Yushi mingyan*, Ch. 16), good friends readily sacrifice their lives to fulfill fraternal love. Yang Jiaoai and Zuo Botao were good friends who lived in the Spring and Autumn period. On a fatally snowy day, Zuo gave up his clothes and provisions so that Yang could have enough sustenance to complete the long journey to their intended destination. Yang became a high official, and had the king build a shrine at Zuo's tomb to honor him. But Zuo's spirit was harassed by the more powerful spirit of the famous third-century BC assassin Jing Ke (this was anachronistic by a few centuries) in a nearby shrine. To assist Zuo in fighting Jing Ke in the nether world, Yang killed himself, since only a spirit could fight spirit.

Fan Juqing and Zhang Yuanbo were sworn brothers who lived in the Han dynasty. Fan was entangled by some trading business in a faraway place when he suddenly remembered an appointment with Zhang. Unwilling to break his promise to visit Zhang on this fixed day, Double Ninth, which was a festival for family reunion and tomb-sweeping, Fan killed himself, because only a spirit could travel instantly. Meanwhile, Zhang was waiting so anxiously for Fan that he refused to dine or sleep until Fan came. When Fan finally arrived at midnight and revealed that he was a spirit and that he had already asked his wife not to bury him until Zhang came, Zhang immediately set off. Upon seeing Fan's body, he joined him in death. Though melodramatic, the two stories remind readers of the good old days when friendship was genuine. Such friendship onto death was in direct contrast to the mercantilism that plagued late Ming society. Feng Menglong laments in the opening of "Wu Baoan Abandons His Family to Ransom His Friend" (*Yushi mingyan*, Ch. 8),

> Friendship, for the ancients, was a contract between hearts;
> Friendship, for people of today, is a contract between faces.
> With united hearts, friends could live and die together;
> With superficial association, how would people share each other's poverty?
> The nine-lane highways are every day thronged with riders;
> Morning and night set no end to the pursuing and visiting.
> At the dinner table men generously give over their wives and children;
> By the wine cup they bow and dance, swearing to be "like brothers."
> But whisper "profit," and friendship turns to loathing.
> How then can you expect to have friends in the hour of peril?
> Don't you see? In the past Yang and Zuo were friends until death;
> Even yet they hold a high place in our annals.[95]

Single-minded devotion with no practical consideration for self-interest is to Feng the essence of *qing*, and *qing* is what makes the world a beautiful place to live. He develops this theory most fully in the *History of Love*, where not just humans but spirits, ghosts, animals, rocks, and woods are capable of *qing*:

> Had heaven and earth had no *qing* they would not have produced the myriad of things. Had the myriad of things had no *qing* they could not have nurtured each other's life circularly. Life nurtures life ceaselessly because *qing* would not cease. The four great elements (earth, water, fire, and wind) are but illusions; only *qing* is neither empty nor false. Where there is *qing* strangers become close; where there is no *qing* close people become estranged. The difference between that with *qing* and that without *qing* is immeasurable.[96]

According to Buddhist theology, the four great elements are what make up the human body and everything else in the universe; these things with forms are all but illusions. *Qing*, though without a form, is what really drives karma forward. People are related to one another because they owed one another some kindness or grudge in the previous existence and need to pay the debts or collect the credits in this existence. Since the account can never be settled, people are caught in the circle of karmic retribution forever. In order to escape the trap, people are advised to disenchant themselves from the snare of *qing*, the greatest illusion of all.

Feng Menglong turns the Buddhist teaching around and gives it a secular, humanitarian spin. He argues that since *qing* is the driving force of karmic motions, *qing* is what really gives life to people and links people together. He would never want to disenchant himself from *qing* and sever that precious link. Even after he dies, claims Feng, he would not cease to love, and would like to become the "Buddha of Boundless Love and Joy." If people have faith in him, he would give them blessings, so that all of their enemies would become their friends. Happiness would abound; hatred and jealousy would disappear.[97]

Feng visualizes a utopia where everybody acts on *qing*:

> I intend to establish a cult of *qing* to teach all who are living, so that a son would treat his father with *qing* and a vassal would treat his lord with *qing*. One can deduce the relations of all the various phenomena from this single point of view. The myriad things are like scattered coins; *qing* is the thread that strings them together. When one strings the scattered coins together, those at opposite ends of the world become

> of one family. When one damages such a union, one is hurting one's own *qing*. Observing the bursting forth of *qing* is like seeing the budding of spring flowers, which brings joy and happiness to all. Robberies and thefts will cease to happen; evil and treason will not arise. The Buddha will have no further use for the teachings of mercifulness and forgiveness, and the Sage will have no further use for the teachings of benevolence and righteousness.[98]

Maram Epstein aptly points out the disharmonious juxtaposition of utilitarianism and romance in the coin imagery.[99] Considering Yuan Huang's (1533-1606) fusion of mercantilism and charity in his *Ledgers of Merit and Demerit*,[100] however, the incongruity appears less surprising. Apparently, both Yuan and Feng regarded materialistic incentive useful in the management of moral order in late Ming China. The above passage implies that when the "teaching of *qing*" takes roots, a kind of mimesis would occur; everybody would treat everybody else with kindness and love. Tension would be non-existent. Therefore, religious preaching would become redundant. This emphasis of the power of *qing* over the effect of orthodox teachings sounds like a distant echo, albeit in a much gentler tone, to Feng's earlier proclamation of "taking the true love between man and woman as an antidote for the fake medicine of nominal rules."

Diminishing hedonism and increasing didacticism can be discerned from *Guazhier* and *Shan ge*, to *Sanyan*, and then to *Qingshi*, along with descending sensuality and ascending spirituality. Comedy was gradually supplemented by tragedy, as Feng aged and the Ming state disintegrated. But Feng's sense of humor and iconoclasm remained a prominent presence, so did his conviction of the romantic and heroic characteristics of *qing*.

## Notes

1. *Taixia xinzou*, 7: 13b.
2. Ibid., 10: 24a.
3. Northrop Frye, *Anatomy of Criticism: four essays* (Princeton: Princeton University Press, 1957), 164.
4. These were referred to in "Yueji," *Liji* (11: 7b) as "the music of fallen states."
5. The airs of Zheng and Wei were referred to in "Yueji," *Liji* (11: 7b) as "the music of the chaotic age." But Feng Menglong here used the airs of Zheng and Wei to represent "expressions of genuine feelings," which Confucius chose to record in the *Shijing*.

6. Feng Menglong, *Shan ge*, "*Xu Shan ge*," 1a-b. Cf. Kathryn Lowry's translation in "Excess and Restraint: Feng Menglong's Prefaces on Current Popular Songs," *Papers on Chinese History* 2 (Spring 1993): 107-08.

7. Oki Yasushi, "Fu Muryu 'Sanka' no kenkyu," 86.

8. Ernestine Friedl, *Women and Men: An Anthropologists' View* (New York: Holt, Rinehart and Winston, 1975), 6-7.

9. Ren Darong, "Guanyu Zhongguo gudai muxi shehui de kaozheng," Mou Runsun, "Chun Qiu shidai muxi yisu Gongyang zhengyi," and Hsü Cho-yun, "Cong Zhouli zhong tuice yuangu de funü gongzuo," in *Zhongguo funü shi lun ji*, ed. Bao Jialin (Taipei: Daoxiang chuban she, 1992), 1-62.

10. E. H. Schafer, "Ritual Exposure in Ancient China," *Harvard Journal of Asiatic Studies* (1951): 130-84.

11. Michael Loewe, *Chinese Ideas of Life and Death: Faith, Myth and Reason in the Han Period (202 B.C.-A.D. 220)* (London: George Allen and Unwin, 1982), 106.

12. Sima Qian, biography of Confucius, in *Shiji*, *Sibu beiyao*, 47: 18b-19a.

13. Ban Gu, "Yiwen zhi," *Qian Han shu*, *Sibu beiyao*, 30: 5a.

14. See Zhang Longxi, "The Letter or the Spirit: The *Song of Songs*, Allegoresis, and the *Book of Poetry*," *Comparative Literature* 39, no. 3 (1987): 193-216.

15. Zhu Xi's theory on the *Shijing* can be seen in *Zhu Zi yulei*, ed. Li Jingde (Taipei: Zhengzhong shuju, 1962), *juan* 80-81.

16. Zhu Xi, *Zhu Zi yulei*, 80: 1a.

17. Sima Qian, autobiography, in *Shiji*, 130: 10a.

18. Zhu Xi, *Zhu Zi yulei*, 80: 2a.

19. Ibid., 80: 10b.

20. Ibid., 80: 2b-3a.

21. Richard John Lynn, "Chu Hsi as Literary Theorist and Critic," in *Chu Hsi and Neo-Confucianism*, ed. Wing-tsit Chan (Honolulu: University of Hawaii Press, 1986), 344.

22. Zhu Xi, *Zhu Zi yulei*, 80: 3b-4a.

23. Li Kaixian's collection of 103 songs is entitled *Shijing yanci* (Amorous Songs in the Market Place).

24. The modern edition of *Guazhier* is without a preface. Tai-loi Ma locates Yu Wanlun's "*Dazaogan* xiaoyin" (Preface to *Dazaogan*) in Yu's *Ziyu ji* (Collection for Self-Entertainment). Yu identifies Feng Menglong as the compiler of the collection for which he is writing the essay, and mentions the term *tongchi* (child's folly) twice. Since "Dazaogan" was an alternate name of the tune "Guazhier," Ma suspects that this essay might have been a preface to an earlier edition of Feng Menglong's *Guazhier*. In the essay Yu praises the collection for its "richness in embellishment," which might mean that Feng makes extensive changes to the songs. See Tai-loi Ma, "Yanjiu Feng Menglong bianzuan min ge de xin shiliao: Yu Wanlun de *Dazaogan* xiaoyin," *Zhonghua wenshi luncong*, 1986.1: 269-72.

25. See Oki Yasushi, "Fu Muryu 'Jo Sanka' ko: Shikyo gaku to minkan kayo," *Toyo bunka* 71 (1990): 121-45.

26. Kathryn Lowry, "Excess and Restraint," 97. A parallel phenomenon in nineteenth-century Europe is studied in Lionel Trilling, *Sincerity and Authenticity* (Cambridge: Harvard University Press, 1971).

27. For a complete translation of "Door God," see Oki Yasushi, "Women in Feng Menglong's 'Mountain Songs,'" 140-42. For his analysis of the song, see Oki Yasushi, *Fu Muryu sanka no kenkyu: Chugoku Mindai no tsuzoku kayo*, 287-90.

---

28. Clunas, *Superfluous Things*, 110-15.

29. See Oki Yasushi, "Zokkyoku-shu 'Ka shiji' ni tsuite—Fu Muryu Sanka no kenkyu, hosetsu," *Toyo Bunka Kenkyujo kiyo* 107 (Oct. 1988): 89-118.

30. Shen Defu (1578-1642), "Shishang xiaoling," *Wanli yehua bian*, *juan* 25 (Taipei: Weiwen tushu chuban she, 1976), 1709-10.

31. See Guan Dedong's preface to *Shan ge*, *Ming Qing min ge shi diao ji*, 1a-2b.

32. Oki Yasushi, "Women in Feng Menglong's *Mountain Songs*," 135-37.

33. For example, Shen Defu, *Wanli yehuo bian*, 1710.

34. Plaks, *Masterworks of the Ming Novel*, 40.

35. Hanan, *Chinese Vernacular Story*, 88.

36. See Guan Dedong's prefaces to *Guazhier* (8b-9a) and *Shan ge* (6b-8a).

37. Oki Yasushi, "Fu Muryu 'Sanka' no kenkyu," 153-62.

38. See the Introduction to *Lang qing nü yi ji—Jiazhutao dingzhen Qianjiashi shan ge* (Hong Kong: Wanli shudian, 1962), 2-4.

39. For a brief discussion of Feng Menglong's authorship and the "hybrid" typography of *Oleander*, see Shuhui Yang, *Appropriation and Representation: Feng Menglong and the Chinese Vernacular Story* (Ann Arbor: Center for Chinese Studies, the University of Michigan, 1998), 39.

40. Introduction to *Lang qing nü yi ji*.

41. For Wang Guowei's view on the "dissolute" and "vulgar" yet "true" poetry see Wang Guowei, *Renjian cihua*, Comment 62, in *Wang Guantang xiansheng quanji* (Taipei: Wenhua chuban gongsi, 1968), vol. 13, 5942-43. For an English translation see Adele Austin Rickett, *Wang Kuo-wei's Jen-chien Tz'u-hua: A Study in Chinese Literary Criticism* (Hong Kong: Hong Kong University Press, 1977), 65-66.

42. Feng Menglong, *Gujin tan gai*, 1: 22b.

43. Marcel Granet, *Chinese Civilization* (New York: Alfred A. Knopf, 1930), 172.

44. "Big brother" is an intimate term for lover.

45. A *zhang* is slightly more than ten feet.

46. Kang-i Sun Chang, *The Late-Ming Poet Ch'en Tzu-lung: Crises of Love and Loyalism* (New Haven: Yale University Press, 1991).

47. "Chun gong yuan," in *Tang shi san bai shou duben*, ed. Chu Yao (Taipei: Taiwan Wenyuan shuju, 1971), 225. An elegant but a bit sketchy translation can be found in Witter Bynner, *Three Hundred Poems of the T'ang Dynasty, 618-906* (n.p., n.d.), 174.

48. Feng Menglong, *Dong Zhou lieguo zhi*, Chapters 81-83 (Taipei: Shijie shuju, 1961), 758-93.

49. Cf. Oki Yasushi's translation, "Seduction," in his "Women in Feng Menglong's *Mountain Songs*," 133.

50. An English translation of the song, "Midnight," can be found in ibid., 132.

51. An English translation of the song, "Clever," can be found in ibid.

52. Cf. Oki, "Beginning Sexual Relations," in ibid., 134.

53. Cf. Oki, "Seduction," in ibid., 133.

54. The ritual is called "*mizuko kuyo*." See Helen Hardacre, *Marketing the Menacing Fetus in Japan* (Berkeley: California University Press, 1997).

55. Stephen Longstreet and Ethel Longstreet, *Yoshiwara: The Pleasure Quarters of Old Tokyo* (Rutland, Vt.: C. E. Tuttle, 1988), 143.

56. Zhao Nanxing, *Xiaozan*, in *Ming Qing xiaohua ji, Guoli Beijing Daxue zhongguo minsu xuehui minsu congshu*, ed. Lou Zikuang, vol. 7 (Rpt. Taipei: The Orient Cultural Service, 1970), 23.

57. Su Zizhong was Su Dan from Puzhou. He was an official in Wu and compiler of poetry collections. See Töpelmann, 132.

58. Feng Menglong, *Qingshi*, 21: 1b; 17: 57a-b. Lee Hua-yuan Mowry, 115.

59. Cheng Yi, *Henan Cheng shi yishu*, 22 *xia*: 4b-5a. In *Er Cheng quanshu*, *Sibu beiyao*.

60. Zhu Xi, *Zhu Zi wenji*, in *Zhu Zi daquan*, *Sibu beiyao*, 62: 28a.

61. *Taisui*, or "Great Year," is Jupiter (Zeus), a baleful star. See Ching-lang Ho, "The Chinese Belief in Baleful Stars," in *Facets of Taoism: Essays in Chinese Religion*, eds. Holmes Welch and Anna Seidel (New Haven: Yale University Press, 1979), 193-228.

62. Raksasi is a female anthropophagous demon in Indian religion.

63. Ann Waltner, "Infanticide and Dowry in Ming and Early Qing China," in *Chinese Views of Childhood*, ed. Anne Behnke Kinney (Honolulu: University of Hawai'i Press, 1995), 193-217.

64. See "Chongding Nanci quanpu fanli xu ji," 1a, in Shen Zijin, *Chongding Nan Jiugong cipu* (1936 Beijing University facsimile copy of 1646 edition).

65. Patrick Hanan, *The Invention of Li Yu* (Cambridge, MA: Harvard University Press, 1988), 186-87.

66. Ling Mengchu (Jikong Guan Zhuren), preface, *Pai an jing qi*, modern facsimile copy of 1628 Shangyou Tang edition (Shanghai: Guji chuban she, 1985), 3-4.

67. For a survey of literature on male homosexuality throughout Chinese history, see Bret Hinsch, *Passions of the Cut Sleeve: The Male Homosexual Tradition in China* (Berkeley: University of California Press, 1990). For a study of homo-erotic fiction in the late Ming, see Giovanni Vitiello, "Exemplary Sodomites: Male Homosexuality in Late Ming Fiction," Ph.D. diss., University of California, Berkeley, 1994.

68. Xie Zhaozhe, *Wu zazu*; Matteo Ricci, *Della entrata della Compagnia di Giesu'e Christianita' nella Cina*. See Vitiello, 51-52.

69. Vitiello, 74.

70. Sommer, *Sex, Law, and Society in Late Imperial China*, 307.

71. Ibid., 308.

72. Ching-sheng Huang, 220-36.

73. Lee Hua-yuan Mowry, *Chinese Love Stories from Ch'ing-shih*, 141.

74. For a complete translation see Mowry, 142-44.

75. Yuan Zhongdao, "Xin lü," translated by Martin Huang in *Desire and Fictional Narrative*, 11.

76. Cf. Mowry, 140-41.

77. For some good discussions of the idealized late Ming courtesan see *Writing Women in Late Imperial China*, eds. Widmer and Chang, 17-143.

78. Susan Mann, *Precious Records: Women in China's Long Eighteenth Century* (Stanford: Stanford University Press, 1997), 121-42.

79. Allan H. Barr, "Jiang Yingke's Place in the Gong'an School," *Ming Studies* 45-46 (2002): 42.

80. This is exactly what happened to the Japanese novelist Ihara Saikaku's (1642-1693) hero Seijuro, who survived his chivalrous courtesan lover Minakawa in "The Story of Seijuro in Himeji." Minakawa's death did not seem to cast a significant

influence on Seijuro, whose love story actually did not start until after Minakawa's death. For the story see Wm. Theodore de Bary, trans., *Five Women Who Loved Love* (Rutland, Vermont: Charles E. Tuttle, 1956), 41-72.

81. Pi-ching Hsu, "Courtesans and Scholars in the Writings of Feng Menglong."

82. For a study of the "guilt" versus "shame" society in late imperial China, see Paolo Santangelo, "Human Conscience and Responsibility in Ming-Qing China," trans. Mark Elvin, *East Asian History* 4 (December 1992): 31-80.

83. *Analects*, 6: 23. *Gu* was a wine vessel used in the ancient ritual of communal wine-drinking. A small-sized goblet, *gu* was meant for moderate drinking in accord with ritual propriety. But people had drink excessively with the vessel. Therefore Confucius lamented that *gu* was unlike *gu*: the name and the reality were divorced.

84. For a discussion of the "mountain man syndrome" see Tsao Jr-lien, "Remembering Suzhou: Urbanism in late imperial China," Ph.D. diss., University of California, Berkeley, 1992, 34-38.

85. A marked example was Xue Gang, who wrote several essays criticizing the mountain men in his *Tianjue Tang ji*. See Chen Wanyi, *Wan Ming xiaopin yu Ming ji wenren shenghuo*, 46-47.

86. Ricci, *Chinese in the sixteenth century*, 81-82.

87. After the cultural hero Yu conquered the great floods at the dawn of Chinese history by draining, he allegedly marked out nine *zhou* (island-provinces, raised land for human inhabitation). So the term "nine provinces" refers to China.

88. Keith McMahon, *Causality and Containment in Seventeenth-Century Chinese Fiction* (Leiden: E. J. Brill, 1988).

89. Donald J. Munro, *Images of Human Nature: A Sung Portrait* (Princeton: Princeton University Press, 1988), 182.

90. Yang Xiang is one of the twenty-four exemplars of filial piety. Her story appears in the Six Dynasties text *Yi Yuan* (Garden of Strange Tales).

91. Feeling ashamed, King Jing confined himself in the palace, refusing to hold an audience at court. At the request of his witty courtier Yan Zi, however, the king awarded the gatekeeper by doubling his salary, exempting his tax, and allowing him to go to court anytime he wanted. The story appears in *Yan Zi*, section *Nei pian*, *Za*, *Shang*. See Wang Gengsheng, ed., *Yan Zi Chun Qiu jinzhu jinyi* (Taipei: Commercial Press, 1987), 229-30.

92. C. T. Hsia, *The Classic Chinese Novel* (New York: Columbia University Press, 1968), 311, 316.

93. Ibid., 315.

94. Chen Jiru, *Chen Meigong xiansheng quanji* (microfilm of Ming edition in the National Central Library, Taiwan), 4: 37a. Translated by Allan H. Barr in idem, "The Wanli Context of the 'Courtesan's Jewel Box' Story," *Harvard Journal of Asiatic Studies* 57, no. 1 (1997): 110.

95. Cf. translation by Cyril Birch, *Stories from a Ming Collection*, 29.

96. Feng's Preface to *Qingshi*, 4a-b. Translation modified from Mowry, 13.

97. Feng's Preface to *Qingshi*, 1b-2a.

98. Feng's Preface to *Qingshi*, 4b-5a. Translation modified from Mowry, 13.

99. Epstein, *Competing Discourses*, 113.

100. Cynthia J. Brokaw, *The Ledgers of Merit and Demerit: Social Change and Moral Order in Late Imperial China* (Princeton: Princeton University Press, 1991).

# 4

# *Treasury of Laughs:*
## Humorous Satire with a Philosophical Undertone

## 笑府

> From past to present all is but talk, and all talk is but laughs. The birth of yin and yang from the original chaos, the voluntary abdication and forceful overthrow of the sage kings—who's ever witnessed this sort of thing? It's nothing more than talk. Future generations will talk about our generation, just as our generation talks about past generations. To talk about something and doubt it is laughable; to talk about something and believe it is even more laughable. Classics, philosophy, and histories are nonsensical talk, and people compete to transmit them. Poetry, rhapsody, and prose are preposterous talk, and people compete to perfect them. Praise or sneers, advocacy or suppression—these are whimsical talk, and people compete to respond to them. Sometimes we laugh at others; other times we are laughed at. Those who laugh at others are in turn laughed at by others. How is there an end to such a cycle of laughter? *The Treasury of Laughs* is a collection of jokes. With all its thirteen chapters, some may still say it's a thin book. If you read it and are delighted by it, please don't be. If you read it and are enraged by it, please don't be. The world from past to present is an immense treasury of laughs; you and I are all in there as laughingstocks. Without talk there're no human beings. Without laughs there's no talk. Without laughs and talk there's no world. Cloth-Sack Monk, you're my master, you're my master.
>
> —Feng Menglong, preface to *Xiaofu*[1]

Cloth-Sack Monk was a tenth-century Chinese eccentric monk who was believed to be a reincarnation of Maitreya, the Buddha of Future. Storing the alms he collected in a cloth sack, this round-bellied, nonsense-talking madman seemed an unlikely prophet, but prophet he was. Invoking Cloth-Sack Monk in the preface to the *Treasury of Laughs* served several purposes. Feng Menglong compared the content of his book to food refuse he collected. Since he was merely a collector, and not the original creator, he was not to be held responsible for the slightly subversive content. Indeed, no original creators of jokes could be identified in the late Ming, because joke books borrowed so heavily from one another. Such practice held the danger of censorship at bay. Meanwhile, Feng was also talking to the "in-group" about the "real" meaning of the compilation. The content might be rejected by straight-faced intellectuals as frivolous, but it was actually good food for thought. The fact that Cloth-Sack Monk was a nonsense-talking prophet implied that this collection was a playful work with a serious intent. Playfulness and seriousness were not mutually exclusive; they were two sides of a coin. The subtlest truth had to be delivered in a hidden message, rather than in the straightforward mode of "serious" utterances. In lieu of this humorous attitude toward the Truth, dogmatic Chinese scholars' attachment to canonized texts and classical genres, their taking "serious" literary endeavor as a vehicle for success in the civil service examinations, and the process whereby such foolishness was transmitted in the Chinese cultural tradition seemed "laughable" indeed.

Lurking beneath the hyperbolic tone of the preface to the *Treasury of Laughs* was an iconoclasm influenced by Li Zhi's theory on the "child-like mind." As discussed before, Li Zhi argued that pursuing "acquired"—as opposed to "innate"—knowledge, conforming to social decorum, and fishing for fine reputation could corrupt one's innocent and instinctive "childlike mind."[2] Here Feng Menglong also hinted that the "orthodox" grooming discouraged critical thinking and spontaneous creativity. Perhaps more to the fore in the preface was a professional writer's apologia in protest against the accepted binary opposition between elite, written, hence more reliable and respectable, literature, and its oral, popular counterpart.

Feng's deconstruction of the oral-literary dichotomy made good sense in the historical context of the rise of Ming vernacular literature. According to Liangyan Ge, an oral-literary reciprocation can be observed in the Ming: "A written version at a certain point of the evolutionary process was the destination of a textualizing movement as well as the starting point for another oralizing movement. It was both prior and posterior to oral delivery, and for that reason it could be both compositional and notational, helping to shape and also being shaped by the oral telling."[3] The relation between oral and written materials was, therefore, dynamic rather than diametrical.

The *Treasury of Laughs* contains 700-odd jokes in simple classical Chinese, a language which W. L. Idema believes to be perhaps easier to read than the vernacular and therefore accessible to a wider audience.[4] While the first two collections of *Child's Folly*, *Hanging Twigs* and *Hill Songs*, have long attracted Western scholars' attention, the *Treasury of Laughs* is among Feng Menglong's more obscure works. It has, however, received high esteem from Japanese scholars. Uemura Koji regards the *Treasury of Laughs* as the best anthology of Chinese Jokes.[5] Muto Sadao praises the anthology for presenting the whole spectrum of traditional Chinese jokes.[6] The *Treasury of Laughs* forms the basis of a Chinese joke book, *Xiaolin guangji* (*Extensive Gleanings of the Grove of Laughter*), which has enjoyed great popularity in China for more than three centuries.

The legacy of *Treasury of Laughs* can also be attested to by the fact that a recent Chinese collection of jokes narrated by a folk storyteller is entitled *Xin Xiaofu* (*New Treasury of Laughs*).[7] Although the narrator Liu Depei (b. 1912) is a semi-illiterate northerner, and his jokes do not overlap with those in the *Treasury of Laughs*, we can discern a thematic continuation to justify the similar titles. Incompetent officials, pedant scholars, magicless Taoist priests, deceptive matchmakers, stupid sons-in-law, and shameless braggadocios are among the common laughingstocks in the two texts separated by time, space, and backgrounds of the collectors. But to historians, the "particulars" are probably of more interest than the "universals." The *Treasury of Laughs* is a useful tool for historical inquiry because it offers a remarkable window on the restless social and intellectual landscape of late Ming China. Although no names are named, the caricature vividly satirizes the thoughts and deeds of Ming people from all walks of life. The commentary also reveals a great deal of Feng Menglong's thoughts. The language is highly witty and humorous, more so than that of *Hanging Twigs* and *Hill Songs*.

## Humor and Wit

The English words humor and wit are both connected with laughter and delightful surprise in their present uses, although they were not in their original meanings. "Humor" was originally a physiological term carrying the meaning of "eccentricity." The meaning of "wit" changed several times, from the earliest "knowledge" to "intellect," "the seat of consciousness," and the "inner senses" in the late Middle Ages, and to "wisdom" and "mental activity" in the Renaissance. And in seventeenth-century literary criticisms, the term "wit" was used to mean "fancy" in the sense of inspiration, originality, and creative imagination. Before 1800 both "humor" and "wit" came to be associated with the laughable, and the two terms became less distinguishable.[8] But differences between the two are recognized to exist. Wit "implies intellectual brilliance and quickness in perception combined with a gift for expressing ideas in an entertaining, often laughter provoking, pointed way, usually connoting the unexpected or apt turn of phrase or idea and often suggesting a certain brittle unfeelingness." Humor, in comparison, "can signify a disposition to see the ludicrous, comical, ridiculous, or absurd or to give it expression or can apply to the expression itself, often suggesting a generalness or a greater kindliness or sympathy with human failings than does wit."[9] While wit and humor are both faculties which enable a person to perceive the incongruities of ideas, speeches, circumstances, characters, and so on, and to express the perception in a laughter-provoking manner, wit is comparatively more playful, sharper, and humor is more sympathetic, gentler. Wit is from the mind, and humor is from the heart.

Feng Menglong produced three compilations on humor and wit. In addition to *Treasury of Laughs*, he compiled an anthology of comic anecdotes in classical language, entitled *Gujin tan gai* (*Survey of Talk Old and New*). Most anecdotes in the *Survey of Talk* are collected from existing *biji* (note-form literature) about famous historical figures. The book also contains contemporary anecdotes, some of which Feng claims to have collected from personal sources. Human folly is a distinctive theme; the folly of "Confucian dogma and obscurantism" is a prominent target. But also can be seen in the *Survey of Talk* are positive qualities which Feng admires, such as "eccentricities of genius," "wit in action," "gallantry," and "magnanimity."[10]

Another text by Feng, entitled *Zhi nang* (*Sack of Wisdom*), is satire of a different kind. It is witty, but not funny or humorous; it has a solemn purpose. As Patrick Hanan points out, the main theme of the *Sack of Wisdom* is "applied intelligence."[11] And it may not be far-fetched to say that the book is about the wisdom of the Huang-Lao Taoist type—the alleged strategies of Huang Di, the Yellow Emperor, and Lao Zi, the founder of philosophical Taoism, which emphasize timeliness and expediency. Feng argues that practical problems require practical solutions; to arrive at practical solutions we need to use our faculty of intelligence smartly; and to use our faculty of intelligence smartly we need to study history comprehensively, to learn from the success and failure of historical precedents.[12] Therefore irrationality and inflexibility on the part of some scholar-officials in charge of public affairs are the main targets of ridicule in the *Sack of Wisdom*, and Feng makes his point using historical sources in the classical language.

*Treasury of Laughs* is a light-hearted jest-book. It is satirical and philosophical, but it is also hilariously funny. The humor might well get in the way of the more serious intent, should the reader be less sensitive. *Survey of Talk* and *Sack of Wisdom*, on the other hand, are more formal and serious in both form and content. Before analyzing *Treasury of Laughs*, the earliest and funniest of the three witty and humorous compilations, a quick look at *Survey of Talk* and *Sack of Wisdom* will give a more complete picture of Feng Menglong's treatment of humor and wit.

## *Survey of Talk*

The *Survey of Talk* first appeared in 1620 under the title *Gujin xiao* (Jokes Old and New), and was probably not widely circulated.[13] The Macheng scholar Mei Zhiyun encouraged Feng to publish it, and Feng did that under the title *Gujin tan gai* (*Survey of Talk Old and New*). The same text was later reissued as *Gujin tan* (*Talk Old and New*), and then *Gujin xiaoshi* (*History of Jokes Old and New*); the latter, with the renowned playwright and novelist Li Yu's preface, sold well.

According to an anonymous preface to *Gujin xiao*, the book was put together by members of the literary society which Feng organized, Yun She. Feng was quoted as saying that laughter could enlarge one's vision and open up one's mind—it was a cure for obscurantism.[14] Patrick Hanan points out that the compilation belongs to the tradition of Liu Yiqing's celebrated *Shishuo xinyu* (*New Account of Tales of the World*) and has close connections with Li Zhi's *Chutan ji* (*Collection of First Pond*) and Xu Zichang's *Pengfu bian* (*Side Splitting Laughter*).[15] Unique personalities and human folly and vice were the main themes of literature in this tradition. Mei Zhiyun stated in his preface to the *Survey of Talk*:

> If a gentleman has his ambition fulfilled, then he can put his ideas into action; if not, then he can only express his ideas in words. Lao Zi says that subtle talk can resolve disputes.[16] But talking is not easy. If you did not have knowledge you would not be competent to talk. If you did not have insight you would not be able to talk. If you did not have courage you would not dare to talk. If you did not have complaints that accumulate in your bosom, which you could find no other ways to vent, then you would not want to talk.[17]

This explains in a nutshell the nature of the *Survey of Talk*. Some entries demonstrated the contributors' knowledge of the material on humor and wit. Others demonstrated the contributors' courage to criticize the intellectual and social phenomena that vexed them. Still others demonstrated the contributors' intelligence in valuing certain human faculties that would help solving contemporary problems.

Not all thirty-six chapters of the *Survey of Talk* are satirical. A glance at the titles of the chapters reveals that the *Survey of Talk* was an encyclopaedia of humor and wit of varied kinds. The chapters are: (1) Obscurantism, (2) Oddity, (3) Craziness, (4) Foolishness, (5) Misunderstanding, (6) Half-Baked Knowledge, (7) Bitter Sea (Poetic Lines Painfully Acquired), (8) Bad Poetry, (9) Obsession, (10) Transcendence of Petty Emotions, (11) Gallantry and Magnanimity, (12) Arrogance, (13) Stinginess, (14) Extravagance, (15) Greed, (16) Tolerance, (17) Love of Beauty, (18) Face, (19) Female Lewdness, (20) Physical Deficiencies, (21) Wiles, (22) Mischief, (23) Wit, (24) Mockery, (25) Linguistic Confrontation, (26) Graceful Sarcasm, (27) Play on Words, (28) Smart Talk, (29) Riddles, (30) Subtle Words, (31) Public Opinion, (32) Miracles, (33) Absurdity, (34) Demons and Extraordinary Phenomena, (35) Non-Human Species, (36) Miscellany.

We would be disappointed if we are looking for a moral lesson in each anecdote, because many of the anecdotes do not seem to have an explicit moral meaning. Their presence in the *Survey of Talk*, rather, showed the inclusive nature of Feng's selection. But in general, we do see an implicit theme underlying the compilation: a revival of the Six Dynasties spirit of admiration for eccentricity and individual freedom, accompanied by a critical attitude toward hackneyed scholarship and rigid modes of behavior in the name of moderation during the late Ming.

### *Sack of Wisdom*

The *Sack of Wisdom* was published in 1626, based on the *Zhi pin* (*Classification of Wisdom*) compiled by an obscure writer named Fan Yuchong and commented on by his brother.[18] As Patrick Hanan points out, Feng's work overshadowed that of his predecessor. While Feng reissued the *Sack of Wisdom* in expanded form (*Zhi nang bu*) in 1634, Fan's text, which was much less lively and interesting, was never reprinted.[19]

In the *Sack of Wisdom*, Feng Menglong continued his attack on hackneyed scholarship and rigid conventions, but not in the vein of "individualism" or "romanticism," as in the *Survey of Talk*. Successful management of public affairs with the aid of individuals' applied intelligence was the overwhelming theme in the *Sack of Wisdom*. Feng advised that substance and trivia be distinguished, the former taking priority over the latter. For example, for the sake of social or national well-being, personal moral integrity might be sacrificed. To carry out effective government, established practices and judicial conventions might be neglected. For Feng, freedom of individual judgment should be allowed when the situation called for expedient action, and each particular situation called for different expedient action: there was no fixed strategy, and there was also no fixed principle.

Feng Menglong seemed to come very close to saying that the end justifies the means when he stated, "Even crafty tacticians, cunning scoundrels, bandits, and thieves can be the saltpeter and spears in my medicine basket. . . . This can be compared to the grand valley, into which all waters flow. The valley does not choose which waters to receive, does it?"[20] The grand valley was Lao Zi's metaphor. In Lao Zi's *Daodejing* (*The Way and Its Power*) it is stated,

> He who knows glory but keeps to disgrace,
> Becomes the valley of the world.
> Being the valley of the world,
> He finds contentment in constant virtue,
> He returns to the uncarved block [the original state of complete simplicity].
> The cutting up of the uncarved block results in vessels,
> Which, in the hands of the sage, become officers.
> Truly, "A great cutter does not cut."[21]

A Confucian sage distinguished between high and low, glory and disgrace, but a Taoist wise man did not. He was inclusive, undifferentiated, and paradoxical. By lying low, he received more; by yielding, he gained.

The valley in the *Daodejing* helps explain Feng's metaphor of the "grand valley." His "valley" was more than inclusive, undifferentiated, and paradoxical. It was almost amoral. But one cannot conclude that Feng was a moral relativist deprived of any principle. He was mildly Machiavellian. A statement in his preface to the *Sack of Wisdom* helps make this clear: "Wisdom is to mankind as water is to land. Without water the land becomes badlands; without wisdom the man becomes a walking corpse. Wisdom is used by mankind in the manner water travels over the land. When there is a cavity in the land, water fills it; when there is a cavity in human affairs, wisdom fills it."[22] From this context it can be inferred that the *Sack of Wisdom* is applicable only when the world is imperfect. If there were no "cavity" in human affairs, there would be no use for the kind of "wisdom," or "applied intelligence," depicted in the book. The end did not always justify the means; expediency was to be employed only under extraordinary circumstances.

Feng classified "applied intelligence" into ten categories, which he then divided into twenty-eight sub-categories. They are:

1. Supreme Intelligence:
   Wide View, Far Sight, Penetrative Insight, Easy Maneuver
2. Enlightened Intelligence:
   Perceiving Incipiency, Speculating Keys, Investigating Doubts, Managing Affairs
3. Perceptive Intelligence:
   Getting at the True Situation, Interrogating Cunning Criminals
4. Bold Intelligence:
   Triumph of Force, Solution by Discernment
5. Quick Wit:
   Sudden Inspirations, Excellent Responses, Sharp Understanding
6. Tactical Intelligence:
   Pretending Politeness and Compliance, Making Up Stories, Taking Expedient Action
7. Linguistic Intelligence:
   Silver Tongue, Eloquent Talk
8. Military Intelligence:
   Winning Without Fighting, Defeating by a Surprise Move, Taking a Surreptitious Route, Employing Strategy
9. Female Intelligence:
   The Wise and Virtuous, The Heroic and Tactical
10. Miscellaneous Intelligence:
    Crafty Cunningness, Petty Tricks.

Feng did not reorganize his entries into different categories in his expanded editions *Zhi nang bu* and *Zengguang Zhi nang bu*; he just added more anecdotes. But the emphasis seemed to shift a bit with the expanded editions: instead of stressing the freedom of individual judgment Feng now stressed the stern measures that were needed to preserve governmental control. As Patrick Hanan points out, the shift of emphasis was related to the historical change that was happening in Ming society: Feng supplemented his *Sack of Wisdom* in a period that saw the start of the devastating rebellions.[23] It is clear that Feng was attentive to the times.

### *Treasury of Laughs*

Feng Menglong evidently made use of existing texts from the Ming and previous dynasties when compiling *Treasury of Laughs*. Among his sources from previous dynasties are *Shishuo xinyu* (*New Account of Tales of the World*) by Liu Yiqing of the Six Dynasties, *Qiyan lu* (*Record of Glee*) attributed to Hou Bai of the Sui dynasty, several Song texts including *Ai Zi zashuo* (*Miscellaneous Tales of Master Ai*) attributed to Su Shi, *Zuiweng tanlu* (*Talks of a Drunkard*) by Luo Ye, *Jichuan xiaolin* (*Grove of Laughter by the River Ji*) by a Master Lu, *Taiping guangji* (*Extensive Gleanings of the Reign of Great Tranquility*) by Li Fang, and *Fuzhang lu* (*Applause Winners*) by Xing Jushi, as well as a Yuan text *Shilin guangji* (*Miscellany of the Scholars*). He also consulted Ming volumes such as Geng Dingxiang's *Quanzi* (*Master of Expediency*), Li Zhi's *Shanzhong yixi hua* (*A Night's Conversations in the Mountain*), Lu Zhuo's *Ai Zi houyu* (*Addendum to the Tales of Master Ai*), Liu Yuanqing's *Yingxielu* (*A Record of the Jocular*), Guo Zizhang's *Xieyu* (*Jocular Talk*), Zhong Xing's (1574-1624) *Xiecong* (*A Collection of the Jocular*), Zhao Nanxing's *Xiaozan* (*In Praise of Laughter*), Jiang Yingke's *Tanyan* (*Gossipy Utterances*), *Xuetao xiaoshuo* (*Petty Talk of Snow Wave*), and *Xuetao xieshi* (*History of Humor of Snow Wave*),[24] Li Zhi's (attributed) *Sishu xiao* (*Jokes on the Four Books*), and the anonymous *Xiaolin ping* (*Commentary on the Glove of Laughter*, preface dated 1611). According to Patrick Hanan, *Treasury of Laughs* drew heavily on the joke section in Deng Zhimo's *Xianxian pian* (*A Book Respectfully Compiled*).[25]

Concerning his source materials, Feng Menglong only mentioned Hulu Sheng (*Xiaofu*, 13: 3b), Zhizhi Sheng (*Xiaofu*, 5: 4a-b), and *Xiaolin ping* (*Xiaofu*, 8: 22b, 13: 13a) by name, and cited variant versions of his jokes or "old jokes" without acknowledging the sources. Many of the jokes in the *Treasury of Laughs* were later copied verbatim into popular joke books in the late Ming, such as Fubai zhuren's *Xiaolin* (*Grove of Laughter*) and Zuiyue Zi's *Jingxuan yaxiao* (*Select Collection of Elegant Jokes*), and in the Qing, such as Chen Gaomo's *Xiaodao* (*Bowled Over with Laughter*, 1718) and Shi Chengjin's *Xiao de hao* (*Have a Good Laugh*, 1739).[26] The *Treasury of Laughs* was also adapted by a certain Youxi Daoren (The Playful Taoist) for his *Xiaolin guangji* (*Extensive Gleanings of the Grove of Laughter*), which is still popular today.[27] In the absence of copyright protection and backed up by convention of anonymity, producers of popular literature freely copied one another, perhaps with little knowledge of and little concern about the identity of the original authors. Besides written sources, Feng noted that some jokes in the *Treasury of Laughs* were collected from oral sources, for example, contemporary hearsay (*Xiaofu*, 1: 2a; 3: 9a-b) and popular jokes circulated in the pleasure quarters (*Xiaofu*, 13: 7a-b).

Despite the inclusion of old jokes from previous times, the *Treasury of Laughs* was still an accurate reflection on Ming society and Ming tastes. Feng Menglong was a seasoned compiler who would not have incorporated jokes that were once funny but did not appeal to the Ming audience. For example, he included several jokes on henpecked husbands and shrewish wives from the *Shishuo xinyu*, but not the jokes on social caste from the same collection.

Jokes and parables were as old as philosophical discourse in Chinese history. As mentioned before, many Warring States (403-221 BC) philosophers such as Mencius, Zhuang Zi, and Han Fei Zi used jokes and parables to express their philosophical ideas. Even their predecessor, the deadly serious Confucius, was at times humorous. George Kao observes that all ancient Chinese philosophers "sought with varying degrees of success to make their moral teachings more palatable by clothing them in the guise of a parable or a fable. It was really more wit than humor, but it was the first time anything that came close to being funny was set down in Chinese writings."[28] Kao further expounds that Chinese humor "sees the ludicrous in the pathos of life. It is the result of a philosophical reaction to adversity coupled with innate optimism about the future."[29] The philosophers bumped along in their journeys but managed not to lose their hope for a better future, and the spirit showed in their writings.

The earliest Chinese text that can be properly termed a jest-book may be *The Grove of Laughs* (*Xiaolin*) compiled by Handan Chun in the state of Wei during the Three Kingdoms period (AD 220-265). Since then, numerous jest-books turned up on the market through the ages. Originally "a verbal mini-art form designed to produce laughter," a jest is "concerned with the accidents and stresses of ordinary life. It is a brief narrative of some piquant reversal or incongruity or smart reply embodying such, appealing to a group of people of similar tastes."[30] According to Derek Brewer, jests tend to be exclusive and politically incorrect; they promote humor and harmony of a group at the expense of "outsiders" such as women, ethnic minorities, disabled people, economic predator, and political oppressors. While the recorded form puts a jest out of context and "deprives it of much of its emotional power, of the privilege and protection of the in-group," it can be historically studied as an index of the culture of humor in a society.[31]

Despite their piquancy, Lu Yunzhong discerns a humanistic touch in Chinese jest-books:

> Writers of humorous stories in ancient China were noted for the sharpness of their observation, the trenchancy of their social criticism and the depth of their concern for human suffering. As to artistic form and technique of expression, they were adept at grasping typical cases and refining the literary raw material gathered from life. In the process of creative writing, they gave full play to their imagination; yet their negative characters, though usually made to look exceptionally stupid and clumsy, were nevertheless true to type. These characters, moreover, were so shown and so brought into action that as little as possible of them had gone to waste. With simple, light touches and in a succinct style, the writers of humorous stories laid bare the true features of certain great personages—hypocrisy, pedantry, avarice, ignorance, incompetence, deceit, indolence, etc and past personages were often used to disparage their present-day counterparts. Therefore, as the writers jibed at the heartless rich and the venal officials, some of us, perhaps, may have the feelings that their thrusts have been directed at them.[32]

In the Ming, many renowned scholars wrote jest-books to satirize laughable phenomena in the world around them, to offer humorous observations on human nature and human relationships, or simply to show off their wit and ability to entertain their audiences. They included such high-profile writers as Xu Wei, Li Zhi, Jiang Yingke, Zhong Xing, and the Donglin party member Zhao Nanxing.[33] Jiang Yingke defended the writing and reading of jokes in his preface to *Xiaolin* (*Grove of Laughter*), "Monks do not use combs, but the world at large does not discard hairbrushes; amputees do not wear shoes, but society does not renounce footwear."[34] In other words, if "orthodox" intellectuals were too lofty to read jokes, that was their choice—and it was not a very popular one.

Sometimes joke-tellers could be carried away and become caustic and offensive. In response to this, the dramatist and literary critic Tu Long (1542-1605) warned, "To be good at satire, fond of humor, and to use off-color language for the sake of entertaining is not terribly harmful. But to reveal others' hidden secrets and discourse on others' personal affairs is not kind. Such deeds result in the accumulation of the teller's faults and the reduction of the teller's blessing; they should be avoided."[35] Tu Long died before the publication of the *Treasury of Laughs*, so his comment was not aimed at this particular work. Certain language in the *Treasury of Laughs* was indeed off-color and offensive; for example, many sex jokes demonized women and homosexual people, and other jokes poked fun at mental and physical handicaps. But against the standards of popular literature in Ming China, Feng Menglong's satire was relatively mild; the bulk of it was neither personal nor malicious, and since it covered a lot of ground, it did not target a specific group.

Feng Menglong divided the seven-hundred-odd jokes in the *Treasury of Laughs* into thirteen categories.[36] They were:

1. Age-Old Envy (The Rich and Powerful)
2. Rotten Scholars
3. The Untouchable
4. Occultism and Medicine
5. Monks, Priests, and Miscellaneous Occupations
6. Extraordinary Faculties
7. Petty Sport (Whoring and Gambling)
8. Vulgarity
9. Sexually Sophisticated Women
10. Body Parts
11. Funny Mistakes
12. Daily Necessities
13. Intercalary Words (Miscellany).

Feng opened each chapter with a short, witty essay, and attached comments or explanatory notes to some entries, although it is not always clear whether these comments and notes were Feng's own writings or those of the original editors of his sources.

In the *Guang Xiaofu* (*Expanded Treasury of Laughs*) Feng (or a later editor)[37] added some new jokes, deleted some old ones, modified a few entries, and reorganized them into the following new categories:

1. Scholars
2. Officials
3. Physicians and Diviners
4. Monks and Priests
5. Appetite for Food
6. Romantic Feelings
7. Greed
8. Temper
9. Obstinacy
10. Sarcasm
11. Remonstration
12. Body Parts
13. Miscellany

14. Appendix (Riddles).

The Shanghai 1935 edition of the *Expanded Treasury of Laughs* has a preface basically the same as that of the *Treasury of Laughs*, except for a short passage elaborating on the vanity of the sages' teachings inserted before the sentence "The world from past to present is an immense treasury of laughs." The copy does not contain any prefatory essays or comments. It is unclear how faithful a reproduction of the Ming original this edition is. Judging from the available copies of *Treasury of Laughs* and *Expanded Treasury of Laughs*, the chapter titles of the *Expanded Treasury of Laughs* are more reader-friendly than the *Treasury of Laughs*, and so are the jokes. The language of *Expanded* is livelier and more comprehensible to general audiences. But the historical values of *Expanded* are reduced, with the omission of prefatory essays, comments, and jokes that are heavily loaded with social and political criticisms. The text of *Expanded* is also cleansed of eroticism. Patrick Hanan doubts that the *Expanded Treasury of Laughs* is Feng's work.[38] Therefore I will focus my discussions on the *Treasury of Laughs*, and cite the *Expanded Treasury of Laughs* only as a supplement.

## Jokes and Analyses

In this section I will translate and analyze selected entries from the *Treasury of Laughs* and occasionally, the *Expanded Treasury of Laughs*, that offer insights to the historical context of late Ming China and are still funny in modern English. In order not to lose the humor of the original entries, I do a faithful, but not necessarily literal rendering in my translation. The colloquial touch to my translation might be achieved slightly at the expense of the classical elegance of the original text. My defense for twice removing the text from its original form is that as a historian, my primary concern is to represent the historical material in such a way as to reconstruct "the content and expression of the argument or narrative during the time of its consumption."[39] The original text, written in simple classical Chinese, was not a mimesis of the colloquial language used by Ming Chinese on a daily basis. But as Idema has suggested, for the Ming readers who had been trained to read classical Chinese since childhood, simple classical Chinese, such as that of the *Treasury of Laughs*, might be even easier to read than the unfamiliar, Mandarin-based vernacular language that Feng Menglong employed for his short stories. For that reason, although it might be more gracious to translate these sixteenth-century Chinese jokes into, say, Shakespearian English, I will represent the jokes in casual modern English. Such strategy, I believe, might be the best way to appreciate the humor of this historical text.

I divide the jokes into ten categories for analytical purposes. Because the titles of the jokes vary slightly in different editions, I do not include them in my translation.

### *1. The Ruling Class:*

In a non-aristocratic society such as the Ming, officials and officers were not nobility. They were nonetheless a privileged class above the common people, sometimes even above the law. *Treasury of Laughs* contained some jokes in which the lofty ruling class was brought low to be ridiculed. But behind the laughter was a cruel reality: historians know all too well the corruption, ineptitude, and incompetence of the ruling class in the late Ming.

> An official is having a birthday. Learning that he was born in the year of the rat, his subordinates each contribute some gold from which a full-scale rat is cast to celebrate his longevity. Much pleased, the official announces, "Did you know that the Mistress's birthday is also coming up? She was born in the year of the ox."
>
> (*Xiaofu*, 1: 6b)[40]

Rats, being sly and clever thefts of agricultural products, have since antiquity symbolized corrupt officials. Apparently not making such an unpleasant connection, the official in the joke not only gladly accepted the gift but also implied that he could accommodate an even bigger one. Mencius distinguished the noble-minded gentlemen from the self-serving people of mercantile mentality by the former's pursuit of righteousness and the latter's pursuit of profit. In the late Ming, with the exception of some incorruptible officials, most notably Hai Rui (1513-1587), who internalized the Mencian distinction perhaps overly rigorously, the opportunity to make profit seemed a stronger motivation for men to enter officialdom than the opportunity to uphold righteousness. Hence the contemptuous discourse on the "mercantile officials." The above joke was on the greed of such an official.

But the "corruption" of Ming officials was not totally unjustifiable. Given the meager salaries and public funds the officials received, soliciting unwilling contributions was a fund-raising resort, almost a necessary evil, that was routinely practiced at all levels of Ming bureaucracy. To cope with this embarrassing situation, in the next dynasty, the Manchu emperor Yongzheng (r. 1723-1735) was to carry out a fiscal reform. A tax surcharge was openly levied partly to award the officials as "money to nourish honesty" and partly to fund local works.[41] Even the emperor acknowledged that honesty was hard to nourish without money.

> An official is looking for a cool location for the summer retreat, about which his subordinates confer enthusiastically. One suggests a secluded and elegant mountain resort. Another suggests a clean and unfrequented temple. Finally an elder announces, "Nowhere is cooler than this very Court." The official asks what he means. He answers, "This place has sky but it has no sun!"
>
> (*Xiaofu*, 1: 7b-8a)

A local official, who was in charge of both administration and justice, was expected to be fair and judicious. Therefore he was called the Lord of the Azure Sky, a human replica of the azure sky god, who, being clear and bright, is the moral judge of people. But when the sky was not brightened up by the sun, which would indicate the absence of the azure sky god, the world under it was understandably gloomy.

The following are a few examples of satirical courtroom drama in the gloomy world of Ming justice:

> As the judge is hearing a case, somebody lets out gas. The judge demands that the source of the noise be brought to him, but is informed by the runner that the task cannot be done. The judge insists, "No cheating! You have to catch the suspect!" The runner wraps up some excrement in a piece of paper, and reports to the judge, "The prime suspect is on the loose. I have hereupon captured his relative."
>
> (*Xiaofu*, 3: 19b)

Despite its unpleasant connotations, gas makes frequent appearances in jest-books. The popularity of flatulence in the jokes might have to do with the generic nature of jokes as a lower form of literature. Gas comes from the lower body and goes into lower literature. The inclusion of such jokes enhances the folkloric touches of the *Treasury of Laughs*. It serves the same function as the bawdy language in some of the more obscene entries in *Hanging Twigs* and *Hill Songs*. But gas is not the focal point of the above joke. The joke hints at the practice of arresting the prime suspect's families when the suspect could not be apprehended. This would have been a violation of human rights today, but it was accepted in Ming China as a means to entice the suspect to surrender to the authorities.

> A man sues somebody for allegedly biting off his ear. The defendant argues, "The plaintiff bit off his own ear. This has nothing to do with me." Behind the judge's seat, the functionary clutches his own ear and turns round and round. The judge senses the motion, turns his head, and shouts at the functionary, "What kind of courtroom manners is this?" The functionary rejoins, "I am doing the fact-finding here, Sir."
>
> (*Xiaofu*, 3: 17a)

The judge did not seem to have a clue that it was physically impossible for a person to bite off his own ear. So the functionary volunteered a hint, which the judge apparently failed to get.

> A man commits a crime and is sentenced to be beaten. He pays his neighbor two *qian* (a *qian* is one-tenth of a tael) of silver to take his place. The neighbor gets the money and happily goes to court. The judge sentences him to thirty strokes. He receives only a few strokes, and already he cannot bear with the pain. So he bribes the executor with the money that he got, and receives lighter strokes for the rest of the process. When he goes home he visits his neighbor to express his gratitude. "Thank you for giving me the money, otherwise I would have been beaten to death!"
>
> (*Xiaofu*, 6: 19b)

In the twists and turns of the joke, the substitute sentence-server was smart for just one moment, that is, when he had the wit to bribe the government runner who was beating him, and to mimic the act of his "benefactor"—getting away with the punishment by using the money. Although the joke seems to be on the stupid man who, mystified by the identity of the criminal he temporarily took on, forgot that he was actually innocent, our sympathy is with him.

This joke is a humorous mask of the grim reality that the judicial system in the Ming fell a prey to money, incompetent officials, avaricious runners, and the slack and sloppy law enforcement. In the actual world of Ming China, convicted criminals were reported to employ poor people to be their replacements in court, as the court did not bother to check their identities before carrying out the punishments and closing the cases. Senior Grand Secretary Zhang Juzheng (1525-1582) noted, "sometimes taxpayers hired paupers to answer summons on their behalf, so that when the latter were flogged by the magistrate for delinquency, the former could let their payments lag further behind."[42] Money indeed talks!

Although the stupid victim in the above joke ended up losing all the money he had gotten for serving the sentence on another person's behalf, he at least got out of the courtroom alive. The victims in the next two jokes were not so lucky:

> A country bumpkin accepts the monetary reward offered by a capital criminal, and takes the criminal's place to be tied up and brought to court. The judge presiding at the court quickly passes on him the sentence of decapitation. The bumpkin's wife and children circle around him, crying, and complain that he shouldn't have craved the money, and now, as a result, he is going to lose his life. To comfort his family, the country bumpkin tells them, "I've learned my lesson. Surely I've suffered a loss of my capital in this transaction. But this will be the only time. I won't do it again, I promise!"
>
> (*Xiaofu*, 6: 19b)

> A man who committed a capital crime coaxes a villager into taking his identity. The villager receives a sentence to be sent to the gallows. While in jail, he sighs, "During this busy agricultural season, how can they sentence me to this 'gallows' thing? I wonder when I'll get to come to the gallows? Damned! Why couldn't they just put me on the gallows now and get it over with! I've got to go home and transplant the rice seedlings!"
>
> (*Xiaofu*, 6: 19b-20a)

It is hilarious that the last two bumpkins seemed not to have the dimmest idea that they would not survive their capital punishments. But the sorry human tragedy awaiting the dupes makes one wonder how the Ming audience could appreciate such dark humor. Henry Wells observes that because of the strong moral sense of Chinese writers, "in traditional Chinese fiction skies are often threatening and dark. Tales are sharply bitter; at least the bitterness remains sufficiently strong to repress the quality that Westerners are accustomed to consider humor."[43] The dark humor in the last jokes may be too wry for modern Chinese readers as well.

> An assistant to the magistrate is illiterate. For the sake of bookkeeping, whenever he makes a purchase he draws a picture of it in his account book. One day the magistrate comes on a tour of inspection. As the assistant has just stepped out, the magistrate casually flips through the account book. Disliking how the bookkeeping is done, he strikes out the pictures with lines of red ink. When the assistant returns and looks at the account book, he frets and fumes. "So your highness has bought

some red candles for your office. Why go recording those all over *my* account book?"

(*Xiaofu*, 1: 9a)[44]

County functionaries were generally not very well educated, but the caricature of an *illiterate* county functionary perhaps revealed more the low social esteem of this class than their real educational levels. Hyperbolically, the assistant's complaint indicated that, without realizing the magistrate's disrespect to his bookkeeping system, he imagined his boss's bookkeeping technique to be as primitive as his.

A military officer engaged in a campaign is on the verge of losing the battle when all of a sudden a superhuman warrior joins his formation so that he ends up winning a great victory instead. The officer prostrates himself before the warrior and asks to know his name. "I am the spirit of the archery target," says the warrior. "What virtue does a humble general like me have that would induce you, O honored spirit, to trouble yourself to come to my aid?" To which the spirit replies, "I was moved by the fact that, in the past, when you practiced on the archery range, you never once wounded me with an arrow."

(*Xiaofu*, 1: 10a)[45]

If the above story were true, then generals in the late Ming must have been better archers than this one; otherwise they would have earned more victories, with the aid of the deity. The late Ming military was in a woeful condition. As Ray Huang points out, degeneration of the hereditary military households system, poor quality of the military service examination, and the subordination of the military to civil government seriously handicapped Ming China's military performance, leading to the eventual Manchu takeover.[46]

A low-ranking officer making his nightly patrol captures a man who violates the curfew. The man claims to be a student going home late from a reading group. The officer says sharply, "Since you are a student, let me give you a test." The student takes on the challenge and asks for the question. The officer thinks for a while and then gives up, shouting, "You got lucky. There's no question tonight."

(*Xiaofu*, 1: 10a-b)

Our knowledge of the student culture in the Ming makes us suspect the lucky student was more likely going home from the pleasure quarters than from a reading group. But the joke might be not so much on the guilty and lying student as on the military officer, whose illiteracy was a popular target of stock jokes on his class.

## 2. *Scholars:*

The Ming government emphasized equal opportunity in upper-class male education. Those who passed the local civil service examinations became students (*shengyuan*, more commonly called *xiucai*). The students studied in the governmental schools established in every locality and the two capitals (Beijing and Nanjing) and received a stipend while preparing for provincial and metropolitan examinations which, if passed, would qualify them for official appointments. In the beginning of the dynasty, there were about 30,000 *shengyuan* out of an approximate population of 65 million. By the end of the dynasty, the ratio increased to about 500,000 *shengyan* in a total population of 150 million. Yet the quotas for degree holders at the provincial and metropolitan levels were fixed. Therefore, the country was full of students who never became officials.[47]

These students could keep on trying their luck in the examination hall, as long as they fulfilled certain requirements. First of all, they had to maintain their student status by passing the triennial evaluation examination. Grades were given on a scale of A-F; A to E were passing grades, but "F" students would lose their student status. Only students who got an "A" or "B" would be allowed to take the qualification examination (the rest had to wait for another three years to take the next turn of examinations); a grade of "A" or "B" in the qualification examination would then qualify the students to take the provincial examination. Students who got a triennial evaluation of A-B would receive material rewards; C, neither rewards nor punishments; D, a good beating; E, a demotion.[48]

Students did not have to study at school full time in order to maintain their student status. While not taking the examinations they could take up the occupations of teachers, tutors, professional writers, and physicians, which were not highly esteemed. Or, they could become busybodies, stirring up disputes, instigating lawsuits, and leading protests. At times their action was motivated by indignation; a good example was their joint protests with the Jiangnan plebeian against the interlocking of property and privilege and the subsequent shift of tax burdens to the disenfranchised.[49] Other times their action was opportunistic, vindictive, or vicious, incurring the notoriety of troublemakers.

Besides students in the school system, there were also "junior students" (*tongsheng*) who did not go to school officially, and those who obtained student status through "protection" via their mandarin fathers, or through purchase. Regular students often looked down upon irregular students, and Feng was no exception. He included several jokes about the irregular students in the *Treasury of Laughs*.

Like Wu Jingzi's (1701-1754) novel *Rulin waishi* (*The Scholars*) (first extant edition 1803),[50] the *Treasury of Laughs* saw in the scholarly class "emotional distortions" and "bureaucratic paralysis," which sprang "from the same source."[51] It was human errors, rather than fundamental problems with the Confucian educational system itself, that caused the students' anomalous behavior. But compared with the extremely sarcastic description of scholars' moral and intellectual decay in *The Scholars*, where even the most filial son turned swindler soon after he tasted the sweetness of academic success, the satire in the *Treasury of Laughs* was a mild mixture of contempt and pity.

Despite the traditional categorization of the "four classes of people"—scholars, peasants, artisans, and merchants—Feng Menglong compared the rating of scholars in the Ming to that in the Mongol Yuan dynasty, when the status of scholars was in the ninth place, below prostitutes and above beggars (*Xiaofu*, 2: 1a). Here are some examples of the jokes about hapless scholars in the Ming:

> A student goes to the temple to do divination prior to the evaluation exam. He prays to the gods, "Please give me the super auspicious sign if I am to get an F, and the super inauspicious sign if I am to get a D." The diviner says, "Sir, you are mistaken. D only means beating [as opposed to F, which means expulsion]. How can D [instead of F] be super inauspicious?" The student says, "You don't understand. If I receive an F and get expelled, then that's the end of it. But if I receive a D, when the executioner looks at my essay, he'll definitely beat me to death!"
>
> (*Xiaofu*, 2: 5b)

> Two *xiucai* meet each other once when they receive their "grade-D" beatings. After a long while, they happen to become in-laws through the marriage of their children. [This is apparently the match-maker's, rather than the men's, arrangement.] When they meet at the wedding, the father of the bridegroom says, "I seem to remember seeing you somewhere before." The father of the bride also says, "The feeling is mutual. I just can't remember. . . ." Then they suddenly become enlightened, "Ah."
>
> (*Xiaofu*, 2: 6a)

Being beaten for bad grades is humiliating, not to mention painful. The student in the first joke is even fearful of his life! The commentary takes advantage of the comic butt with the remark, "Judging from his correct self-assessment, this must be a smart student, who regrettably is unwilling to work hard" (*Xiaofu*, 2: 5b). Writers in the Ming must have felt strongly about the scandalous "grade-D beating," judging from the frequent references to it in jokes and folksongs. But the second joke about the two—quite compatible, it turns out—in-laws probably brings a smile to the audiences' faces rather than heaping serious contempt on the two embarrassed dupes.

> A student fails the civil service exams several times. His wife, who has been experiencing difficult labor, comments, "To pass the exam is as difficult as to give birth." The student sighs, "However, you *do* have something in your belly."
>
> (*Xiaofu*, 2: 5a)

In the above joke, the early juxtaposition of the husband's struggles in the examination hall and the wife's struggles in the birthing room anticipates the wife's analogy. What is less anticipated is the punch line, the husband's candid confession that his belly—where people are supposed to store their learning—is actually empty. The *Expanded Treasury of Laughs* records a more elaborate version of the same joke:

> A *xiucai* is about to take the exams. Day and night he is apprehensive. His wife tries to console him, "I can see how excruciating it is for you to compose an essay, it's like me giving birth to a child." The husband gives a sigh, "It's actually easier for you guys to give birth." The wife asks, "How come?" The husband answers, "You have something in your belly. I don't."
>
> (*Guang Xiaofu*, 1: 14)

The above is a rare example of jokes in the *Expanded Treasury of Laughs* which seem to have been modified from the *Treasury of Laughs* originals. Most jokes in the *Expanded Treasury of Laughs* are either copied verbatim from the *Treasury of Laughs* or are brand-new additions. In this version, the wife tries to express her sympathy with her husband by making the analogy between composition/exam success and labor/childbirth, both painful and difficult. But the husband is not comforted. He dryly makes the confession that his problem lies not so much in the final stage (labor) as in the beginning stage (conception): he has no learning in his belly to be productive.

The next joke also has to do with the connection between learning and belly:

> The father of a child complains to his tutor about the poor quality of his teaching. The tutor retorts, "Do you want me and your son to both die?" The father does not understand him. The tutor explains, "I have exhausted my teaching methods, unless you want me to get into your son's belly. In that case I will be smothered to death, and your son will be glutted to death."
>
> (*Xiaofu*, 2: 15a)

The tutor would not admit that he is bad at teaching; the pupil's failure to absorb his instructions is all that is to blame. Since the child has trouble digesting what he is taught, protests the tutor, if the parent really wishes the child to have learning in his belly, the tutor himself (with his full stomach of learning) will have to enter into the pupil's belly physically.

The student would not become learned even if he has in his belly all the learning of the teacher in the next joke:

> A tutor initiates his pupil by teaching him the *Great Learning*. When he gives instructions on the sentence "Alas (*Wu hu*)! Do not forget the former kings," he mistakenly reads *wu hu* as *yu xi*, as the two characters are usually pronounced. The patriarch in the family corrects him, "You are mistaken, sir. The two characters should be read *wu hu*." The tutor complies. In the winter, they are studying an annotation to the *Analects*, "Although the exorcising dance of *no* is a ritual of ancient origin, it is close to drama (*yu xi*)." The tutor, remembering the last experience, reads *yu xi* as *wu hu*. The patriarch says, "You are mistaken again. These two words should be read *yu xi*." Greatly vexed, the tutor goes to his friend and complains, "This boss is really difficult. He's giving me a hard time over the two simple characters *yu xi* from the beginning of the year to the end of the year!"
>
> (*Xiaofu*, 2: 12b)

The grammar and lexicon of Classical Chinese are generally acknowledged to be very difficult, and, to make it even harder, some characters are not pronounced in the usual way when they carry different meanings. These are called the *po yin* (literally "broken sound") words. Even an erudite person is in danger of mispronouncing a word if it has several possible pronunciations, including some obscure ones. But the knowledge about the alterant *wu hu* and the usual *yu xi* is elementary enough to make the above tutor's mistake inexcusable. The buffoon makes a complete fool of himself when he exposes, through his complaint to the friend, that even after having been corrected twice, he still does not get it.

In addition to mispronunciation, the *Treasury of Laughs* also includes jokes on mispunctuation, misinterpretation, and misidentification of words that have similar configurations. Poking fun at the buffoons' mistakes, the jesters flaunt their own erudition, and invite the audience to join in the show of superiority by having a good laugh at the buffoons. But the jesters have to be cautious. If the mistake is too transparent, it fails to entice a substantial sense of superiority in the audience. If, on the other hand, the mistake takes too much time to figure out, it frustrates the audience. The editor therefore has to take into consideration the educational level of his prospective readership when he edits such "scholarly" jokes. Judging from the level of linguistic and textual incongruities employed in the *Treasury of Laughs*, its target readers do include people who are more than rudimentarily educated—some jokes need to be elaborately annotated before they make sense to modern readers. This brought the readers to the world of parody.

For Bakhtin, parody is a "double-voiced word," designed to be interpreted as the expression of two speakers. The author of parody appropriates the utterance of another and subverts it "by inserting a new semantic orientation into a word which already has—and retains—its own orientation."[52] In order to create a maneuverable space between the two utterances, the parodist sometimes quotes the original utterance out of context, and other times quotes it in "too much" context. Gary Morson observes,

> While the parodist's ironic quotation marks frame the linguistic form of the original utterance, they also direct attention to the occasion (more accurately, the parodist's version of the occasion) of its uttering. The parodist thereby aims to reveal the otherwise covert aspects of that occasion, including the unstated motives and assumptions of both the speaker and the assumed and presumably sympathetic audience. Unlike that audience, the audience of the parody is asked to consider why someone might make, and someone else entertain, the original utterance.[53]

Parody, therefore, could potentially target a huge portion of the scholarly class.

> A teacher dozes off during class hours. When he wakes up he tells his student, "I was dreaming of the Duke of Zhou." [The Duke of Zhou was an important figure in the formation of Chinese rituals, of whom Confucius reportedly often dreamed (*Analects*, VII.5).] The next day the student also dozes off during the class. The teacher strikes him with

a ruler and scolds him, "How could you fall asleep?" The student says, "I, too, was dreaming of the Duke of Zhou." The teacher challenges him, "Oh, really? What did the Duke of Zhou say?" "He said he did not see you yesterday," answers the student.

(*Xiaofu*, 2: 11a)

We recognize this as yet another smart student who is unwilling to work hard!

A second joke about daydreaming makes reference to the famous passage in *Analects*, V.10. Confucius' disciple Zai Yu, well known for his eloquence,[54] slept during the day. Disappointed and annoyed, Confucius compared Zai Yu to rotten wood which could not be sculptured and an efflorescent wall (*fentu zhi qiang*) which could not be painted; he did not even care to rebuke him. The phrase *fentu zhi qiang* is curious. *Fen* is manure. *Tu* is earth or dirt. Could Confucius have been so abusive as to compare his student to something as dirty and stinking as "a wall of manure"?[55] The Master would have been an overrated teacher if that were what the phrase meant. *Fentu zhi qiang* in fact refers to an earthen wall that effloresces, or changes to a whitish, mealy substance, due to the deposit of crystalline salts when moisture evaporates on the inside surface of the wall. This condition is cancerous; the health of the wall is seriously compromised. The imagery of the efflorescent wall parallels that of rotten wood. The subject might not start as bad material—people were born with innate goodness—but lamentably it has deteriorated to the extent that it cannot be treated, and has to be given up.

One wonders why Confucius was so upset by Zai Yu's sleep during the day. Did Zai Yu take an afternoon nap, which was taken by Confucius to be a sign of laziness? Did he oversleep in the morning and was late to the class? Was he caught sleeping during the Master's lecture? Or, did Confucius simply disapprove of any sleep during the daytime because it violated the rule of cosmic operation—to work as the sun rises and rest as the sun sets? The *Analects*, as usual, does not provide a clue. But regardless of the circumstances, the severity of Confucius' criticism seems to have won Zai Yu extensive sympathy among Chinese students.

So the joke goes:

Confucius berates Zai Yu with the remarks about rotten wood and efflorescent walls. Zai Yu finds this unacceptable and retorts, "I wanted to see the Duke of Zhou myself [just like you]. How could you blame me?" Confucius says, "In broad daylight is not the right time to dream of the Duke of Zhou." Zai Yu responds, "But the Duke of Zhou is also

> not the kind of person who is willing to visit in the darkness of the night."
>
> (*Xiaofu*, 2: 11a-b)

Feng Menglong was apparently unsympathetic toward Confucius in this incident when he cited in his commentary an extremely pedantic essay elaborating on the conflict between Confucius and Zai Yu (*Xiaofu*, 2: 11b-12a). The great length Confucius goes to lash at Zai Yu, who interrupts the Master's lunch with thundering snore, is hyperbolic. To make the "anti-teacher" point even clearer, Feng quoted another, much less pedantic, joke. A teacher likes to sleep in the day. His student thereupon asks the teacher, "How do you interpret the four words *Zai Yu zhou qin*?" The teacher says, "*Zai* is to kill. *Yu* is I. *Zhou* is in the middle of the day. *Qin* is to take a nap." The student asks the teacher how he is going to put this all together. The teacher answers, "Even if I am to be killed, I take no heed of what you said. I just have to take a nap in the middle of the day." (*Xiaofu*, 2: 11b)

"Dreaming of the Duke of Zhou" in class has been a popular theme of jokes in Chinese schools for centuries. Long school hours and tedious drills make it very difficult for school children to resist the summons of "the Duke of Zhou" to the dreamland. While contemporary school kids poke fun at their classmates who "dream of the Duke of Zhou" in class, interestingly, in the Ming jokes the teacher is more often the target of ridicule. The fact that comedians took so much advantage of Ming teachers might shed some light on the low social esteem of teachers in the Ming.

> In a classroom, the topic of the day is King Wen's imprisonment in Youli. Because the teacher has to leave early to answer a call, he is unable to finish the lecture. A student goes home with a heavy heart and a sorrowful countenance. A friend sees him on the road and asks him why he looks so sad. The student answers, "This morning my teacher lectured on the great sage, King Wen. He is thrown in jail by the tyrant Zhou. I pity him, for he's innocent." The friend comforts him. "King Wen would be released soon. He was not to grow old in prison." "I am not worried that he will not be released. I am just worried that he will have a hard time tonight in jail."
>
> (*Xiaofu*, 6: 7b)

The Grand Historian Sima Qian saw the imprisonment of King Wen as a moment of crisis that engendered his "frustrated energy." When his pent-up frustration was suddenly released in writing, it was transformed into turbulent literary creativity. The end product was the fantastic *Book of Changes*.[56] In Sima Qian's re-creation, the tragic element of King Wen's imprisonment was significantly toned down by the happy ending. But the student in the above joke had a more mundane response to King Wen's crisis. Confusing historical time and contemporary time, the student treated King Wen's imprisonment as a "current" affair, literally, and the teacher's early departure from the classroom suspended King Wen's release.

The satire on poorly equipped students and teachers reflects an objective reality: many students and teachers in the late Ming were indeed under-educated and/or not serious about education, a phenomenon that alarmed quite a few scholars and officials.[57] The satire might also project Feng's self-image: being a student and tutor forever, Feng might have wanted to distinguish himself, an unrecognized rather than unqualified candidate for an examination degree, from his truly inferior colleagues by including such jokes.

But Feng did have sympathy for his unfortunate peers. In a joke of black humor, a rich man asked an impoverished scholar to give his newborn son a name. The son, named "Gold Boy," soon died. The rich man then had a second son, whom the scholar named "Silver Boy." But the baby also died. The third time around, the rich man begged the poor scholar to name his son after something that was cheap but lasting, and the scholar named the baby "Professor" (*Xiaofu*, 2: 16b). Many of us can probably relate to the joke!

### *3. Fake Neo-Confucian Moralists:*

Feng Menglong made a distinction between true Neo-Confucian moralists (*zhen dao xue*) and fake Neo-Confucian moralists (*jia dao xue*). While expressing due respect to true Neo-Confucian moralists, whose words and deeds complied with the essence of moral principle, he was contemptuous of fake Neo-Confucian moralists, who merely wore the masks of "learners of the Way" (*dao xue*) but neither understood nor incorporated the essence of moral principle. Many jokes in the *Treasury of Laughs* mocked the fake moralists' meaningless disputes and abstract discourse, and their phony moralizing, pedantry, pretension, and blind imitation of the Sage. Here are some examples:

> Two people exchange abusive language on the street. A says, "You have a deceitful mind." B says, "You have a deceitful mind." A says, "You are lacking in heavenly principle." B says, "You are lacking in heavenly principle." A Neo-Confucian hears this and tells his disciples, "Listen! These are sounds of scholarly discourse." One disciple asks,

> "They are but reviling one another, why does our master call this scholarly discourse?" The master explains, "When men speak of 'mind' and 'principle,' it cannot be anything but scholarly inquiry." "But if this is scholarship," ventures the student, "then wherefore all the abuse?" To which the teacher replies curtly, "Look, nowadays how many Neo-Confucians are at peace with one another?"
>
> (*Xiaofu*, 2: 17b)[58]

The "mind" and "principle" in the joke refer to the Wang Yangming school Learning of the Mind and the Cheng-Zhu school Learning of Principle, two rival Neo-Confucian schools in the Ming. The former, emphasizing self-awakening of the mind—an immanent moral authority, was more subjective or idealistic. The latter, emphasizing investigation of the principle through book learning and rigorous discipline, was more objective or realistic. Although commonality was evident in the philosophical essence of the two variants of Neo-Confucianism, followers of the two schools in the Ming often engaged in intellectual bickering and, occasionally, political struggles. The above joke apparently did not show sympathy with either school as far as their doctrinal disputes were concerned.

> Two Neo-Confucians have some disagreement on their theories. Both claim to be the true "learner of the Way" and accuse the other party of falsehood. They argue for a long while without reaching a conclusion, so they ask Confucius to be their judge. Confucius descends the stairs, bowing and showing his respect to them, and says, "Our Way is enormously broad. Why do you have to have the same opinion? Both of you are true learners of the Way and I always admire you. How can you be false?" The two delightedly retreat. The disciples ask Confucius, "Why did you flatter them to such an extent?" Confucius answers, "Such people! I only care to coax them to leave me alone. Why mind them?"
>
> (*Xiaofu*, 2: 18a)

Feng Menglong often depicted Confucius as a wise man who did not stick to rules, contrary to the fake moralists, who were described as stupid and stubborn. In the *Sack of Wisdom*, Feng cited the following anecdote about Confucius: Once when Confucius traveled, his horse fled and grazed in a field. The farmer was angry and detained the horse. Confucius' disciple Zi Gong, who was eloquent, negotiated humbly with the farmer but failed to bring back the horse. Confucius then asked his horseman to go and say to the farmer, "It is not like you are tilling on the east of the sea and I am traveling on the west of the sea. [Since we are in the vicinity of each other] how could my horse not intrude your field?" The farmer accepted the argument and released the horse. Feng commented that talking about the *Book of Odes* and the *Book of Documents* with the illiterate was how vulgar schoolmasters ruined the country: they did not know how to communicate properly.

Confucius' strategy worked, Feng argued, because he sent the right person to say the right words. But why did Confucius make Zi Gong negotiate with the farmer at first? Feng thought that it was because if Confucius had asked the horseman to negotiate in the very beginning, Zi Gong would have been unhappy. Feng praised Confucius for being able to understand the *qing* (emotional responses) of different individuals, therefore being capable of using them properly. Feng then reflected upon the current system of civil service recruitment: "Later generations confined people with literary styles, limited people with qualifications, and expected people to have general capacities, to be able to do everything. How can the affairs of the world be managed successfully?" (*Zhi nang*, 1: 1b) Since *qing* varied with each individual and each circumstance, people who understood *qing* would observe and respect individual differences, and should therefore be more flexible in managing human affairs. Literary styles, qualifications, and general capacities, on the other hand, were fixed and impersonal requirements which lacked in flexibility; people who stuck to these requirements when making personnel decisions might not use the right man. The *dao xue* moralists were producers and products of the more rigid system.

Some *dao xue* moralists were genuinely cultivated. But there were also "fake" ones who only appeared cultivated. The following joke pokes fun at a fake moralist who cares too much about how he looks:

> A *dao xue* is caught in the rain. He keeps his hands down, his paces slow, and his countenance solemn. When he turns a corner and enters an alley, he asks his page boy, "Is anyone back on the street looking at us?" The boy says, "No." The *dao xue* then starts running. "Since no one notices us," he says, "Let's get out of the rain."
>
> (*Xiaofu*, 8: 10a)[59]

The next joke is about stupid imitation of Confucius. It is stupid because the imitation is superficial:

> A *dao xue* official's stable is on fire. After the servants put out the fire he inquires of them, "Is anybody hurt?" They reply, "Fortunately nobody is hurt. But the tail of the horse is burnt a little bit." The *dao xue*

> angrily has them punished. The servants request to know what they have done wrong, to which the *dao xue* replies, "Haven't you learned that [when Confucius' stable was on fire] Confucius did not ask about the condition of the horse? (*Analects*, X.12) How dare you mention the horse to me?"
>
> (*Xiaofu*, 2: 18a-b)

The indication of the horse episode in the *Analects* is that Confucius cared more about human lives than about the horse, even though the horse was a gift from the King. The *dao xue* in the joke was funny because he did not truly understand the moral of the episode; he only cared about the superficial fact that Confucius did not show concern about the horse, so neither should he or his servants.

As Christoph Harbsmeier has pointed out, stupid imitation of Confucius was a popular subject in joke books in late imperial China, and such jokes had an early precedent in the *Book of Rites*.[60] In the "Tan gong" section of the *Book of Rites*, it is recorded that Confucius was once standing together with his disciples. He held his hands, placing the right one above the left one. His disciples also all placed their right hands above their left hands. Confucius mocked them, "How you love to imitate! I [hold my hands this way] because I am mourning my elder sister." The disciples then all placed their left hands above their right hands.[61]

Arthur Schopenhauer attributes pedantry to lack of confidence. Unsure about the thoroughness of his understanding, a pedant "puts it entirely under the control of the reason, and seeks to be guided by reason in everything; that is to say, he tries always to proceed from general concepts, rules, and maxims, and to confine himself strictly to them in life, in art, and even in moral conduct. Hence that clinging to the form, to the manner, to the expression and word which is characteristic of pedantry, and which with it takes the place of the real nature of the matter."[62] This analysis seems to apply beautifully to the phony "learners of the Way," who talk about reason and principle and consult their books all the time, as if they do not have their independent thoughts and feelings.

The next joke contains sexually explicit language: Parental discretion is advised.

> A moralist goes to bed with his wife. After taking off his underwear he folds his hands and makes a solemn speech, "I am doing this not for sex, but for continuing sacrifices to my ancestors." Thereupon he thrusts once. He then makes another speech, "I am doing this not for sex, but for increasing the population of the nation," followed by a

second thrust. Then the third speech, "I am doing this not for sex, but for expanding creation between heaven and earth," followed by a third thrust. You may ask, "I wonder what his next speech will be?" The answer is, "How could such a moralist make it to the fourth speech?"

(*Xiaofu*, 2: 18b-19a)

This joke is not only erotic but also cynical: it is not very kind to make fun of people's deficiencies. But an attitude toward sex is revealed here at least as much as a jest about sexual deficiency. Feng would have argued that sex is part of human nature. It is not something to be ashamed of if one does it on the spur of spontaneous emotions toward one's partner. The moralist in the joke is ridiculed because he is too bookish to be spontaneous.

Observing sex-segregation and curbing non-procreative sex are prescribed in ancient ritual texts such as the *Book of Rites*. By focusing on the obscene, the joke radically inverts the privileged discourse on morals and the unprivileged discourse on sexual desire, the former being used by the moralist in the joke to shield the latter. On another level of the joke, the juxtaposition of the moralist's high-flown language and wealth of textual authority above and his low-level performance and lack of potency below creates a grotesque incongruity, perfect to invoke folkloric laughter.[63] The timeless and absolute truth in the classical text apparently could do little to solve the practical problem the moralist had in his bedroom.

Feng Menglong often mocked the sexual behavior of Neo-Confucian moralists. In the *Survey of Talk Old and New*, he cited an anecdote in the *Guochao shiyu* (*Complement to the Dynastic History*) about the Neo-Confucian philosopher Chen Xianzhang (1428-1500). Chen allegedly always asked for his mother's blessing for successful production of offspring whenever he entered his wife's bedroom. His superior reprimanded him for doing that. His mother was widowed. Therefore it was unfilial for him to keep on reminding her of what happened in the bedroom.[64] In another entry, in a slightly different vein Feng recited a story about the two Cheng brothers. The brothers went to a dinner party. When Cheng Yi found that there were courtesans serving the wine in the party he angrily left, but his elder brother Cheng Hao (1032-1085) stayed throughout the party. The next day Cheng Yi visited Cheng Hao in his study and was still angry about the incident. Cheng Hao said, "Yesterday there were courtesans in the seats, but there were no courtesans in my mind. Today there are no courtesans in my study, but there are courtesans in your mind." Cheng Yi had to admit that he was inferior.[65] Courtesans represent not only sexual temptation but also pollution of one's ethical reputation. There are two morals in this story. First, you do not have to let your concern with reputation confine your behavior. Second, it will not do to avoid the temptation or to suppress the desire; all you need to do is channel your desire so that you will not succumb to the temptation.

### *4. Medicine:*

The satire in the *Treasury of Laughs* was not exclusively oriented toward the gentry. Physicians, pharmacists, fortune-tellers, merchants, servants, cooks, butchers, musicians, painters, barbers, tailors, shoe makers, carpenters, silversmiths, matchmakers, brokers, functionaries, prostitutes, actors, and even beggars all came in for their share of mockery. The dupes were ridiculed mostly because they could not or would not perform their jobs right, due to incompetence or poor work ethics. Here are a couple of preposterous examples:

> A shoe repairman has used only one pair of leather bottoms throughout his career. He always glues the leather bottoms to the shoes so superficially that after the customer leaves his shop, the bottoms will drop for sure. Trailing the customer, he would retrieve his leather. One day, after following a customer for a distance, he fails to find his leather. Lamenting and crying over his permanent loss, he returns to the shop, and is delighted to see that the leather had already been dropped even before the customer stepped outside.
>
> (*Xiaofu*, 5: 15a)

> An apprentice barber just begins to learn how to shave heads. Every time he cuts his customer's skin through a slip of his razor he uses his finger to cover the injury. After a while the cuts are too many to be covered. Woefully he laments, "I didn't know shaving heads is so difficult. It takes the thousand-armed Bodhisattva Guanyin to do the job."
>
> (*Xiaofu*, 5: 13b)[66]

Although the jokes are hilarious, given the exuberant Ming writings about the cunning traits of the Jiangnan businessmen and the low-scale professionalism of the workers, there might be a grain of truth behind the laughter.

Of the miscellaneous occupations, the medical vocation had the lion's share of mockery, as the following examples illustrate:

> Yama, the King of Hell, dispatches his runners to search for great physicians in the world of the living with the instruction, "If you find a

> physician whose clinic is not haunted by unrequited ghosts, he must be good." Now every clinic the runners visit is crowded with unrequited ghosts. But finally they come to a clinic with only five ghosts lingering about. They decide that this physician must be a good one—until, that is, they learn that the doctor just hung out his shingle yesterday.
>
> (*Xiaofu*, 4: 3b)[67]

The joke is of course on doctors. But it is also funny that even Yama, the King of Hell, needs a doctor, and he does not have a handy list of good doctors himself!

Yama is not a mortal human being, and we would assume that he is immune from the infliction of human ailments. Why, then, is Yama looking for reputable doctors in the human world? Is Yama really sick, and in need of the medical care of a doctor from among the living (rather than from among his hellish staff)? Or is the King of Hell calling a meeting with the human physician to exchange some thoughts on the tremendous power over people's life and death, which they both possess? Yama is the god who, as the Chinese proverb goes, would not allow a person to live past the fifth watch of the night, if he has ordained the person to die at the third watch. And the medical doctors are stereotyped by skeptics as the human agents who contribute to their patients' death either out of their incompetence or out of their unethical behavior of delaying treatment in order to extract more money from the patients' families. Clearly the above joke was based on this stereotype and made buffoons out of the mediocre and/or greedy doctors, who killed their patients with remarkable speed. What the jester did not suggest was the possibility that besides incompetence and questionable medical ethics, the sense of frustration and guilty conscience over the insurmountable limitations of medical knowledge, technology, and resources could also create in the minds of conscientious doctors unrequited ghosts of the patients who had lost their lives under their care. A recent Taiwan short story, for example, fictionalizes a doctor who is driven first to madness, then to suicide, because he is haunted by the long queue of ghosts of his former patients, who line up behind him, waiting to be treated by the single available medical device that could have saved their lives.[68]

The gloomy conscience of a good doctor was hardly fit material for a joke, and certainly not in the Ming, when the legends of the godlike physician Bian Que of the Warring States era and the marvelous surgeon Hua Tuo at the end of the Han dynasty were things of the past. In many Ming jokes, the physician was Yama in person, as we shall see in the next few jokes.

A physician kills a patient by mistake and is detained by the victim's family, but he manages to escape at night and swim a long way home. When he gets home his son is reading the *Pulse Diagnosis*. He advises the youngster, "First things first, my son. You may put aside the book for a while. It's more urgent to learn how to swim."

(*Xiaofu*, 4: 3a)[69]

A baby cries uncontrollably at night, so a doctor is called in. After giving the baby some medicine, the doctor is asked to stay for the night. In the middle of the night, he sends his page boy to take a peep and see if the baby has stopped crying. The boy returns with the report, "The baby is not crying, but the baby's mother is."
(Appendix) In a variant version, the boy reports, "The child is not crying, but the adults are." The doctor says, "Go ask the adults if they also want to take the medicine."

(*Xiaofu*, 4: 1b)

On his way back from gathering firewood, a woodcutter stumbles into a physician with his heavy load. The physician gets angry and is about to wave his fist, when the woodcutter kneels down and pleads, "Please kick me instead." Bystanders are puzzled by this strange request. The woodcutter explains, "The chances for me to survive the touch of his hand are absolutely minimal."

(*Xiaofu*, 4: 5b)[70]

Some doctors did not kill their patients, but did not do their patients much good either, as in the next joke.

A man invites a monk to stay overnight in his study. The monk doesn't feel well, so the host calls in a doctor. Upon entering the elegant room, the doctor assumes this must be a boudoir of a fine lady. Therefore when he reads the patient's pulse from behind the curtain, he talks about menstrual disorders, parturient and postpartum ailments, and suchlike symptoms. The monk draws the curtain, looks the doctor up and down, and has a good laugh. The doctor says to the monk, "Don't laugh, my young master. I was talking about the very origin of your ailments, tracing back to your mother."

(*Xiaofu*, 4: 6a-b)

The doctor's witty explanation did little to hide the fact that he was not competent enough to tell a man and a woman apart by reading the pulse. According to the classical *Canon of Problems* and *Canon of the Pulse*, "gender was presumed to influence the movement of energy along the cardinal channels as detected when a healer took his patient's pulse. A well-trained physician would be expected to read the pulse by pressing at varying depths on three separate locations on each arm and wrist, and to identify two dozen or even more distinct types of energy flow, along the channels beneath the skin." Because "the specifically female pulse pattern was a yin one," "doctors normally were expected to know their patients' sex by pulse alone."[71] It is noteworthy that the doctor in the joke not only failed to detect his patient's sex, but also failed to identify the "gender" of the setting. It was the mistaken gender of the setting that led to the mistaken gender of the person, although he probably could not read the pulse very accurately anyway. By having the doctor mistake a man's study to be a woman's bedroom, the jester implied that the doctor was not learned enough to recognize a study. That can be regarded as an attack on the cultural status of the physician class, and may also be a comment on the ambiguous gender status of monks.

> A pharmacist does not have many customers. By and by, his medicine chest is infested with worms. One day a customer comes to buy some drugs. Catching sight of the worms in the chest he demands to know what they are. The pharmacist dashes off a reply, "Oh, these are dehydrated silkworms." "But why are they alive?" asks the customer. "Because they take my drugs."
>
> (*Xiaofu*, 4: 4a)

In Chinese medical fields, the division of labor between physicians and pharmacists was not clear-cut. Physicians often doubled as pharmacists, as in the case here. The physician certainly has quick wits, but that does not save him from the sarcasm of the commentator of the joke, who exclaims, "I am afraid if the customer takes the drug, *he* will become a dehydrated silkworm!"

The dehydrated silkworm is a popular ingredient in medicinal soups treating gynecological and pediatric disorders. Silkworms are raised primarily for sericulture. They are very picky about environment. The room has to be properly heated for them to prosper. But silkworms that die of cold are not wasted. They are collected in the late spring for medical purposes. The dead silkworms are naturally dehydrated and would not decay.[72] But it would have been scary if they come back to life!

> A physician advertises his fantastically formulated cream for scabies. One day a customer comes to his clinic and inquires about the cream. The physician points to the calabash on the shelf and asks the customer to pour out some cream himself. The customer complains about the

physician's laziness, to which the physician responds, "I have scabies." "Then why don't you apply the cream?" "I did, and that's how I got it."

(*Xiaofu*, 4: 6a)

Now we know what the physician means by "cream for scabies"!

Paul Unschuld's study of medical ethics in imperial China shows that Confucian skepticism about the competence and honesty of medical doctors had a very long history in China.[73] Robert Hymes' analysis of an independent dramatic skit (*yuanben*) produced in the Jurchen Jin (1115-1234) or the Song and popular in the Yuan, entitled "The Two Battling Doctors" (*Shuang dou yi*),[74] shows that status, in addition to competence and honesty, was at issue. The two doctors in the comedy appeared as buffoons, who were professionally incompetent, morally greedy, and culturally pretentious. They wished to mask their low status and to appear to be more respectable and cultivated than they were. What this comic piece reflected, Hymes believes, was the prejudice that medicine was not quite a gentlemanly occupation.[75]

According to Angela Leung, skepticism about medicine in Ming and Qing China was even stronger than in previous ages because of the slackening of bureaucratic intervention and popularization of medical knowledge.[76] Amateur healers practiced medicine with only rudimentary knowledge learned from cheap medical handbooks, and the government did very little to constrain them. Even the great physician Wang Kentang (b. 1553, *jinshi* 1589) wrote in his *Liu ke zhunsheng* (*Criteria of the Six Medical Specialties*), "Now that there are medicine and drugs, people in the country no longer die from diseases, but from medicine and drugs. So it is wisely said, 'If in case of a disease someone does not take any drugs at all, the results still resemble the success of treatment by a mediocre physician.'"[77] The jokes in *Treasury of Laughs*, though hyperbolic, did reflect the apprehensions about medicine in their day.

### 5. *Clergy:*

Buddhist asceticism, especially the clergy's abstinence from sex, meat, and alcohol, has been a subject of popular suspicion and religious apologia. The more doubtful people get about the clergy's ability to stick to the taboos, the more vigorously the religious community turns up stories of monks who resolutely resist any temptations presented to them.[78] Because of this tension, Buddhist asceticism has long been one of the favorite themes Chinese comedians enjoy taking on for mockery. Highly cultivated monks and nuns appear too sainted to be human. Certainly, they are also flesh and blood, and ascetic suppression could have had the negative effect of amplifying their animal drive.

The incongruity between the saintly virtue of ideal Buddhist clergy and the misconduct of the less ideal clergy provides a fertile ground for many a comic caricature. But the comedy is not merely entertaining fabrication. Here, as in many other instances, literature is informed by history. The fictional transgression of the clergy was at times reflected in the criminal behavior of some religious practitioners who reportedly seduced, abducted, or raped women, or swindled them out of money. Such cases inspired the suspicion of lawmakers in late imperial China that "clerical celibacy was a disingenuous facade, designed to facilitate sexual aggression and other predatory behavior by disarming gullible people."[79] At the juncture where life and art negatively conformed to each other, a monk in a humorous tale was often "a Gargantuan clown, the antithesis of all that a monk should be."[80] He was more prone to human vices than ordinary human beings.

> A monk sleeps with a prostitute. When he fondles with the front and back of her lower body, he suddenly calls out in amazement, "How strange! How marvelous! Her front is like that of a nun, and her back is like that of my apprentice."
>
> (*Xiaofu*, 5: 1a-b)

In China, a Buddhist reformation in the fashion of Shinran's (1173-1262) True Pure Land Sect, which allowed Japanese clergy to get married, never occurred. Chinese monks and nuns have to abstain from sex and live outside the secular family system. Rigid rules of clerical celibacy enhance the monks' vulnerability to suspicions of sexual transgression, imagined or real. In the above joke, the monk not only occasionally sleeps with a prostitute, but also regularly sleeps with a nun, and a young monk! But the last revelation should not surprise us too much: sodomy in the monastery is taken for granted in jest-books, as well as in "serious" literature, almost universally.

> A man asks, "What's the most potent aphrodisiac?" His friend answers, "Flour gluten and tofu. These two are absolutely superb." The first person expresses his surprise at this absurd answer, to which the second man responds, "If you don't believe me, just look at the monks!"

(Zhizhi Sheng comments) How could these monks be eating flour gluten and tofu? I'm afraid they're taking aphrodisiac, after all.

(*Xiaofu*, 5: 4a-b)

The joke mocks the Buddhist clergy's sexual prowess. This theme must be popular enough for Feng Menglong to include two tales of clerical promiscuity in his *Sanyan* collection of vernacular stories. "He Daqing Remorsefully Leaves Behind the Mandarin-duck Kerchief" (*Xingshi hengyan*, Ch. 15) tells the story of an amorous young man whose life expires after dallying with nuns whose insatiable sexual desires overwhelm even this Don Juan. "Magistrate Wang Sets Fire to the Precious Lotus Temple" (*Xingshi hengyan*, Ch. 39) depicts how virile monks impregnate unwitting housewives who stay overnight in the temple to pray for babies. The reward for these "sperm donors" is that their temple gets burned down at the order of the indignant magistrate.

The reference to flour gluten and tofu deserves a little bit of discussion. Flour gluten and tofu are not just healthy foods; they are an important part of a vegetarian diet. A strict vegetarian diet, which excludes any meat, poultry, fish, seafood, and even strong spices such as onions, garlic, and chives, is practiced not only by the Buddhist clergy but also by many devout lay Buddhists. A famed gourmet, and by no means a pious Buddhist, Feng Menglong refuses to endorse vegetarianism. In *Treasury of Laughs* (12: 9b-11b) he includes several jokes on vegetarians and comments lengthily on the belief that by keeping a strict vegetarian diet one can accumulate good karma. He tells stories of villains who keep a vegetarian diet and chant Buddha's name, convinced that this would redeem their sins—that is why the lowest hell is full of vegetarians! After citing the Buddhist theory that if you killed and ate a chicken in this life you would become a chicken in the next and in turn get killed and eaten, he proceeds to quote a counter argument. Skeptics claim that if indeed you are to be what you eat, then vegetarianism is actually disadvantageous, because it is more fun to be reborn as an animal, bird, or fish than a turnip or vegetable. Although Feng admits that the latter argument stretches too thin, he firmly supports what he deems a Confucian attitude: moderate consumption of meat is ritualistically and ecologically appropriate. It is quite all right to sacrifice animals, and to hunt and fish for food, so long as we take only the necessary quantities and in the right seasons.

> A gentleman visits the temple and inquires of a monk if he eats meat. The monk answers, "Not much. On the occasion of wine-drinking, I would eat a little bit of meat." The gentleman is taken aback, "So you drink?" The monk answers, "Not much. On the occasion of the visit of my father-in-law and brother-in-law, I would drink a little bit of wine along with them." The gentleman snaps in a rage, "So you even have a wife! You are not like a monk at all! Tomorrow I shall talk to the magistrate to revoke your certificate of ordainment." The monk replies, "I do not dare to lie to you. The certificate was already revoked a couple of years ago, when my crime of theft was exposed."
> (Comment) Recently the Five Commandments of the Buddhist clergy have all but gone with the wind. But this monk at least still follows that one commandment against lying.
>
> (*Xiaofu*, 5: 5a-b)

The gentleman might be a degree-holder, a retired official, a landholding philanthropist, a noted scholar, or the patriarch of a family of long standing—somebody who commanded certain respect in the locality. Being a member of the "gentry society," he felt a special responsibility and privilege, as he had the ear of local government officials, who had jurisdiction over the religious institutions, to correct the misconduct of the phony monk. But alas, the monk was beyond correction. The Buddhist Five Commandments are: slay not, steal not, lust not, lie not, and taste not intoxicants and meat. Although the monk did not kill, by eating meat he indirectly took the life of the slain animal. So that indeed left only one commandment which he could not be accused of violating. The monk could be a trickster who concealed sanctity with eccentricity, like the Cloth-Sack Monk. However, he was probably more likely a phony monk devoid of sanctity. On the other hand, because the monk seemed at ease with his transgression, the gentleman's indignation appeared out of place, so he might also be slightly mocked.

> A scholar tours a Buddhist temple. When he goes to the western chamber, he is badly received by a monk. He leaves in anger, and goes to the eastern chamber, where he sees a monk chanting the sutra of repentance. The scholar asks the monk for whom he is doing the repentance. The monk answers, "I am chanting the sutra to keep the repentance in stock. If a pious layman gives us alms, we will then attribute the repentance to him." The scholar suddenly knocks on the monk's head incessantly. The monk asks, "What have I done wrong?" The scholar tells him, "Just now I was offended by that heinous baldhead in the western chamber. You may attribute the beating to him."

> (Appendix) Qiu Jun [a junior minister in the Song dynasty, namesake of a prominent Ming official] once paid a visit to Abbot Shan. The abbot dealt with him arrogantly. A while later, the son of the subprefectural general also visited the temple. Abbot Shan received him with utmost respect. Jun expressed his annoyance at the discrimination. Shan argued, "To receive is not to receive. Not to receive is to receive." Jun stood up in rage, struck Shan several times, and said, "Don't be mad, Abbot. Not to strike is to strike. To strike is not to strike."
>
> (*Xiaofu*, 5: 6a)

The main joke mocks the first monk's arrogance and the second monk's commercialized practice of selling repentance. The appendix criticizes the abbot's snobbishness, and also pokes fun at a favorite Zen paradox: to be is not to be.

The above snapshots illustrate the antagonism between Confucian scholars and Buddhist monks. Historically, Confucian scholars often regarded Buddhist monks as anti-social parasites, who contributed nothing to their families and societies, and furthermore competed with the state for precious metals, wealth, and manpower to enrich their churches. Although some temples were also the sites of religious learning and philosophical discourse, general education for poor children, and all sorts of charitable activities, scholarly skepticism concerning the Buddhist institution remained strong.

> On his way back after collecting alms, a monk comes across a tiger. When the tiger approaches him, he becomes frightful and throws one cymbal at it. The tiger holds the cymbal in its mouth and, after putting it aside, approaches the monk again. The monk throws the other cymbal at the tiger, but the tiger repeats its previous response. The monk then throws his scroll of scripture at the tiger. The tiger hurriedly returns to its cave. The other tiger in the cave asks, "What is going on?" The first tiger answers, "I met an impudent monk. I have simply received two pieces of crackers from him, and he goes so far as to produce an alms-soliciting book. I have no choice but to run."
>
> (Appendix) In another version, after the monk throws the scripture at the tiger, the tiger again holds its trophy in the mouth, puts it aside, and re-approaches the monk. The monk thereupon removes his cap, and charges at the tiger with his shaven head. In response the tiger withdraws in a hurry. The monk returns to his quarters and tells the story. The person who hears the story says, "Oh, I know. This must be a tigress." This latter version is even more zestful.
>
> (*Xiaofu*, 5: 6b-7a)

The message seems clear enough: begging monks were not welcomed. The alternate version has a sexual connotation, which expresses a further contempt for the mendicant monks.

> In a particularly chilly winter, a boat loaded with pearls is stuck in the frozen Lake Dongting. The food supply is completely gone, and the people in the boat are about to be starved to death when they see in the vicinity a boat with a nun in it, loaded with plenty of rice. The pearl merchant tells the nun he is willing to trade his pearls at a reduced price for the rice. The nun is just then beating the wooden fish drum while chanting Buddhist scriptures. Amidst her Buddha chanting she utters, "No, No." The merchant says, "I would be willing to trade a decaliter of pearls for a hectoliter of rice." The nun still says, "No. No." Finally, the merchant is willing to trade a liter of pearls for a liter of rice. But still the nun says, "No. No." The merchant asks, "On what terms would you consent to trade your rice?" Without stopping chanting the Buddhist scriptures the nun says, "When you guys are all starved to death, wouldn't the whole boat of pearls be all mine?"
>
> (*Xiaofu*, 5: 10a-b)

The gender of the clergy is deliberately chosen to sharpen the irony. Women are expected to be compassionate. Buddhists are expected to renounce worldly profit. The nun's response is therefore doubly incongruous.

No jokes about clergy would be complete without some references to the Taoists. Unlike the Buddhist clergy, Taoist priests do get married and often pass on the priesthood to their sons (with the marked exception of Quanzhen Taoists, who are celibate). The Taoist priests seldom assume a puritanical and Spartan attitude. But they have a different sort of comic potential: they are known for magic. Through the uses of talismans, incantations, sword dancing, sacred water, and animal blood, the Taoists perform exorcism for their clients, sometimes as a substitute for medical treatment, and other times as a means to ward off evil spirits and other undesirable beings.[81] Apparently the magic works in the minds of tens of thousands of people, as the practice continues well into the modern era. But it never works in humorous tales.

> A Taoist priest walks by the graveyard of a princely residence, where he is possessed by a spirit. Fortunately a passerby helps him break away from the grip of the spirit and brings him safely home. To show his appreciation the priest tells his savior, "I am truly grateful for your rescue. Here is an exorcising talisman. Please take it as a thank-you gift from me."

(*Xiaofu*, 5: 12a)

> A Taoist priest claims his talismans can ward off mosquitoes. A man buys one but he is still bothered by mosquitoes. When he makes an inquiry to the priest, the priest asks him where he put the talisman. He answers, "I pasted it on the wall." The priest says, "No wonder it didn't work. You have to put it on the back of the mosquito."
>
> (*Guang Xiaofu*, 4: 47-48)

Very cunning words indeed! Unfortunately, it is commonsensical that Taoist talismans are to be pasted on the wall for the purpose of exorcism, so the customer cannot be blamed for not following the manufacturer's manual.

### 6. *Social Manners:*

The economic prosperity of Jiangnan brought about extravagant lifestyles and philistine social customs. The importance of "face" created all sorts of abnormal social behavior, which in turn triggered abundant cynical comments from the quick-eyed and quick-eared observers.

> Old woman Wang is rich and vain. On her deathbed she pays a Taoist priest dearly and asks him to inscribe a glorious title on her spiritual tablet to honor her clan. The priest thinks very hard, but cannot think of anything glorious about her. Finally he comes up with "Official So-and-so's Neighbor Madame Wang."
>
> (*Xiaofu*, 8: 12a)

What woman Wang failed to realize was that money could not buy status. Notwithstanding this, people continued to pay a high price for vanity. Feng Menglong cited a popular saying in *Hanging Twigs*, "Even if you are as innocent as Prince Boyi, you won't be short of a horrible piece of writing to send you to the woods. Even if you are as evil as Robber Zhi, you won't be short of a wonderful piece of writing to send you to the nether" (*Guazhi'er*, 6: 2a). Feng enlightened his readers that the former referred to the impeachment and the latter, the epigraph.

Prince Boyi was a virtuous hermit who died of starvation. His biography headed the biographies section of Sima Qian's *Records of the Grand Historian*. Robber Zhi was a cruel and unruly terrorist who lived to a ripe age. Sima Qian cited him in the biography of Boyi as a foil. Feng Menglong told us that, however incorruptible you were, you could still be impeached by a slanderer and forced to retire in disgrace; however infamous you were, you could still be romanticized by a money-hungry epigraph writer and die in honor—all because of the power of the written word. As a much sought-after writer who received fabulous commissions to produce formulary texts such as temple inscriptions, prefaces, congratulatory notes, and eulogies, Feng should know this well.

> When a millionaire orders his cowherd to dry his Confucian cap in the sun, the cowherd hangs the cap on the horn of an ox. While drinking at a stream the ox is startled by its own odd reflection and stampedes off into the distance, leaving the cowherd to trail behind and ask around, "Have you seen an ox wearing a cap?"[82]
> (Comment) This ox knows its lot in life and is therefore far superior to its owner.
>
> (*Xiaofu*, 1: 1b)

According to Ming sumptuary law, only students (*shengyuan*) were allowed to wear Confucian caps. The cap symbolized the honor the students earned through diligent study. Rich merchants could demonstrate their artistic cultivation through possession of *objets d'art* and association with painters, calligraphers, and writers, but this did not make them literati. By suggesting that an arriviste rich merchant could not even compare to an ox in social sensibility, the joke ridiculed the entire rich merchant class for their crudity.

A cultural artifact (such as the Confucian cap) being hung on the horn of an ox was a recurrent image in the Ming. After the publication of the dynastic founder's *Great Proclamation*, which all students were required to memorize, according to a poem,

> Heaven's words are earnest, sure in guiding men's fortunes:
> Wind swirls, thunder frightens, the spirits are startled to listen.
> Hanging the text on the ox's horns, reading it at the field's edge,
> How delightful that the farmer can also read simple writing.[83]

Perhaps that explained the ox's social sensibility—it remembered the sumptuary rules in the *Great Proclamation*, which its ancestor mysteriously internalized.

> A man sends a letter to a rich man to borrow his ox. The rich man happens to be entertaining a guest. Hating to reveal his illiteracy, he opens the envelope, pretends to read the letter, and then says to the courier, "I see. I'll go over there myself in a short while."

> (Comment) Although he doesn't recognize the words, his response happens to match perfectly.
>
> (*Xiaofu*, 1: 1b)

The comment compares the rich man to a "big stupid ox," as the Chinese animal lore goes. This harsh criticism for a flawed but somewhat excusable desire to appear better than one really is tells a great deal about the way the men of letters felt about their more wealthy but less "respectable" peers.

In the appendix to the above joke, Feng Menglong looked at the false pride of the illiterate rich man from a more benign angle. He reported,

> A rich man that I know holds a contract up side down when he shows it to his debtor to collect the money. The debtor laughs at his mistake. Annoyed, the rich man counterattacks. "I am holding the contract so that *you* can read it from across, not for myself to read!" On another occasion, when he is entertaining a guest, a note is delivered from a neighbor. He opens the envelope to read the note. The guest knows he is just faking, and mischievously asks him what the note is about. He answers, "The neighbor is going to treat me to some wine." The courier contradicts him, saying, "No. He is asking to borrow your gong and drum." The rich man smiles. "Wouldn't he have to treat me to some wine after borrowing my gong and drum?" Henceforth people are even more impressed by his quick wits.
>
> (*Xiaofu*, 1: 2a)

Instead of ridiculing the pretentious rich man, Feng Menglong expressed his admiration for his quick wits. The rich man would not allow himself to be poked fun at just because he was illiterate and was inclined to hide this shortcoming. Quick wits and a good sense of humor more than compensated his illiteracy and his vanity. Furthermore, he also had the good fortune to be the personal acquaintance of Feng's. Otherwise, a less friendly report was not entirely impossible in a world where blurring social lines sharpened the literati's sense of discrimination.

> A rich man has an obsessive craving for antiques. On several occasions he is presented with forgeries which are claimed to be the lacquered bowl made by King Shun, the stick with which the Duke of Zhou struck Bo Qin, and the mat on which Confucius sat when he lectured at the Apricot Altar. He pays a thousand pieces of gold each to obtain the artifacts. His funds depleted, the man holds King Shun's bowl in his left hand and Duke of Zhou's stick in his left hand, and throws on

Confucius' mat. Begging in the market thus equipped, he calls out, "Please, give me a penny of Jiang Taigong's Nine Treasury coins."
(*Xiaofu*, 6: 20b-21a)

The *Guang Xiaofu* contains a modified version of the joke (8: 102), which locates the rich man in the Qin dynasty (221-207 BC). He exposed his vulnerability to antiques when he generously exchanged his farmland for a tattered mat, on which Confucius (551-479 BC) allegedly sat when he lectured in the famous Apricot Altar, a site which had since become an emblem of the teaching profession. This transaction attracted a second vendor who, holding what he claimed to be the stick of King Wen of the Zhou dynasty (around the first millennium BC), came to the rich man's door and argued that his stick was several centuries older than Confucius, hence more valued. Thereupon the rich man exhausted his personal assets to acquire the stick. Then came a third vendor with the lacquered bowl, who proclaimed that his bowl, made in the time of King Shun (around the second millennium BC), was even older than the stick and the mat. The rich man exchanged his real assets for the bowl, thus depleting all his wealth. The punch line is that after having foolishly given away his property for a bunch of junk, he was still not cured of the obsession with antiques. Instead of begging for useful money, he was begging for another antiquarian artifact, but this one might have some cash value—a Nine Treasury coin minted by the legendary wise man Jiang Taigong.

The late Ming obsession with antiques was phenomenal. From mid-sixteenth century on, "the 'enjoyment of antiquities' shifted its role from being a personal predilection, one of a number of potential types of privileged cultural activities, to being an essential form of consumption which was central to the maintenance of elite status."[84] Since it was no longer acceptable for the educated man not to be a lover of antiques, everybody had to cultivate this expensive hobby, and while the real thing was of limited supply, forgery mushroomed to respond to the need of the market, at very high prices. In this market, where the authentic and the bogus were hard to tell apart, true connoisseurship in antique collection was a trademark of a refined sense of discrimination, a singular passion for artistry, and a unique personality. Only a true connoisseur could be a gentleman, and only a true gentleman could be a connoisseur. Yuan Hongdao proclaimed, "As I observe around the world, those who sound insipid and look tedious are all people who do not have any passion for connoisseurship. If they did, they would have indulged it, even at the expense of their lives. How would they have the leisure to concern themselves with such trivia as money, servants, officialdom, and commerce?"[85]

Judith Zeitlin correctly points out that in the face of the ordinary Jiangnan *nouveau riche*'s shallow vogue for obsession, the late Ming literati's glorification of their purely spiritual and practically useless misplacement of energies was a demonstration of their "ideal of unswerving commitment and genuine integrity that [was] incompatible with worldly success." It was "a deliberately unconventional and eccentric pose" that set themselves off from the dust-stained world.[86] Here, as elsewhere, there were things that money could not buy. The wealthy man in the above joke was mocked because he was not entitled to play the literati game of "antique obsession." Foolishly, he threw his money away on forgery. And still more foolishly, he did not wake up even after he had lost all of his money.

> A beggar has pus in his ailing leg. When he lies at the foot of a statue in a Buddhist temple, a dog goes and licks his leg. The beggar snaps, "Impatient beast! After I die, it's all yours."
> (Comment) Someone recounts the joke and interprets it to be about prodigal sons. I say it's rather a joke on the father of the prodigal son. "Why do you say so?" He asks me. My answer is, "The father must be a miser who carries on like a penniless beggar to raise a son like that beast."
>
> (*Xiaofu*, 3: 8a)

Beggars were a social menace in Ming China. They were believed to possess a dark, liminal power, and on New Year's Day, the local government would call on the hereditary and endogamous beggar households to perform the ancient *nuo* ritual to exorcise evil spirits, as well as other ritual plays to bring good fortune to the community.[87] That was probably the only occasion when beggars were welcome. But the above joke, as the commentary makes clear, is not exactly about beggars, but about miser fathers and prodigal sons. The dog could not wait until the death of the beggar to steal a mouthful of his body, just as a prodigal son could not wait until the demise of his father to steal the old man's hard-earned money and waste it. The original teller of the joke saw the sarcasm to be more on the dog/son, but Feng Menglong saw the sarcasm to be more on the beggar/father.

Cautionary tales often warned wealthy people if they were extremely reluctant to part with their money, their sons would go to the other extreme and would not flinch a bit from throwing the money away. Frugality was a virtue, but stinginess was a vice. In the universe of cautionary tales, it was a divine retribution for a stingy man to have a prodigal son who would wring his heart. Misers are universally popular dupes in humorous tales, but there is also a particular late Ming implication here. Perhaps the miser in the tale reminded the storyteller of a wealthy man who had refused to patronize his writing, for which sin he deserved to be compared to a penniless beggar who was about to become the meal of a stray dog.

> A "pure houseman" complains to his friend during summer time about home management. "As the saying goes, when you open the door, you are facing the task of acquiring the seven daily necessities. But nowadays the way of the world calls for nine items, which makes the management of household budget even more difficult." When asked what the two additions are, he replies, "You cannot get by in the morning without a few jasmine flowers. You cannot go through the night without a roll of mosquito-repelling incense."
> (Comment) There are only two items on the shopping list of the "pure houseman"—jasmine flowers and mosquito-repelling incense. What's the fuss about "nine items"? If you ask me why I say so, I would tell you his firewood, rice, oil, salt, soy sauce, vinegar, and tea are all provided for by somebody else.
>
> (*Xiaofu*, 7: 5b)

A "pure houseman" was an unemployed man of letters taken in by a host family without specific job assignments, hence the appellation "pure houseman." Like the hungry warrior in late Tokugawa Japan who nevertheless always had a toothpick between his lips, the above "pure houseman" in late Ming China attempted to cover up the disparity between his livelihood and his gentry status. He gave the impression that he was complaining about home economy, whereas his real intention was, first, to appear as if he *had* a home, and second, to brag about how well he kept up with the elements of gentility. Jasmine flowers and mosquito-repelling incense are both fragrant and graceful. The incense might have a practical use, but the same thing cannot be said about the jasmine flowers. The commentator sarcastically left these two non-essential items alone to highlight the parasitic nature of the "pure houseman." It must be with an awareness of such social contempt that the "pure houseman" gave the pretentious speech.

The next joke is a rich piece of satire:

> Twenty years ago, in the Suzhou area, whenever there was occasion for a funeral, the family of the deceased would hire Confucian students to entertain the guests. It so happened that a funeral ceremony occurred when it was time for the students to take their triennial evaluation ex-

> amination, so there was no real student around. The family therefore hired an "honorary *xiucai*" (village gentry) and an "ex-*xiucai* " (disqualified student) to carry out the task. A cynic composed a poem in jest: "Yesterday a family entertained their guests. There trotted out two Confucian caps. One was 'Empty field, real title.' The other was 'Property gone, taxation remains.'"
>
> (*Xiaofu*, 2: 6b-5a)

The multiple meaning of the above satire on "guest entertainers" may not be immediately clear; the last two phrases require interpretation. According to Ming law, if your farmland was flooded and the situation was reported to the authorities, your land would be registered as an "empty field." The taxation would be reduced by half and spread among landowners of the county: you yourself would get tax exemption for that piece of land. The social reality was that some rich and powerful families registered their productive lands as "empty fields," so that, although they had substantial land titles, they did not have to pay the tax. Powerless people, on the other hand, might still be levied taxation for the estate that was actually flooded: the authorities just did not care to straighten out the registry.[88] This joke reflects discrepancies between reality and name on several levels: families that did not produce Confucian students wanted to pretend that they did; people who were not Confucian students were taken to be Confucian students; and finally, property and taxation did not match each other and were allowed not to.

> Sima Wengong's given name was Guang. One day he summoned some monks to perform the religious ceremony of chanting the name of Buddha Yao Shi Guang (Buddha of Medicine and Light). The monks, according to the ritualistic taboo against making reference to the master's name, replaced the "Guang" (light) in the Buddha's name with its synonym "Jiao" (moonlight). Sima Guang came out to burn incense and heard the strange chanting of "Yao Shi Jiao." He made an inquiry and learned that the monks were observing the etiquette of avoiding uttering the master's name. He laughed and asked them to relax the rule, saying, "If I didn't come out to burn the incense, I don't know how long you guys will continue to fool around (*jiao*, written in a different form)."
>
> (*Guang Xiaofu*, 5: 67)

In imperial China, it was dictated that any character in the current emperor's given name be avoided (*hui*) in all writings and speeches. When the character was part of an established phrase, it had to be dropped or replaced with a synonym. The Bodhisattva Guanshiyin therefore became Guanyin to avoid a "collision" with Li Shimin, the great emperor Taizong of the Tang dynasty. The new name Guanyin somehow stuck and was more popular than the original name Guanshiyin. The rule of "avoidance" also caused the Taoist philosopher Zhuang Zi to appear in some written texts as Yan Zi, "*zhuang*" and "*yan*" both meaning "solemnity." But in the case of Zhuang Zi the alternate name did not stick. This ritualistic taboo was preposterous. But the tyranny cut both ways. To save people from the trouble of having to use replacement words too frequently, most Chinese emperors were given very obscure characters for their names. The poor emperors were victimized by the rules that were meant to hold them in reverence. Some gentry took the rule of avoidance so seriously that they extended it to the names of their forefathers and superiors to show the depth of their piety, hence the above joke.

Yao Shi Guang, the Buddha of Medicine and Light, was a Buddhist king who vowed to save people of the world from all kinds of diseases and illusions. This Medicine King was aided by two ministers—the Bodhisattva of Sunlight and the Bodhisattva of Moonlight. The three of them formed a trinity.[89] Sima Guang was a renowned Song statesman and scholar. He was known to be a traditionalist who made great effort to find textual evidence in order to rationalize ritual tradition. He was also known to argue strongly against the use of Buddhist rituals, which he regarded as heterodoxy. In the joke, however, Sima Guang was transformed into a liberal Ming person who did not seem to be serious about either sabotaging Buddhist rituals or observing the *hui* taboo.

Timothy Brook shows that, although since the sixteenth century many Confucian-minded gentry abandoned the commonly used Buddhist services and sought alternative authority for funerary ritual in Zhu Xi's *Family Rituals*, some gentry still preferred Buddhist services to Neo-Confucian rituals. Brook points out four factors related to the preferences for Buddhist rituals: Buddhist services were more family-centered; they were associated with popular culture; they were less costly; and they provided both the living and the dead with religious atonement. Neo-Confucian rituals, on the other hand, were more lineage-centered; they were associated with high culture; they were more costly; and they provided some emotional relief but little religious atonement.[90] The teller of the joke apparently was not sympathetic to the Neo-Confucian position represented by Sima Guang when he transformed Sima Guang into his own opposite.

### 7. ***Master-Servant Relationships:***

According to the law, commoners were not allowed to own bondservants. But as always, law was one thing and practice was another. An official report included in a statute of 1479 stated, "When moving about ["powerful magnates" who are honorary officials] ride in sedan chairs or on horses and take along a group of three to five bondservant companions (*puban*) who follow them on their rounds. Relying on their power and wealth they conspire to occupy the landed property of small peasants (*xiaomin*), forcefully drag away cows and horses and make the children of free people into bondservants (*nu*)."[91] Other people got around the law and acquired bondservants in the name of adoption.[92] Ideally, the master-servant relationship should have been paternal—the master nurtured the servant as if the servant were his child and the servant served his master as if the master were his father. However, this was often not the case, even if the servant grew up in the master's family. The situation was still further from ideal in late Ming Suzhou, where adults often attached themselves to powerful families to seek protection, avoid taxation, or to share their masters' prestige, so there was very little bond of affection to begin with.[93]

Toward the end of the Ming dynasty, in the lower Yangzi and southeastern coastal areas, class-based social unrest led to riots and rebellions.[94] Scholarly opinions differ as to what caused the rebellion: whether the masters mistreated their servants, so the servants were forced to rebel in self-defense, or because the government lost control of the social order, the servants seized the opportunity to rebel. In either case, the master-servant relationship was less than perfect, which is reflected in the *Treasury of Laughs*:

> A man newly attaches himself to a master. He is embarrassed by this new, lowly status, so he makes an agreement with the master: whenever they go out he would not carry anything for the master. One day the master is going out and cannot find anyone to carry his bamboo box, so he forces this newcomer to carry it. The man finds it difficult to violate his master's wishes, so he attaches a big "For Sale" sign to the box, pretending to be a vendor. When they walk on the street someone (apparently an interested customer) calls to him, "Come here, box-vendor." The man points to his master, "Sorry, this gentleman already bought it."
>
> (*Xiaofu*, 3: 8b)

The funny behavior of the new servant reveals his fears of downward mobility and false pride. He regarded servile status in a big household as worse than being a self-employed small vendor, and shielded himself in this expedient disguise.

> A servant ran away because his master was poor. Then the master passed the examinations, so now the servant wants to come back. The master refuses to take him, but he persists. The master angrily summons him in, has him beaten, and drives him out. When he reaches the door he refuses to leave. The gatekeeper hurries him. He says, "I am now his 'flesh-and-blood' family member (*jiaren*). You can't drive me out." The gatekeeper says, "Since he had you beaten, he would by no means use you. How could you be his 'family member'?" The servant argues, "If I were not his family member, how could he beat me?"
>
> (*Xiaofu*, 3: 8b-9a)

The servant was snobbish, since he left his master when the master was poor and came back when the master gained power, and cunning, since he refused to leave the master's household arguing that because he had been subject to the punishment of a "family member" he should be allowed to stay. "Family member" (*jiaren*) was an ordinary term for servant in the Ming. When a person became a family servant, he gained intimacy with his master's family; this intimacy also subjected him to their violence. But in an ironic twist, the servant in the joke cited violence as evidence of intimacy. The joke may be more a commentary on the servant's cunning than a commentary on the terror of servitude, but it is still a reminder of the precarious relation a Ming servant had with his master and also of the relationship of violence and intimacy.

> A man serving tea to a visitor is naked except for the piece of tile hanging in front of his privy parts. The astonished visitor asks his host who that was, to which the host replies, "That was my humble servant." When asked how long the servant has been employed, the host answers, "It has been more than a year now. He takes care of his own meals. We only supply his clothing."
> (Appendix) In another version of the joke, after a while, the servant comes to serve a second round of tea, this time wearing a lotus leaf to cover the same spot. The host complains to his guest, "He does ok as a servant. But I resent his sense of pride. The economy is doing so badly, and he's changing clothes!"
>
> (*Xiaofu*, 12: 1b)

The *naked* truth cannot be more transparent.

> A master is very mean to his servant, who is often short of food and clothing. In the autumn, the servant hears the chirp of a cicada. He asks his master, "What is this?" The master answers, "Cicada." "What does the cicada eat?" asks the servant. "Only wind and dew," answers the master. "Does the cicada wear any clothes?" asks the servant. The master says no. The servant says, "the cicada would be a perfect servant for you, my master."
>
> (*Guang Xiaofu*, 5: 63)

There is no ambiguity as to which party the joke is on. One only wonders if the master would be awakened to his conscience by this smart servant, who clearly knew the art of roundabout remonstration.

The next joke is not exactly about master-servant relations, but it hints at the social reality of late Ming land-tenure system.

> Two brothers till the land jointly. When the rice is ripe, they confer on how to divide the harvest. The elder brother tells the younger brother, "I'll take the part above the ground and you take the part below the ground." The younger brother protests, "This isn't fair!" The elder brother says, "No problem. Next year, you'll take the upper part while I take the lower part." The next year, the younger brother urges his elder brother to sow the seeds of the grain. The elder brother suggests, "Let's plant taro this year."
>
> (*Xiaofu*, 8: 9a-b)

The land-tenure system in the late Ming was confusingly complex. The rights to a land could be shared by two or three different parties; for example, the absentee landlord living in the city, the local landlord living on the farm, and the tiller. Sometimes the landlord retained "subsurface" right to the soil while transferring the "surface" right to the tiller who brought the bad land into production. Other times, one landlord had the "subsurface" right and another had the right to harvest the crops for a specific period of time. Still other times various parties had claims to various produce of the land.[95] The above joke reflects possible disputes over the land rights under such circumstances.

## *8. Folly of Various Kinds:*

Human folly is the most basic and universal ingredient of comedy. Ming writers were especially fascinated by this topic. They did not regard all folly as undesirable. When a member of the gentry circles was obsessed with a hobby to the extent of eccentricity, for example, or if he possessed a strange temperament which set him apart from the "ordinary" fellows, he was to be complimented. Many literati glorified passion (*chi*), obsession (*pi*), laziness (*lan*), craziness (*han*), madness (*kuang*), stupidity (*yu*), and folly of such kinds, as indications of unique personalities, and freely adopted them as parts of their literary and artistic names.[96] Feng Menglong, who named his studio "Ink-Crazy Studio," was among them. Zhang Dai claimed, "Do not befriend a person with no obsessions, for he lacks deep feelings (*qing*). Do not befriend a person with no flaws, for he lacks true psycho-physical vitality (*qi*)."[97] Nothing was more dreadful than being a person with no extraordinary characteristics.

In the context of the late Ming fascination with folly and eccentricity, it is no surprise the *Treasury of Laughs* contains numerous jokes on a wide range of human folly, such as hot temper, quick temper, sluggish disposition, indolence, timidity, amnesia, alcoholism, obtuseness, addiction, stinginess, greed, bragging, affectation, jealousy, lying, excessive self-effacement, and litigiousness. Some jokes are "romantic," others are "satirical," depending on whether one can find in one's heart a tender spot for the victims of the mockery.

> As a merchant is about to go on a business trip, his wife asks him to buy her a comb in town. He asks her what a comb looks like. She points to the new moon in the sky. After the merchant is done with his business and is on his way home, he suddenly remembers his wife's request. He looks up and sees a full moon in the sky. Thereupon he buys a mirror. When he comes home, he presents the mirror to his wife. The wife looks into it and snaps, "Why did you buy a concubine instead of a comb?" Hearing the clamor, the man's mother comes to intervene. She looks into the mirror and is upset. "My son, since you've taken pains to spend the money, how come the woman you're bringing home so old?" Hence the case is brought to court. When the policeman comes to summon the parties to court, he looks into the mirror and becomes nervous. "How come there's a guy arresting people who are late on tax payment?" When the case is on trial, the mirror is put on the bar for examination. The judge looks into the mirror and flies into a rage. "This is just a trivial case of conjugal disharmony. How on earth is there a need to ask a local grandee to intercede?"
>
> (*Xiaofu*, 11: 3a-b)

The joke is funny because none of the dupes recognize themselves in the mirror. The simple philosophical meaning is that it is foolish not to see oneself in one's mirror image. Yet paradoxically, few people do. One can often see other people's shortcomings and strengths but not one's own. That was why Socrates regarded knowing the self as the greatest wisdom, and that was why the search for the "authentic self" caused many a Ming thinker a high level of internal anxiety.

The joke also reveals some external anxieties in late-Ming society: the wife's anxiety over the husband's infidelity, the mother's anxiety over the son's unwise investment in his harem, the policeman's anxiety over the duty to enforce timely tax collection, and the judge's anxiety over local gentry's intercession at the request of the plaintiff and/or the defendant. This was certainly not a relaxing environment.

The next couple of jokes develop the theme of confusion of identities in a different way. The jesters playfully manipulate the juncture between actor and character and create comic butts who fail to separate the physicality of the actors from the dramatic personae they take on.

> In the stage performance of "Story of the Lute," the cast includes an actress who has previously appeared in another play, "Forced Marriage of the Thorny Hairpin." A man in the audience suddenly exclaims, "It is imperative to go to the theater—so educational! Not until today do I know that the mother of Cai Bojie is the mother-in-law of Wang Shipeng."
>
> (*Xiaofu*, 6: 9b)

> When performing the "Story of the Lute," the troupe assigns the leading role to the actress who has played Diao Chan, the Three Kingdoms period beauty slain by General Guan Yu. A villager watches the play and laments in tears, "What a pity! This wonderful woman is a filial daughter-in-law. She toils all life long, and ends up being killed by that red-faced barbarian."
>
> (*Xiaofu*, 6: 9b)

"The Romance of the Thorny Hairpin" and "The Story of the Lute" were both great masterpieces of Southern Drama (*chuanqi*) in the late Yuan-early Ming period. The authorship of "Hairpin" was unclear. "Thorny hairpin" refers to the wife in a poor household. In the story, Wang Shipeng was an impoverished student who could only offer his mother's old hairpin as an engagement gift to Qian Yulian. In Wang's absence, a wealthy and wicked man forced Qian to marry him. To keep her chastity Qian Yulian drowned herself. Fortunately, a high official rescued her and adopted her as his daughter. Meanwhile, Wang Shipeng became a prospective scholar. By coincidence, a match was made between the two young people, who both steadfastly refused to marry, until they learned of each other's identity. Tragedy turned comedy as a testimony to their true love—even God was moved to help them out.

"The Story of the Lute" was a romance of another star-crossed couple, Cai Bojie and Zhao Wuniang. This famous Han dynasty story was dramatized by Gao Ming (1305?-1370?). Cai Bojie was a poor scholar. When he went to the capital to take the civil service exam (although it was actually not yet instituted in the Han Dynasty), his hometown was struck with a famine. Cai's wife Zhao Wuniang served her parents-in-law gruel everyday. The mother-in-law suspected that Zhao Wuniang was reserving rice for herself, so she stole a look when the young woman had her meal in the kitchen. Alas, Zhao Wuniang was only eating the husk. Despite Zhao's sacrifice, the aging in-laws finally died of starvation. Zhao Wuniang cut her beautiful hair and sold it in order to give her in-laws a proper burial. With a painting of her in-laws and a lute in hand, she sang her way to the capital in search of her husband. But Cai Bojie had already passed the exam with flying colors and was more or less coerced into marrying the Prime Minister's daughter. The faithless lover was, however, rewarded with two wives in the end, thanks to the good will of the new wife.[98] What could be regarded as male fantasy did not hurt the popularity of such story lines in the traditional Chinese theater, where it was up to the women to earn their respect in a patriarchal world.

In contrast to the impeccably chaste Zhao Wuniang, Diao Chan, who lived at the end of the Han dynasty, was presented to a series of powerful men for political purposes. Like Xi Shi before her, Diao Chan sacrificed her chastity for the sake of loyalty. But in a nonextant Yuan drama, Diao Chan's life ended at the hands of Guan Yu, the War God in Chinese folk religion otherwise marked for his moral integrity. In various versions of the drama, Guan Yu killed Diao Chan either out of jealousy, because he and Cao Cao both wanted Diao Chan, or out of righteousness, as he was disgusted by Diao Chan's promiscuity. Critics found neither motivation convincing.[99]

These different stories are fused through the embodiment of the actor in the above jokes. The buffoons are funny because they confuse actor and mask, life and art, and by extension, illusion and reality. Yet again, boundaries between actor and mask, life and art, and illusion and reality are fluid rather than clear-cut, leaving room for imagination.

Dreams, mirrors, and plays are popular subjects in a literature that plays with the idea of seeking the authentic self in a world where one is lost in constant role-playing. The philosophical connection between *Child's Folly* and Li Zhi's theory of the recovery of "child-like mind" makes clear why dreams, mirrors, and plays pop up here and there in *Child's Folly*.

> A self-proclaimed expert chess-player once loses three games in a row to an opponent. A short while later, he is confronted by an inquisitive acquaintance. "How many games did you play with that guy the other day?" asks the friend. "Three," the player answers. When asked how the games went, the player says, "I didn't win the first game. He didn't lose the second game. As for the third game, I would like to settle with a tie, but he didn't want to."
>
> (*Xiaofu*, 13: 10a-b)

What a tactical answer! Having taken pride in the superiority of his skill, the chess-player finds it difficult to admit outright he is not *that* superior. When performance does not match expectation, the safest response is not to confront the sense of failure directly.

> A dilatory man and his friends sit and chat around the fireplace in the wintertime. Observing that the tail of a friend's gown has caught fire, the dilatory man addresses his friend in a leisurely tone, "I have observed a phenomenon for a while. I wanted to tell you, but was afraid you might become anxious. But if I did not tell you, I was afraid you might get hurt. To tell or not to tell? That is the question!" The friend asks, "What is it that you observed?" The dilatory man answers, "Your gown has caught fire." The friend hastily puts out the fire on his clothes and upbraids the dilatory man, "Why didn't you tell me earlier?" The dilatory man retorts, "I said that you are precipitate, and indeed you are!"
>
> (*Xiaofu*, 6: 2b)

The tardiness of the above person is in sharp contrast with the hastiness of the people in the next joke:

> An impetuous person often tells his wife, "If there are people in the whole wide world who are more impetuous than I am, then I would be so irritated I could die." One day he enters a noodle shop and demands that noodles be served to him instantly. The shopkeeper brings him a bowl of noodles, pours the content on the table, and says, "Here, help yourself. I have to hurry up and wash the bowl." The impetuous man goes home in a rage, tells his wife what has just happened to him, and cries, "I am going to die for certain." Hearing this, the wife instantaneously leaves him and marries another man. The day after the wedding, the woman's second husband is asking for a divorce. The wife is taken by surprise. "Honey, what did I do wrong?" Her second husband explains, "I am mad that you haven't delivered me a son!"

(*Xiaofu*, 6: 1b-2a)

The world population would probably explode if babies could be made overnight! But under different circumstances, the second husband's request for a divorce would not be completely groundless—according to classical ritual texts, the wife's failure to produce an heir for the patriline could indeed constitute a ground for her expulsion. In real life, however, people rarely divorced their wives on the ground of their barrenness. Concubinage and adoption were more popular remedies for men who failed to produce offspring with their wives. The above joke is of course on an impetuous man whose impetuosity is unexpectedly surpassed, in escalation, by first the owner of the noodle shop, then his own wife, and then her new husband. But the ritual texts' citation of heirlessness as a ground for a woman's expulsion from her husband's family, regardless of the source of the problem, is also casually poked fun at.

> There is a man who is extremely impulsive. On one occasion he sees a man wearing a felt hat in the month of June. Greatly disturbed by the man's out-of-season attire, the impulsive man throws himself at the hatted man. He is about to give the offender a good licking when mediators stop him and persuade him to let go. Upon returning home, he is taken ill by the pent-up fury. It takes him a long while before he regains his health. Then it is December. His little brother accompanies him to go out and enjoy the New Year festivities, so as to relax his nerves. Unfortunately, the little brother spots a man at a distance who is wearing an unseasonal cap made of horsehair. Hurrying up, the little brother approaches the capped man and implores him, "My big brother just got a little better. Please, I beg you, hide yourself!"
>
> (*Xiaofu*, 6: 2a-b)

If triviality such as a stranger's unseasonal headgear can trigger an outburst of rage in the man, he is not just impulsive; he is weird, and perhaps mentally ill. But the joke avoids making any unpleasant connections to real problems. Because the impulsive man in the joke can still be stopped from using violence against the object of his fury, his impulsiveness only victimizes himself, and in a smaller way his little brother. While in reality the situation might not be so funny, comedy is comedy because it puts together all the comic elements without also hinting at the possibly tragic consequences.

> Mr. X always uses pure silver to pay for his expenditure. Mr. Y advises Mr. X to remold his silver into alloy of 80-90 % silver. This

> way, says Mr. Y, Mr. X can gain some economic advantage. Mr. X thereupon takes out a silver ingot and entrusts Mr. Y to transform it into alloy of 80 % silver. Mr. Y has known very well that Mr. X is foolish, so he takes advantage of Mr. X and only returns to him 40 taels of silver. Mr. X asks, "How much silver is this?" Mr. Y answers, "40 taels." Mr. X is puzzled. "Is my original ingot 50 taels?" Mr. Y says, "Yes." Mr. X's confusion grows. "How come my 50 taels of silver have been reduced to 40 taels?" Mr. Y explains, "This is 80 % silver. 5 times 8 equals 40." Mr. X exclaims, "I am mistaken by you! There is absolutely no economic advantage to use this kind of silver."
>
> (*Xiaofu*, 6: 7b-8a)

The appendix to the joke revealed that Mr. X was Zhou Yongzhai, who was famous for being a dummy. But despite numerous stories about his slow wits, Zhou managed to acquire a *jinshi* degree through his unbelievably exquisite essays. This was an excellent example of a man whose literary talents did not translate into administrative wisdom, or any practical intelligence. Yet the ability to produce great essays was what won a man his *jinshi* degree and important governmental post. Feng Menglong was not just telling a joke about a dullard. He was questioning the wisdom of the Ming system of official recruitment.

Adulterated silver money (in the form of alloy) appeared in *Child's Folly* more than once, indicating its popularity. The circulation of the adulterated silver money was a result of the Ming government's failure to regulate silver currency. In the early years of the Ming dynasty, paper currency was the primary medium of exchange and coin served as a subsidiary currency. The paper notes posed a serious economic problem, as the paper currency was not backed up by gold or silver reserve. Although in the early fifteenth century the government finally abandoned paper currency and allowed the use of silver money, throughout the entire Ming dynasty the state did not mint silver dollars. In the absence of coined silver, the precious metal "was always handled in ingots, chunks, and bits."[100] Richard von Glahn informs us that the worth of uncoined silver "was determined solely by its intrinsic value, which could be ascertained only through cumbersome measurement of its weight and purity. Easily adulterated, poor in fungibility, silver constituted a mediocre instrument of exchange, especially as a fractional currency."[101] Again, the joke sounded an alarm on the government's management of the state of affairs.

> A man orders his servant to go to the Maple Bridge to check the price of wheat. As the servant approaches the Bridge, he hears someone calling, "Please come and have some noodles." He thought the noodles were free of charge, so he eats three hearty bowls in a row, then stands up and walks straight away. The noodle-vender, not getting his payment, angrily tails after the servant and slaps him on the cheeks nine times. The servant hurries home and reports to his master, "I didn't get information on the price of wheat, but I did check out the price of noodles." "How much?" asks the master. "Three slaps in the face for a bowl of noodles," answers the servant.
>
> (*Xiaofu*, 6: 16b)

The servant is not a complete fool—he apparently does his mathematical calculation quite well. But his master may not appreciate it.

In the *Guang Xiaofu*, a similar version of the above joke—sort of a sequel to the original—appears, and it is even more hilarious:

> A country bumpkin goes to town. When he walks by a noodle stand he is cordially invited to sit down and eat. He takes it to mean that the noodles are free of charge, so he heartily eats three bowls. When he is asked to pay the bill, the profusely embarrassed bumpkin cannot produce any money. The angry vendor curses him incessantly and takes his shoulder pole to strike the bumpkin eight or nine times before throwing him out. When the country bumpkin returns home, he reports to his fellow villager, "In the town there are deliciously hot and spicy noodles. Three strokes of the shoulder pole for one bowl." When the fellow villager goes to town, he finds the noodle-vendor and asks him, "I already know the price of the noodle. But do I get to eat first, or do I get beaten first?"
>
> (*Guang Xiaofu*, 5: 63)

With a price like this, the noodles are indeed "hot and spicy"! It is hard to tell which bumpkin is more stupid—the one who has had the noodles, or the one who is about to. But they are stupid in a funny and inoffensive way. Perhaps even the noodle-vendor will be amused.

> A man brings a knife to the bamboo grove to cut bamboo. He suddenly has an urge. So he puts the knife on the ground and enters the bamboo grove to go. While he is relieving himself, he incidentally lifts his head and thinks to himself, "We can use some bamboo at home. There is some nice bamboo here. Unfortunately I didn't bring a knife." After he's done, he sees the knife and is overjoyed. "Gods follow the wishes of humans. There happens to be a knife here." As he is searching for the right bamboo to apply the knife, he spots the manure. Vexed, he

complains, "Who emptied his bowels all over the ground? It almost dirties my feet!"

(*Xiaofu*, 6: 4a-b)

Amnesia is troublesome in real life, but it can also be funny from the mouth of a comedian.

Feng Menglong pointed out that the folly of naive and stupid people was funny, but the most laughable folly was that of "smart" people who did not realize how foolish their behavior really was (*Xiaofu*, 6: 1a), like the people below:

A miser is having a religious service at home. He orders a Taoist priest to invite the gods to come down for a feast, so that he can offer his prayer.[102] The priest sends a petition inviting the gods in the two Capitals. The miser asks the priest why he's sending for gods so far away. The priest replies, "The gods nearby all know you. They won't believe you're treating them to a feast."

(*Xiaofu*, 8: 2a)

A poor man bumps into an old friend on the road. The friend has achieved immortality and acquired magic power. After some chitchat the friend points his finger at a brick on the roadside, turning it into gold, and gives it to the poor man. The man is not satisfied. The friend turns a huge stone lion into gold and gives it to the poor man. The man is still not satisfied. The immortal asks, "What on earth do you want?" The man says, "I want this finger of yours."

(*Xiaofu*, 8: 7b)

A stingy man never stands treat. One day a neighbor gets his permission to use his dining hall as a site for a banquet. A spectator curiously inquires of the stingy man's servant, "Boy! Is your master hosting a dinner party today?" The servant sniffs, "It'll be another lifetime when you will hear of my master hosting a dinner party!" Overhearing what the servant has just said, the master curses, "Hey! Who gave you leave to fix a date with him?"

(*Xiaofu*, 8: 1b)

The stingy man evidently takes rain checks, even the ones that cross lifetimes, very seriously. Like most servants in jest-books, the stingy man's servant has an intimate knowledge of his master's personality flaws. This knowledge empowers the servant to ridicule his master, hence a carnivalesque reversal of the hierarchical positions of the master and servant. But ultimately, it is the master's curse, an attempt to reclaim his hierarchical superiority, that draws him down to the rock bottom of the respectability spectrum.

> A master instructs his servant, "When you go out, you should talk up everything at home to gain face for our family." The servant nods his head. On running into somebody who marvels at the magnificence of the "Palace of the Three Pure Ones" (Taoist temple), the servant exclaims, "It's just as big as our rental house." Another man remarks on the enormous size of the "dragon-robe boat" (emperor's boat). The servant declares, "It's just as big as our business boat." Yet another man comments on the gigantic stomach of a castrated bull. The servant announces, "It's just as big as the stomach of my master."
>
> (*Xiaofu*, 8: 10a-b)[103]

The punch line is, of course, the one about the *castrated* bull, although the comparison between his master's business boat and the emperor's boat is dangerous enough.

> Two men are bragging. One says, "Our family has a drum. When it is beaten, the rumbling sound can be heard a hundred *li* (a *li* is about one-third of a mile) away." The other says, "Our family has an ox. When it drinks water on the southern bank of the Yangzi River, its head leans on the northern bank of the Yangzi River." The first man shakes his head in disbelief, "How on earth can there be an ox so big?" The second man says triumphantly, "If there isn't an ox as big as ours, how do they get the hide big enough to cover that drum of yours?"
>
> (*Xiaofu*, 8: 10b)

The second braggart wins the day. He improvises his tall talk on the basis of that of the first braggart. Thus, his opponent cannot dismiss his tale without dismissing his own at the same time. Very smart indeed!

In Feng Menglong's categorization, stinginess, greed, bragging, and the like illustrated the folly of people who were far from naive. Their folly was motivated by their pursuit of self-interest with no concern for others or their attempt to appear better than themselves. These butts deserved no sympathy.

### *9. Children's Naiveté:*

Despite its title, *Child's Folly* was no children's literature. In fact, children rarely appeared in *Child's Folly*. This is appropriate, for the compilation celebrates the "child-like mind," and only adults can be properly described as "child-like." But no joke book would be complete without tales of children. Children are a natural source of humor in the eyes of adults. The minds of children and adults operate on different tracks of logic. What seems to be logical for children often appears incongruous to adults. Sometimes adults look at children's naiveté with envy. Children do not need to make compromise with etiquette and are allowed to act spontaneously. Other times children's naiveté brings into embarrassing relief the fallacy and affectation of the adult world.

> A child is playing shuttlecock. Incidentally he kicks the shuttlecock down a well. Looking down the well, he sees his own reflection and cries, "Return the shuttlecock to me!" His father comes to investigate. The boy complains that the child in the well retains his shuttlecock. The father goes over to the well. Looking down, he also sees his own reflection, and is agitated by that unreasonable father down there. "Your son wants to play the shuttlecock. And my son doesn't?"
>
> (*Xiaofu*, 11: 1b-2a)

This joke calls to mind the one about the mirror, but is simpler. As the saying goes, "Like father, like son." Unfortunately, what is regarded naive in the child would be judged foolish in the father.

> A dummy is looking after his father's store when the latter is out on business. A customer appears and asks, "Is the reverent elder around?" The dummy says no. The customer then asks, "How about the reverent hall?" The dummy again says no. When his father returns and learns what has come to pass during his absence, he says, "The 'reverent elder' refers to me, the 'reverent hall' refers to your mother. How could you say we are not around (are deceased)?" The son, annoyed, exclaims, "How was I to know the two of you are both for sale?"
>
> (*Xiaofu*, 6: 6a)[104]

Although the honorable appellations employed by adults to refer to Mom and Dad apparently evade the simple-minded child, he is not willing to admit it. Maybe he is a bit too smart in this regard.

> A man is going out of town. Before he leaves, he instructs his son, "If somebody inquires about the 'excellent venerable,' you may respond, 'My father went out to run some errands. Please, come in for a cup of tea.'" Fearing that the son may be too dumb to remember the lines, he writes them down on a piece of paper and gives it to him. The son puts the paper in the inner lining of his sleeve and from time to time nervously takes it out to read. For three days nobody comes. Relieved by

> the thought that there might be no use for the paper after all, he burns it at the lamp. On the fourth day, a man unexpectedly turns up to inquire about the "excellent venerable." The son searches his sleeve but cannot find the paper, so he announces, "It's gone!" The guest is stunned. "When was he gone?" "Last night. I burned it."
>
> (*Xiaofu*, 6: 6a-b)

This joke is possible because in classical Chinese, when the object of a sentence is a pronoun, it is omitted. Therefore "he" and "it" in the conversation are not in the original text to prevent confusion.

> A father draws a horizontal line and teaches his little boy, "This is the character 'one.'" The next day, the father is wiping the table when the boy happens to stand nearby. The father takes this opportunity to test his little pupil. He draws a line on the table with the wet towel and asks his son to identify it, but the boy fails the test. "This is the character 'one' I taught you yesterday. Remember?" The boy opens his eyes widely. "How come it grows so big overnight?"
>
> (*Xiaofu*, 6: 6b)[105]

> A wealthy household has been marred by illiteracy for generations. At the advice of a friend, the father hires a tutor to teach his son how to read and write. When the tutor reports to work, the first lesson he gives is how to use the writing brush to copy down the characters in a model. As the child draws a horizontal line, the tutor teaches him, "This is 'one.'" As the child draws two horizontal lines, the tutor teaches him, "This is 'two.'" As the child draws three horizontal lines, the tutor teaches him, "This is 'three.'" At this point the child puts down the brush and self-complacently tells his father, "I have learned it all. There is no further need for the trouble of the tutor." The poor tutor thereupon loses his job. Then one morning the father plans to invite a kinsman by the name of Wan (literally, "ten thousand") for a drink. When his son arises from bed, he asks him to fill in the name Wan on the invitation note. The son works on it for a long while and still hasn't finished it, so the father goes to hurry him. The son is very unhappy. "There are so many surnames. Why does the guy have to be named Wan? From morning till now I have only managed to complete over five hundred strokes!"
>
> (*Xiaofu*, 1: 3b)

The child has a long way to go before he finishes with all ten thousand strokes of the character "Wan" in his configuration! Had he had a little more patience, he would have learned that the simple principle of denoting numerals by drawing horizontal lines is applicable only to the numbers one through three. Afterwards artifice takes over. To the smart yet simple-minded child, perhaps the primitive method of denotation makes much more sense than the intricate art of etymology.

> A woman steals her neighbor's sheep, hides it under the bed, and instructs her son not to tell anybody. When the neighbor clamors up and down the street, cursing the thief, the boy professes, "My Mom didn't steal your sheep." Annoyed by the unwitting troublemaker, the woman darts a warning glance his way. The boy points his finger at his mother's eye and excitedly says to the neighbor, "Did you see it? This eye of my Mom's looked exactly like the eye of the sheep under our bed."
>
> (*Xiaofu*, 11: 6a-b)

Protected by their youth, children need not lie and need not be held responsible for their ignorance. Adulthood takes that privilege away.

The Song scholar-official Su Shi, known for quick wits, had many ups and downs in his political career. During his banishment following a defeat in a factional struggle, he wrote a playful yet biting poem to commemorate his month-old son's ceremony of first bath:

> Families, when a child is born
> Wish the little bundle to be blessed with intelligence.
> I, through intelligence,
> Having wrecked my whole life,
> Only have this wish for my son:
> May he prove dumb and doltish,
> So no setbacks or hardships will obstruct his path
> To the highest court posts.[106]

This might be a tongue-in-cheek mockery of his victorious political enemies, for they owed their success to stupidity, or it could be a self-mockery, for he could not bring himself to hide his brilliance in order to avoid political troubles. The wish he jotted down for his son could not have been genuine—he should have known very well the perpetual glorification of children's naiveté ceased to apply as the children turned adults.

### *10. Husband-Wife Relationships:*

*Mencius* acknowledges, "The desire for food and sex is natural."[107] This line appears in a discussion between the Confucian philosopher Mencius and his disciple Gao Zi about whether humanity and righteousness are as intrinsic to human nature as the desire for food and sex. They conclude that humanity, generated internally, is intrinsic, whereas righteousness, imposed from the outside, is not intrinsic. While the focus of the original conversation is on humanity and righteousness, the above line is often quoted out of context to justify indulgence in food and sex.[108] There is therefore little wonder that food and sex, and especially the latter, constitute the most popular themes of jokes on husband-wife relationships. Apparently oriented toward entertaining a male audience, the *Treasury of Laughs* contained many sexual jokes made at the expense of women, including stock jokes about jealous shrews, sexually insatiable wives, and the weeping brides who actually could not wait to join their husbands in matrimony. Unwittingly, the jokes might have revealed a certain degree of male anxiety over their private as well as public lives: if a man was overpowered by women in a domestic setting, there is the possibility that he cannot take up leadership at work.

The selection of this section begins with a joke that echoes nicely with the song cited at the opening of the book.

> A woman is having a rendezvous with a neighbor at night, when her husband suddenly comes home. The neighbor hurriedly jumps through the window, but the husband manages to grab his shoe. Cursing his wife endlessly, the husband pillows his head on the shoe and threatens to settle the issue in the morning, when the owner of the shoe may be identified. While the husband is soundly asleep, the wife replaces the incriminatory shoe with the husband's shoe. The husband resumes his row when he gets up the next morning. The wife calmly asks the husband to examine the shoe. Seeing that it's his own shoe, the husband relents, "Sorry. My mistake. It was I who jumped over the window last night."
>
> (*Xiaofu*, 6: 12b)

While the adulteress in "Playing Double-Sixes" sweats, this one does not.

> A bride is leaving her natal home for the first time. While she is wailing miserably, the sedan chair bearers are having a hard time finding the carrying poles. "Oh, My Dear Mother!" stammers the bride between sobs, "The carrying poles are in the corner of the door."
>
> (*Xiaofu*, 9: 2a)[109]

Social customs required that a bride weep as markedly as possible to express her deep sorrow over the difficult separation with her natal family. Since parentally arranged village exogamy was the norm, the bride's anxiety over marrying a total stranger in a faraway place almost certainly made the weeping genuine. In the above joke, however, while feigning sorrow, the bride was keen enough to locate the carrying poles and give useful instructions so as to expedite the wedding procession. Apparently, she was eager to go.

> On the way to her husband's home, a bride has the mishap of having the bottom of her sedan chair suddenly fall off. The sedan chair bearers confer among themselves, saying, "The bride is not supposed to arrive at her new home on her own two feet. But it's a long way if we are to go back and get a replacement sedan chair. Now what?" The bride hears the discussion and says, "I have a plan." The bearers happily inquire what plan she's got. She answers, "You guys go ahead and carry the sedan chair on the outside; inside I will walk on my own."
>
> (*Xiaofu*, 9: 3a)

The wedding ritual demanded that a bride be carried in a bright red sedan chair, accompanied by loud music and a caravan of dowry, to flaunt her dignified status as the principal wife. Even a concubine, who came quietly and usually without dowry, had to be carried in a sedan chair, albeit of a much plainer style and color. The sedan chair was crucial for "keeping the bride from touching the earth or being seen by Heaven on her wedding day."[110] The point was to protect the bride from direct contact with any gods or spirits that would awe her, hence the taboo against the bride being on her own two feet. The bride in the above joke, by proposing to walk inside of a sedan chair, observed the ritual only nominally.

From the tales of the brides we now turn to the tales of the wives.

> A couple heard that blowfish are in season, so they thought they would buy and taste the famous delicacy. After the dish is done, they suspect the fish might be poisonous, so they each urge the other to try it first. After a long tug of war, the wife gives in. Before she lifts the chopsticks, she tells her husband in tears, "I'll eat it first all right. But please, look after our son and daughter. If they get to grow up, tell them don't ever buy blowfish to eat."
>
> (*Xiaofu*, 12: 17b-18a)

The deliciousness of the blowfish is legendary. But if not prepared with utmost care, a poisonous essence called TTX contained in the fish could be deadly. As in the cases of many other food items, the Chinese passion for blowfish has been shared and expanded by the

Japanese. Today Osaka is the city most renowned for gourmet blowfish dishes, and the occasional occurrence of blowfish-related deaths seems to reinforce the attractiveness of the exciting food. But very little excitement is detected in the above joke. The husband's refusal to be the brave one was incongruous. Ideally he should be the leader in the patriarchal family. But here he seemed to use his leadership only to boss around the wife. Being the subordinate, and perhaps also having fewer muscles, the wife was forced to be the guinea pig. She did manage to voice a weak protest before her possible demise. But one doubts that her worry about the children's likelihood to survive without a mother's care would change her husband's mind.

The *Expanded Treasury of Laughs* gives another example of marital friction related to food preparation. But here, no fatal decision needs to be made.

> A man is very stingy and emotionally unreliable. One day he buys a small piece of meat and asks his wife to cook a broth with it. The meat sinks to the bottom of the bowl, and the fat floats on the surface of the broth. The man sees only the fat, and not the meat. So he angrily shouts at his wife, "You and I were enemies in our previous life. Leave me right now!" When he puts his chopsticks in the broth, however, he finds the meat. He then merrily pats on his wife's back and says, "You and I have been destined to be husband and wife since five hundred years ago."
>
> (*Guang Xiaofu*, 5: 66)

Influenced by Buddhism, the Chinese believe that marriage is predestined. Some couples are happy together because they have cultivated good karma over several lifetimes, while others are unhappy because they held a serious grudge against each other in previous existence. In the above joke, the husband saw his wife as friend or foe, in the current as well as previous lives, simply based on his vision of the meat broth. The audience's sympathy should be with the poor wife, who had to put up with her husband's temper and apparently had very little say in their relationship.

But women who have little say in their marital relations are the minorities in the *Treasury of Laughs*. Most women in the collection have a lot of say.

> A man is poor and is no drinker. When he leaves home, he looks drunk after having had only two cookies made of dregs of wine. One day, he encounters a friend in his topsy-turvy state. The friend asks him if he has drunk in the morning; he says, "No, I just had wine-sediment

cookies." When he goes home he reports this to his wife. His wife advises him, "You should have said, 'Yes, I have drunk.' This would make you look good." The husband nods his head. Next time, when he sees the friend and is asked the same question, he answers that he has drunk. The friend presses on, "Do you drink it hot or cold?" He answers, "Baked." The friend laughs, "You had wine-sediment cookies, as before." He goes home, reports what has happened, and is nagged by his wife. "How can you say you drink the wine baked? You should say you drink it hot." The husband assures his wife he has really got it. The next time he meets the friend, he brags, without having been asked, "This time I have my wine hot." The friend asks how much he has drunk. He shows two fingers, "Two pieces."
(Comment) A bundle of heavenly naiveté, spoiled by the "smart" advice of the philistine woman.

(*Xiaofu*, 6: 11b-12a)

The commentator, very likely Feng Menglong, was wrong to blame the philistine wife for spoiling her husband's naiveté. The husband wanted to put on the appearance of being able to afford alcohol as much as his wife, once he was enlightened by her on the social connotation of the conversation with his friend. He simply was not smart enough to tell a good lie. His stupidity does not make him innocent of philistinism. However, it may be true that without the nagging of his philistine wife, his philistine nature might not have been awakened.

A man returns after a prolonged sojourn away from home to find his wife raising three small kids unknown to him. When he expresses surprise at his wife's conception without the aid of a husband, she explains, "I miss you so much that my longing for you must have congealed to form the embryos. That's why the names I give to our kids all have profound meanings. I named the first child Yuanzhi ("Remembering the one afar," or "Polygala"), because my thought was focused on the sorrow over your departure. I named the second child Danggui ("Should be back," or "Ligusticum"), because my thought was focused on the wish of your return. I named the third child Huixiang ("Return to the village," or "Fennel," written differently), because my thought was focused on the anticipation of your home-coming." The husband exclaims, "If I stay away for a few more years, we'll be able to open a new herbal medical shop!"

(*Xiaofu*, 9: 11b)

It is hard to tell if the husband means to be sarcastic, but the jester certainly does. The joke is a smart word play based on the homophones connecting the kids' names in association with the wife's professed longing for the absent husband, and the names of some Chinese herbal medicine. But it also draws from a curious theory of gestation in traditional Chinese medicine. In his celebrated *One Hundred Questions on Medicine for Females* (*Nüke baiwen*, preface dated 1220), Qi Zhongfu explained that chaste women could indeed get pregnant in the absence of male agency. According to Qi, female victims of depletion fatigue, especially widows and nuns in the imperial palace, were vulnerable to emotional affliction which took the form of "dreams of intercourse with ghosts," resulting in possible "ghost pregnancy." Such medical construction of pregnancy outside of matrimony protected the women from the blame of not only the conception but also the erotic fantasy, since it was all due to an outside agency beyond the women's control. As Charlotte Furth aptly observes, "Respectful of the honor of their upper class clients, medicine showed a concern for female chastity."[111] Given the existing medical construction, the wife in the joke is even less to blame than the widows and nuns of the palace. The agent of her supernatural conception is not a ghost, but a far more appropriate entity; rather than being a passive victim, she takes the initiative to invoke him, all because of matrimonial love. However, the jester is unlikely to buy the theory. In a roundabout way, he seems to be mocking traditional Chinese medicine via mocking the sensual woman and her "herbal" children.

> During a dinner party a guest happens to mention that sponge gourds might effect impotence; it is better to have chives, which could enhance potency. A while later, the host calls for more wine, but the wine keeps on not coming. The host asks his son what is going on. The son answers, "Mother has gone to the vegetable garden." "What for?" "She's going to pull up the sponge gourds and plant chives."
>
> (*Xiaofu*, 9: 6b)

The wife did not say anything, but her action was quite telling. According to Charlotte Furth, Ming sexual manuals such as *To Benefit Yin* stressed "feminine shame" and "indirection and reserve" in an eroticized woman, who was "caught between modesty and instinct."[112] Women were imagined to be sexually passive; they needed the guidance of their husbands to be blessed with sexual pleasure and successful conception. Vernacular fiction and sexual jokes, on the other hand, often put women on the dominant side of the erotic arts. Here are a couple more examples:

> A man's ailment is traced to excessive drinking and too much sex. The doctor cautions him with the words, "You have 'hacked the wood with

two axes' (burned the candle at both ends). From now on, you need to constrain yourself." Taking a hint from the wife's slant, the doctor quickly moderates his advice, "If you find it difficult to abstain from sex, at least try to abstain from wine." To which the patient responds, "The harm of sex exceeds the harm of wine, so sexual moderation should take priority." "How can you get well if you don't listen to the doctor?" retorts the wife.

(*Xiaofu*, 9: 8a-b)[113]

Husband and wife are in bed. The husband is sexually aroused. But the wife rejects him, saying, "Early tomorrow morning you're going to the temple to burn incense. You should straighten your mind in utmost sincerity." After he goes to sleep she is terribly regretful. Then she suddenly hears the raindrops outside the window. She immediately kicks her husband, waking him up, and says, "Listen. Listen. You got lucky."

(*Xiaofu*, 9: 9b)

Jokes about women refusing sex and really wanting it poke fun at women's pretentiousness as well as their inappropriate claim of power over men, who are not masculine enough to control women.[114] In this regard both the male and the female are ridiculed for transgression of sexual hierarchy.

A prostitute teases her patron, "You are having fun here, leaving your wife a widow at home." The patron protests, "She's by no means 'widowed.'" "Why not?" "Think about it. If she were really 'widowed' over there, how would she have released me to come here?"
(Comment) Such malicious jokes serve as excellent excuses for jealous wives.

(*Xiaofu*, 7: 1b)

The commentary, again very likely Feng Menglong's, indicated that prostitution was not a serious sin, but to joke that the wife must have herself had a rendezvous was just too much. Such malicious jokes, the commentator warned, only justified the jealous wife's forbidding her husband access to other women. In the end, men had to pay for telling such jokes.

A man has a concubine. During intercourse with his wife, the wife says, "Your body is here, but I bet you your mind is over there." The husband retorts, "If it is so, would you rather that my body is over there, and my mind is over here?"

(*Xiaofu*, 13: 9a)

According to the Ming law, a commoner could acquire a concubine only if he was over forty and still heirless, in which case the continuation of the family line made it necessary to seek sexual partnership with another, usually much younger woman. But the law was rarely enforced, and it was not unusual for well-to-do men under forty to have one or more concubines and handmaids for reasons other than procreation. The wife in the above joke could not prevent her husband from acquiring a concubine, but she wanted to express her jealousy in a coquettish manner, so as to induce her husband to comfort her. However, she was in a no-win situation: her husband simply turned her words around to stop her nagging.

Susan Purdie contends, "Psychologically, women who nag, or refuse, or sexually demand can all be seen as 'threatening' and the male involved is constructed as a butt in his inadequate masculinity."[115] Keith McMahon demonstrates in his study of eighteenth-century Chinese fiction that the jealous shrew is both sexually insatiable and emasculating. Even if she bears no son she demands that her husband have sex only with her, disregarding the risk that the family might become extinct. The polygamist thus tries to "avoid the shrew by pretending she is not there": he "finds new and submissive or opportunistic women"; such alienation, however, only makes the jealous wife even more shrewish.[116] A similar dynamic can also be found in the seventeenth-century jokes. The husband in the above joke refuses to be a victim of a "threatening" or "shrewish" wife: he confronts and tames her. But the next few husbands are not so assertive: they are clearly comic butts who are overpowered by their wives.

> A and B are both henpecked. B comes to A with the following complaint. "My wife has recently become even more ferocious. At night she goes so far as to order me to collect the chamber-pot." A pushes up his sleeves indignantly. "This is too much! If it were I. . . ." Before he has the chance to finish his sentence, his wife shouts from behind, "If it were you, what would you do?" A involuntarily falls on his knees. "If it were I, I would have collected the pot."
>
> (*Xiaofu,* 8: 16a)

In another joke, the night pot, whose shape resembles female genital and is therefore used as a tool of masturbation, becomes the target of a wife's jealous rage—she smashes it to pieces when she finds one in the household (*Xiaofu*, 8: 17a). The erotic implication of the night pot is also invoked in *Hanging Twigs* (8: 8b) and *Hill Songs* (6: 46b), indicating the popularity of the theme.

> A group of henpecked husbands are holding a conference to figure out a counter-henpecking method, so as to reassert their "husband's authority." A busybody interrupts the meeting with the frightening news, "Gentlemen! Your wives have gotten wind of your conference, and they're ganging up to come down here and give you guys a good beating." Flabbergasted, the mob flees in all directions, with the exception of one man, who resolutely stays put. Wondering if this man alone is fearless of his wife, the fellows go over to investigate, and find that he's already scared to death, literally!
>
> (*Xiaofu*, 8: 18b)

While painting a farcical picture of the coward among cowards in the husbands' camp, the joke does not paint a flattering picture of the wives either. It is frightening to visualize the scene of a stampede in which a troop of ferocious women charge at their helpless, trembling husbands.

The fear of the shrew infected not only the commoners, but also the gentry, as we shall see in the next two jokes from the *Guang Xiaofu*.

> A henpecked functionary is one evening scratched on the face by his wife. When he goes to work the next day the magistrate inquires about the scratch. The functionary replies, "Last night, I was taking in the cool of the night air, when the grapevine trellis suddenly fell down, cutting my face." The magistrate does not believe him. "This must be the work of your wife. Runners, go catch the wife." Unexpectedly the magistrate's wife has been eavesdropping, and is now rushing at her "chauvinistic" husband. The magistrate hurriedly instructs the functionary, "Court's in recess. You may withdraw. The grapevine trellis in my backyard is also falling down."
>
> (*Guang Xiaofu*, 2: 32-33)[117]

This joke must have already been popular prior to the Ming. An art song (*sanqu*) by the Yuan playwright Guan Hanqing (second half of the thirteenth century) entitled "Recording what I saw" sang the praises of a maidservant who accompanied her newly wed mistress to her marital home. The maid had beautiful black hair and rosy cheeks; she was of admirable bearing, was sensitive and understanding, and was a great converser. What was implied was that she outshone her mistress the bride. The last line of the song read, "If she were mine, the grapevine trellis will fall down."[118] Without the knowledge that the falling of the grapevine trellis was an allusion to the bout of a jealous or shrewish wife, this last line would have made no sense to the reader.

By the Ming and the Qing, the allusion had probably become common knowledge. The phrase "havoc of grapevine trellis" appeared time and again in novels on polygamous families, such as *The Plum in the Golden Vase* (*Jin Ping Mei*) and *A Marriage that Awakens the World* (*Xingshi yinyuan zhuan*), without much of an explanation.[119] Thanks to the inclusion of the above joke in the *Expanded Treasury of Laughs*, modern readers will not stumble over the fallen grapevine trellis when reading these stories.

> A wife is jealous. Her husband tries to reason with her. He cites the "Jiumu" and "Zhongsi" poems in the *Book of Odes*. ("Jiumu" praises the queen for being not jealous, so that imperial consorts can get along. "Zhongsi" praises the queen for being not jealous, so that the king can have numerous offspring.) The husband then sighs, and says to his wife, "You see, the virtuous women in the imperial court of old were not jealous." The wife asks him who wrote the poems. The husband answers, "The Duke of Zhou." The wife says, "No wonder. If it were the Duchess of Zhou, she wouldn't have written the poems this way."
>
> (*Guang Xiaofu*, 6: 85)

The above joke seems to be a combination of two historical anecdotes.[120] The husband failed to persuade his wife because the textual evidence he cited was not gender-neutral, a fact his smart wife found out in no time. One wonders whether the joke was more on the bookish husband who was henpecked or on the witty wife who was shrewish.

According to Yenna Wu, the theme of marital strife with the stock figures of shrewish wives and henpecked husbands can be traced back to the fifth century, but it was not until the seventeenth century that this theme reached the peak of its popularity. She proposes that "although writers caricature shrewish behavior to reflect a certain amount of social reality and to convey moral concerns, they turn to the shrew figure mainly for its comic-satirical potential."[121] But art and life often imitate each other, and they can be studied in the light of each other. There is a possible historical explanation for the upsurge of the literary theme. Wu hints at some of this in her study. In terms of social reality, from the mid-Ming on, women had been playing a greater role in religious, social, and literary activities, which might have alarmed socially conservative males. The growing trend toward polygamous families also intensified male suspicion of female jealousy, factual or imagined. In terms of intellectual climate, the philosophical discourse on spontaneous emotions and the blossoming of vernacular fiction focusing on family and marriage heightened awareness of proper gender relations. Because shrewish, jealous, and aggressive wives posed a significant threat to the traditional concept of patriarchy and harmony within the family, they were portrayed negatively to serve a comic-satirical purpose. From the psychological perspective, jokes on shrewish wives and henpecked husbands could release the tension of polygamous men, who empathized with the fictional victims, as well as wifeless men, who found solace in the plight of the comic butts.

Otherwise acknowledging women's intelligence and moral integrity, Feng Menglong shared his male contemporaries' intolerance of female jealousy. In the *Survey of Talk Old and New,* Feng argued that desire and jealousy went hand in hand: if a man did not have strong desire for wealth and power, he would not be jealous of other men, his competitors for wealth and power. Likewise, if a woman did not have strong sexual desire, she would not be jealous of other women, her competitors for the love of the man she desired.[122] The association of female jealousy and sexual insatiability was in tune with the stock fiction of shrewish wives and henpecked husbands in Keith McMahon's study.[123]

However, women's jealousy of sex appeared a bit more understandable, though still unacceptable, when Feng put it in parallel with men's jealousy of wealth and power. Inspired by Feng's remark, one wonders if there was a possible link between male jealousy in real life and female jealousy in fiction. In China's time-honored lyrical tradition of *meiren xiangcao* (beauty and flower), the beauty serves the function of what Martin Huang terms "literati indirect self-re/presentation"[124] or what Shuhui Yang terms "ventriloquism through women characters."[125] The beauty who, despite being wronged by her master, still held on to her undying loyalty, was the invented Other, the romantic mirror image of the idealized Self, the faithful but unfortunate talent who was not recognized by his lord. In light of this allegorical tradition, the jealous shrew in late Ming popular literature can be seen as the mirror image of the green-eyed writer, who was jealous of his socially more respectable peers.

If the male writers indeed projected their own jealousy onto their fictional creations, they were apparently unaware of it. Many of them, including Feng Menglong, seemed to worry genuinely about the erosion of male authority in the face of shrewish wives. In the preface to his play, entitled "Wan shi zu (All Is Well)," about the taming of a shrew, Feng estimated unjealous women to number a mere one or two in a thousand, but among the jealous women, he believed eighty percent were jealous only on the outside and only twenty percent were jealous through and through. Most could be persuaded and transformed. He thus ascribed the shrewishness of jealous wives to the husbands' failure in containment due to emotional indulgence or dispositional weakness.[126]

However, not all henpecked men were being ridiculous. In the *History of Love*, Feng cited the famous story of the Lady Lu, wife of Fang Xuanling, emperor Tang Taizong's (r. 626-649) prime minister.[127] The emperor offered Fang a beauty as a gift, but Fang repeatedly declined the offer. Knowing that Fang's wife was famous for jealousy, the emperor summoned Lady Lu to court. He gave her two options: she could allow her husband to take the beauty as a concubine, or she could stand firm and drink the poisonous wine he prepared for her. Lady Lu consumed the cup without any hesitation. She did not die; the "poisonous wine" turned out to be vinegar. The emperor was amazed by the extremity of her jealousy and gave up. For centuries "eating vinegar" became a metaphor for jealousy, and Fang was mocked as a henpecked husband. But Feng Menglong thought he knew the real story behind all this. Before Fang rose in power, he was once fatally ill. He instructed the young Lady Lu to remarry. To demonstrate her determination not to marry another man, the lady gouged out an eye to make herself undesirable. This dramatic act won her Fang's lifelong fidelity after he recovered.[128] Although Feng Menglong's main point was to defend Fang Xuanling's henpecking, Lady Lu's jealousy was at the same time justified. But Lady Lu had to pay a high price to win her right to be jealous.

## Interpreting the Humor in *Treasury of Laughs*

Jokes can be inspired by tensions. The jokes in the *Treasury of Laughs*, though humorous and hyperbolic in tone, vividly reveal the tensions within the political and educational systems, within intellectual circles, between men and women, among different classes, between ideals and practices, and between appearance and reality. The jokes ridicule unqualified military officers and civil officials. They mock pseudo scholars—unsatisfactory products of Ming popularization of education. They satirize the loopholes in administration and justice. They express impatience with didacticism, pedantry, and vulgar culturalism. The jokes suggest male anxiety about the increasing importance of female activities in late Ming society, and perhaps also male anxiety over sexual performance in a time when success in a romantic relation was a marked attribute. They reflect a deep-seated distrust of religious practitioners with regard to their asceticism and their wonder-working. They reveal the elite apprehension of the amateurishness of medical doctors. They also show how pride (in a negative sense), shame, stinginess, affectation, among other emotions of this sort, work against spontaneity, honesty, and generosity, and create oddities in one's social behavior.

The *Treasury of Laughs* seems to embody certain defiant characteristics of Bakhtin's "carnival laughter."[129] The humor is directed at everything and everyone: no one is excluded from the mockery and derision of debased human folly, and no one is excluded from the merry extolling of the innocent "child's folly." Bakhtin sees a subversive effect in carnival's inversion of symbolic hierarchies; others see carnival as an authorized transgression and argue that in the long run carnival is more constraining than liberating.[130] Whether the world of the *Treasury of Laughs* is subversive or not is a complicated issue. Some sexual humor might well have served the Freudian function of providing socially acceptable release of repressed impulses,[131] in effect discouraging sexual transgression. In this regard such jokes might function as a "safety valve," an outlet for frustration and aggression that in the end helps to maintain the status quo. But there are also many jokes which strip human folly and social ailments so naked that they force upon the audience a sharp realization that something is deadly wrong with the current world. The *Treasury of Laughs* is not intended to undercut the entire social and cultural structure of China. It is meant to expose the discrepancy between the social and cultural values which Feng Menglong upheld, and the vulgar culturalism and social disruption which are rampant in his times.

The modern Korean scholar Cho Dong-il divides humor into two categories: satirical and comic. He explains that "Both kinds of humour arise from iconoclastic exposure of what ought to be and, in its place, affirmation of what is. Where iconoclasm is more to the fore, we have satire, and where affirmation is more to the fore, we have comic humour. Comic humour, in that its main concern is affirmation of what is, resembles elegance or appears to be compounded of humor [sic] and elegance. In satire there is an inescapable awareness of the antagonistic object the speaker must struggle against: what has been taken as what ought to be."[132] Along the same lines another Korean scholar Lee Jae-son distinguishes between "a harmless laughter," "a smile which is filled with peerless refinement," and "a laughter of satire," "a laughter concealing a dagger ready for one mighty stroke."[133] The *Treasury of Laughs* contains both the comic, harmless humor that is socially inconsequential—jokes on oversexed women, nearsighted men, idiotic sons, and the like, and the satirical humor which awakens in the audience an awareness of the difference between what is and what ought to be.

The *Treasury of Laughs* is at once entertaining and reflective. Besides a good laugh, the modern reader also gets something extra from the Ming emulator of the eccentric Cloth-Sack Monk. Far from being an island apart, as advocated in modern Western individualism, Feng Menglong was a member of the "gentry society," whose qualification included a "combination of individual integrity and conformity to principle, expressing itself in social or political nonconformity."[134] Critical of contemporary society and politics, he nevertheless remained engaged in their betterment rather than removing himself from them. Unlike the early modern Western Great Artist who was locked in a self-destructive struggle to replace God the Creator, Feng did not manipulate the universe to create order out of chaos.[135] He responded to the imperfect circumstances with a sense of humor. He pointed out the irregularity and called for sanity. While Ming China was falling apart, Feng Menglong exemplified an individualism and romanticism in the Ming style, and left behind a historical record of a tension-felt society through his sharp lens.

## Notes:

1. Cf. Translation by Eva Hung, "Preface to *The Hall of Laughter*," *Renditions: A Chinese-English Translation Magazine* nos. 33-34 (1990): 189. Portions of this chapter were published in my article "Feng Meng-lung's *Treasury of Laughs*: Humorous Satire on Seventeenth-Century Chinese Culture and Society," *The Journal of Asian Studies* 57, no. 4 (1998): 1042-67; used by permission of the Association for Asian Studies.
2. Li Zhi, "Tongxin shuo," in *Fen shu*, 97-99.
3. Liangyan Ge, *Out of the Margins: The Rise of Chinese Vernacular Fiction* (Honolulu: University of Hawai'i Press, 2001), 109-10.
4. W. L.Idema, *Chinese Vernacular Fiction*, LIII-LIV.
5. Uemura Koji, "The Study of *Hsiao-fu*," *Bungaku kaishi* 3:2 (1952): 54-64.
6. Muto Sadao and Matsueda Shigeo, eds., *Chugoku showa sen: Edo kobanashi to no majiwari* (Tokyo: Heibonsha, 1964), 357.
7. Wang Zuodong, ed., *Xin Xiaofu: Minjian gushi jiangshujia Liu Depei gushi ji* (Shanghai: Shanghai wenyi chuban she, 1989).
8. *A Handbook to Literature*, by C. Hugh Holman, based on the original by William Flint Thrall and Addison Hibbard, 3rd edition (Indianapolis: The Odyssey Press, 1972), 557-59.
9. *Webster's Third New International Dictionary of the English Language*, 2625.
10. Hanan, *The Chinese Vernacular Story*, 84.

11. Ibid., 83.

12. The relation between learning and the use of intelligence is made clear by Feng in his preface to the *Sack of Wisdom*, in which he compared wisdom to water. The water hidden underground was like the latent faculty of intelligence; it required learning to draw it forth. See *Zhi nang* (Guanban edition preserved in Harvard-Yenching Library), *xu*: 5b.

13. Shanghai Library has the original issue of *Gujin xiao* of 36 *juan* printed by Feng Menglong himself. Each page has nine lines, and each line has twenty-one characters. Feng's preface was dated spring of 1620.

14. The writer of the preface called himself "The Fifth Member of Yun She." The preface is reprinted in Ju Jun, ed., *Feng Menglong shih wen*, 26.

15. Hanan, *The Chinese Vernacular Story*, 223, notes 38, 39.

16. This is a quotation from *Shiji*, "Guji liezhuan" (Biographies of Jesters). See Sima Qian, *Shiji*, *Sibu beiyao*, 126: 1b.

17. Mei Zhiyun, preface to Feng Menglong, *Gujin tan gai* (Beijng: Wenxue guji kanxing she, 1955), 1a-b.

18. Copies of the edition are preserved in Naikaku Bunko, the Library of Congress, and the Gest Collection at Princeton. The prefaces are dated 1605 and 1614.

19. Hanan, *The Chinese Vernacular Story*, 83.

20. Feng Menglong, preface to *Zhi nang*, in *Zhi nang*, *xu*: 6a-b.

21. *Daode jing*, translated in Wm. Theodore de Bary, Wing-tsit Chan, and Burton Watson, comps., *Sources of Chinese Tradition* (New York: Columbia University Press, 1960), Vol. 1, 57.

22. *Zhi nang*, *xu*: 1a.

23. Hanan, *Chinese Vernacular Story*, 84.

24. Allan Barr discusses and translates several of Jiang Yingke's jokes in "Jiang Yingke's Place in the Gong'an School," 49-63.

25. Hanan, *The Chinese Vernacular Story*, 225, n. 67.

26. For good collections of pre-modern Chinese jokes see Wang Liqi, *Lidai xiaohua ji* (Jokes of Past Dynasties) (Hong Kong: Hsin-yüeh ch'u-pan she, 1962), and Lou Zikuang, ed., *Ming Qing xiaohua ji* (Jest Books During 1368-1911 A.D.), in *Guoli Beijing Daxue Zhongguo minsu xuehui minsu congshu* (The Folklore and Folk Literature Series of National Peking University and Chinese Association), vol. 7 (Rpt. Taipei: The Orient Cultural Service, 1970).

27. Herbert Giles translates 200-odd Chinese jokes from a text which he does not identify. See Herbert A. Giles, *Quips from a Chinese Jest-Book* (Shanghai: Kelly and Walsh, 1925). I suspect his source may be the *Xiaolin guangji*.

28. George Kao, ed, *Chinese Wit and Humor*, xx.

29. Ibid., xxi.

30. Derek Brewer, "Prose Jest-Books Mainly in the Sixteenth to Eighteenth Centuries in England," in *A Cultural History of Humor*, eds. Bremmer and Roodenburg, 90.

31. Ibid., 91.

32. Lu Yunzhong, *100 Chinese Jokes Through the Ages* (Hong Kong: Commercial Press, 1985), 6-7.

33. Xu Wei, *Xieshi* (History of Humor); Li Zhi, *Shanzhong yixi hua* (One Night's Talk in the Mountain); Zhao Nangxing, *xiaozan* (Commentaries on Jokes); Jiang Yingke, *Xuetao xiaoshuo* (Snow Wave's Minor Talk) and *Xuetao xieshi* (Snow

Wave's History of Humor); Zhong Xing, *Xiecong* (Anthology of Humor). This list is not exhaustive. There are more than a dozen famous joke books in the Ming. For a brief discussion of Ming jokes, see Cao Shujuan, *Wan Ming xingling xiaopin yanjiu*, 245-48.

34. Cited by Allan Barr in "Jiang Yingke's Place in the Gong'an School," 48.

35. Tu Long, *Suoluo Guan qingyan*, quoted in Cao Shujuan, 248.

36. There are believed to be only two original copies of *Treasury of Laughs* today, one in Manchuria, the other in Naikaku Bunko. I am using a 1985 facsimile edition.

37. The *Guang Xiaofu* that I use is a modern production edited by Jinxia Ge Zhuren in the series *Guoxue zhenben wenku* 1.7 (Shanghai: Zhongyang shudian, 1935). A large number of jokes in the *Xiaofu* that are erotic, offensive, or too heavy to be funny are cut. This use of scissors was possibly done by the modern editor or editors before him. But since the compiler of *Guang Xiaofu* changed the classification of the jokes, he might have done some deletion himself to fit the new categories.

38. Hanan, *The Chinese Vernacular Story*, 225, n. 67.

39. Robert F. Berkhofer, Jr., *Beyond the Great Story—History as Text and Discourse* (Cambridge: The Belknap Press of Harvard University Press, 1995), 108-09.

40. This translation is modified from Victor H. Mair, "The Wife Who Was Born Under the Sign of the Ox," in *The Columbia Anthology of Traditional Chinese Literature*, ed. Idem (New York: Columbia University Press, 1994), 662.

41. Madeleine Zelin, *The Magistrate's Tael: Rationalizing Fiscal Reform in Eighteenth-Century Ch'ing China* (Berkeley: University of California Press, 1984).

42. Ray Huang, *1587*, 62.

43. Wells, *Traditional Chinese Humor*, 218.

44. Cf. Jon Kowallis, trans., "The Account Book," in *Wit and Humor from Old Cathay*, 97.

45. The translation is slightly modified from Victor Mair, "The God of the Archery Target Helps Win the War," in idem, *Columbia Anthology*, 662-63.

46. Ray Huang, *1587*, 156-88.

47. Benjamin A. Elman, "Political, Social, and Cultural Reproduction via Civil Service Examinations in Late Imperial China," *The Journal of Asian Studies* 50, no. 1 (1991): 7-28.

48. The Chinese terms for the "grades" are "yi deng" (first rate, A), "er deng" (second rate, B), etc. For details of this grading system see *Ming shi, juan* 69, 1687. For more information on Ming education see Benjamin A. Elman and Alexander Woodside, eds., *Education and Society in Late Imperial China, 1600-1900* (Berkeley: University of California Press, 1994).

49. Richard von Glahn, "Municipal Reform and Urban Social Conflict in Late Ming Jiangnan," *The Journal of Asian Studies* 50, no. 2 (1991): 280-307.

50. For an English translation of *Rulin waishi*, see Yang Hsien-yi and Gladys Yang, trans., *The Scholars* (New York: Grosset and Dunlap, 1972).

51. Wells, *Traditional Chinese Humor*, 222.

52. Mikhail Bakhtin, *Problems of Dostoevsky's Poetics*, trans. R. W. Rotsel (Ann Arbor: Ardis, 1973), 156.

53. Gary Saul Morson, *The Boundaries of Genre: Dostoevsky's Diary of a Writer and the Traditions of Literary Utopia* (Austin: University of Texas Press, 1981), 113.

54. *Analects*, XI.3.

55. Roger T. Ames and Henry Rosemont, Jr., *The Analects of Confucius: A Philosophical Translation* (New York: Ballantine, 1998), 97.

56. Sima Qian, *Shi ji, juan* 130. Durrant, *Cloudy Mirror*, 13.

57. Hai Rui's critical attitude toward unworthy students is discussed in Joanna F. Handlin, *Action in Late Ming Thought*, 58-59. Hai Rui's criticism was later echoed by Gu Yanwu in his "Shengyuan lun," in Gu Yanwu, *Tinglin wenji*, in *Gu Tinglin xiansheng yishu shi zhong* (Taipei: Jinxue shuju, 1969), 1: 17a-22a.

58. Cf. Kowallis's translation of the same joke from Fubai Zhuren's *Xiaolin* in *Wit and Humor from Old Cathay*, 67-68. In Liu Yuanqing's *Ying xie lu*, the Neo-Confucian master in the joke is Wang Yangming, and the last sentence reads, "These two only know others' faults but not themselves'." See Wang Liqi, 163.

59. This joke may be a combination of two jokes told by the Neo-Confucian Luo Hongxian (1504-1564), which Geng Dingxiang cites in his *Quan Zi zazu*. In one joke a man is learning to walk like a *dao xue*; he gets tired and quits, but not before asking his servant to be sure that nobody is looking. In the other joke a man gives up his *dao xue* walking manner and runs when caught in the rain. After realizing that he has lost his manner, however, he returns to where he started running and resumes his slow walking posture, in order to make up for his mistake. Luo criticizes the first man for falsity and the second for pedantry. See Wang Liqi, 143.

60. Christoph Harbsmeier, "*Confucius Ridens*: Humor in the Analects," *Harvard Journal of Asiatic Studies* 50, no. 1 (1990): 152.

61. *Liji*, *Sibu beiyao*, 2: 11a-b.

62 Arthur Schopenhauer, *The World as Will and Idea*, trans. R. B. Haldane and John Kemp, 6th edition (London: Routledge and Kegan Paul, 1907-09), Book I, Section 13.

63. I owe this insight to communication with Hu Ying, March 1995.

64. *Gujin tan gai*, 1: 21a.

65. Ibid., 1: 22a.

66. Cf. Kowallis, trans., "Needing a Thousand Hands," *Wit and Humor*, 115.

67. Cf. Kowallis, trans., "Locating a Noted Doctor," ibid., 106.

68. Hou Wenyong, "Siwang zhi ge," in *Hou Wenyong duanpian xiaoshuo ji* (Taipei: Crown Publishing Company, 1996), 87-97.

69. Cf. Kowallis, trans., "Learn First Things First," *Wit and Humor*, 107.

70. Cf. Kowallis, trans., "A prayer to Be Kicked," ibid.

71 Charlotte Furth, *A Flourishing Yin: Gender in China's Medical History, 960-1665* (Berkeley: University of California Press, 1999), 50, 51.

72. Li Shizhen, *Bencao gangmu*, Insect Section, *juan* 39, in *Li Shizhen yixue quanshu*, ed. Liu Changhua (Beijing: Zhongguo zhongyiyao chubanshe, 1999), 1279-81.

73. Paul U. Unschuld, *Medical Ethics in Imperial China: A Study in Historical Anthropology* (Berkeley: University of California Press, 1979).

74. For an English translation of "The Battling Doctors" see William Dolby, *Eight Chinese Plays: From the Thirteenth-Century to the Present* (New York: Columbia University Press, 1978), 21-29. For excerpts of some Chinese plays on doctors see T'ao Lee, "The Doctor in Chinese Drama," *Chinese Medical Journal* 68 (1950): 34-43.

75. Robert P. Hymes, "Not Quite Gentlemen? Doctors in Sung and Yuan," *Chinese Science* 8 (1987): 9-76.

76. Angela Ki Che Leung, "Organized Medicine in Ming-Qing China: State and Private Medical Institutions in the Lower Yangzi Region," *Late Imperial China* 8, no. 1 (1987): 134-66.

77. Wang Kentang, *Shanghan zhunsheng*, in *Liuke zhunsheng* (Shanghai: Hongbao Zhai shuju, 1923), preface: 1a; Unschuld, 68.

78. John Kieschnick, *The Eminent Monk: Buddhist Ideals in Medieval Chinese Hagiography* (Honolulu: University of Hawai'i Press, 1997), 17-28.

79. Sommer, *Sex, Law, and Society in Late Imperial China*, 100.

80. Wells, *Traditional Chinese Humor*, 119.

81. For a study of the social functions of Taoist ritual of exorcism in medieval China see Edward L. Davis, *Society and the Supernatural in Song China* (Honolulu: University of Hawai'i Press, 2001).

82. Cf. Kowallis's translation of the same joke from Fubai Zhuren's *Xiaolin* in *Wit and Humor from Old Cathay*, 66.

83. Xie Yingfang, *Guichao gao*, 8.13a, cited in Brook, 65.

84 Clunas, *Superfluous Things*, 108.

85. Yuan Hongdao, "Shi: Haoshi," in his *Ping shi*, in *Yuan Hongdao ji jianjiao*, ed. Qian Bocheng (Shanghai: Shanghai guji chuban she, 1981), 826.

86. Judith T. Zeitlin, "The Petrified Heart: Obsession in Chinese Literature, Art, and Medicine," *Late Imperial China* 12, no. 1 (1991): 3-4.

87. Tsao Jr-lien, "Remembering Suzhou: Urbanism in Late Imperial China," 94.

88. Gu Yanwu, *Tianxia junguo libing shu*, *Tushu jicheng chubian*, 14: 7b; 14: 11b-13a.

89. *Fo xue da cidian*, edited by Ding Fubao (Taipei: Huayan lian she, 1969), 2837.

90. Timothy Brook, "Funerary Ritual and the Building of Lineages in Late Imperial China," *Harvard Journal of Asiatic Studies* 49, no. 2 (1989): 465-99.

91. *Huang Ming tiaofa shilei zuan*, cited in Joseph W. Esherick and Mary Backus Rankin, eds., *Chinese Local Elites and Patterns of Dominance* (Berkeley: University of California Press, 1990), 5.

92. Ann Waltner, *Getting an Heir: Adoption and the Construction of Kinship in Late Imperial China* (Honolulu: University of Hawaii Press, 1990), 85-88.

93. Evidence of such practices is ample. For example, see Xu Sanzhong, "jia ze," *Mingshan quanbian*, and Gu Yanwu, "Jia tong," *Ri zhi lu*, cited in *Gujin tushu jicheng*, Vol. 330, 41a.

94. See, for example, Susumu Fuma, "Late Ming Urban Reform and the Popular Uprising in Hangzhou" (translated by Michael Lewis), and Paolo Santangelo, "Urban Society in Late Imperial Suzhou" (translated by Adam Victor), in Linda Cooke Johnson, ed., *Cities of Jiangnan in Late Imperial China* (New York: State University of New York Press, 1993), 47-79, 81-116.

95. For discussions of the complex land-tenure system, see Fu Yiling, *Ming Qing nongcun shehui jingji* (Beijing: Sanlian shudian, 1961); Ye Xian'en, "Ming Qing Huizhou dianpu zhi shi tan," *Zhongshan Daxue xuebao* (1979/2): 71-73.

96. Chen Wanyi, *Wan Ming xiaopin*, 80.

97. Zhang Dai, "Qi Zhixiang pi," in *Taoan mengyi*, *Congshu jicheng chubian*, 34.

98. For a brief description of the two stories, see Josephine Huang Hung, *Ming Drama* (Taipei: Heritage Press, 1966), 87-94.

99. For a discussion of the controversy see Hu Ying, "Angling with Beauty: Two Stories of Women as Narrative Bait in *Sanguozhi yanyi*," *Chinese Literature Essays Articles Reviews* 15 (1993): 103-04, 111-12.

100. Ray Huang, *Taxation and Government Finance in Sixteenth-Century Ming China* (Cambridge: Cambridge University Press, 1974), 79.

101. Richard von Glahn, *Fountain of Fortune: Money and Monetary Policy in China, 1000-1700* (Berkeley: University of California Press, 1996), 83.

102. For more information on Taoist rituals see Kristofer Schipper, *The Taoist Body*, trans. Karen C. Duval (Berkeley: University of California Press, 1993), 72-99.

103. Cf. Kowallis, trans., "The Master's Belly," *Wit and Humor*, 99.

104. Cf. Kowallis, trans., "Parents for Sale," *Wit and Humor*, 95-96.

105. Cf. Kowallis, trans., "How Did the Character Grow?" *Wit and Humor*, 96.

106. Translation modified from Arthur Waley, trans., "On the Birth of His Son," in *Asian Laughter*, ed. Feinberg, 83, and Patricia Buckley Ebrey, *The Cambridge Illustrated History of China* (Cambridge: Cambridge University Press, 1996), 140.

107. *Mencius*, VI A: 4.

108. For a discussion of this line from the *Mencius* and its modern applications see Judith Farquhar, *Appetites: Food and Sex in Post-Socialist China* (Durham: Duke University Press, 2002), 1-3.

109. Cf. Kowallis, trans., "Mounting the Sedan Chair," *Wit and Humor*, 114.

110. Margery Wolf, *Women and the Family in Rural Taiwan* (Stanford: Stanford University Press, 1972), 135.

111. Ibid., 90.

112. Charlotte Furth, *A Flourishing Yin*, 209-10.

113. Cf. Kowallis, trans., "A 'Double-Axe Hacking,'" *Wit and Humor*, 100.

114. Susan Purdie, *Comedy: The Mastery of Discourse* (Toronto: University of Toronto Press, 1993), 135-36.

115. Ibid., 136.

116. Keith McMahon, *Misers, Shrews, and Polygamists: Sexuality and Male-Female Relations in Eighteenth-Century Chinese Fiction* (Durham, N.C.: Duke University Press, 1995), 56.

117. Cf. Kowallis, trans., "Collapsing Trellises," *Wit and Humor*, 102.

118. Guan Hanqing, "Shu suo jian," quoted in Li Jinghua, "Guanyu 'Dao le putao jia,'" *Wenxue yichan* (1991.2): 5.

119. Martin Huang discusses the references to the grape arbor in these two novels in *Desire and Fictional Narrative*, 148-50. Because Huang interprets grape arbor as a metaphor for sexual escapade, the discussion is a bit confusing.

120. In Luo Ye, *Zuiweng tan lu*, Yang Langzhong was recorded to cite the "Jiumu" poem to his wife Madame Zhao. In *Shishuo xinyu*, XIX.23, and *Taiping yulan*, 521.6a, Xie Daifu (Xie An, 320-385) was recorded to cite the "Zhongsi" poem to his wife Madame Liu.

121. Yenna Wu, "The Inversion of Marital Hierarchy: Shrewish Wives and Henpecked Husbands in Seventeenth-Century Chinese Literature," *Harvard Journal of Asiatic Studies* 48, no. 2 (1988): 363-64.

122. Feng Menglong, *Gujin tan gai*, prefatory essay to the chapter on "Female Lewdness," 19: 1a.

123. McMahon, *Misers, Shrews, and Polygamists*, 55-81.

124. Martin W. Huang, *Literati and Self-Re/Presentation: Autobiographical Sensibility in the Eighteenth-Century Chinese Novel* (Stanford: Stanford University Press, 1995).

125. Shuhui Yang, *Appropriation and Representation*, 99-152.

126. Feng Menglong, "Wan shi zu," in *Mohan Zhai dingben chuanqi*, vol. 1 (Beijing: Zhongguo xiqu chuban she, 1960), preface: 1a-4a.

127. In *Gujin tan gai* 19: 8a Feng Menglong cites exactly the same story but identifies the heroine as Ren Gui's wife, the Lady Liu.

128. Feng Menglong, *Qingshi*, 1: 9b-10a.

129. Mikhail Bakhtin, *Rabelais and His World*, trans. Helene Iswolsky (Bloomington: Indiana University Press, 1984).

130. Umberto Eco, "The Frames of Comic 'Freedom,'" in *Carnival!*, ed., Thomas A. Sebeok, Approaches to Semiotics 64 (Berlin: Mouton, 1984), 1-9. Purdie, 126-27.

131. Sigmund Freud, *Jokes and Their Relation to the Unconscious*, trans. James Strachey (New York: W. W. Norton, 1960).

132. Cho Dong-il, "Humour in Folk Poetry," in *Humour in Korean Literature*, ed. Chun Shin-Yong (Seoul: International Cultural Foundation, 1977), 56.

133. Lee Jae-son, "Laughter in the Literature of Enlightenment Period," in *Humour in Korean Literature*, ed. Chun Shin-Yong, 70.

134. Wm. Theodore de Bary, *Learning for One's Self: Essays on the Individual in Neo-Confucian Thought* (New York: Columbia University Press, 1991), 233.

135. For a comparative study of Ming and Western romanticism, see Jonathan Chaves, "The Expression of Self in the Kung-an School: Non-Romantic Individualism," in *Expressions of Self in Chinese Literature*, eds. Robert E. Hegel and Richard C. Hessney (New York: Columbia University Press, 1985), 123-50.

# Epilogue

# 跋

The late Ming was a curious historical moment. So many things went so wrong for so long that when the dynasty finally did collapse it came almost as a surprise to its people. Modern historians may be amazed that an institution as decayed as the Ming imperial court could have sustained over a half century of faulty governance. But many Ming intellectuals who survived the fall of the dynasty sullenly admitted they did not see it coming. If China could have survived the reigns of the absentee Wanli emperor and the mentally disabled Tianqi emperor, then there was no reason why it could not survive under the more enlightened Chongzhen emperor. And yet most Ming intellectuals might simply have been blinded by hedonism, moral relativism, and escapism, their conscience being numbed by political corruption and social injustice. Wei Yong, who lived around the seventeenth century, justified his indulgence in sensual pleasure by placing the blame on the bottleneck of job placement. "If a man's capabilities went unnoticed, his full bosom of true feelings would not have the chance to be brought to use in fulfillment of his ambition to make a name for himself," said Wei. "He then has no alternative but to lodge his feelings in beautiful women, so as to vent his anguish."[1] Wei bifurcated male desires. Politics was the more respectable site of male desire, whereas women's bodies provided the less honorable, although still recognized site of male desire. When men's political ambitions were stifled, the legitimacy of men's desire for women ascended. Sex became a socially acceptable object of male desire, as men withdrew from the political arena and escaped to women's quarters to indulge in sensuality.

It was in this atmosphere of general moral decadence that Feng

Menglong compiled his literary works. The greatest appeal of Feng's works, which made them so successful in the commercial press of late Ming China, appears to be eroticism—it is everywhere and very eye-catching. In *Hill Songs*, peasant men and women immerse themselves in titillating sexual orgy with little hint of guilt or shame. In *Hanging Twigs*, flirtatious prostitutes and courtesans stop at nothing to entice their clients. In the *Treasury of Laughs*, small children fall from the top of the bunk beds in the local earthquake created by their parents' ecstasies. In the *Sanyan*, nervous virgins pass out in the excitement of their secretive sexual debut; a chaste widow involuntarily mounts the naked body of her servant boy when she sees his penis standing erect in his erotic dream. These men and women are fleshy and hot-headed; they are governed more by animal drive than by reason. Even the most admirable romantic heroes and heroines are sensationally described as having fair skin, handsome looks, alluring figures, charming smiles, and amorous impulse. These otherwise gentle and reserved love birds are made to have sexual intercourse under the voyeurist gaze of the audience, albeit in dim light and for just a fleeting moment.

But what is not there is perhaps as important as what is there. Absent from Feng Menglong's works are lengthy, provocative close-ups of masturbation, sex perversion, and violent rape. Feng does not build a story line around the glorification of sexual conquest, debauchery, or polygamy. Promiscuity and infidelity do not go unpunished. There is no pretense that the whole spectrum of carnal love has to be fully explored before its illusive nature is exposed. Not sharing the religious agenda of novels such as the *Dream of the Red Chamber*, Feng Menglong, the self-proclaimed "Buddha of Boundless Love and Joy," has no interest in preaching disenchantment through enchantment, to borrow Wai-yee Li's metaphor.[2]

Eroticism might be Feng Menglong's trademark, but it was an uncomfortable trademark. After all, Feng aspired to a political career and could not afford to be reputed as a producer of frivolous literature. While exploring human sexuality in a satisfying fashion as a canny commercial author/publisher, Feng also needed to elevate his literature above and beyond eroticism if he was to be taken seriously in the elite circles. What he came up with was an advocacy of healthy and guiltless sex, happy sex if you will—although he was not always convincing. As long as sex was the corporeal manifestation of genuine love and single-minded devotion, argued Feng, it was respectable. On the other hand, sex without love or out of control was unhealthy and sinful. A lustful person could not truly enjoy sex. Rather, s/he would be plagued by it and from which there was no redemption.

Feng Menglong was not the only erotic writer to claim a moral high ground above and beyond eroticism. Others made similar claims, but some were little more than sugarcoating. A particularly interesting comparison to Feng's *Child's Folly* and *History of Love* is *History of Debauchery* (*Langshi*), whose commentator, perhaps more than coincidentally, styled himself Tongchi (Child's Folly). Since the only publication information available on the *History of Debauchery*, which is no longer extant, is that it had appeared before 1620,[3] it is hard to tell between Feng Menglong and Tongchi who influenced whom, or who inspired whom. Not surprisingly, the preface to the *History of Debauchery* contains a statement reminiscent of the *History of Love*, "*Qing* is first nurtured in the inner chamber; then it will expand and develop in a person to enable him to become a loyal minister as well as a filial son."[4] Despite the rhetoric, as Martin Huang aptly points out, the *History of Debauchery* is fundamentally different from the *History of Love*. "*Langshi* concentrates on the sexual adventures of the male protagonist—how he conquers various female beauties and finally becomes a Taoist immortal after achieving ultimate sexual gratification. As represented in this novel, *qing* refers to the pursuit of sexual gratification through promiscuity and has little to do with the values of *qingzhen* (fidelity in love) that Feng Menglong advocated."[5]

Feng Menglong's *Tongchi* also bears little resemblance to the Tongchi of *History of Debauchery*. In esoteric Taoism, sexual orgy without seminal ejaculation, or "plucking the *yin* to nourish the *yang*," is a technique to achieve longevity and immortality.[6] By absorbing the *yin* energy of the unwitting female participant, the domineering male practitioner augments his own life force. Since the man does not ejaculate, technically he retains his virginity (*tongzhen*, literally, "child's chastity"). The ideal female partner was also a virgin, a neophyte full of energy. She would only supply, but not consume, the vitality throughout the process. Perhaps that was the rationale for the pen name Tongchi, commentator of *History of Debauchery*—the book was about a male virgin's (*tong*) obsessive (*chi*) sexual quest for foolish (*chi*) female virgins (*tong*).

Feng Menglong's *Tongchi*, on the other hand, did not invoke the sexual orgy of esoteric Taoism. Undeniably, sexual orgy was prominent in *Hanging Twigs*, *Hill Songs*, and *Treasury of Laughs*. But by naming the collection *Child's Folly* and writing didactic prefaces and commentaries, Feng was claiming innocence of transgression. To borrow Christian terminology, what happened between the lovers in

*Child's Folly* was prelapsarian; it was not sinful. Since the concept of Original Sin was absent from the Chinese tradition, it might be a bit imprecise to describe the universe of *Child's Folly* as "prelapsarian," but Feng did try to recall a more primitive, amoral time prior to the onslaught of Confucian cultural colonialism. The romanticization of the pre-Confucian state of non-duality went back to Lao Zi's Taoist classic *Daodejing*, where the "heart-and-mind of the naked baby" was celebrated. Lao Zi's primordial "naked baby" was neither good nor bad, one to whom a moral standard was inapplicable. Given Lao Zi's "romantic" intellectual inclination, it was no coincidence that Feng Menglong invoked Lao Zi in many of his pseudonyms. Feng's *zi* (courtesy name) was Youlong, Ziyou, and Eryou, and his *hao* (literary name) was Long Ziyou. All four names allude to Lao Zi, whom Confucius was said to have praised as "resembling a dragon" (*you long*).[7]

But Feng Menglong's protest against Confucian orthodoxy was not meant to discredit Confucian ethics completely. When Feng vowed to "take the true love between man and woman as an antidote for the fake medicine of nominal rules," his stated intent was to make the claim that by oppressing sex and marginalizing erotica, the pedantic moralists had driven them underground and contributed to their debasement. He therefore followed the lead of Confucius, who was more "enlightened" than later Confucians, and compiled *Child's Folly* in the spirit of the *Book of Odes*, so as to bring love songs and the discourse of *qing* back to the mainstream, for the sake of sanity.

It was smart indeed of Feng to invoke both Lao Zi and Confucius. However, his claim begs the question of whether the love songs in *Child's Folly* reflected the "prelapsarian" state of "true love between man and woman" or the decadent state of sexual promiscuity after the "lapse." After all, the songs were collected long after Confucianism had been canonized and love songs marginalized. This inherent ambiguity gave Feng a space to play his double-role of a popular author and a conscientious member of the "gentry society." Straightforward depictions of the obscene satisfied the voyeurism of audiences of pornographic literature. But refreshing materials that threw light on the jarring gap between empty moralizing and actual practices and between daily reality and sexual fantasy legitimized the volumes in the eyes of audiences who appreciated the tension. In the late Ming, these two groups of audiences did not even need to be mutually exclusive.

Highlighting social and intellectual tension was where humor came into play in *Child's Folly*. Humorists spotted the tension and magnified it in a hyperbolic manner, so that the audience would not fail to see it. Because the hilarious material could have a potentially serious intent, the ambiguity gave Feng the edge to include speeches that could be indecent or dangerous under normal circumstances, but would be all right under the cover of humor. Again, Feng was allowed to play the double-role of popular and conscientious editor. Using a low form of language to tackle tabooed subjects, the authors of *Child's Folly* committed a literary transgression, either to entertain or to educate, or both. Victoria Cass puts it well in the following passage: "As philologists love to tell us, the logos of the insignificant also commands listeners. Public speech is helpful, positive, informative; but private speech reveals."[8]

Humorous utterances function like private speeches. They are informal, but revealing. Even obscene jokes reveal deep-seated fear and anxiety in the human psyche and in human sexual behavior. They are not just funny. While the pedants only claimed to be mindful of people's well-being, conscientious humorists had true compassion for people's mental and physical health. Carnal love was the most prominent taboo, so it took up most space in *Hanging Twigs* and *Hill Songs*. But non-erotic subject matters such as social and political criticisms also made their way into the song collections, albeit in small numbers. In *Treasury of Laughs*, non-sexual materials gained distinctive prominence to cover a wide spectrum of social, cultural, political, and economic phenomena. Nothing seemed to escape the keen eyes of the humorist.

*Child's Folly* had its flaws. Distinct from the sexy playthings in most hedonistic literature of the late Ming, the heroines in *Hanging Twigs* and *Hill Songs* were not always objectified as the site of male desire. Often women were the subjects of sexual desire, and they were applauded for their courage to pursue the objects of their desire. But still, the materials in *Child's Folly* seemed to be catering more to the enjoyment of a male audience than to that of a female audience. When women took the initiative in a romantic relationship, they were willing to shoulder the burden entailed by that relationship, hence releasing the men from possible responsibilities. Sexual jokes at the expense of women popped up here and there in the *Treasury of Laughs*. Women's jealousy was poked fun at even in the seemingly pro-feminine song collections. The message seemed to be that women should have their own desires and their own minds, as long as they posed no serious threat to the comfort of men.

Similarly, *Child's Folly* exposed the evil of social injustice and sympathized with the socially disadvantaged in their plight, but defended the exclusive prestige of the gentry. Again, the message seemed to be that people of the lower class should be treated fairly and compassionately, so long as they did not go overboard and presume to be the gentry's social equals.

We may not approve of some of the attitudes and sentiments expressed in *Child's Folly*. But if we can suspend our moral and value judgment, we may be able to appreciate the text as an excellent record of the material and spiritual lives of late Ming people. We know what they ate, what they drank, what they wore, what they owned, and what they wished they owned. We know how they went about their daily routines. We know their beliefs, their superstitions, their skepticism, their hopes, and their misgivings. We hear their laughs. We see their tears. We glance at the expanse of "liberal" trends in the late Ming. We also notice their limits. If nothing else, *Child's Folly* preserves vast tabooed materials that were marginalized by the mainstream culture and would have been hidden from our sight at the collections' absence.

Gu Jiegang, an Avant-garde May Fourth folklorist, proposed two possible perspectives to view the erotic songs in the *Hill Songs* (about one-third of the total content). One was to see the songs as honest reflections of the healthy love lives of Ming people. The other was to see the songs as sexual fantasies of pathologic people whose desires were suppressed by orthodox teachings. From the former perspective, if readers found the graphic descriptions of sexual intercourse offensively obscene, that was because the readers themselves had obscene minds. From the latter perspective, readers should sympathize with the pitiable souls who could be licentious only in the mind, and not in real life.[9] Whether as reflections of objective or subjective realities (albeit in a more condensed and exaggerated form), these songs were celebrated as valuable records of the "voice of the people."

But was this truly the "voice of the people," repressed by Confucian orthodoxy, rescued by Feng Menglong, victimized by Qing inquisition, and finally rehabilitated by May Fourth intellectuals? Haiyan Lee cautions that because a pristine form of popular culture is inaccessible without elite mediation, the "voice of the people" should be regarded as a hybrid of folk oral tradition and elite scriptural labor. It is a product of "folklore movements that both reify the heterogeneous voices in writing and legitimize writing in the name of orality."[10]

Elite contributions to *Child's Folly*, however, went beyond rescue and reinvention. Intellectuals in the Ming not only reinterpreted the folk material; they participated in the production of the folk material. *Hanging Twigs*, *Hill Songs*, and *Treasury of Laughs* recorded works of both commoners and literati. From a historical perspective, such active elite participation in the dialogue between the popular culture and the learned culture helped to mold a culture for all Chinese and to sustain Chinese civilization through the tyranny of history.

The question remains: can *Child's Folly* still be regarded as "folk literature"? They may not if we see the presence of works by literati authors as "contamination" of the integrity and authenticity of folk literature. But they can if we adopt the definition of "folk" by Alan Dundes, who contends,

> Folk is not a synonym for peasant (as it was in the nineteenth century), nor is it limited to one stratum of society, for example, the *vulgus in populo*, or the lower class. Nor is it the illiterate in a literate society. The term "folk" can refer to *any group of people whatsoever* who share at least one common factor. It does not matter what the linking factor is—it could be a common occupation, language or religion—what is important is that a group formed for whatever reason will have some traditions which it calls its own.[11]

Feng Menglong would have agreed. Like his namesake Lao Zi over a millennium ago, Feng Menglong, the man who aspired to roam as free as a dragon, despised binary oppositions. He endeavored to break down the barriers between high and low, central and marginal. He looked for a common link between his authors from various strata of society, and he found one—a spark of naiveté that he termed "child's folly." Ideally, these "folks" with "child's folly" mediated between high and low cultures and transcended them both. They were neither elitist nor vulgar. Their minds were bare of social sophistication and literary intricacy when they sang the songs or told the jokes. Their swift and humorous insights allowed them to be amused by the multifarious incongruities of their world, and their simple yet refreshing language allowed them to transfer that amusement down to us, even after a lapse of almost four centuries. Meanwhile, they revealed, unwittingly, their own ambivalence with regard to, for example, sexually aggressive women, homosexuals, and the *nouveau riche.* No matter how open-minded these possessors of "child's folly" were, there was a limit to their social and cultural tolerance. Even the conscientious compiler Feng Menglong could not completely escape from this provincialism of the late Ming collective consciousness. So as Feng had anticipated, the ones who laughed are in turn laughed at when we read *Child's Folly* in the twenty-first century.

After the laughter dies down, let us ponder. What kind of world does the *Child's Folly* present to us? Was it a world with plenty supply of eccentric, ludicrous, mediocre, depraved, and credulous people? Yes. Was it a world of eerie tensions and troubling problems? Yes.

Was it a world of alarming moral, social, and cultural crises? Yes. But was it a world on the road to national catastrophe? It seemed unlikely. The world of *Child's Folly* appeared too merry to be doomed, despite all the negative factors. Murray Davis contends, "Laughter saves the integration of the self from the disintegration of the world. People laugh when they suddenly recognize that something does not fit into the larger pattern of their cosmos while simultaneously removing the self from this contradiction to a safe distance."[12] When the Ming world disintegrated, what better weapon could the Ming people find than laughter to save themselves from disintegration along with the world around them? Laughter lifted the people above the inconsistency in the cosmos, and allowed them to maintain a somewhat consistent view of the sane self and the sane cosmos. Was this escapism, or was it transcendence? There may not be a definite answer. Shall we congratulate the Ming people for their ability to laugh while the time was less than ideal? Or shall we pity them for their inability to foresee what the future had in store for them? Perhaps it depends on whether we see "optimism" or "blind optimism" in the humor of *Child's Folly*.

To conclude, I would like to quote Bakhtin:

> The epic and tragic hero is the hero who, by his very nature, must perish. Popular masks, on the contrary, never perish: not a single plot in Atellan, Italian or Italianized French comedies provides for, or could ever provide for, the actual death of a Maccus, a Pulcinello or a Harlequin. However, one frequently witnesses their fictive comic deaths (with subsequent resurrections). These are heroes of free improvisation and not heroes of tradition, heroes of a life process that is imperishable and forever renewing itself, forever contemporary—these are not heroes of an absolute past.[13]

Bakhtin's comment, directed toward the artistic structure of two distinctive heroic images, reflects his prejudice against classicism. But one may apply his comment to human history and arrive at a feasible conclusion: those who can laugh in the face of adversity have better chances of surviving it than those who are locked in the mood of melancholy.

## Notes:

1. Wei Yong, *Yuerong bian*, in *Xiang yan congshu*, 1: 2.1a.
2. Wai-yee Li, *Enchantment and Disenchantment*.

3. *Langshi* is mentioned in a preface (dated 1620) to the Tianxu Zhai edition of *Sansui Pingyao zhuan* (*Quelling the Demons' Revolt*). See Martin Huang, *Desire and Fictional Narrative*, 69.

4. *Langshi*, *Si wu xie hui bao* series (Taipei: Taiwan Daying baike, 1995), 37. Translated in Martin Huang, *Desire and Fictional Narrative*, 68.

5. Martin Huang, *Desire and Fictional Narrative*, 70.

6. Charlotte Furth, "Rethinking Van Gulik: Sexuality and Reproduction in Traditional Chinese Medicine," in Gilmartin et al., eds., *Engendering China*, 125-46.

7. Sima Qian, *Shiji*, 63: 2a.

8. Victoria Cass, *Dangerous Women: Warriors, Grannies and Geishas of the Ming* (Lanham: Rowman & Littlefield, 1999), xi.

9. Gu Jiegang, preface, 5a-6b, in *Shan ge* (Shanghai: Chuanjing tang, 1935).

10. Haiyan Lee, "Tears That Crumbled the Great Wall," 59.

11. Alan Dundes, *Folklore Matters*, 11.

12. Murray S. Davis, *Smut: Erotic Reality/Obscene Ideology* (Chicago: The University of Chicago Press, 1983), 226.

13. Bakhtin, "Epic and Novel," in *Dialogic Imagination*, 36.

# Bibliography

## A. Chinese and Japanese Sources:

Ban Gu. "Yiwen zhi." *Qian Han shu. Sibu beiyao.*

Bao Jia-lin. *Zhongguo funü shi lun ji.* Taipei: Daoxiang chuban she, 1992.

Cao Shujuan. *Wan Ming xingling xiaopin yanjiu.* Taipei: Wenjin chuban she, 1988.

Chen Jiru. *Chen Meigong xiansheng quanji.* Microfilm of Ming edition in the National Central Library, Taiwan.

---. "Pidian Mudanting tici." In *Tang Xianzu ji*, edited by Xu Shuofang, 1544-45. Beijing: Zhonghua shuju, 1962.

Chen Jisheng. *Tianqi Chongzhen liang chao yishi.* Rpt. Beijing: Zhonghua shuju, 1958.

Chen Wanyi. *Wan Ming xiaopin yu Ming ji wenren shenghuo.* Taipei: Daan chuban she, 1988.

Chen Xuewen. "Ming dai yici shimin yishi di xin juexing: Wanli shi nian Hangzhou bingbian he minbian yanjiu." *Zhejiang shehui kexue* (February 1992): 61-64.

Cheng Pei-kai. "Wan Ming Yuan Zhongdao di funü guan." *Research on Women in Modern Chinese History* 1 (June 1993): 201-16.

Cheng Yi, and Cheng Hao. *Er Cheng quanshu. Sibu beiyao.*

Feng Menglong. *Chun Qiu daquan.* Benya cangban edition preserved in Harvard-Yenching Library.

---. *Chun Qiu hengku.* Jiren Tang edition preserved in Harvard-Yenching Library.

---. *Dong Zhou lieguo zhi.* Taipei: Shijie shuju, 1961.

---. *Feng Menglong quanji.* Compiled by Wei Tongxian. 43 Vols. Shanghai: Guji chuban she, 1993.

---. *Gujin tan gai.* Beijing: Wenxue guji kanxing she, 1955.

---. *Gujin xiaoshuo* (*Yushi mingyan*). Shijie wenku facsimile reproduction of Tianxu Zhai edition.

---. *Guazhier.* In *Ming Qing min ge shi diao ji*, Vol. 1. Shanghai: Shanghai guji chuban she, 1987.

---. *Guang Xiaofu. Guoxue zhenben wenku* 1.7. Shanghai: Zhongyang shudian, 1935.

---. *Jiashen jishi.* In *Xuanlan Tang congshu.*

---. *Jingshi tongyan*. Shijie wenku facsimile reproduction of Jianshan Tang edition.
---. *Lang qing nü yi ji—Jiazhutao dingzhen Qianjiashi shan ge*. Hong Kong: Wanli shudian, 1962.
---. *Linjing zhiyue*. In *Feng Menglong quanji*, compiled by Wei Tongxian, Vols. 1-2. Shanghai: Guji chuban she, 1993.
---. "Madiao pai jing." In *Xu Shuofu, jiu* 39, edited by Tao Ting, 1759-62. Rpt Taipei: Xinxing shuju, 1964.
---. *Mohan Zhai dingben chuanqi*. 3 Vols. Beijing: Zhongguo xiqu chuban she, 1960.
---. *Qingshi leilue*. Late Ming edition preserved in The University of Chicago Library.
---. *Qingshi leilue*. Qing Jiezi Yuan edition preserved in Harvard-Yenching Library.
---. *Qingshi leilue. Ming Qing shanben xiaoshuo congkan chubian*. Taipei: Tianyi chuban she, 1985.
--- (Qile Sheng). *San jiao ou nian*. Modern facsimile edition in *Guben xiaoshuo congkan*. Beijing: Zhonghua shuju, 1990.
---. *Shan ge*. Shanghai: Chuanjing Tang, 1935.
---. *Shan ge*. Beijing: Zhonghua shuju, 1962.
---. *Shan ge. Ming Qing min ge shi diao ji*, Vol. 1. Shanghai: Shanghai guji chuban she, 1987.
---. *Shouning daizhi*. In *Feng Menglong quanji*, compiled by Wei Tongxian, Vol. 14. Shanghai: Guji chuban she, 1993.
---. (Xiangyue Ju Guqu Sanren). *Taixia xinzou*. Modern facsimile edition without a preface, n.d.
---. *Xiaofu. Ming Qing shanben xiaoshuo congkan chubian*. Taipei: Tianyi chuban she, 1985.
---. *Xingshi hengyan*. Shijie wenku facsimile reproduction of Ye Jingchi edition.
---. *Zhi nang*. Guanban edition preserved in Harvard-Yenching Library.
---. *Zhongxing weilue*. Japanese edition preserved in Harvard-Yenching Library.
*Fujian tongzhi*, 1871 edition.
*Funing fuzhi*. Edited by Li Ba.
Fu Yiling. *Ming Qing nongcun shehui jingji*. Beijing: Sanlian shudian, 1961.
Gao Hongjun. "*Guazhier* chengshu kao ji Feng Menglong, Hou Huiqing lianli yuanwei." *Tianjin Shida xuebao, sheke ban*, 1992.2: 39-44.
Gu Yanwu. *Gu Tinglin xiansheng yishu shi zhong*. Taipei: Jinxue shuju, 1969.

---. *Rizhi lu jishi. Sibu beiyao.*

---. *Tianxia junguo libing shu. Tushu jicheng ju* 1901 edition.

Guo Moruo. "'Chimi pian' de yanjiu." *Nuli zhi shidai*, 2nd edition, 148-201. Beijing, 1973.

Hou Wenyong. "Siwang zhi ge." In *Hou Wenyong duanpian xiaoshuo ji*, 87-97. Taipei: Crown, 1996.

Hu Xiaowei. "*Jin Ping Mei* quanben zaoqi shoucang zhe Liu Jinwu kao." *Wenxue yichan*, 1992.1: 90-96.

Hu Wanchuan. "Feng Menglong yu Fu She renwu." In *Zhongguo gudian xiaoshuo yanjiu quanji*, Vol. 1, 123-36. Taipei: Lianjing chuban shiye youxian gongsi, 1979.

*Jiangnan tongzhi*, 1737 edition.

Jin Demeng. "Feng Menglong sheji kao." *Zhonghua wenshi luncong*, 1985.1: 281-84.

*Jiu Tang shu*. Compiled by Liu Xu. *Sibu beiyao.*

Ju Jun, ed. *Feng Menglong shiwen*. Fuzhou: Haixia wenyi chuban she, 1985.

Kaikou Shiren. *Jueying sanxiao*. Ming edition preserved in the College of Liberal Arts in Tokyo University.

*Langshi. Si wu xie hui bao* series. Taipei: Taiwan Daying baike, 1995.

*Liji. Sibu beiyao.*

Li Jinghua. "Guanyu 'Dao le putao jia.'" *Wenxue yichan* (1991.2): 5.

Li Shizhen. *Li Shizhen yixue quanshu*. Edited by Liu Changhua. Beijing: Zhongguo zhongyiyao chubanshe, 1999.

Li Yu. *Li Yu quanji*. Zhejiang: Zejiang guji chuban she, 1992.

Li Zhi. *Fen shu*. Taipei: Heluo tushu chuban she, 1974.

Lin Ying, and Chen Yukui. "Feng Menglong si nian zhixian shenghuo di shilu: *Shouning daizhi* pingjie." *Zhonghua wenshi luncong*, 1983.1: 199-211.

Lin Yutang, *Qingsuan yueliang: Yutang youmo wenxuan*. Edited by Lin Taiyi. Taipei: Lianjing chuban shiye youxian gongsi, 1994.

Ling Mengchu (Jikong Guan Zhuren). *Pai an jing qi*. Modern facsimile copy of 1628 Shangyou Tang edition. Shanghai: Guji chuban she, 1985.

Liu Zhiqin. "Wan Ming shifeng manyi," *Shehui xue yanjiu* (March 1992): 107-11.

Liu Yonglong, and Su Conglin. *Jiuling xiaohua*. Taipei: Yushu tushu chuban youxian gongsi, 1994.

Lou Zikuang, ed. *Ming Qing xiaoshuo ji* (Jest Books During 1368-1911 A.D.). In *Guoli Beijing Daxue Zhongguo minsu xuehui minsu congshu*, Vol. 7. Rpt. Taipei: The Orient Cultural Service, 1970.

Lu Ji. *Jianjia Tang zazhu zhaichao*. In *Jilu huibian*, 204: 3a-b.

Lu Shulun. “Feng Menglong de ‘yi yan de zui’ han ‘shu ji gou dang.’” *Liaoning Daxue xuebao, zhexue shehui kexue ban*, 1981.6: 83-84.

---. *Feng Menglong yanjiu*. Shanghai: Fudan Daxue chuban she, 1987.

---. *Zhongguo lidai zhuming wenxuejia pingzhuan*, Vol. 4. Jinan: Shandong jiaoyu chuban she, 1985.

Lu Xun. “Cong fengci dao youmo.” In *Lu Xun xuanji*, 194-95. Hong Kong: Wencai chuban she, 1968.

Ma Tai-loi. "Feng Menglong youpeng jiaoyou shi kaoshi." In *Zhongguo tushu wenshi lunji*, 329-36. Taipei: Zhengzhong shuju, 1991.

---. “Feng Menglong yu Wen Zhenmeng.” *Zhonghua wenshi luncong*, 1984.1: 137-39.

---. "Yanjiu Feng Menglong bianzuan min’ge de xin shiliao: Yu Wanlun de *Dazaogan* xiaoyin." *Zhonghua wenshi luncong*, 1986.1: 269-72.

Ma Youyuan (Y. W. Ma). "Feng Menglong yu Shouning daizhi." In *Xiaoshuo xiqu yanjiu*, Vol. 3, 141-80. Taipei: Lianjing, 1990.

Mao Jin. “He youren shijuan.” In *Yinhu yigao*, *Yushan congke*, 6b-7a.

Mao Xiaotong, ed. *Tang Xianzu yanjiu ziliao huibian*. Shanghai: Shanghai guji chuban she, 1986.

*Ming shi*. Edited by Zhang Tingyu. In *Xin jiaoben Ming shi bing fubian liu zhong*, edited by Yang Jialuo. Taipei: Dingwen shuju, 1975.

Muto Sadao and Matsueda Shigeo, eds. *Chugoku showa sen: Edo kobanashi to no majiwari*. Tokyo: Heibonsha, 1964.

Nagasawa Kikuya. "'Sangen' 'Nihaku' ni tsuite." *Shibun* 10, no. 9 (1928): 12-36 & 11, no. 5 (1929): 21-29.

Niu Xiu. "Yingxiong judong." *Gusheng xubian*. In *Biji xubian*, Vol. 39, 256-58. Taipei: Guangwen shuju, 1969.

Oki Yasushi. "Fu Muryu 'Jo Sanka' ko: Shikyo gaku to minkan kayo.” *Toyo bunka* 71 (1990): 121-45.

---. "Fu Muryu 'Sanka' no kenkyu.” *Toyo Bunka Kenkyujo kiyo* 105 (Feb. 1988): 57-241.

---. *Fu Muryu sanka no kenkyu: Chugoku Mindai no tsuzoku kayo*. Tokyo: Keiso shobo, 2003.

---. "Fu Muryu to Gijo,” *Hiroshima Daigaku bungakubu kiyo* 48 (January 1989): 71-91.

---. "Minmatsu Konan ni okeru shuppan-bunka no kenkyu.” *Hiroshima Daigaku Bungakubu kiyo* 50 Tokushugo no. 1 (1991): 122-32.

---. *Minmatsu no hagure tsishikizin: Fu Muryu to sosu bunka*. Tokyo: Kodanshya, 1995.

---. "Zokkyoku-shu 'Ka shiji' ni tsuite—Fu Muryu Sanka no kenkyu, hosetsu." *Toyo Bunka Kenkyujo kiyo* 107 (Oct. 1988): 89-118.

Otsuka, Hidetaka. "*Zetsuei Sansho* ni tsuite," *Todai Chutetsubun Gakkai ho* 8 (June 1983): 159-62.

Qian Qianyi. *Muzhai chuxue ji*. In *Jindai Zhongguo shiliao congkan*, edited by Qian Zeng. Taipei: Wenhai chuban she, 1984-87.

*Qing dai jinhui shumu si zhong*. *Guoxue jiben congshu si bai zhong*.

Rao Zongyi. "Lun xiaoshuo yu baiguan: Qin jian zhong 'baiguan' ji Ru Chun cheng Wei shi wei 'ouyu wei bai' shuo." In *Wenche*, edited by idem, Vol. 1, 253-60. Taipei: Xuesheng shuju, 1991.

Rong Zhaozu. "Ming Feng Menglong de shengping ji qi zhushu." *Lingnan xuebao* 2, no. 2 (1931): 61-91.

---. " Ming Feng Menglong de shengping ji qi zhushu xu kao." *Lingnan xuebao* 2, no. 3 (1932): 95-124.

Shen Defu. *Wanli yehuo bian*. 5 Vols. Taipei: Weiwen tushu chuban she, 1976.

Shen Zijin. *Chongding Nanjiugong cipu*. 1936 Beijing University facsimile copy of 1646 edition.

---. *Nanci xinpu*.

Shinoya On. "Min no shosetsu 'Sangen' ni tsuite." *Shibun* VIII (1926), no. 5: 309-19, no. 6: 375-96, no. 7: 468-79.

*Siku quanshu zongmu tiyao*. In *Guoxue jiben congshu si bai zhong*, edited by Wang Yunwu. Taipei: Commercial Press, 1968.

Sima Qian. *Shiji*. *Sibu beiyao*.

*Suzhou fuzhi* (1743). Compiled by Xi Jun.

Tan Zhengbi. *Sanyan Liangpai ziliao*, 2 Vols. Shanghai: Shanghai guji chuban she, 1980.

Tang Xianzu. *Tang Xianzu ji*. Edited by Xu Shuofang, 4 Vols. Beijing: Zhonghua shuju, 1962.

Uchiyama Chinari. *Mindai bunjinron*. Tokyo: Mokujisha, 1986.

Uemura Koji. "The Study of *Hsiao-fu*." *Bungaku kaishi* 3, no. 2 (1952): 54-64.

Wang Gengsheng, ed. *Yan Zi Chun Qiu jinzhu jinyi*. Taipei: Commercial Press, 1987.

Wang Guowei. *Renjian cihua*. In *Wang Guantang xiansheng quanji*. Taipei: Wenhua chuban gongsi, 1968, Vol. 13.

Wang Jingchen. *Si hou bian*, 1924 edition.

Wang Kentang. *Shanghan zhunsheng*. In *Liuke zhunsheng* by idem. Shanghai: Hongbao Zhai shuju, 1923.

Wang Liqi. *Lidai xiaohua ji.* 4 Vols. Hong Kong: Xinyue chuban she, 1962.

Wang Ting. "Wan Feng Youlong." In *Liyou ji*, edited by Chen Hu. *Qiaofan Lou congshu*, *shang*: 16b-17a.

Wang Zuodong, ed. *Xin Xiaofu: Minjian gushi jiangshujia Liu Depei gushi ji.* Shanghai: Shanghai wenyi chuban she, 1989.

Wei Yong. *Yue rong bian.* In *Xiangyan congshu*, Vol. 1.

*Wu xian zhi*, 1933 edition. Rpt. Taipei: Chengwen chuban she, 1970.

*Xin Tang shu.* Compiled by Ouyang Xiu and Song Qi. *Sibu beiyao.*

*Xu Biaozhong ji.* Taipei: Chengwen chuban she, 1971.

Xu Bo. "Shouning Feng fumu shi xu." In *Hongyu Lou ji.* Manuscript preserved in Shanghai Library.

Xu Qin. *Ming hua lu.* In *Congshu jicheng chubian*, Vol. 317.

Xu Sanzhong. "Jia ze." *Mingshan quanbian.* In *Gujin tushu jicheng*, Vol. 330.

Xu Wei. "Xiaofu shi xu." In *Xu Wenchang san ji*, 19: 29b-30a Taipei: Central Library, 1968.

Xu Zichang. *Shuzhai manlu.*

Yao Zheng. "Feng Menglong yu Yun She chengyuan mingdan." *Zhonghua wenshi luncong*, 1987.1: 279-82.

Ye Ru (Lu Shulun). "Guanyu Feng Menglong de shenshi." In *Ming Qing xiaoshuo yanjiu lunwen ji*, 34-38. Beijing: Renmin wenxue chuban she, 1959.

---. "Guanyu Sanyan de zuanji zhe." In *Ming Qing xiaoshuo yanjiu lunwen ji*, 29-33.

Yuan Hongdao. *Yuan Hongdao ji jianjiao*, edited by Qian Bocheng. 2 Vols. Shanghai: Shanghai guji chuban she, 1981.

Yuan Zhongdao. *Kexue Zhai qianji.* 5 Vols. Taipei: Weiwen tushu chuban she, 1976, modern facsimile edition of the original preserved in the Central Library, Taipei, Taiwan.

Zhang Dai. "Qi Zhixiang pi." In *Taoan mengyi*, *Congshu jicheng chu bian.*

Zhang Han. "Baigong ji." *Songchuang mengyu*, preface dated 1593. In *Wulin wangzhe yizhu*, *Congshu jicheng san bian.*

Zhao Nanxing. *Xiaozan.* In *Ming Qing xiaohua ji. Guoli Beijing Daxue Zhongquo minsu xuehui minsu congshu*, edited by Lou Zikuang. Vol. 7. Rpt. Taipei: The Orient Cultural Service, 1970.

Zhoyuan Ting Zhuren. *Zhao shi bei.* In *Han ben Zhongguo tongsu xiaoshuo congkan.* Taipei: Tianyi chuban she, 1974.

Zhou Dunyi. *Tongshu.* In *Zhou Lianxi ji. Congshu jicheng chubian*, Vol. 369.

Zhu Xi. *Zhu Zi wenji.* In *Zhu Zi daquan. Sibu beiyao.*

---. *Zhu Zi yulie*. Edited by Li Jingde. Taipei: Zhengzhong shuju, 1962.
Zhu Yizun. *Ming shi zong*. N.p., n.d.

**B. Western-Language Sources:**

Ames, Roger T., and Henry Rosemont, Jr. *The Analects of Confucius: A Philosophical Translation*. New York: Ballantine, 1998.

Anderson, Mary M. *Hidden Power: The Palace Eunuchs of Imperial China*. Buffalo: Prometheus Books, 1990.

Atwell, William S. "From Education to Politics: The Fu She." In *The Unfolding of Neo-Confucianism*, edited by Wm. Theodore de Bary, 333-67. New York: Columbia University Press, 1975.

---. "International Bullion Flows and the Chinese Economy Circa 1530-1650." *Past and Present* 95 (May 1982): 68-90.

---. "Some Observations on the 'Seventeenth-Century Crisis' in China and Japan." *Journal of Asian Studies* 45, no. 2 (1986): 223-44.

Bakhtin, Mikhail. *The Dialogic Imagination: Four Essays by M. M. Bakhtin*. Edited by Michael Holquist. Translated by Caryl Emerson and Michael Holquist. Austin: University of Texas Press, 1981.

---. *Problems of Dostoevsky's Poetics*. Translated by R. W. Rotsel. Ann Arbor: Ardis, 1973.

---. *Rabelais and His World*. Translated by Helene Iswolsky. Bloomington: Indiana University Press, 1984.

Barr, Allan H. "Jiang Yingke's Place in the Gong'an School." *Ming Studies* 45-46 (2002): 41-68.

---. "The Wanli Context of the 'Courtesan's Jewel Box' Story." *Harvard Journal of Asiatic Studies* 57, no. 1 (1997): 107-41.

Berkhofer, Robert F. Jr. *Beyond the Great Story—History as Text and Discourse*. Cambridge: The Belknap Press of Harvard University Press, 1995.

Birch, Cyril, trans. *Mu-tan t'ing—The Peony Pavilion*. Bloomington: Indiana University Press, 1980.

---. *Stories from a Ming Collection: The Art of the Chinese Story-Teller*. New York: Grove Weidenfeld, 1958.

Birrell, Anne. *Popular Songs and Ballads of Han China*. London: Unwin Hyman, 1988.

Bishop, John Lyman. *The Colloquial Short Story in China: A Study of the San-Yen Collections*. Harvard Yenching Institute Series 14. Cambridge, MA: Harvard University Press, 1956.

Bol, Peter K. *"This Culture of Ours": Intellectual Transitions in T'ang and Sung China*. Stanford: Stanford University Press, 1992.

Bremmer, Jan, and Herman Roodenburg, eds. *A Cultural History of Humour: From Antiquity to the Present Day*. Cambridge: Polity Press, 1997.

Brewer, Derek. "Prose Jest-Books Mainly in the Sixteenth to Eighteenth Centuries in England." In *A Cultural History of Humour: From Antiquity to the Present Day*, edited by Jan Bremmer and Herman Roodenburg, 90-111. Cambridge: Polity Press, 1997.

Brokaw, Cynthia J. *The Ledgers of Merit and Demerit: Social Change and Moral Order in Late Imperial China*. Princeton: Princeton University Press, 1991.

Brook, Timothy. *The Confusions of Pleasure: Commerce and Culture in Ming China*. Berkeley: University of California Press, 1998.

---. "Funerary Ritual and the Building of Lineages in Late Imperial China." *Harvard Journal of Asiatic Studies* 49, no. 2 (1989): 465-99.

---. *Praying for Power: Buddhism and the Formation of Gentry Society in the Late Ming*. Cambridge, MA: Harvard University Press, 1993.

Bynner, Witter. *Three Hundred Poems of the T'ang Dynasty, 618-906* (n.p., n.d.).

Carlitz, Katherine. "Desire, Danger, and the Body: Stories of Women's Virtue in Late Ming China." In *Engendering China: Women, Culture, and the State*, edited by Christina K. Gilmartin, Gail Hershatter, Lisa Rofel, and Tyrene White, 101-24. Cambridge, MA: Harvard University Press, 1994.

---. "The Social Uses of Female Virtue in Late Ming Editions of *Lienü Zhuan*." *Late Imperial China* 12, no. 2 (1991): 117-48.

Cass, Victoria. *Dangerous Women: Warriors, Grannies and Geishas of the Ming*. Lanham: Rowman & Littlefield, 1999.

Chaffee, John W. *The Thorny Gates of Learning in Sung China: A Social History of Examinations*. Cambridge: Cambridge University Press, 1985.

Chan, Hok-lam. "The White Lotus-Maitreya Doctrine and Popular Uprisings in Ming and Ch'ing China." *Sinologica* 10 (1969): 211-33.

Chang, Kang-i Sun. *The Late-Ming Poet Ch'en Tzu-lung: Crises of Love and Loyalism*. New Haven: Yale University Press, 1991.

Chaves, Jonathan. "The Expression of Self in the Kung-an School: Non-Romantic Individualism." In *Expressions of Self in Chinese Literature*, edited by Robert E. Hegel and Richard C. Hessney, 123-50. New York: Columbia University Press, 1985.

Cheng, Pei-kai. "Reality and Imagination: Li Chih and T'ang Hsien-tsu in Search of Authenticity." Ph.D. diss., Yale University, 1980.

Cho Dong-il. "Humour in Folk Poetry." In *Humour in Korean Literature*, edited by Chun Shin-Yong. Seoul: International Cultural Foundation, 1977.

Chou, Chih-p'ing. *Yüan Hung-tao and the Kung-an School*. Cambridge: Cambridge University Press, 1988.

Clunas, Craig. *Superfluous Things: Material Culture and Social Status in Early Modern China*. Urbana: University of Illinois Press, 1991.

Dardess, John W. *Blood and History in China: The Donglin Faction and Its Repression*. Honolulu: University of Hawaii Press, 2002.

---. *Confucianism and Autocracy: Professional Elites in the Founding of the Ming Dynasty*. Berkeley: University of California Press, 1983.

Davis, Edward L. *Society and the Supernatural in Song China*. Honolulu: University of Hawai'i Press, 2001.

Davis, Murray S. *Smut: Erotic Reality/Obscene Ideology*. Chicago: The University of Chicago Press, 1983.

de Bary, Wm. Theodore. "Individualism and Humanitarianism in Late Ming Thought." In *Self and Society in Ming Thought*, edited by idem, 145-247. New York: Columbia University Press, 1970.

---. *Learning for One's Self: Essays on the Individual in Neo-Confucian Thought*. New York: Columbia University Press, 1991.

---, trans. *Five Women Who Loved Love*. Rutland, Vermont: Charles E. Tuttle, 1956.

---, and Irene Bloom, eds. *Principle and Practicality: Essays in Neo-Confucianism and Practical Learning*. New York: Columbia University Press, 1979.

---, Wing-tsit Chan, and Burton Watson, comps. *Sources of Chinese Tradition*. 2 Vols. New York: Columbia University Press, 1960.

*Dictionary of Ming Biography (1368-1644)*. Edited by L. Carrington Goodrich, and Chaoying Fang. 2 Vols. New York: Columbia University Press, 1976.

Dimberg, Ronald G. *The Sage and Society: The Life and Thought of Ho Hsin-yin*. Honolulu: The University Press of Hawaii, 1974.

Ditmanson, Peter. "Intellectual Lineages and the Early Ming Court." *Papers on Chinese History* 5 (1996): 1-17.

Dolby, William. *Eight Chinese Plays: From the Thirteenth-Century to the Present*. New York: Columbia University Press, 1978.

---. *The Perfect Lady by Mistake and Other Stories by Feng Menglong (1574-1646)*. London: Elek, 1976.

Douglas, Mary. *Implicit Meanings*. London: Routledge & Kegan Paul, 1975.

Dundes, Alan. *Folklore Matters*. Knoxville: The University of Tennessee Press, 1989.

Durrant, Stephen W. *The Cloudy Mirror: Tension and Conflict in the Writings of Sima Qian*. Albany: State University of New York Press, 1995.

Duus, Peter. "Presidential Address: Weapons of the Week, Weapons of the Strong—The Development of the Japanese Political Cartoon," *The Journal of Asian Studies* 60, no. 4 (2001): 965-97.

Eco, Umberto. "The Frames of Comic 'Freedom.'" In *Carnival!*, edited by Thomas A. Sebeok, 1-9. Approaches to Semiotics 64. Berlin: Mouton, 1984.

Eisenstadt, S. N., ed. *The Origins and Diversity of Axial Age Civilizations*. New York: State University of New York Press, 1986.

Elman, Benjamin A. *From Philosophy to Philology: Intellectual and Social Aspects of Change in Late Imperial China*. Cambridge, MA: Harvard University Press, 1984.

---. "Political, Social, and Cultural Reproduction via Civil Service Examinations in Late Imperial China." *The Journal of Asian Studies* 50, no. 1 (1991): 7-28.

---, and Alexander Woodside, eds. *Education and Society in Late Imperial China, 1600-1900*. Berkeley: University of California Press, 1994.

Epstein, Maram. *Competing Discourses: Orthodoxy, Authenticity, and Engendered Meanings in Late Imperial Chinese Fiction*. Cambridge, MA: Harvard University Press, 2001.

Esherick, Joseph W., and Mary Backus Rankin, eds. *Chinese Local Elites and Patterns of Dominance*. Berkeley: University of California Press, 1990.

Fang, Lienche Tu. "Ming Dreams." *Tsing Hua Journal of Chinese Studies* 10, no. 1 (1973): 55-73.

Farmer, Edward L. *Early Ming Government: The Evolution of Dual Capitals*. Cambridge, MA: Harvard University Press, 1976.

---. "The Dragon's Tether: Theoretical Limits on Imperial Power in Ming China." Paper presented in the Conference on "Absolutism and Despotism in Early Modern Eurasia" at University of Minnesota, October 26-28, 1989.

Farquhar, Judith. *Appetites: Food and Sex in Post-Socialist China*. Durham: Duke University Press, 2002.

Feinberg, Leonard, ed. *Asian Laughter: An Anthology of Oriental Satire and Humor*. New York: John Weatherhill, 1971.

Freud, Sigmund. *Jokes and Their Relation to the Unconscious*. Translated by James Strachey. New York: W. W. Norton, 1960.

Frye, Northrop. *Anatomy of Criticism: four essays*. Princeton: Princeton University Press, 1957.

Furth, Charlotte. *A Flourishing Yin: Gender in China's Medical History, 960-1665*. Berkeley: University of California Press, 1999.

---. "Rethinking Van Gulik: Sexuality and Reproduction in Traditional Chinese Medicine." In *Engendering China: Women, Culture, and the State*, edited by Christina K. Gilmartin, Gail Hershatter, Lisa Rofel, and Tyrene White, 125-46. Cambridge, MA: Harvard University Press, 1994.

Ge, Liangyan. *Out of the Margins: The Rise of Chinese Vernacular Fiction*. Honolulu: University of Hawai'i Press, 2001.

Giles, Herbert A., trans. *Quips from a Chinese Jest-Book*. Shanghai: Kelly & Walsh, 1925.

Granet, Marcel. *Chinese Civilization*. New York: Alfred A. Knopf, 1930.

Gurevich, Aaron. "Bakhtin and His Theory of Carnival." In *A Cultural History of Humour: From Antiquity to the Present Day*, edited by Jan Bremmer and Herman Roodenburg, 54-60. Cambridge: Polity Press, 1997.

Guy, R. Kent. *The Emperor's Four Treasuries: Scholars and the State in the Late Ch'ien-lung Era*. Cambridge, MA: Council on East Asian Studies, Harvard University, 1987.

Hanan, Patrick. *The Chinese Short Story: Studies in Dating, Authorship, and Composition*. Cambridge, MA: Harvard University Press, 1973.

---. *The Chinese Vernacular Story*. Cambridge, MA: Harvard University Press, 1981.

---. *The Invention of Li Yu*. Cambridge, MA: Harvard University Press, 1988.

Handlin, Joanna F. *Action in Late Ming Thought: The Reorientation of Lü K'un and Other Scholar-Officials*. Berkeley: University of California Press, 1983.

Harbsmeier, Christoph. "*Confucius Ridens*: Humor in the Analects." *Harvard Journal of Asiatic Studies* 50, no. 1 (June 1990): 131-61.

Hardacre, Helen. *Marketing the Menacing Fetus in Japan*. Berkeley: California University Press, 1997.

Hegel, Robert E. "Unpredictability and Meaning in Ming-Qing Literati Novels." In *Paradoxes of Traditional Chinese Literature*, edited by Eva Hung, 147-66. Hong Kong: The Chinese University Press, 1994.

Hinsch, Bret. *Passions of the Cut Sleeve: The Male Homosexual Tradition in China*. Berkeley: University of California Press, 1990.

Ho, Ching-lang. "The Chinese Belief in Baleful Stars." In *Facets of Taoism: Essays in Chinese Religion*, edited by Holmes Welch and Anna K. Seidel, 193-228. New Haven: Yale University Press, 1979.

Ho, Ping-ti. *The Ladder of Success in Imperial China: Aspects of Social Mobility, 1368-1911*. New York: Columbia University Press, 1962.

Holman, C. Hugh. *A Handbook to Literature*, based on the original by William Flint Thrall and Addison Hibbard. 3rd ed. Indianapolis: The Odyssey Press, 1972.

Holquist, Michael. *Dialogism: Bakhtin and His World*. London: Routledge, 1990.

---. "The Politics of Representation." In *Allegory and Representation*, edited by Stephen J. Greenblatt, 163-83. Baltimore: The Johns Hopkins University Press, 1981.

Hsia, C. T. *The Classic Chinese Novel*. New York: Columbia University Press, 1968.

---. "Time and the Human Condition in the Plays of T'ang Hsien-tsu." In *Self and Society in Ming Thought*, edited by Wm. Theodore de Bary, 249-90. New York: Columbia University Press, 1970.

Hsu, Pi-ching. "Celebrating the Emotional Self: Feng Meng-lung and Late Ming Ethics and Aesthetics." Ph.D. diss., University of Minnesota, 1994.

---. "Courtesans and Scholars in the Writings of Feng Menglong: Transcending Status and Gender." *Nan Nü* 2, no. 1 (2000): 40-77.

---. "Feng Meng-lung's *Treasury of Laughs*: Humorous Satire on Seventeenth-Century Chinese Culture and Society." *The Journal of Asian Studies* 57, no. 4 (1998): 1042-67.

Hu, Ying. "Angling with Beauty: Two Stories of Women as Narrative Bait in *Sanguozhi yanyi*." *Chinese Literature Essays Articles Reviews* 15 (1993): 99-112.

Huang, Ching-sheng. "Jokes on the Four Books: Cultural Criticism in Early Modern China." Ph.D. diss., University of Arizona, 1998.

Huang, Martin W. *Desire and Fictional Narrative in Late Imperial China*. Cambridge, MA: Harvard University Asia Center, 2001.

---. *Literàti and Self-Re/Presentation: Autobiographical Sensibility in the Eighteenth-Century Chinese Novel*. Stanford: Stanford University Press, 1995.

Huang, Ray. *1587: A Year of No Significance*. New Haven: Yale University Press, 1981.

---. "Fiscal Administration during the Ming Dynasty." In *Chinese Government in Ming Times: Seven Studies*, edited by Charles O. Hucker, 73-128. New York: Columbia University Press, 1969.

---. *Taxation and Government Finance in Sixteenth-Century Ming China*. Cambridge: Cambridge University Press, 1974.

Hucker, Charles O. *The Ming Dynasty: Its Origins and Evolving Institutions*. Papers in Chinese Studies no. 34. Ann Arbor: Center for Chinese Studies, the University of Michigan, 1978.

---. "Su-chou and the Agents of Wei Chung-hsien, 1626." In *Two Studies on Ming History* by idem, 41-83. Michigan Papers in Chinese Studies no. 12. Ann Arbor: Center for Chinese Studies, University of Michigan, 1971.

---. "The Tung-lin Movement of the Late Ming Period." In *Chinese Thought and Institutions*, edited by John K. Fairbank, 132-62. Chicago: University of Chicago Press, 1957.

Hung, Eva. "Preface to *The Hall of Laughter*." *Renditions: A Chinese-English Translation Magazine* nos. 33-34 (1990): 188-89.

Hymes, Robert P. "Not Quite Gentlemen? Doctors in Sung and Yuan." *Chinese Science* 8 (January 1987): 9-76.

Idema, W. L. *Chinese Vernacular Fiction: The Formative Period*. Leiden: E. J. Brill, 1974.

*The Indiana Companion to Traditional Chinese Literature*. Edited by William H. Nienhauser, Jr. Bloomington: Indiana University Press, 1986.

Jacobs, N. J. *Naming-Day in Eden*. London: Gollancz, 1958.

Kao, George. *Chinese Wit and Humor*. New York: Coward-McCann, 1946.

Kieschnick, John. *The Eminent Monk: Buddhist Ideals in Medieval Chinese Hagiography*. Honolulu: University of Hawai'i Press, 1997.

Ko, Dorothy. *Teachers of the Inner Chambers: Women and Culture in Seventeenth-Century China*. Stanford: Stanford university Press, 1994.

Koestler, Arthur. *The Act of Creation*. London: Arkana, 1989.

Kowallis, Jon. *Wit and Humor from Old Cathay*. Beijing: Panda Books, 1986.

Kuhn, Philip A. *Soulstealers: The Chinese Sorcery Scare of 1768*. Cambridge, MA: Harvard University Press, 1990.

Le Goff, Jacques. "Laughter in the Middle Ages." In *A Cultural History of Humour: From Antiquity to the Present Day*, edited by Jan Bremmer and Herman Roodenburg, 40-53. Cambridge: Polity Press, 1997.

Le Roy Ladurie, Emmanuel. *Montaillou: The Promised Land of Error*. Translated by Barbara Bray. New York: Vintage Books, 1979.

Lee, Haiyan. "Tears That Crumbled the Great Wall: The Archaeology of Feeling in the May Fourth Folklore Movement." *The Journal of Asian Studies* 64, no. 1 (2005): 35-65.

Lee Jae-son. "Laughter in the Literature of Enlightenment Period." In *Humour in Korean Literature*, edited by Chun Shin-Yong. Seoul: International Cultural Foundation, 1977.

Lee, T'ao. "The Doctor in Chinese Drama." *Chinese Medical Journal* 68 (1950): 34-43.

Leung, Angela Ki Che. "Organized Medicine in Ming-Qing China: State and Private Medical Institutions in the Lower Yangzi Region." *Late Imperial China* 8, no. 1 (1987): 134-66.

Lévy, André. *Inventaire Analytique et Critique du Conte Chinois en Langue Vulgaire*, Mémoires de l'Institut des Hautes Etudes Chinoises, Vols. 8-1, 2, 3, 4. Paris: Presses Universitaires de France, 1978, 1979, 1981, 1991.

Levy, Howard S., ed. *Chinese Sex Jokes in Traditional Times*. Taipei: The Orient Cultural Service, 1974.

Li, Wai-yee. *Enchantment and Disenchantment: Love and Illusion in Chinese Literature*. Princeton: Princeton University Press, 1993.

Liu, James J. Y. *Chinese Theories of Literature*. Chicago: The University of Chicago Press, 1975.

Liu, Kwang-ching. "World View and Peasant Rebellion: Reflections on Post-Mao Historiography." *The Journal of Asian Studies* 40, no. 2 (1981): 295-326.

Loewe, Michael. *Chinese Ideas of Life and Death: Faith, Myth and Reason in the Han Period (202 B.C.-A.D. 220)*. London: George Allen and Unwin, 1982.

Longstreet, Stephen, and Ethel Longstreet. *Yoshiwara: The Pleasure Quarters of Old Tokyo*. Rutland, Vt.: C. E. Tuttle, 1988.

Lowry, Kathryn. "Excess and Restraint: Feng Menglong's Prefaces on Current Popular Songs." *Papers on Chinese History* 2 (Spring 1993): 94-119.

Lu Yunzhong. *100 Chinese Jokes Through the Ages*. Hong Kong: Commercial Press, 1985.

Lynn, Richard John. "Alternate Routes to Self-Realization in Ming Theories of Poetry." In *Theories of the Arts in China*, edited by Susan Bush and Christian Murck. Princeton: Princeton University Press, 1983.

---. "Chu Hsi as Literary Theorist and Critic." In *Chu Hsi and Neo-Confucianism*, edited by Wing-tsit Chan, 337-54. Honolulu: University of Hawai'i Press, 1986.

Ma, Y. W., and Joseph S. M. Lau, eds. *Traditional Chinese Stories: Themes and Variations*. New York: Columbia University Press, 1978.

Mair, Victor H., ed. *The Columbia Anthology of Traditional Chinese Literature*. New York: Columbia University Press, 1994.

Mann, Susan. *Precious Records: Women in China's Long Eighteenth Century*. Stanford: Stanford University Press, 1997.

Mather, Richard B. *Shih-shuo hsin-yü: A New Account of Tales of the World*. Minneapolis: University of Minnesota Press, 1976.

McDermott, Joseph P. "Friendship and Its Friends in the Late Ming." In *Family Process and Political Process in Modern Chinese History*, 67-96. Taipei: Institute of Modern History, Academia Sinica, 1992.

McElrath, Miles Kenneth Jr. "The Seisuisho of Anrakuan Sakuden." Ph.D. diss., University of Michigan, 1971.

McMahon, Keith R. *Causality and Containment in Seventeenth-Century Chinese Fiction*. T'oung pao Monographie 15. Leiden: E. J. Brill, 1988.

---. *Misers, Shrews, and Polygamists: Sexuality and Male-Female Relations in Eighteenth-Century Chinese Fiction*. Durham, N.C.: Duke University Press, 1995.

Miyazaki Ichisada. *China's Examination Hell: The Civil Service Examinations of Imperial China*. Translated by Conrad Schirokauer. New York: Weatherhill, 1976.

Morson, Gary Saul. *The Boundaries of Genre: Dostoevsky's Diary of a Writer and the Traditions of Literary Utopia*. Austin: University of Texas Press, 1981.

Mowry, Hua-yuan Li. *Chinese Love Stories from Ch'ing-shih*. Hamden: Archon Books, 1983.

Mulkay, Michael. *On Humor: Its Nature and Its Place in Modern Society*. Oxford: Basil Blackwell, 1988.

Munro, Donald J. *Images of Human Nature: A Sung Portrait*. Princeton: Princeton University Press, 1988.

Nan, Huai-Chin. *The Story of Chinese Zen*. Translated by Thomas Cleary. Boston: Charles E. Tuttle, 1995.

Oki, Yasushi. "Women in Feng Menglong's 'Mountain Songs.'" In *Writing Women in Late Imperial China*, edited by Ellen Widmer and Kang-i Sun Chang, 131-43. Stanford: Stanford University Press, 1997.

Parsons, James Bunyan. *Peasant Rebellions of the Late Ming Dynasty*. Tucson: The University of Arizona Press, 1970.

Plaks, Andrew. *The Four Masterworks of the Ming Novel: Ssu-ta ch'i-shu*. Princeton: Princeton University Press, 1987.

Purdie, Susan. *Comedy: The Mastery of Discourse*. Toronto: University of Toronto Press, 1993.

Qian, Nanxiu. *Spirit and Self in Medieval China: The Shih-shuo hsin-yü and Its Legacy*. Honolulu: University of Hawai'i Press, 2001.

Redferm, Walter. *Puns*. Oxford: Basil Blackwell, 1984.

Redfield, Robert. *Peasant Society and Culture*. Chicago: University of Chicago Press, 1956.

Ricci, Matteo. *China in the Sixteenth Century: The Journals of Matthew Ricci: 1583-1610*. Translated by Louis J. Gallagher. New York: Random House, 1953.

Rickett, Adele Austin. *Wang Kuo-wei's Jen-chien Tz'u-hua: A Study in Chinese Literary Criticism*. Hong Kong: Hong Kong University Press, 1977.

Santangelo, Paolo. "Human Conscience and Responsibility in Ming-Qing China." Translated by Mark Elvin. *East Asian History* 4 (Dec., 1992): 31-80.

---. "Urban Society in Late Imperial Suzhou." Translated by Adam Victor. In *Cities of Jiangnan in Late Imperial China*, edited by Linda Cooke Johnson, 81-116. New York: State University of New York Press, 1993.

Schafer, E. H. "Ritual Exposure in Ancient China." *Harvard Journal of Asiatic Studies* (1951): 130-84.

Schipper, Kristofer. *The Taoist Body*. Translated by Karen C. Duval. Berkeley: University of California Press, 1993.

Schopenhauer, Arthur. *The World as Will and Idea*, 6th edition. Translated by R. B. Haldane and John Kemp. London: Routledge and Kegan Paul, 1907-09.

Skinner, G. William. *The City in Late Imperial China*. Stanford: Stanford University Press, 1977.

Smith, Kidder Jr., Peter K. Bol, Joseph A. Adler, and Don J. Wyatt. *Sung Dynasty Uses of the I Ching*. Princeton: Princeton University Press, 1990.

Sommer, Matthew H. *Sex, Law, and Society in Late Imperial China*. Stanford: Stanford University Press, 2000.

Spence, Jonathan D. *Treason by the Book*. New York: Penguin, 2001.

Struve, Lynn A. *The Southern Ming 1644-1662*. New Haven and London: Yale University Press, 1984.

Susumu Fuma. "Late Ming Urban Reform and the Popular Uprising in Hangzhou." Translated by Michael Lewis. In *Cities of Jiangnan in Late Imperial China*, edited by Linda Cooke Johnson, 47-79. New York: State University of New York Press, 1993.

Swatek, Catherine Crutchfield. "Plum and Portrait: Feng Meng-lung's Revision of the Peony Pavilion." *Asia Major* 3rd series, 6: 1 (1993): 127-60.

Taylor, Romeyn. "Rulership in Late Imperial Chinese Orthodoxy." Paper for the Conference on "Absolutism and Despotism in Early Modern Eurasia" at University of Minnesota, October 26-28, 1989.

T'ien Ju-k'ang. *Male Anxiety and Female Chastity: A Comparative Study of Chinese Ethical Values in Ming-Ch'ing Times*. Monographies du T'oung Pao, Vol. XIV. Leiden: E. J. Brill, 1988.

Tong, James W. *Disorder Under Heaven: Collective Violence in the Ming Dynasty*. Stanford: Stanford University Press, 1991.

Töpelmann, Cornelia. *Shan-ko von Feng Meng-lung: Eine volksliedersammlung aus der Ming-zeit*. Wiesbaden: Franz Steiner, 1973.

Trilling, Lionel. *Sincerity and Authenticity*. Cambridge: Harvard University Press, 1971.

Tsao Jr-lien. "Remembering Suzhou: Urbanism in late imperial China." Ph.D. diss., University of California, Berkeley, 1992.

Unschuld, Paul U. *Medical Ethics in Imperial China: A Study in Historical Anthropology*. Berkeley: University of California Press, 1979.

Vitiello, Giovanni. "Exemplary Sodomites: Male Homosexuality in Late Ming Fiction." Ph.D. diss., University of California, Berkeley, 1994.

Von Glahn, Richard. *Fountain of Fortune: Money and Monetary Policy in China, 1000-1700*. Berkeley: University of California Press, 1996.

---. "Municipal Reform and Urban Social Conflict in Late Ming Jiangnan." *The Journal of Asian Studies* 50, no. 2 (1991): 280-307.

Wakeman, Frederic Jr. "China and the Seventeenth-Century Crisis." *Late Imperial China* 7, no. 1 (1986): 1-26.

---. "The Price of Autonomy: Intellectuals in Ming and Ch'ing Politics." *Daedalus* 101, no. 2 (1972): 35-70.

---. "The Shun Interregnum of 1644." In *From Ming to Ch'ing: Conquest, Region, and Continuity in Seventeenth-Century China*, edited by Jonathan D. Spence and idem, 39-87. New Haven and London: Yale University Press, 1979.

Waltner, Ann. *Getting an Heir: Adoption and the Construction of Kinship in Late Imperial China*. Honolulu: University of Hawaii Press, 1990.

---. "Infanticide and Dowry in Ming and Early Qing China." In *Chinese Views of Childhood*, edited by Anne Behnke Kinne, 193-217. Honolulu: University of Hawai'i Press, 1995.

*Webster's Third New International Dictionary of the English Language, Unabridged*. Edited by Philip Babcock Gove and the Merriam-Webster Editorial Staff. Springfield, MA: Merriam-Webster, 1986.

Wells, Henry W. *Traditional Chinese Humor: A Study in Art and Literature*. Bloomington: Indiana University Press, 1971.

Wilson, Thomas A. *Genealogy of the Way: The Construction and Uses of the Confucian Tradition in Late Imperial China*. Stanford: Stanford University Press, 1995.

Wolf, Margery. *Women and the Family in Rural Taiwan*. Stanford: Stanford University Press, 1972.

Wong, Siu-kit. "*Ch'ing* in Chinese Literary Criticism." Ph.D. diss., Oxford University, 1969.

Wu, Pei-yi. *The Confucian's Progress: Autobiographical Writings in Traditional China*. Princeton: Princeton University Press, 1990.

Wu, Yenna. "The Inversion of Marital Hierarchy: Shrewish Wives and Henpecked Husbands in Seventeenth-Century Chinese Literature." *Harvard Journal of Asiatic Studies* 48, no. 2 (1988): 363-82.

Yang Hsien-yi, and Gladys Yang, trans. *The Courtesan's Jewel Box: Chinese Stories of the Xth-XVIIth Centuries*. Peking: Foreign Languages Press, 1957.

---. *Lazy Dragon: Chinese Stories from the Ming Dynasty*. Peking: Foreign Languages Press, 1994.

---. *The Scholars*. New York: Grosset and Dunlap, 1972.

Yang, Lien-sheng. "Economic Justification for Spending—An Uncommon Idea in Traditional China." *Harvard Journal of Asiatic Studies* 20, nos. 1-2 (1957): 36-52.

Yang, Shuhui. *Appropriation and Representation: Feng Menglong and the Chinese Vernacular Story*. Ann Arbor: Center for Chinese Studies, the University of Michigan, 1998.

---, and Yunqin Yang, trans. *Stories Old and New*. Seattle: University of Washington Press, 2000.

---, and Yunqin Yang, trans. *Stories to Caution the World*. Seattle: University of Washington Press, forthcoming.

Ye, Yang. *Vignettes from the Late Ming: A Hsiao-p'in Anthology*. Seattle: University of Washington Press, 1999.

Zeitlin, Judith T. "The Petrified Heart: Obsession in Chinese Literature, Art, and Medicine." *Late Imperial China* 12, no. 1 (1991): 1-26.

Zelin, Madeleine. *The Magistrate's Tael: Rationalizing Fiscal Reform in Eighteenth-Century Ch'ing China*. Berkeley: University of California Press, 1984.

Zhang Longxi. "The Letter or the Spirit: The *Song of Songs*, Allegoresis, and the *Book of Poetry*." *Comparative Literature* 39, no. 3 (1987): 193-216.

# Glossary of Chinese Characters

| | |
|---|---|
| *Ai Zi houyu* | 艾子後語 |
| *Ai Zi zashuo* | 艾子雜說 |
| Anhui | 安徽 |
| *baiguan* | 稗官 |
| Ban Gu | 班固 |
| *bi* | 鄙 |
| *biji* | 筆記 |
| *bian* | 變 |
| Bian Que | 扁鵲 |
| *Bieben Chun Qiu daquan* | 別本春秋大全 |
| *Bie Huiqing* | 別慧卿 |
| *bingshen* | 丙申 |
| Bo Qin | 伯禽 |
| Boyi | 伯夷 |
| Cai Bojie | 蔡伯喈 |
| Cao Cao | 曹操 |
| Changzhou | 長洲 |
| Chen Gaomo | 陳皋謨 |
| Chen Jiru | 陳繼儒 |
| Chen Xianzhang | 陳獻章 |
| Chen Zilong | 陳子龍 |
| Cheng Hao | 程顥 |
| Cheng Yi | 程頤 |
| *chi* | 癡 |
| *Chimi pian* | 侈靡篇 |
| Chongzhen | 崇禎 |
| *Chutan ji* | 初潭集 |
| *chuanqi* | 傳奇 |
| *Chun Qiu* | 春秋 |
| *Chun Qiu dingzhi canxin* | 春秋定旨參新 |
| *Chun Qiu hengku* | 春秋衡庫 |
| *ci* | 詞 |
| Da | 答 |
| *daya* | 大雅 |
| *Dazaogan* | 打棗竿 |

| | |
|---|---|
| Dantu | 丹徒 |
| Danggui | 當歸 |
| *Daodejing* | 道德經 |
| *dao xue* | 道學 |
| Deng Zhimo | 鄧志謨 |
| Diao Chan | 貂蟬 |
| *Dongchang* | 東廠 |
| Donglin | 東林 |
| Dong Sizhang | 董斯張 |
| Dongting | 洞庭 |
| *Dong Zhou lieguo zhi* | 東周列國志 |
| Du Xunhe | 杜荀鶴 |
| Duan'er yibie | 端二憶別 |
| *er nong* | 二弄 |
| Eryou | 耳猶 |
| *fan'an* | 番案 |
| Fan Juqing | 范巨卿 |
| Fan Li | 范蠡 |
| Fan Qiuer | 范鰍兒 |
| Fan Yuchong | 樊玉衝 |
| Fang ge zeng ren | 放歌贈人 |
| *fang xia* | 房下 |
| Fang Xiaoru | 方孝孺 |
| Fang Xuanling | 房玄齡 |
| *Fen shu* | 焚書 |
| *fentu zhi qiang* | 糞土之牆 |
| *feng* | 風 |
| Feng Menggui | 馮夢桂 |
| Feng Menglong | 馮夢龍 |
| Feng Mengxiong | 馮夢熊 |
| Feng Yu | 馮熉 |
| Feng Xisheng | 馮喜生 |
| Fubai zhuren | 浮白主人 |
| Fu Chai | 夫差 |
| Fujian | 福建 |
| Funing | 福寧 |
| *Funing fuzhi* | 福寧府志 |
| Fu She | 復社 |
| *fuxin* | 負心 |
| *Fuzhang lu* | 拊掌錄 |

| | |
|---|---|
| Fuzhou | 福州 |
| Ganhuai shi | 感懷詩 |
| Gao Hongjun | 高洪鈞 |
| Gao Ming | 高明 |
| Gao Zi | 告子 |
| Geng Dingxiang | 耿定向 |
| Gong'an | 公安 |
| *gongsheng* | 貢生 |
| *gongzi* | 公子 |
| Gou Jian | 句踐 |
| *gu* | 觚 |
| *guji* | 滑稽 |
| Guji liezhuan | 滑稽列傳 |
| Gu Jiegang | 顧頡剛 |
| *Gujin tan* | 古今談 |
| *Gujin tan gai* | 古今談概 |
| *Gujin xiao* | 古今笑 |
| *Gujin xiaoshi* | 古今笑史 |
| *Gujin xiaoshuo* | 古今小說 |
| *guazhier* | 掛枝兒 |
| *Guazhier* | 掛枝兒 |
| Guan Hanqing | 關漢卿 |
| Guanshiyin | 觀世音 |
| Guanyin | 觀音 |
| Guan Yu | 關羽 |
| *Guan Zi* | 管子 |
| Guang | 光 |
| Guangdong | 廣東 |
| Guangji | 廣濟 |
| Guangling | 廣陵 |
| *Guang Xiaofu* | 廣笑府 |
| *Guochao shiyu* | 國朝詩餘 |
| Guofeng | 國風 |
| Guo Zizhang | 郭子章 |
| Hai Rui | 海瑞 |
| *han* | 憨 |
| Handan Chun | 邯鄲淳 |
| Han Fei Zi | 韓非子 |
| *Han shu* | 漢書 |
| Han Wudi | 漢武帝 |

| | |
|---|---|
| Hangzhou | 杭州 |
| *hao* | 號 |
| *hao wai pi* | 好外癖 |
| He Daqing | 赫大卿 |
| *hong* (clamoring) | 鬨 |
| *hong* (coaxing) | 哄 |
| *hong* (heating) | 烘 |
| Hong Chengchou | 洪承疇 |
| Hongwu | 洪武 |
| Hongyu Lou | 紅雨樓 |
| Hou Bai | 侯白 |
| Hou Huiqing | 侯慧卿 |
| Hubei | 湖北 |
| Hulu Sheng | 胡盧生 |
| Hua Tuo | 華佗 |
| Huang'an | 黃安 |
| Huang Di | 黃帝 |
| Huang Zongxi | 黃宗羲 |
| Huang Zunsu | 黃尊素 |
| *hui* | 諱 |
| Huiqing | 慧卿 |
| *huixiang* | 回鄉（茴香） |
| *huixie* | 詼諧 |
| Huizhou | 徽州 |
| *Jichuan xiaolin* | 籍川笑林 |
| *jia dao xue* | 假道學 |
| Jiajing | 嘉靖 |
| *jiaren* | 家人 |
| *Jiashen jishi* | 甲申紀事 |
| Jiaxing | 嘉興 |
| *Jiazhutao* | 夾竹桃 |
| Jianshan Tang | 兼善堂 |
| Jiangnan | 江南 |
| Jiang Taigong | 姜太公 |
| Jiang Yingke | 江盈科 |
| Jiao (moonlight) | 皎 |
| *jiao* (to fool around) | 攪 |
| Jinjiang | 錦江 |
| *Jin Ping Mei* | 金瓶梅 |
| *jinshi* | 進士 |

| | |
|---|---|
| *jinyi wei* | 錦衣衛 |
| Jingdezhen | 景德鎮 |
| Jing Ke | 荊軻 |
| *Jingshi tongyan* | 警世通言 |
| *Jingxuan yaxiao* | 精選雅笑 |
| Jiumu | 樛木 |
| *juan* | 卷 |
| *Jueying sanxiao* | 絕纓三笑 |
| *kaozheng* | 考證 |
| *Kexue Zhai qianji* | 珂雪齋前集 |
| *Kong Cong Zi* | 孔叢子 |
| *kuang* | 狂 |
| *lan* | 懶 |
| *Langshi* | 浪史 |
| Lao Zi | 老子 |
| *li* (one-third of a mile) | 里 |
| *li*(principle) | 理 |
| *li*(ritual propriety) | 禮 |
| *li* (rustic) | 俚 |
| Li Fang | 李昉 |
| Li Kaixian | 李開先 |
| Li Shimin | 李世民 |
| *lixue* | 理學 |
| Li Yu | 李漁 |
| Li Zhi | 李贄 |
| Li Zicheng | 李自成 |
| Linchuan | 臨川 |
| *Linjing zhiyue* | 麟經指月 |
| Ling Mengchu | 凌濛初 |
| Lingnan | 嶺南 |
| Ling Yutang | 林語堂 |
| Liu Depei | 劉德培 |
| Liu Hanxiang | 劉含香 |
| *Liu ke zhunsheng* | 六科準繩 |
| Liu Pian | 劉翩 |
| Liu Yiqing | 劉義慶 |
| Liu Yuanqing | 劉元卿 |
| Longchang | 龍場 |
| Long Ziyou | 龍子猶 |
| Lu Ciyun | 陸次雲 |

| | |
|---|---|
| Lu Ji | 陸楫 |
| Lu Shulun | 陸樹崙 |
| Lu Xun | 魯迅 |
| Lu Zhuo | 陸灼 |
| Lü Kun | 呂坤 |
| Luo Ye | 羅燁 |
| Macheng | 麻城 |
| *Madiaojiao li* | 馬吊腳例 |
| *meiren xiangcao* | 美人香草 |
| Mei Zhiyun | 梅之熉 |
| *ming jiao* | 名教 |
| *Ming shi* | 明史 |
| *nei* | 內 |
| Neize | 內則 |
| *ni shan ge* | 擬山歌 |
| *nu* | 奴 |
| Nü Gua | 女媧 |
| *Nüke baiwen* | 女科百問 |
| *nuo* | 儺 |
| Ouyang Xiu | 歐陽修 |
| *Pai an jing qi* | 拍案驚奇 |
| *Paijing* | 牌經 |
| *Pengfu bian* | 捧腹編 |
| *pi* | 癖 |
| Pingyao zhuan | 平妖傳 |
| *po yin* | 破音 |
| Pu | 濮 |
| *puban* | 僕辦 |
| *qi* (marvel) | 奇 |
| *qi* (psycho-physical energy) | 氣 |
| Qi | 齊 |
| Qi Zhongfu | 齊仲甫 |
| *Qiyan lu* | 啟顏錄 |
| *qian* (one-tenth of a tael) | 錢 |
| *qian* (transparent) | 淺 |
| Qianlong | 乾隆 |
| Qian Qianyi | 錢謙益 |
| Qian Yulian | 錢玉蓮 |
| *qing* | 情 |

| | |
|---|---|
| *Qingjiang yin* | 清江引 |
| *Qingshi leilue* | 情史類略 |
| Qing wai | 情外 |
| *qingzhen* | 情貞 |
| Qiu Jun | 丘濬 |
| Qiu Tianshu | 丘田叔 |
| Qiu Ying | 仇英 |
| *qu* | 趣 |
| Quanzhen | 全真 |
| *Quanzi* | 權子 |
| Rao Zongyi | 饒宗頤 |
| Rong Zhaozu | 容肇祖 |
| Rulin waishi | 儒林外史 |
| *Sanguo zhi yanyi* | 三國志演義 |
| *san nong* | 三弄 |
| *sanqu* | 散曲 |
| *Sanyan* | 三言 |
| Shan | 珊 |
| *shan ge* | 山歌 |
| *Shan ge* | 山歌 |
| *Shanren* | 山人 |
| *Shanzhong yixi hua* | 山中一夕話 |
| Shaonan | 召南 |
| Shen Jing | 沈璟 |
| Shen Zhou | 沈周 |
| *shengyuan* | 生員 |
| *shi* | 詩 |
| Shi Chengjin | 石成金 |
| *Shiji* | 史記 |
| Shiji | 誓妓 |
| *Shilin guangji* | 事林廣記 |
| *Shishuo xinyu* | 世說新語 |
| Shouning | 壽寧 |
| *Shouning daizhi* | 壽寧待志 |
| *Shouning xianzhi* | 壽寧縣志 |
| *Shuang dou yi* | 雙鬥醫 |
| *Shuihu zhuan* | 水滸傳 |
| Shun | 舜 |
| Shunzhi | 順治 |

| | |
|---|---|
| *Sida qishu* | 四大奇書 |
| *Siku quanshu* | 四庫全書 |
| Sima Qian | 司馬遷 |
| Sima Wengong | 司馬溫公 |
| *Sishu xiao* | 四書笑 |
| *Sishu zhiyue* | 四書指月 |
| Song Maocheng | 宋懋澄 |
| Su Shi | 蘇軾 |
| *Su yi* | 蘇意 |
| Suzhou | 蘇州 |
| *Suzhou fuzhi* | 蘇州府志 |
| Su Zizhong | 蘇子忠 |
| *Taixia xinzou* | 太霞新奏 |
| Taizong | 太宗 |
| Taizu | 太祖 |
| *Tanyan* | 談言 |
| Tang Pozi | 湯婆子 |
| Tang Xianzu | 湯顯祖 |
| Tianqi | 天啟 |
| Tongcheng | 桐城 |
| Tongchi | 童癡 |
| *Tongchi* | 童癡 |
| *tongsheng* | 童生 |
| *tongxin* | 童心 |
| *tongzhen* | 童貞 |
| Tu Long | 屠隆 |
| *wai* | 外 |
| Wan | 萬 |
| Wanli | 萬曆 |
| Wan Sheng zhuan | 萬生傳 |
| Wan shi zu | 萬事足 |
| Wang Guowei | 王國維 |
| Wang Ji | 王畿 |
| Wang Kentang | 王肯堂 |
| Wang Shipeng | 王十朋 |
| Wang Shizhen | 王世貞 |
| *wangsi cheng* | 枉死城 |
| Wang Yangming | 王陽明 |
| Wang zhi | 王制 |
| Wei | 衛 |

| | |
|---|---|
| Wei Yong | 衛泳 |
| Wei Zhongxian | 魏忠賢 |
| *wen* | 文 |
| Wen Zhenmeng | 文震孟 |
| Wu | 吳 |
| *Wu chao xiaoshuo* | 五朝小說 |
| *wu er* | 巫兒 |
| *wu hu* | 於戲（嗚呼） |
| *Wuji baimei* | 吳姬百媚 |
| Wujiang | 吳江 |
| Wu Jingzi | 吳敬梓 |
| Wu Sangui | 吳三桂 |
| Wu Sansi | 武三思 |
| Wuxian | 吳縣 |
| Wu Zetian | 武則天 |
| Xi Shi | 西施 |
| *Xiyou ji* | 西遊記 |
| *Xianxian pian* | 洒洒篇 |
| Xiangxia ren | 鄉下人 |
| *Xiaodao* | 笑倒 |
| *Xiao de hao* | 笑得好 |
| *Xiaofu* | 笑府 |
| *Xiaolin guangji* | 笑林廣記 |
| *Xiaolin ping* | 笑林評 |
| *xiaomin* | 小民 |
| *xiaopin* | 小品 |
| *xiaoshuo* | 小說 |
| *Xiaozan* | 笑贊 |
| *Xiecong* | 諧叢 |
| *Xieyu* | 諧語 |
| Xie Zhaozhe | 謝肇淛 |
| Xin Bo | 辛伯 |
| *Xin Lieguo Zhi* | 新列國志 |
| *Xin Pingyao zhuan* | 新平妖傳 |
| *Xin Tang shu* | 新唐書 |
| *Xin Xiaofu* | 新笑府 |
| *xinxue* | 心學 |
| *xing* | 性 |
| Xing Jushi | 邢居實 |
| *Xingshi hengyan* | 醒世恆言 |

| | |
|---|---|
| *Xingshi yinyuan zhuan* | 醒世姻緣傳 |
| Xiong Tingbi | 熊廷弼 |
| *xiucai* | 秀才 |
| Xu Bo | 徐渤 |
| Xu Wei | 徐渭 |
| Xu Zichang | 許自昌 |
| Xue Gang | 薛岡 |
| *Xuetao Ge Waiji* | 雪濤閣外集 |
| *Xuetao xiaoshuo* | 雪濤小說 |
| *Xuetao xieshi* | 雪濤諧史 |
| *ya* | 雅 |
| *yan zhi* | 言志 |
| Yan Zi | 嚴子 |
| Yang Jiaoai | 羊角哀 |
| Yang Tingshu | 楊廷樞 |
| Yang Xiang | 楊香 |
| Yao Shi Guang | 藥師光 |
| Yao Ximeng | 姚希孟 |
| *Yezi xin dou pu* | 葉子新門譜 |
| *yi nong* | 一弄 |
| *yin* | 淫 |
| Ying She | 應社 |
| *Yingxielu* | 應諧錄 |
| Yongle | 永樂 |
| Yongzheng | 雍正 |
| Youhuai | 有懷 |
| Youli | 羑里 |
| *you long* | 猶龍 |
| Youlong | 猶龍 |
| *You Min yincao* | 游閩吟草 |
| *youmo* | 幽默 |
| Youxi Daoren | 游戲道人 |
| *yu* (desire) | 欲 |
| *yu* (stupidity) | 愚 |
| Yu Huali | 俞華梨 |
| Yu Shaoyu | 余邵魚 |
| *Yushi mingyan* | 喻世明言 |
| *Yutao ji* | 鬱陶集 |
| Yu Wanlun | 俞琬綸 |
| *yu xi* | 於戲 |

| | |
|---|---|
| *yuanben* | 院本 |
| Yuan Hongdao | 袁宏道 |
| Yuan Huang | 袁黃 |
| *Yuanli ci* | 怨離詞 |
| *Yuanli shi* | 怨離詩 |
| Yuanmeng | 怨夢 |
| *yuan qing* | 緣情 |
| *yuanyang* | 鴛鴦 |
| Yuanzhi | 遠志 |
| Yuan Zhongdao | 袁中道 |
| Yue | 越 |
| Yun-Gui | 雲貴 |
| Yun She | 韻社 |
| Zai Yu | 宰予 |
| *Zai Yu zhou qin* | 宰予晝寢 |
| *Zengguang Zhi nang bu* | 增廣智囊補 |
| *Zhanguo ce* | 戰國策 |
| Zhan Jingfeng | 詹景鳳 |
| *zhang* | 丈 |
| Zhang Boqi | 張伯起 |
| Zhang Cai | 張采 |
| Zhang Dai | 張岱 |
| Zhang Fengyi | 張鳳翼 |
| Zhang Han | 張瀚 |
| Zhang Juzheng | 張居正 |
| Zhang Pu | 張溥 |
| Zhang Qianren | 張千仞 |
| Zhang Runsan | 張潤三 |
| Zhang Shicheng | 張士誠 |
| Zhang Youwen | 張幼文 |
| Zhang Yuanbo | 張元伯 |
| Zhao Nanxing | 趙南星 |
| Zhao Shijie | 趙世傑 |
| Zhao Tingji | 趙廷璣 |
| Zhao Wuniang | 趙五娘 |
| Zhejiang | 浙江 |
| *zhen* | 真 |
| *zhen dao xue* | 真道學 |
| *zheng* | 正 |
| Zheng | 鄭 |

| | |
|---|---|
| Zheng Dan | 鄭旦 |
| Zhengde | 正德 |
| Zheng Mengge | 鄭孟哥 |
| Zhi | 跖 |
| *Zhi nang* | 智囊 |
| *Zhi nang bu* | 智囊補 |
| *Zhi pin* | 智品 |
| *zhiyin* | 知音 |
| Zhizhi Sheng | 至至生 |
| Zhongsi | 螽斯 |
| Zhong Xing | 鍾惺 |
| Zhongxing shilu | 中興實錄 |
| Zhongxing weilue | 中興偉略 |
| Zhongzong | 中宗 |
| Zhounan | 周南 |
| Zhou Shunchang | 周順昌 |
| Zhou Yongzhai | 周用齋 |
| Zhu Furen | 竹夫人 |
| Zhu Xi | 朱熹 |
| Zhu Yizun | 朱彝尊 |
| Zhu Yuanzhang | 朱元璋 |
| Zhuang Zi | 莊子 |
| *zi* | 字 |
| Zi Gong | 子貢 |
| Zi Shang | 子上 |
| Ziyou | 子猶 |
| *Zuiweng tanlu* | 醉翁談錄 |
| Zuiyue Zi | 醉月子 |
| Zuo Botao | 左伯桃 |

# Index

# About the Author

## 徐碧卿

**Pi-ching Hsu** is Associate Professor in the Department of History at San Francisco State University. She holds a B.A. in Foreign Languages and Literature from National Taiwan University, an M.A. in Chinese Literature from University of Minnesota, and a Ph.D. in History from University of Minnesota. Her research interests include gender, social, cultural, and intellectual history of premodern China.